Software Testing
with Visual Test™ 4.0

Software Testing
with Visual Test™ 4.0

by Thomas R. Arnold, II

IDG Books Worldwide, Inc.
An International Data Group Company

Foster City, CA ♦ Chicago, IL ♦ Indianapolis, IN ♦ Southlake, TX

Software Testing with Visual Test™ 4.0

Published by
IDG Books Worldwide, Inc.
An International Data Group Company
919 E. Hillsdale Blvd.
Suite 400
Foster City, CA 94404

www.idgbooks.com (IDG Books Worldwide Web Site)
http://www.dummies.com (Dummies Press Web Site)

Library of Congress Catalog Card No.: 96-76233

ISBN: 0-7645-8000-0

Printed in the United States of America

10 9 8 7 6 5 4 3 2 1

1B/QX/QY/ZW/FC

Distributed in the United States by IDG Books Worldwide, Inc.

Distributed by Macmillan Canada for Canada; by Contemporanea de Ediciones for Venezuela; by Distribuidora Cuspide for Argentina; by CITEC for Brazil; by Ediciones ZETA S.C.R. Ltda. for Peru; by Editorial Limusa SA for Mexico; by Transworld Publishers Limited in the United Kingdom and Europe; by Academic Bookshop for Egypt; by Levant Distributors S.A.R.L. for Lebanon; by Al Jassim for Saudi Arabia; by Simron Pty. Ltd. for South Africa; by Pustak Mahal for India; by The Computer Bookshop for India; by Toppan Company Ltd. for Japan; by Addison Wesley Publishing Company for Korea; by Longman Singapore Publishers Ltd. for Singapore, Malaysia, Thailand, and Indonesia; by Unalis Corporation for Taiwan; by WS Computer Publishing Company, Inc. for the Philippines; by WoodsLane Pty. Ltd. for Australia; by WoodsLane Enterprises Ltd. for New Zealand. Authorized Sales Agent: Anthony Rudkin Associates for the Middle East and North Africa.

For general information on IDG Books Worldwide's books in the U.S., please call our Consumer Customer Service department at 800-762-2974. For reseller information, including discounts and premium sales, please call our Reseller Customer Service department at 800-434-3422.

For information on where to purchase IDG Books Worldwide's books outside the U.S., please contact our International Sales department at 415-655-3172 or fax 415-655-3295.

For information on foreign language translations, please contact our Foreign & Subsidiary Rights department at 415-655-3021 or fax 415-655-3281.

For sales inquiries and special prices for bulk quantities, please contact our Sales department at 415-655-3200 or write to the address above.

For information on using IDG Books Worldwide's books in the classroom or for ordering examination copies, please contact our Educational Sales department at 800-434-2086 or fax 817-251-8174.

For authorization to photocopy items for corporate, personal, or educational use, please contact Copyright Clearance Center, 222 Rosewood Drive, Danvers, MA 01923, or fax 508-750-4470.

 is a trademark under exclusive license to IDG Books Worldwide, Inc., from International Data Group, Inc.

To my parents, Thomas and Dorothy Arnold. Words cannot express the love I feel for you and how blessed I am to have you as my parents. Thank you for always being there for me.

Welcome to the world of IDG Books Worldwide.

IDG Books Worldwide, Inc., is a subsidiary of International Data Group, the world's largest publisher of computer-related information and the leading global provider of information services on information technology. IDG was founded more than 25 years ago and now employs more than 8,500 people worldwide. IDG publishes more than 270 computer publications in over 75 countries (see listing below). More than 90 million people read one or more IDG publications each month.

Launched in 1990, IDG Books Worldwide is today the #1 publisher of best-selling computer books in the United States. We are proud to have received eight awards from the Computer Press Association in recognition of editorial excellence and three from *Computer Currents*' First Annual Readers' Choice Awards. Our best-selling *...For Dummies*® series has more than 25 million copies in print with translations in 30 languages. IDG Books Worldwide, through a joint venture with IDG's Hi-Tech Beijing, became the first U.S. publisher to publish a computer book in the People's Republic of China. In record time, IDG Books Worldwide has become the first choice for millions of readers around the world who want to learn how to better manage their businesses.

Our mission is simple: Every one of our books is designed to bring extra value and skill-building instructions to the reader. Our books are written by experts who understand and care about our readers. The knowledge base of our editorial staff comes from years of experience in publishing, education, and journalism — experience which we use to produce books for the '90s. In short, we care about books, so we attract the best people. We devote special attention to details such as audience, interior design, use of icons, and illustrations. And because we use an efficient process of authoring, editing, and desktop publishing our books electronically, we can spend more time ensuring superior content and spend less time on the technicalities of making books.

You can count on our commitment to deliver high-quality books at competitive prices on topics you want to read about. At IDG Books Worldwide, we continue in the IDG tradition of delivering quality for more than 25 years. You'll find no better book on a subject than one from IDG Books Worldwide.

John J. Kilcullen

John Kilcullen
President and CEO
IDG Books Worldwide, Inc.

Foreword

Test automation is growing up.

Automation tools for graphical user interfaces used to be one of the most over-hyped and under-delivered technologies in the business. Yahoo! Robots can find the bugs while you sleep! Up to a few years ago, the only tools available were either intrusive software-only products or cumbersome and expensive hardware emulators. Their ability to check test results was usually limited to simple screen shots, making them oversensitive to minor changes in the tested software. An entire test suite could be invalidated by a single change in the background color of a main window. Worst of all, few companies knew how to use test automation tools as part of a responsible test strategy.

Times are changing. Three trends are converging to bring test automation out of the dark ages: better operating systems, better tools, and more experience with automation. Modern multitasking operating systems provide facilities that protect applications from each other, greatly reducing the intrusiveness of software-only test tools. The tools themselves have caught up with the technology, and now provide much richer facilities for executing, analyzing, and reporting test results. There's a lot more test automation experience out there, and people who are willing to share it. The major software companies, at least, are getting wiser about what, when, and how to automate.

This book is a good example of those trends in action. Its subject matter is one of the best tools available. Visual Test is a versatile and sophisticated automation platform that takes full advantage of the capabilities of Windows 95 and Windows NT. This is the tool that Microsoft uses in their own test efforts. But, technology aside, Tom has infused this book with his experience and judgment. Tom created the training course that Microsoft uses to teach its own people about Visual Test. I, for one, found his materials to be much more helpful than the Visual Test manual.

Also, when it comes to developing test suites, Tom has been there and done that. So pay special attention to the cautionary notes that he's included in this book. Success in test automation requires careful planning and design work, and it's not a universal solution. Tom points out that automated testing should not be considered a replacement for hand testing, but rather as an enhancement. This runs counter to the hype that sometimes surrounds automated testing, but it rings true to automation veterans.

Before you reach the brie and champagne stage of operating a highly effective, computer-aided test suite, you will have to go through the Doritos and Jolt stage of building it. This book is one way of getting through that stage as quickly and painlessly as possible. Good luck.

James Bach
Chief Scientist at ST Labs, Inc.

Preface

It was in January, 1992, when I was first introduced to — what was then called — Microsoft Test. It was a Beta of the 1.0 version, and because Asymetrix and Microsoft had strong ties with each other, we were on Microsoft's beta program.

I was the Senior Test Lead on the ToolBook 3.0 project at Asymetrix, responsible for leading the quality assurance effort for that product. The Director of Development had heard of this new tool and how it would automate testing. He asked me if I would be interested in putting together a demonstration for the company's founder, Paul Allen, who co-founded Microsoft with Bill Gates those many years ago. "Er... uh... No, I think I'll pass on that one," was my first reply, mostly because I didn't want to be put on the spot in front of Paul, but also because I was busy getting our testing effort under way for the latest version of ToolBook.

Then he posed the question to me differently. Actually, the question became more of a command. "Let me put it this way: Learn how to use Microsoft Test and be ready with a demo for Paul on Friday." You can probably guess my second reply: "Uhm, sure! Happy to!" Considering it was a Wednesday, there was a bit of pressure to get this done. So, I cleared the decks, sat down in front of my computer, installed and ran Microsoft Test, and... where to start? I wasn't sure.

It seemed a simple task: Learn what the product is about and what it can do for our development teams. Simple, yet the cursor in the Microsoft Test editor just kept blinking at me, offering neither help nor direction on how to proceed. It just kept flashing, waiting for me to do something, anything!

I fumbled around with different approaches and ideas until I pieced together something for Paul based on the examples that came with the Test 1.0 Beta and my background in programming. Fortunately he had to cancel the Friday meeting, so I had the entire weekend to continue to prepare for the demo that had been moved to the following Monday.

The Demonstration

As much as I'd like to say my scripting and layout were works of art, they weren't. It was my first attempt at an automated script. I wasn't sure to what degree I should be testing the product using automation, and I didn't have any idea of how much time it would take me to automate an entire product. Even so, the presentation left the executives with high hopes in what automation promised in delivering a quality product to market.

A successful demonstration, then, right? Well, no. Not really, because they weren't given the entire picture. And I wasn't in the position to give them the entire picture because of my newness to the realm of Test Automation. What wasn't impressed upon them was the time it took to come up to speed with the tool, the effort to write automated scripts, and the number of people it would take to not only guarantee that the product received the same level of testing it had before, but that also allowed for the scripts to be written correctly and maintained over the full product cycle.

The Commitment

After that, using Microsoft Test became a part of Asymetrix's testing efforts. Unfortunately, the number of testers didn't increase. We were to provide the same level of testing that we'd given before this new tool made its debut and begin putting our testing into automated scripts.

We did our best, shared our efforts with other testing teams at the company, and figured out what worked and what didn't. We even started building some common utilities and scripting libraries that we could share throughout the company. And, we refined our efforts from there.

The Vicious Cycle

We were encouraged to automate the entire product. Because script development is truly a parallel development project, it takes time to develop scripts to automate some or much of the testing on a product. Because the number of testers wasn't allowed to increase, the bug count dropped — we were spending all of our time automating. We were then asked to increase the bug count to help keep a high intensity level on the developers. Because we were still laying the groundwork for our automated scripts, and still understanding the full potential of this automation tool, we weren't at a point where the scripts would help test the product. So, we returned to manual testing. The result was an increased bug count. But then it was noticed that the script development effort was slowing, so we were then asked to increase the number of automated scripts. The result was the bug count dropping again. A vicious and all too common cycle at companies setting up test automation.

Doing it Right

Since my first efforts in working with Microsoft Test, I've been fortunate enough to have been on projects where we were given the time we needed to do the job right. One such job was with Microsoft Consulting Services (MCS).

After three years of a great experience at Asymetrix Corporation, I moved on to a job with MCS in August 1993 as an automation script developer using Microsoft Test 2.0. The project was a very interesting one. MCS was hired to write the software for the passenger and flight attendant terminals that have gone into United Airlines' shipments of the new Boeing 777. It was my job to write the underlying utilities to be used by the script development team and write all the scripts to automate the testing of the program running on the terminals found in all the passenger seats.

Microsoft had prototyped the product in Visual Basic so that United Airlines could sign off on the design before the product was re-written in C++. Not only did it make it easy on the developers to have a frozen specification to code against, it gave the script developers a prototype on which to write tests. The result was that a large percentage of our scripts were written and running by the time the first build of the C++ version of the product was made available to us. We also had a realistic approach to combining some automation with some manual testing instead of assuming that the entire product could be fully automated. By focusing on what automation does well and what testers do well, a solid product was released to the customer.

The Course

After six months of script development, and a number of side weekend and evening automation projects, I started working on a project in my spare time for Microsoft's Worldwide Products Group. Rob Arnold, a founder of a fledgling company called Software Testing Laboratories (STLabs), pitched the idea to Microsoft. Then he and I proceeded to put it all together. The end result was a complete course on learning and using Microsoft Test 2.0 that I then taught to Microsoft employees. The course was then updated to Microsoft Test 3.0 and recently to Microsoft Visual Test 4.0.

Because we constructed a contract with Microsoft that allowed us to use the course outside of Microsoft under our own company name, I have had the honor of teaching the course throughout the United States and Canada to employees from such companies as Hewlett-Packard, Compaq, Peachtree, Intel, MCI, Traveling Software, Starwave, Edmark, Corel, Entergy, IBM, Spry/CompuServe, Aldus/Adobe, Delrina, and, of course, Microsoft. The uses of the Visual Test tool were as varied as the companies to which I presented the course. These variances were a bonus because it allowed us to constantly update and revise our course based on common questions and pitfalls that employees from these companies encountered.

I'm looking forward to sharing with you what I've learned over the past four years of using and teaching Microsoft Visual Test.

The Goal of this Book

The goals of this book include helping the reader to understand some of the common misconceptions shared by management, what the realities and limitations of Microsoft Visual Test 4.0 are, and how to approach an automation project realistically and flexibly. It is also meant to be used after the reader has become familiar and comfortable with Visual Test and is ready to move on to advanced topics. In short, this book is meant to stay with you as you grow in your knowledge and abilities as a Visual Test programmer. Quality Assurance topics and methodologies are no more than lightly touched upon, since many excellent books are already available that discuss these concepts in depth.

Acknowledgments

A few people deserve to be recognized because I consider them key to the creation of this book. First I'd like to thank Rick Fant of Microsoft Consulting Services. Rick gave the testing team the time we needed to develop robust and maintainable scripts for the Boeing 777 project. I'd also like to thank Bill Barry, James Tierney, and Rebecca Reutter of the Microsoft Worldwide Products Group for the opportunity to develop courses on Microsoft Test and Visual Test for Microsoft and its employees. Thank you to Steve Fuchs (Program Manager), Bob Saile (Development Manager), Michael Scheele (Product Manager), and the rest of the Visual Test 4.0 team for their help on answering my questions on how to push the envelope of their great tool. Thanks to Gregg Brown (President, STLabs) for putting the ball into motion with Nu-Mega and Microsoft to make this book possible, and for offering constant encouragement that I tend to need. Thank you to Cory Low, my ski buddy and author of three successful Internet books. It was Cory's guidance and willingness to act as a sounding board during our skiing and chair-lift rides that helped keep me sane. Michelle Drewien, thank you for your graphics-artist abilities and sparing the readers of this book from my diagrams. Thank you to everyone at IDG Books who put this book together, especially Amy Pedersen, John Osborn, Jim Sumser (my editor-extra-ordinaire), and Tim Lewis, who helped me appear to be a somewhat coherent writer. Thanks to Dan Hodge, a fellow Visual Test instructor, for doing the technical edits on this book. And finally, thank you to Rob Arnold (CEO, STLabs), Tye Minckler (CFO, STLabs), James Bach (Chief Scientist, ST Labs) for your thoughts on automation, Cem Kaner for looking over the drafts of this book, and all of my fellow employees at STLabs for their encouragement and support in my writing this book.

Thomas R. Arnold II
WWW: *http://www.stlabs.com/*
E-MAIL: *TomA@STLabs.com, TomA@WebSoln.com*

Contents at a Glance

Table of Contents

P A R T

Introduction

Why Automate Software Testing?

ver the last few years, testing software has become increasingly complex and fraught with danger. Windows NT and Windows 95 both represent much more intricate programming needs and so the opportunity for bugs and poor software performance is very real. Yet the time taken to check for them all, in the present cutthroat software development market, means that a product's success depends on quickly and efficiently removing these problems. This, in turn, makes automatic testing an essential tool.

Because of this, automatic testing is now becoming integrated into the general development cycle. We shall look, first, at the cycle as a whole, then at the role and benefits of automatic testing within it. Finally, we shall consider three of the perceived drawbacks of test automation.

I would like to say up front, before we get too far into this book, that no test automation tool is a silver bullet. Automation takes time, effort, and commitment from all involved, including management understanding the realities of what automation can and cannot do. The purpose of this book is provide you with a *how to* approach to using Visual Test 4.0. These approaches and side comments about the realities of automation are based on my experiences and those experiences of people whom I've spoken with who've participated on test automation teams.

Attitude Is Everything

An important aspect of this book for me is the attitude in which it is written. I am as much a student as you are. I had to pick up how to use Microsoft Test on my own and then had to defend when it did and did not make sense to use it in a particular way. To a certain extent, I was feeling my way along a dark passage without a flashlight.

(continued)

Attitude Is Everything *(Continued)*

Fortunately, as it turned out, when I started creating a class on Visual Test and started teaching that class, the people I spoke to who were getting the most out of their automation happened to be doing it the same way that I was. This reinforcement of my methods helped me realize how best to use this tool and how to share with others the approaches to take to get the most out of Visual Test.

Be like them: Be open minded; be willing to try some of these ideas; be willing to fail; be willing to dive in, move forward, make mistakes, and come back later and tweak the work you've already done.

If you aren't willing to do that, then you're making your job harder than it needs to be. Whether you're making mistakes or writing code that Bill Gates would be proud of, the only way you're going to learn is to start putting down some code and tweaking from there.

The first thing I would ask you to do is be willing to try different things and be willing to fail. If you're not making mistakes, you're not learning. Even those of you who think you already know much of this should at least browse the next chapters. Even if you think you know most of it, you might pick something up along the way. Every time I go into a company using an automation tool, I learn a new approach that can be added to my bag of tricks. In turn, they also learn tricks and methods from me to help them improve upon their existing processes.

The Development Cycle

Development cycles for computer software vary from company to company and depend on how long a firm has been in the software development business. For the sake of establishing the big picture, in this chapter I will only include a broad overview of the development process. I'm speaking broadly about the development cycle because of how it varies between companies. This book is about how to automate portions of testing through Visual Test, so please pardon some of the broad strokes.

To begin with, a group of people get together and decide to build a product. This group is run by a *Program Manager*, who orchestrates the development process by managing the Quality Assurance (QA), Development, and Technical Writing Leads, as shown in Figure 1-1.

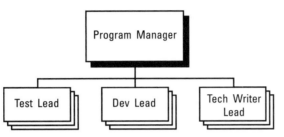

Figure 1-1
The product development group.

Usually, the process starts with the engineers telling the marketers, or *Product Manager*, what features they can get into the product based on the suggested timeline. If the team has been through enough development cycles in the past, and has learned from those efforts, it'll then put together a *functional specification* that outlines the features and milestones of the product.

Note

The Product Manager, not to be confused with the Program Manager, works on the marketing side taking care of building the marketing messages, artwork, timelines with manufacturers, and advertising. Depending on which company you work for, usually the Product Manager is reporting to the Director of Marketing, while the Program Manager is reporting to the Director of Development.

The quality assurance engineers then come on the scene — some argue that they should be involved from the beginning, but that's a matter of program management style and depends on how mature the company is in its experience in developing software — and begin designing their overall *test plan* for the features of the product. The documentation team will also come in around the same time as the quality assurance team and will begin designing its approach to documenting the product.

The goal is to have the test plan and checklists laid out and ready to be manually stepped through by the test engineers when each feature is completed by the programmers. Each item on a test checklist is considered a *scenario* and related scenarios are grouped into *test cases*. These test cases are organized into *suites* of tests that focus on such testing concerns as benchmarks, stress testing, functionality testing, and so on.

The other part of that goal is to have the documentation reach completion at the same time as the developers and testers are finalizing the development of the product. This is basically the theory of how the development cycle works, not including the marketing side of things.

The Real World

The reality of what tends to happen in the development cycle, especially in a young software company, is that a group of people get together over hamburgers, decide to develop a product, get a lead developer to put the product together, and then decide that it needs to be documented and tested before it is released onto the market. Quality Assurance and Documentation find themselves on the back end of the development cycle, where all the time pressures exist because of under-estimating the schedule.

It can be argued that this is a cynical view, but I guarantee that a high percentage of the people reading this book are nodding their heads and saying, "Yup; that's exactly what happens!"

An experienced Program Manager knows to not only have as accurate a project time line as possible, but to also add time for "feature-creep" caused by overzealous developers, marketing-types, and, sometimes, the company's owner. She also keeps in mind the bugs that can be caused by junior developers, incompatibility issues with another company's software or hardware, staff turnover, and other potential complications.

While this padding can help take some of the pressure off those who find themselves on the back end of the schedule, that pressure still exists to some degree. In many cases, though, it is actually positive, since it keeps everyone focused and moving forward on getting the product finished and out the door on time and with high quality. The trick is finding the fine line between the amount of pressure being positive, as opposed to negative — where everyone on the team is thrashing around in their efforts to reach their intended goals.

The Role of Test Automation

What is the role of automatic testing in this process? What benefits can it produce for those harried test engineers and for the over-stretched and understaffed development process as a whole? First, let's take a look at what test automation is, and then at its benefits.

What Is Test Automation?

A number of people, when first hearing about test automation, assume it's meant to replace the human aspect of testing. As it turns out, the opposite is true. Automated tests are helpful in performing tests quickly and precisely, but they don't replace the human tester, who has to run the tests, check that all is going satisfactorily and *think* about what other items need to be checked to ensure quality. Where automation wins is in doing the same steps the same way over and over again. As a way of catching errors early and allowing for much more reliable software, it can cut up to 80 percent from testing time, as Microsoft has boasted in the results its projects have realized.

Simply put, test automation emulates user actions such as clicking on buttons, typing, dragging and dropping, and selecting menus. Above all, it provides speed and reliability to tedious, repetitive tasks. It also makes sure that those tasks are repeated in the same order again and again, helping to verify that features are working as documented and that known bugs aren't recurring.

Take, for example, a test to verify the state of an application's menus. Test automation can run through this for you, checking that the accelerator keys haven't changed from the previous build, verifying that menu items haven't been added or removed, and ensuring that the menus still display the dialog boxes that they displayed in the build from the previous week. This alone is a powerful mechanism providing the tester with a reasonably good idea about what sections of the product may have changed that weren't reported by the development team. It also validates portions of the program, letting the tester know that the features that worked in a previous build appear to still be hooked up.

But pushing a button and clicking on a menu item does not a test make. Writing tests to verify that menus haven't changed are helpful in identifying changes, but they don't delve deeply into the functionality of a product. A structure must be built by someone using Visual Test (from now on referred to as a *Test programmer*) that will exercise key components of a product. A decision must also be made by the Program Manager and Test Lead as to how much of the testing will involve automation. As you continue to read through this book you will begin to understand the task ahead of you in automating testing. Take care to weigh the advantages and disadvantages of automation which are both discussed next, beginning with the benefits of automation.

Benefits of Automation

Imagine yourself near the end of a project. Management has you in late every evening and on weekends, pounding on the code; your family hasn't seen you for three months; the developers are complaining about the testers and the fact that bugs are being found now that should have been found earlier; new code drops and releases of the code are being thrown over the wall to the testers every hour, on the hour.... Everything's going nuts!

It is in the final days of a project where test automation can really pay off. Imagine being able to run through the majority of your known list of system problems or bugs every time the programmers provide a new compilation of the product. Not only being able to run through a huge portion of the known bugs, but to be able to verify that those bugs are still closed in a fraction of the time it would take someone to perform such a verification by hand. Further imagine being able to run whatever tests have been created for testing the product on a number of machine configurations, all at the same time, all using the same steps, and all at a fraction of the time it would take to perform those tests manually. The result is being able to quickly determine whether or not a build provided by the development team is stable enough to be accepted by the testing team. If it doesn't pass specific tests deemed important by the QA group, it goes back over the wall to the programmers to fix the major bugs that have broken the build. Not only that, but the scripts can be included to provide a way of reproducing those problems for the developers.

VISUAL TEST

Specifically, Visual Test offers considerable benefits over and above those just mentioned. Not only can it provide a means with which to automate testing, it's a powerful tool that will allow you to build other tools that can help in the testing process.

Visual Test is truly a development tool that has the capabilities of building stand-alone applications (with help from a run-time engine) that can be used by one's fellow test engineers. An example of this capability is Software Testing Laboratories' *Digger* utility which was written completely in Visual Test. This utility, which reads in an executable file and spits out a Visual Test template based on that file's menus and dialog boxes, shows how capable Microsoft's test automation tool really is.

Microsoft has taken care to move Visual Test up the ladder to keep it current through integrating it with the Developer Studio, the same integrated development environment (IDE) that Visual C++ uses. It's been updated so that its network scripts can communicate with and synchronize hundreds of machines to perform the same or different tests at the same time. Its scenario recorder has been updated to be more robust in its script generation capabilities. And, its report generation capabilities allow for writing to a simple text file on up to writing to a database-compatible file.

Advanced programmers who are already aware of Visual Test's capabilities appreciate how open-ended this tool really is. It supports such advanced features as pointers to functions, pointers to variables, linking to the user's own dynamic libraries, and working with Windows APIs. In other words, it's extensible such that you can write your own utilities in C and use them from Visual Test as if those routines are a part of Visual Test's own language.

So, Why Use an Automation Tool?

What's making the idea of automating tests such a big deal? A big part of it is management buying into the marketing hoopla: "You'll get higher quality products out to the market faster if you automate your testing." And it's true: Once a testing team really gets an automation library built and a process in place, automation can play a big part in getting a quality product to the market. It's just that the initial investment required isn't part of that marketing message.

So, your firm decides to try it out.

Consider this scenario: You are on a testing project and someone comes to you and suggests that you look into automating your testing. Maybe it's the Director of Development of your company, who'd like to standardize the testing efforts on using an automation tool. Or perhaps it's the Program Manager, who thinks she can help you get your testing done more quickly and effectively. Or, maybe you're in the lucky minority and your QA Manager, who has a realistic view of automation, has broken the testing team into two groups: those who will automate and those who will perform manual testing.

Whatever's the case, most likely your first response will be the same as mine was, and you'll think that you have enough to do as it is: You've got a product to test, not much time to do it in, and you want to make sure you get the best darned product out to market. Why do you want to spend what little time you have learning how to automate your testing, when you have tight deadlines to meet? This is a fair question.

So, let's look at some of the key reasons for using an automation tool like Visual Test:

▶ Regression testing

▶ Reproducible steps

▶ Compatibility testing

▶ Accurate benchmarking

▶ Re-using scripts

▶ Specialized needs

REGRESSION TESTING

On most development projects, a time is set for when the developers can expect to make a *build* (a particular version of the software product) that will be handed off to the testing team. As a result, the development team is pushing to have their bugs fixed and new features checked in, so that testing can continue on the product.

Once the build is finished, it is then handed off to the testing team to verify whether it's a good build or not. Typically, this happens once a week. If it's not any good, the testers will stay with the previous version and usually ask the development group to fix the high-priority bugs. Eventually, a build is accepted by the testing team, so that testing can be done for yet another week on the latest and greatest build of the product.

Bugs have a tendency to resurface, or a programmer will fix one problem within the system only to cause a new bug to surface. By fixing that new bug, it might break the previous fix of a feature someplace else in the system — perhaps in an area that is seemingly unrelated.

If the testing team sets up a process, such that all known and reported bugs in the system are put into an automated test file, those tests can be run with each new release of the product. This process is commonly referred to as *regression testing*: The process of stepping through all known bugs to verify that they have either been fixed, or remain fixed from the last time they were regression tested.

By the end of the project, when thousands of bugs have been filed on the product, running a group of regression tests is a valuable tool to determine the stability of the product.

REPRODUCIBLE STEPS

After receiving a new build from the development team, tests that exercise the main features of the product are usually run. If, after a few minutes of the tests running, an error occurs that causes your application to shut itself down, a critical bug has been found. Because the testers wrote their scripts such that they logged each step taken during the testing, a list of steps now exists that can be used in tracking that bug down.

If you re-run that script, and the error occurs again in the same place, count yourself among the fortunate, because you have a reproducible error and a script that can reproduce it. Using the script, the error can be tracked down by working backwards from where the error occurred. Was it as simple as displaying the Open dialog box, or was it crucial that the user selected New Document just before doing so? You can track this down by retracing your automated script's steps.

Once these steps are refined to the minimum reproducible case, a problem report (*bug*) can be communicated to the developer who owns the area where the error was found.

COMPATIBILITY TESTING

Imagine yourself on a project where you need to verify that the product you are testing works on a number of different configurations: low memory, low disk space, a specific video board, a particular printer driver, a sound board that has given your company fits in the past, a particular computer brand, and so on. Now, imagine taking a number of tests that you and the other test automation engineers have written and running them on each machine configuration. The workload is enormous. But with test automation, in addition to running those key tests, you have the time to test specific areas of concern by hand.

Compatibility testing is a definite area to focus on when automating tests. The intention of it isn't to automate the entire product, it's to automate some of the key features that can be tested on the different configurations. This gives testers the time they need to use their skills to their fullest. They can pound on the areas of concern they know have caused problems in the past. And they can do this while the automated tests are busily exercising the mundane pieces of the product, verifying that the obvious pieces of the product haven't deteriorated unexpectedly.

BENCHMARKING

Just like many other testers, I've performed benchmarking by using a hand-held stop watch. This is effective on really slow sections of a program where time can be accurately estimated in tens of seconds.

It's not so effective when dealing with two seconds or less and it is in this area that Visual Test comes in very handy. Let's take a drawing program as an example. Say there is a particular picture that takes up to five seconds to draw because of the graphical richness involved in it: multiple irregular polygons, ellipses, shading, layers, and so on. Let's also assume that efforts are being made by the developers to optimize their code to speed up that drawing process.

Setting up an automated test to load a complicated picture and cause it to redraw a number of times is a breeze with test automation. Not only that, but it will do it multiple times, performing the exact same steps, so that an average time can be computed, resulting in cutting down on the timing errors relating to benchmarking. These results can be saved and compared with future versions of the product to determine if it is truly being sped up by the efforts of development.

Once that speed is finally realized, the last thing you want to happen is to have it drop back to a slower speed again. If a suite of tests exists that determines the speed of specific risk areas in the product, each build can be tested to verify that something hasn't changed to cause the drawing or imaging to become slow once more.

Bugs can occur in more ways than one. They can be obvious bugs, such as a crash that brings the product down, or a bug in logic that causes the imaging of a program to slow to such a slight degree that a human operator might not notice any change between builds of the product, but which becomes very noticeable with complex drawings. Test automation can spot these changes, in a way that human testers might not be able to.

RE-USING SCRIPTS

The internationalization teams in software companies typically have the hardest jobs on the shortest time lines. The software has been written, all they have to do is translate it into a foreign language. What's the big deal?

Take someone from your company's international team to lunch some day and ask them about their job. You'll find that they have one of the shortest timelines of any group in the company. You think documentation and quality assurance folks have it tough since they're commonly on the back end of the development cycle? These folks have it tougher because the domestic version of the product is out and the owners of the software company are eager to get a localized version for foreign markets selling as soon as possible.

Let's take just two typical nightmares.

Because a number of resources need to be changed to allow for another language, an executable file needs to be recompiled so that resources can be re-attached. If even a small change is made, or if somehow the build that was released to manufacturing is not the same as that given to the international team, you're no longer certain exactly where you stand on the stability of that product.

And what happens if a word that only took eight characters in English takes 12 in another language? Is there anything hard-coded in the code base that relies on the size of that character string? When the developers made the changes for the internationalization group, did they use the same *compiler flags* that specify *code compaction* and *optimization*? You can't be sure.

Now, imagine how nice it would be if there were automated scripts available from the original domestic testing teams that the internationalization group could run on the builds of the localized product they're testing. Also, think how handy automated tests could come in for a quick check on the stability of a product. In addition, if the testing team working on the domestic version of the product has programmed with flexibility in mind, the internationalization team can make use of those scripts in helping them bring their localized product to market faster.

These scripts do not replace the need for manual testing, however, they merely act as a virtual tester that painstakingly checks the same sections of a product that were checked in the domestic version of the product. The manual testing must still be done to verify that other problems haven't surfaced.

SPECIALIZED NEEDS

Other, more specialized needs can be met by using an automated script. An example is testing a database when there is high network traffic. A good way of testing this is to have a test suite running on multiple machines, hitting the same area of a database, allowing the tester to verify, manually on another machine, that record-locking on a database is working.

There are countless specialized needs that can be met with an automation tool. One business in New Orleans where I provided training used Microsoft Test as a way of installing new versions of software across the company network. When a new version of a product came out, it would run this script and distribute the latest version onto everyone's machines. Pretty slick, but not your typical use of a test automation tool.

Note

This can be a reality of test automation if the proper amount of effort is placed up front from the beginning of the development cycle and carried throughout to its completion. As you will find when reading through this book, automation is much like a parallel development cycle that is carried out at the same time as the development of the product itself. Because of this, it is necessary to have testers that focus on manual testing and those who focus on automation. Focusing solely on automation will lead to a poorly tested product because of the time and effort it takes to write, debug and maintain automated scripts.

Automation Rears Its Ugly Head

Of course, nothing wonderful in this world is without a few attendant difficulties. Let's look at two of the main problems encountered with automation:

▶ It's too time-consuming to learn the testing tool and it will use up valuable extra resources.

▶ If the team is new to automation, no one is sure where to begin.

Each of these worries is valid. Let's look at them individually.

Test Automation Consumes Time and Resources

It's a fact that automating tests does take time; a fact that has to be embraced rather than avoided. First you have to sit down and learn how to use the automation tool, whether it's Visual Test or some other one. Next, you need to figure out exactly the approach you want to take. Then you need to assess how dedicated your company is to automating testing on the product. And, finally, you need to either hire automation engineers or bring your existing team up to speed on an automation tool.

Furthermore, test automation does not replace testers, although this is a common belief in some companies. What it allows you to do is automate repetitive tasks so that those tests can be run automatically and allow you to work smarter as a software testing engineer. Let me restate that: *It doesn't replace testers, it increases testers' effectiveness.* In fact, it is necessary to have automatic testing run in parallel with normal "human" testing.

All this takes time and money. But this unspoken message about needing initial investment isn't necessarily what the management of a software company wants to hear. It just wants to get the product out the door in a reasonable amount of time, so it can grab more market share than the competition. This is a fair goal for management to have, but cannot be achieved without adding more resources to a development team to make automation come together and function correctly.

It takes time and it takes commitment to learn a tool and get an automation process in place. Plus, it takes *more* people, not less, if you are on any kind of critical path. This is because you need the regular number of testers to do the manual testing that was already being done, and a separate group of testers to put the automation in place.

The company's production goal can be attained if the time and resources (in other words, people) required to put together a realistic automated testing approach are available. If your Development Managers are thinking they can pick up a test automation package and increase productivity and bug count without adding to the head count of the testing department, they will soon realize their error. If they don't have the resources to spare, they should reassess whether or not they really want to automate all, or even just part of the testing of a product.

It is your job as a test engineer to communicate the realities of test automation to the company's management. Automation pays off big at the end of a project and also when a product is internationalized to another market, but as the saying goes, you can't get something for nothing.

Note

It is my humble opinion that very little automation should be done on a 1.0 version of a product. This is because the testing staff is setting up its test plan, checklists, and generally understanding what it is they are helping to create. On a 2.0 version of a product, automation can be started using the 1.0 version while the developers are busy pulling the guts out of what will turn into version 2.0. When the 2.0 version begins to settle and come together, many of the scripts that were written using the stable 1.0 version can then be moved over and executed on the more stable builds of the new version.

Where Do We Begin?

This is the question everyone asks themselves when they sit down with an automation tool: "Where do I begin my automation approach?" It doesn't matter which tool you use, it's always a challenge to figure out where to start.

Buying this book was certainly a good move. With it spread out on the desk beside you, you can begin by typing in some code, trying to run it, and tracking down the errors from there. Hopefully, this book will get you past some of the obvious hassles facing you and point you in the right direction. Above all, you need to keep your scripts flexible, both for your own benefit and for the benefit of those who will be charged with maintaining your code in the future.

Your best bet is to work carefully through this book, working with the examples as we go along, and then going back and sorting out glitches as you come to understand them. Chapter 2, "History of Visual Test," and Chapter 3, "Synopsis of Visual Test," provide you with the background on how this quality tool came about, and what you can look forward to in the next chapters of this book. Chapter 4, "Visual Test User Interface," introduces you to the basic development environment you will be using when building your scripts. Chapter 5, "Visual Test Language," introduces you to what Visual Test offers as a programming language, while Chapter 6, "Visual Test Utilities," explains the Scenario Recorder, Window Information Utility, Screen Utility, and the Suite Manager.

We will specifically look at a beginning example of a simple script in Chapter 7. In Chapters 8 through 12 you'll be taken, step by step, through the creation of automated tests for a common Windows text editor. And finally, the last chapters focus on some of the more advanced areas of this tool.

Ignore the Man behind the Curtain

Don't be pulled in by all the magic and promises of automated testing. They may not all turn out to be feasible. Test automation is *not* meant to replace existing testing methodologies, only to enhance them. It is a tool to be used in addition to your regular testing. And the level of this enhancement depends strictly on the skills and thoroughness of those that wrote the automated tests.

You're not going to be able to write tests that will find all the bugs in your program. Not all bugs show up by simply clicking on a feature of the product. Sometimes it requires something specific to have occurred just before a particular action is taken. This is a big part of a tester's job, to think about what's going on underneath; to figure out what the developer of the product has missed. To ask himself, "I wonder if she thought to put a check in her code for this situation?" This isn't something an automated test can do and reinforces the old axiom that computers will never be able to replace humans.

On the other hand, you can certainly achieve a significant number of beneficial returns when using an automated testing tool, as I've explained in this chapter. It takes time and effort, though, to put automation together.

Summary

At present, the reality of the development process is that testing a product is considered at the last moment, and there is never enough time given to it. This is where test automation can help. It can provide significant benefits, in terms of speed, reliability, regression testing, creating reproducible steps, compatibility testing, benchmarking, re-using scripts, and meeting specialized needs. In particular, Visual Test offers specific advantages, such as providing the Test programmer with a common editor used by other Microsoft development tools, the capability to extend the language through the use of dynamic libraries (DLLs), and the same advantages of other programming languages, such as the use of pointers.

CHAPTER

History
of Visual Test

had the opportunity to talk with Bob Saile, Development and
Quality Assurance Manager for the Microsoft Visual Test 4.0 team,
about the history of Visual Test and how it was started. The reason
Microsoft Visual Test—known as Microsoft Test for versions 1.0 through
3.0—became a product was because enough of Microsoft's customers
asked for it to be made available to them, instead of being used exclu-
sively by Microsoft Corporation as an internal testing tool.

At the end of the 1980s, Microsoft was working on ways to automate
some of its testing efforts. Specifically, it was interested in capturing
mouse movements and keystrokes. Its first efforts were with a hardware
device it termed the Versatile Computer Recorder (VCR) which was to
be used for testing DOS applications and worked by plugging the mouse
and keyboard directly into the VCR hardware. This project was overseen
by Byron Bishop, the development lead, and Marv Parsons, the test
manager.

Used on the predecessor to Microsoft Access, the VCR tool was responsible for blazing the trail into the area of test automation and was responsible for new levels of tracking and finding system problems (commonly
referred to as *bugs*). It's biggest task was ensuring that problems fixed in
the software didn't recur as the development cycle came to an end.
Breaking Microsoft's project bug-count records, the value of automation
was realized early on by Microsoft and its quality assurance groups.

After realizing the potential of test automation, Saile approached Mike
Maples, then Vice President of Development at Microsoft, to increase the
head count in Saile's group, so that he could improve upon the existing
automation schema. It wasn't possible because there weren't any projects that could afford to lose developers at that time. Test automation
advances were temporarily put on hold.

A few months later, Saile was approached by an internal tools group at Microsoft that wanted him to help develop a software version of the VCR system. After ten months of development time, and feedback from over 300 testers at Microsoft who had played with the tool, it developed a new system it referred to as WATT: the Windows Application Testing Tool. The team had taken what it had learned from the VCR hardware used under DOS, avoided the problems the VCR system had faced, and created a new tool that worked in the Windows 3.0 environment.

All of this was going on around the spring of 1990, the time that Windows 3.0 made its debut. A number of Windows 3.0 developers outside Microsoft were developing new programs that would run under this latest version. One of Microsoft's major clients heard word of the tool and decided to use it to help the software development efforts for its new Windows 3.0 product. The client fell in love with the tool and provided feedback to Saile's team to help improve it even further.

Later that same year, Saile presented the tool at a Microsoft Windows developers' conference in Seattle, Washington. Those attending were intrigued by the possibilities and wanted to hear more about it; then they wanted copies of it, so they could use the tool in their development cycles.

Because it was such a small group of people, Microsoft wasn't interested in turning it into a product. They decided to release it to developers as an unsupported tool. Saile's group's only focus was to support the 300 to 400 testers at Microsoft; there wasn't enough time to support those outside the company. Incredibly, the WATT group was made up of only two developers, two testers, one group leader, and a program manager.

The next thing that happened was a crucial turning point in the decision as to whether or not the product would remain an internal tool, unsupported for developers outside of Microsoft. The outside developers continued to call Saile and Steve Fuchs, the Program Manager of WATT, telling them that they would pay for support on the tool. They were using it, liked it, and wanted to continue to get updates on it. Plus, they wanted some kind of technical support to help them with their questions.

It was then that Maples approached Saile and asked him how much effort was needed to enhance the documentation and add a script recorder to turn the tool into a shipping product. Microsoft Test was born.

Today, the Microsoft Visual Test team supports 900 internal testers at Microsoft and over 50,000 external users. The team has, of course, increased its number of developers and testers; but the same six people that were on the original team survived to this latest version of the product.

Microsoft Test 1.0

Microsoft Test 1.0 showed up around the end of 1991 in beta form, and as a fully fledged product in the spring of 1992. It provided the ability to work with Microsoft Windows controls, capture and compare dialog boxes and screens, and generate Test Basic scripts using a script recorder. As a result, Test 1.0 was a good first version of an automation tool (see Figure 2-1 and Figure 2-2).

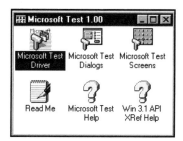

FIGURE 2-1
Test 1.0 installation.

FIGURE 2-2
The Microsoft Test 1.0 About box.

The first version included tools for capturing the contents of the screen and the controls of dialog boxes. It also came with some simple scripts that served as examples of how to use the tools.

Microsoft Test itself was considered the *test driver* (a program that steps through and runs a group of test scripts); it wasn't until version 2.0 that a driver which ran each test script file in turn appeared. And when it did, the driver itself was considered a sample script. Version 1.0's main window can be seen in Figure 2-3.

FIGURE 2-3
The Microsoft Test 1.0 main window.

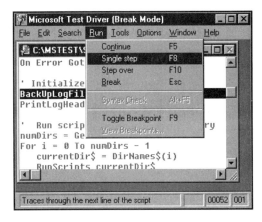

Microsoft Test 1.0 was a pretty good starting point and gave developers and testers an automation tool with which to begin their work. What it lacked in a programming environment (for example, no way to view the values of local or global variables, and no way to force a variable to be explicitly declared, which resulted in mis-typed variables being automatically declared as new variables), it made up for in what it offered for its $99 retail price.

Microsoft Test 2.0

In 1993, the 2.0 version hit the market. It was a big leap forward, offering a number of new features for automating Windows 3.1 products (see Figure 2-4).

The new *integrated development environment* (IDE) made its appearance, allowing users to access all the product's different tools from one window. Also included with this version was the latest advance in user interface (UI) design, including a scalable toolbar, a status bar, and child windows for tracking the values of the local and global variables used in a script.

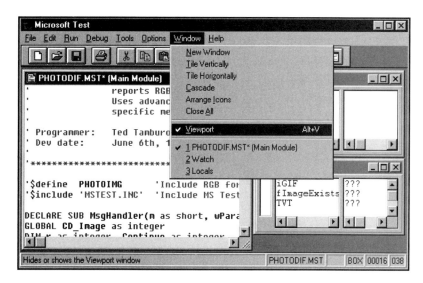

FIGURE 2-4 Test 2.0 offered a number of welcome new features.

FastTest, a feature of Microsoft Test 1.0 that allowed for the quick development of test suites, went undocumented in the 2.0 version to encourage testers to move over to the normal Test Basic scripting language. In version 3.0, FastTest was removed completely.

One of the biggest features of Microsoft Test 2.0 was the ability to pre-compile large declaration files into *header files*. By having large blocks of declarations and utilities compiled into one pre-compiled file, the compilation time decreased dramatically. The theory was, "Why re-compile sections of code that aren't changing between executions of the scripts?"

Along these same lines was the ability to compile scripts into a pseudo-code file, or a *.pcd* file. This further decreased the compilation time because the scripts were already in a compiled state. It didn't increase the run-time speed, however, because scripts were interpreted just as they were when a non-PCD file was compiled and run. However, it did allow them to be run without re-including external files, perform syntax, and parse-time checks. It also opened up another possibility. Tests the automation engineer didn't want modified without his or her knowledge could now be distributed in compiled form for other testers to use.

Context-sensitive help was also added, a foreshadowing of what was to come with documentation. Microsoft was slowly moving its documentation online; a controversial move made company-wide that was encouraged by many users, but discouraged by others. The printed documentation was slowly shrinking.

Personally, after getting the general idea of how to lay out an automated test suite, I never returned to the book. The online help described how each feature worked and offered a number of coding examples to clarify how each Test Basic command was used.

Some new and enhanced *dynamic link libraries* (DLLs) were added to version 2.0. These allowed three specific functions:

▶ Automation of DOS applications with DOS Virtual Machine (VM) routines

▶ Communication between other Microsoft applications using Dynamic Data Exchange (DDE)

▶ Remote distributed testing using the new Test Talk routines, which allowed for running tests on more than one machine across a Network Basic input/output system (NetBIOS)-compatible network

Making its first appearance was a driver that would allow testers to specify which tests to run. While it was thought to be hideous by many because of the colors used in its user interface, it definitely served a positive purpose in providing a way to run multiple scripts and served as an example of how to create a test driver. The test case driver is shown in Figure 2-5.

This first implementation of the test driver was written using Microsoft Test's own language: Test Basic. It was a useful tool for batch-running all automated tests and provided an excellent example of how to use the latest feature of Microsoft Test: the User Interface Editor. Test 2.0 made it possible for testers to add dialog boxes and menus to their test scripts. They could now either use the driver that was included with Microsoft Test or design their own. In addition, they could create countless other tools that required a user interface of some kind.

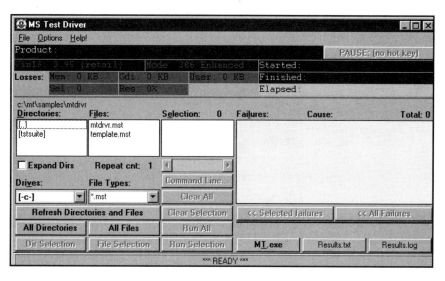

FIGURE 2-5 The Microsoft Test 2.0 test case driver.

Microsoft Test 3.0 and 3.0a

The following version of Microsoft Test, version 3.0, was born in the fall of 1994. Its installation program can be seen in Figure 2-6.

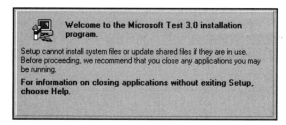

FIGURE 2-6
The Microsoft Test 3.0 instal-lation program.

When it was launched, Microsoft Test 3.0 didn't seem to be much of an upgrade from 2.0. Actually, it looked very similar, at first glance, to the previous version. However, when people looked a little deeper they found that Microsoft had been busy once again.

All of the DLLs had been re-written to be compatible with 32-bit versions of Microsoft Windows. As a result, those software companies that were busily upgrading their 16-bit applications to 32-bit found this latest version of Test invaluable. They could now take their existing scripts and run them on a 32-bit platform, with little or no modification.

The error numbers were another big change to the way Microsoft Test worked. Previously, each DLL had returned error numbers specific to itself. In some cases, tracking down an error number was tricky because some DLLs would begin numbering their errors in the same range as another DLL's routines. Some would return negative numbers for their error return values, others would return large positive numbers. And then, the Test Basic language itself would return its own run-time error numbers.

In Test 3.0 this issue was addressed by assigning a base number to each DLL as it was loaded and by having all DLLs start numbering their error return values at zero (0). The return value was then added to the base number assigned to the DLL returning the error, to arrive at a unique error number. This solution was very creative because it provided automation programmers with a unique error numbering system, and it left the error numbering scheme open-ended for future expansion.

While no discernible change was made to the Test Talk routines that allowed for distributing tests across a network, the name that collectively referred to those routines was changed to Network Distribution Libraries.

Note

Network Distribution Libraries was, in turn, changed to Network Distribution Procedures in Visual Test 4.0.

Lastly, the screen capture and comparison utility was updated. A screen no longer needed to be referred to as an index position in the capture file; screen captures could now be associated with a string describing the image. A new user interface was given to the capture utility as well. No modifications were made to the dialog capture and comparison utility, however. This was a foreshadowing of what was to happen to the dialog comparison utility in version 4.0; that is, the dialog utility was not included with Visual Test 4.0.

In the spring of 1995, a 3.0a version of Test was made available, which added support for Windows 95 controls. It was now possible to work with the new desktop layout, tree controls, tabs, sliders, spinners, and so on.

Microsoft Visual Test 4.0

As Microsoft's language group was moving into all-visual tools, it was decided that Microsoft Test 4.0 should go into that same group. The result was to rename the product Microsoft Visual Test and move it to a different development environment. An example of this new, visual approach can be seen in Figure 2-7, with the splash screen.

FIGURE 2-7 The splash screen displayed when starting Visual Test. Depending on what programming tools are installed and using the Developer Studio, different sections of this splash screen highlight.

Microsoft Developer Studio

Part of creating this vision of Visual Tools was having them share one integrated development environment (IDE). Therefore, now they all use the Microsoft Developer Studio, including some of Microsoft's other development tools that will soon hit the market, such as Microsoft's own Java compiler code-named *Jakarta*. (Visual Basic, however, remains the rogue development tool that uses its own specialized development environment. For the moment, anyway.)

The result is, that when working with most of the visual tools, you need only learn one programming environment and you have access to all your tools in one place.

32-bit Only

This latest version of Microsoft Test only works on 32-bit versions of Microsoft Windows: Windows NT and Windows 95. To make sure that 16-bit users weren't forgotten, however, the Microsoft Visual Test team followed Visual C++'s example by including the previous 16-bit version (Microsoft Test 3.0) on the installation CD-ROM.

Snap-On Parts

This latest version makes Visual Test more modular than before. If Visual C++ is installed at a later date, it integrates right into the Developer Studio. If version control is an issue, and the 2.0 version of SourceSafe is installed, it snaps into place in the "studio" as well. NuMega Technologies worked closely with Microsoft, so BoundsChecker 3.0 integrates into the IDE for use by both Visual C++ and Visual Test. Additionally, Software Testing Laboratories created an add-on tool (Test Now 2.0) for Visual Test that snaps into place on the Tools menu, just like BoundsChecker, so that the goal of having all tools available in one place is realized.

The Competition

It's been a good run for the Microsoft Test group, and there's plenty of competition to keep it on its toes. There are a number of test automation tools on the market for automating test cases under Microsoft Windows, with the most well-known being:

▶ WinRunner, by Mercury Interactive

▶ QA Partner, by Segue Software

▶ SQA TeamTest, by SQA, Inc.

Microsoft Visual Test has the edge on them all, however, since the tool isn't solely developed for Microsoft's external customers, it's also used internally by Microsoft's QA teams. The result is a full-featured tool that's always in the lead, as opposed to one catching up on the latest needs in test automation. This is why I've chosen to use Microsoft Visual Test as my own main automation tool: It's been developed by testers for testers, with access to the engineers who created the platform on which it's used to automate testing.

Summary

Visual Test was known as Microsoft Test for versions 1.0 to 3.0a. It started as a purely internal development tool, but when external clients became interested in it, it was developed as a product for wider use. It gradually improved its user interface, and Version 2.0 introduced header files, pseudo-code (*.pcd*) files, and context-sensitive help. Version 3.0 re-wrote the DLLs and updated the screen capture and comparison utility. Finally, version 4.0, Visual Test, instigated a fully visual set of tools, all available on the same screen, giving full support for Windows 95 and Windows NT.

3

Synopsis
of Visual Test

This chapter gives you an overview of the book and where particular topics about Visual Test 4.0 are discussed:

▶ We start by examining what happens when you fully install the product. This gives you a general idea of what it consists of and points you to those chapters that go into more depth about its specific features.

▶ After looking at the installation of the product, the remaining sections of this book are described, to help you decide where to begin your reading.

▶ The last part of this chapter provides definitions for some of the more common terms used in this book.

By default, Visual Test is installed into a directory called MSDEV on your main hard disk drive (for example, C:\MSDEV). Figure 3-1 shows all the files and folders that are installed into that main directory. Most of these topics are covered in Part II, "Overview of Visual Test" But let's step through them briefly here, so that we're familiar with what's available and where all of Visual Test's components can be found.

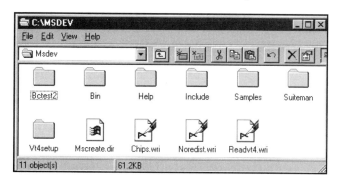

FIGURE 3-1
MSDEV folder.

Visual Test's Folders

The Bctest2 folder contains the new BoundsChecker 3.0 technology by NuMega Corporation. NuMega and the Microsoft Visual Test group got together to include some of BoundsChecker's *error-trapping technology* in the latest version of Visual Test. We discuss how to use this new feature in Chapter 13, "Beyond the Basics." Until then, there's nothing in this folder that you need worry about. It contains run-time libraries for both Windows NT and Windows 95 that are automatically linked into by Visual Test.

The Bin folder contains the guts of Visual Test. That is, all the *binaries*, or executable files, are found in this directory. It is where the Microsoft Developer Studio and Visual Test-related libraries and utilities are kept. It is also where the run-time program, *MTRun*, can be found which allows you to compile and distribute your test scripts. This will be discussed further in Chapter 13 and Chapter 14, "Working with Resources."

This folder is self-explanatory. It contains the help files used by Visual Test's context-sensitive help. The context sensitivity is very useful in tracking down exactly how to use a particular routine. Simply click on a keyword in the editor and press the F1 key. Help on how to use that keyword is then displayed.

The Include folder is where the declarations are kept for working with Windows *application programming interfaces* (APIs) and for allowing Visual Test to be backward-compatible with scripts written with previous versions of Microsoft Test. Visual Test has this folder in its search path so that when a script names an include file to be included, this is the folder that is searched. We'll go into more detail on these include files in Chapter 5, "Visual Test Language."

The samples found in this folder play a big part in learning how to use the Visual Test product. Take some time to go through them and dissect the examples to get a better idea of how to go about writing test scripts. This book does not go over these samples at all. Instead, we go over examples that we've included on the disk that's attached to the inside back cover of this book. Our examples include some of the details that the Visual Test tutorial suggests, along with other tricks of the trade that have been picked up over the years.

In Microsoft Test 2.0 and 3.0, a Suite Manager was included that served both as a sample script and as a tool for organizing all your test files. Microsoft has improved upon this utility and made it even more useful. It's no longer a sample script, it's a true stand-alone application. You'll note, however, that it is a .PCD file, meaning that it was written using the Test language, but compiled into this pseudo-code form restricting us from modifying its behavior.

Suiteman

We briefly go over the Suite Manager in Chapter 6, "Visual Test Utilities," and Chapter 12, "Overview." Only briefly, though, because the tutorial that comes with Visual Test introduces you to it. In Chapter 14, "Working with Resources," I show you what it looks like to build your own driver, so that if you find you need more flexibility than the Suite Manager provides, you can build your own version.

This last folder is made available so that you can re-run the installation program. If you didn't install a portion of the product when originally setting up the program, or a sample file was deleted or altered, this allows you to re-install all or part of the product. So, go nuts! Tear the samples apart, dig in! Don't worry about messing anything up because you can always re-install the program.

Vt4setup

Fortunately, you don't have to remember all of these directories and what is contained in each. Microsoft installed the necessary files in the Startup menu for Windows 95 users, and in the Visual Test 4.0 program group for Windows NT users. However, when it becomes necessary to go looking for a particular file, for whatever reason, it's helpful to know where to find it. Plus, by telling you what's in each folder, you have a better idea of the entire product.

Note

When other utilities, such as Software Testing Laboratories' Test Now 2.0, are added to the MSDEV folder, they will typically place their files into the appropriate existing folders. For example, Test Now's *Help* file could be found in the C:\MSDEV\HELP directory after that product had been installed. (See Appendix A, "Products for Visual Test 4.0 Users.")

The Remainder of this Book

By going through the folders in the above section, it's clear where the particular parts of the product I'll talk about will come. As mentioned before, most of these topics are covered in Part II, "Overview of Visual Test 4.0." Here is a brief description of the sections that make up the remainder of this book:

▶ **Part III, "Building a Test Suite":** In this part, I take you through building a test suite. If you've already spent a week or so playing with Visual Test, you might want to skim over Part II and move directly to here. Topics covered are

   — **Common Coding Guidelines**: With these, you can start building robust scripts.

   — **Defining an Approach:** You see the process involved in deciding where to start.

   — **Writing Simple Test Cases:** This gives you a first-hand look at banging out some code.

   — **Common Utilities and Routines:** You get an idea of the underlying utilities you have to create for your automation project.

   — **Review of the Final Test Suite:** This gives you a summary of what you've accomplished in writing your tests.

▶ **Part IV, "Advanced Topics":** Visual Test is a very capable product. There's always room to grow when using the tool. If you get to the point where you want your test suites run in a certain way, Visual Test has the full ability to allow you to build stand-alone applications.

In addition, if you are a tester with a computer science degree and want to get closer to programming in Windows, you have this ability with Visual Test.

This part describes how to take your scripts to a higher level by adding a user interface to them, working with advanced features of the Test language, and creating scripts to manage testing on multiple machines across a network.

▶ **Part V, "Appendixes":** There are five appendixes that give you other paths you can follow including a lot of source code listings so that you have a lot of examples at your fingertips.

— **Appendix A:** *"Products for Visual Test 4.0 Users"*
— **Appendix B:** "James Bach's *'Features of a Test Automation System'*"
— **Appendix C:** "Other Materials Relating to Software Quality Assurance"
— **Appendix D:** Listing of our test suite's main include file: NOTEMAIN.INC
— **Appendix E:** The common utilities you will find yourself writing when first starting an automation project: NOTEUTIL.INC
— **Appendix F:** The actual files that make up a test suite: assorted test case files for testing the common Windows editor.
— **Appendix G:** The log file generated from running our test cases.

Definitions

You should now have a pretty good idea of where to start your reading, based on your background in testing automation. However, before you move on to the other sections, let me first make sure we are using the same definitions for words that will be used throughout this book.

Before getting into the definitions, let me first explain the general method of how tests are organized. When a single test is written to verify a specific behavior of a feature of a product, that single test is commonly referred to as a *scenario*. A grouping of one or more scenarios for a given feature or area is referred to as a *test case*. And finally, a grouping of one or more test cases is what is referred to as a *test suite*, as shown in Figure 3-2. Furthermore, it is possible to have multiple test suites around for testing a single product, as you will see in the following definitions.

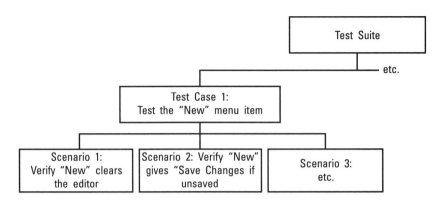

FIGURE 3-2 The hierarchical relationship of individual tests, their relationship to test cases, and how they all make up an overall test suite.

▶ **Benchmark Suite:** A benchmark suite is a group of test cases that checks the speed and performance of an application. Frequently, this has to do with searching, sorting, and graphic-imaging routines.

▶ **Full Functionality Suite:** This is the most common test suite that companies focus on. It is made up of test cases that check every feature of the product. It is usually the largest and most complex suite and is also the hardest to put together during the early, unstable stages of a product's development.

▶ **Regression Suite:** I briefly mention regression tests in Chapter 1. A regression suite is made up of test cases that verify that previously reported system problems (*bugs*) have not reappeared in the product. Sometimes, the more nasty bugs are included in the smoke suite.

▶ **Smoke Suite:** A smoke suite is run immediately after a new build of the product is received from the development team. If the tests don't find any problems in the major portions of the product, the build is usually accepted after a few manual checks are made. Otherwise, it's thrown back over the wall to development with a list of problems for it to fix before the testing team accepts it as a testable build of the product.

▶ **Smoke Test:** A test scenario in the smoke suite that tests the broad areas of the product. It's a test that doesn't go too deeply but verifies key areas of concern that, if found to have problems, would cause the build to be rejected. It's especially used on a product that is in its early, unstable stages. I've heard the term employed throughout the halls of Microsoft. It's a very good, descriptive term, and one the company is using in the tutorial that accompanies Visual Test 4.0.

▶ **Test Case:** A test case is a grouping of test scenarios. Usually there is a test case for each area of the product. These vary in their scope. For example, a test case could be for an entire menu (such as the File menu), or for a specific menu item. It just depends on the way the test automation team sets things up and to what granularity or level the test case focuses.

▶ **Test Driver:** A test driver is a program that steps through and runs a grouping of test scripts. These scripts might be test cases or test scenarios. Either way, the driver's sole purpose is to step through a list and run each file in its list.

▶ **Test File:** (See Test Script.)

▶ **Test Hierarchy:** The relationship of the test suite, test case files, and test scenarios that make up a test case. In the test hierarchy, the test suite is the parent of the test cases and the test cases are the parents of the test scenarios that relate to those test cases.

▶ **Test Scenario:** The test scenario is the lowest point of the automation test hierarchy. This is where a specific test is written and the results are checked.

▶ **Test Script:** I use test script, *test file*, and test case file interchangeably. Basically it's a file that contains either a specific test scenario or a grouping of test scenarios (in the case of a grouping, the test script is a test case). It can also be a program that runs other test scripts (that is, a test driver). In general, a test script is simply source code written in the Test language.

▶ **Test Suite:** A test suite is a group of test cases and test scenarios that test a product. On a simple project there may be only one test suite. On larger projects there can be any number. Some typical test suites are: benchmark, full functionality, regression and smoke. The test suite is found at the top of the test hierarchy since it owns all of the test cases and scenarios.

Summary

This chapter summarizes what is covered in the rest of the book. First, it looks at the contents of the MSDEV folder and goes through all the files and folders that are installed in that main directory. It then briefly walks through Parts III, IV, and V. Finally, it defines the basic testing terms used throughout the book.

PART II

Overview of Visual Test

41

Visual Test User Interface

4

Microsoft's test automation tool has been given a major face lift between versions 3.0 and 4.0. Where previous versions of Microsoft Test had their own integrated development environments (IDE), Microsoft Visual Test now integrates directly into a common IDE used by Microsoft Visual C/C++, Microsoft Fortran Power Station, and the Microsoft Development Library. Rumors are that Microsoft's Java development tool, currently named *Jakarta*, will also be using this IDE when it is released in the summer of 1996. This IDE is called the Microsoft Developer Studio (see Figure 4-1) and is an exciting step forward by Microsoft by having their development products use a single development environment.

If you have already used Visual C++ from version 2.0 and up, you may be familiar with the features of the IDE and you can quickly browse this chapter looking for the key components of Microsoft Visual Test that are different. If you've not done any development using the Developer Studio IDE, then you'll probably want to read every section of this chapter so that you have a good overall understanding of what it offers.

Note

In the interest of clearly communicating what features are available through the Developer Studio IDE when used with Visual Test, the IDE is looked at and discussed as if only Visual Test is installed. For Microsoft Visual C/C++ users, you will notice some differences depending on whether you are working on a C/C++ project or a Test project.

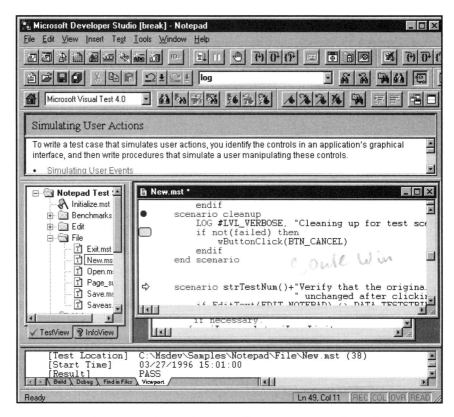

FIGURE 4-1 The Microsoft Developer Studio is an integrated development environment (IDE) used by many of Microsoft's development tools. This is a positive step forward because now programmers need only learn a single editor, debugger, and common supporting utilities.

The IDE Views

There are four principal windows that appear in the Developer Studio's main window:

▶ **Project Workspace:** The Project WorkSpace shows a graphical representation of the project's file hierarchy, making it easier to organize all related files in the test suite. It also provides easy access to the online documentation that is displayed in the InfoViewer Topic window.

▶ **InfoViewer Topic:** The InfoViewer Topic window is the interface into the online help for looking up information about features of the Test language and related topics.

▶ **Output:** The Output window provides a container for information on errors encountered while compiling the script, text written out by the test script, and other information.

▶ **Source:** The Source window is where the actual programming is done. This window acts as a text editor allowing you to type in your test script. As keywords are typed into this window they highlight depending on their functionality.

These windows provide easy access to information about the script you're writing and testing. We shall now look at each one in more detail.

Project Workspace

The Project Workspace window has two separate views, allowing users to see the hierarchical representation of their automation projects and the online documentation, which is helpful when learning a new feature of the product. In Figure 4-2, the InfoView tab is selected to show the online documentation.

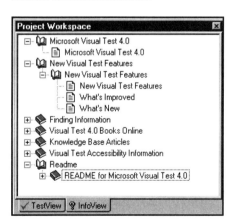

FIGURE 4-2
The Project Workspace provides easy access to online documentation and provides a hierarchical representation of the automation project.

In some cases, the window won't appear as shown in Figure 4-2. Instead, it will appear *attached* to the IDE's main window. This is known as the Docking View and is a difficult view to work in when using the IDE at a low resolution (800x600, or less). To get out of this docking mode, right-click anywhere in the project window and select the Docking View menu item, so that it toggles the check mark off. The window becomes a separate MDI (multiple document interface) window, or *child window*. You can now minimize it when it's in the way: It will appear as an icon at the bottom of the IDE's main window.

If you are working at a high resolution (1024x768 and up) you can tear off the window so that it isn't even a part of the IDE's main window. To do this:

1. Return it to the docking view mode by right-clicking on the contents of the window.

2. Select the Docking View menu item, so that the check mark toggles on.

3. Go to the empty gray space just to the right of the InfoView tab. Click on that area and drag the window out of the IDE's main window to make it a separate window.

Optionally, the Project Window can be moved to snap to the other side of the IDE's main window.

Tip

To avoid the now-detached window's attempt to re-attach to the IDE main window when moving it across the Developer Studio's window, hold the control key down while dragging.

Note

The InfoViewer Topic and Output windows can also be manipulated through the same methods as described for the Project Workspace window, and can therefore be torn off or minimized in the main window.

InfoViewer Topic

The InfoViewer Topic window (see Figure 4-3) works in conjunction with the InfoView tab found in the Project Workspace window. By double-clicking on a topic in the InfoView area of the Project Workspace window, the InfoViewer Topic window displays the information about that selected item.

FIGURE 4-3
The InfoViewer Topic window provides online help information on topics selected via the InfoView section of the Project Workspace window.

Output

The Output window (see Figure 4-4) has five separate tabs that provide different kinds of information to the Test programmer. The first tab, 1) *Build*, provides information about the progress and results of the compilation of the source code. If an error occurred while the script was compiling, double-clicking on the line displaying the error information will cause the Source window to display the line of code causing the error. 2) The *Debug* tab displays information generated by the debugger. The *Find* 3) *in Files* tab displays the results of the last search for information in a file by using the Find in Files menu item under the File menu. The fourth 4) tab, *Profile*, displays information generated by the Profiler. This is a tool associated with C++ development so it will have no effect when using Visual Test. The final tab is the *Viewport* tab which provides a place for 5) common output information and replaces the Viewport window that was used in previous versions of Test.

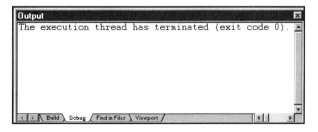

FIGURE 4-4
The Output window communicates information back to the user about compilation errors and run-time test information.

47

Tip

If an error occurs during the compilation of your script and your attempts to double-click on the error message in the Build section of the Output window don't take you to the line of code causing the problem, save the file so that it isn't considered an untitled file. This should fix the problem.

Although the Viewport is still available as a separate executable (MTVIEW.EXE) that can be run by a script, it now appears as a tab in the Output window providing a place for common output to go when the PRINT statement is used in a test script. The MTVIEW.EXE version of the Viewport is also used by the *Visual Test Suite Manager*, which provides a way to run multiple scripts one at a time. The Suite Manager will be discussed more fully in Chapter 6.

Source

The Source window is where the scripts are written using the Test language. As keywords are typed in they will highlight themselves depending on their usage. By default, keywords appear in blue, comments appear as green text, the keywords of the language that existed in separate DLLs in version 1.0 to 3.0 of Microsoft Test appear as red, and so on. In this editor is also where the Test programmer places breakpoints to cause the script to halt and bookmarks to simplify the process of relocating sections of code.

Toolbars

There are seven main toolbars available with the Visual Test installation in the Developer Studio. More may be added as other development tools are installed. Also, users can create their own toolbars via the Customize... menu item found under the Tools menu. Focusing on the toolbars specific to Visual Test, shown in Figure 4-5, the seven toolbars are:

▶ Standard

▶ Resource

▶ Edit

▶ Debug

▶ Test

▶ InfoViewer

▶ InfoViewer Contents

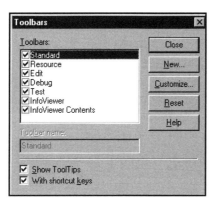

FIGURE 4-5
The Toolbars dialog box allows the user to control which dialog boxes are displayed in the environment.

Each toolbar is described briefly in this section.

If the toolbars in your installation of Visual Test don't appear the same as the toolbars in this book, it could be because you either have other development tools installed that work with the Developer Studio, or you're not working with a fresh installation of Visual Test and the toolbars have been modified.

Standard

The Standard toolbar is basically just that: the standard toolbar you find in most every application that uses toolbars. This can be seen in Figure 4-6. It provides a shortcut for creating new files, opening files, saving files, and saving all of the opened files in the environment. It also has shortcuts for the Edit menu allowing the user to cut, copy, paste, and multiple levels of undo and redo.

It also has search capabilities, which often aren't on a standard toolbar, but are available on this toolbar. These features allow you to search for items in the current window or across multiple files.

The last item on the toolbar makes it easy for the user to hide and show the Project Workspace window.

FIGURE 4-6
The Standard toolbar.

Resource

The Resource toolbar is put to use in the Advanced Topics section of this book (see Chapter 14 for more detailed information). Its purpose is to provide easy access to the resource editor that comes with the Developer Studio. By using this toolbar and the resource editor, dialog boxes, menus, and even toolbars can be added to make test scripts easier to use (see Figure 4-7).

FIGURE 4-7
The Resource toolbar.

Edit

The first four icons on the Edit toolbar are ones that I use frequently when editing a test case file in the development environment (shown in Figure 4-8). These icons, shown as flags, allow the programmer to place bookmarks on individual lines of source code. The reason for doing this is that many times it is necessary to jump from one section of the file to another, but it's a hassle to relocate where you were in the source window. Setting a bookmark lets the programmer mark important locations (such as declaration blocks to determine the type of a variable, or parameters of a function) so that they can be jumped to quickly. These four icons allow for setting a bookmark, jumping to the next or previous bookmark, and removing a bookmark.

FIGURE 4-8
The Edit toolbar.

The next grouping of buttons makes it easier to indent and un-indent text. Highlighting a block of text makes these buttons active. The same thing can be accomplished using the keyboard by pressing the Tab key to indent and the Shift+Tab keys to un-indent a block of text when it is selected.

The last buttons on this toolbar specifically affect the windows and their views. One causes a duplicate window of the same source code to be opened, so that work can be done in the same file at different locations. The other buttons allow you to split the views of the windows to accomplish this same task, except using a single window. The last set of buttons affect how the windows in the development environment are arranged: whether they're cascaded, stacked, or tiled vertically.

Debug

The Debug toolbar makes it possible to control stepping through a file's source code, line by line, so that errors can be tracked down more easily. The toolbar's buttons are shown in Figure 4-9. The first button on the toolbar turns off debugging mode. The next three are Step Into, Step Over, and Step Out. These relate to functions and subroutines for which source code is available.

FIGURE 4-9
The Debug toolbar.

When stepping through a file's source code, and a subroutine or function name is encountered, it's sometimes preferable to step into the source code for the subroutine so that every single line being executed can be observed. This is where the Step Into button comes in handy.

Tip

Many of these toolbar buttons have keyboard equivalents. For example, the Step Into function is also available through the keyboard using the F8 key, as shown in the Test menu.

However, there are times when it *isn't* necessary to step into a subroutine's or function's section of code. Perhaps you know that the routine isn't the source of the problem, so why look at its code? This is where the Step Over button comes in handy. The keyboard equivalent for this button is the F10 key, as can be seen under the Test menu.

Finally, for those occasions when it's no longer necessary to step through the code of a subroutine or function, the Step Out button allows the function or subroutine to continue its execution. In this situation, the debugger will stop on the line of source code that immediately follows the function or subroutine call. The keyboard equivalent to the Step Out button is Shift+F7.

Test

The Test toolbar is demonstrated in Figure 4-10. It contains buttons for running a script that is under development. The first button compiles and runs the script (its keyboard equivalent is F5). The second button will *break* or stop the script, so that programming can be done. The third button (it shows a hand) is used to mark *breakpoints* in the script. For further information on breakpoints, see the sidebar.

FIGURE 4-10
The Test toolbar.

The next three buttons on the toolbar are the same as those found on the Debug toolbar. They allow you to step into, over, or out of a function or subroutine.

The last few buttons are shortcuts to running the Scenario Recorder, Window Information (Winfo) utility, Suite Manager, and Screen utility. These utilities are discussed later in Chapter 6 and Chapter 12. You'll also notice that the menu items for accessing these utilities are found under the Test menu.

InfoViewer

The InfoViewer (Figure 4-11) provides a top-level search interface to the Visual Test 4.0 documentation and the Windows 32-bit Software Development Kit (Win32 SDK). Selecting one of these two Help files will affect which are used during the search for help on any given topic.

The first icon on this toolbar displays the top-level home screen for the Visual Test 4.0 Help file when clicked upon. This is yet another way to access help on Visual Test and is the same information that appears in the Project Workspace when the InfoView tab is selected.

FIGURE 4-11
The InfoViewer toolbar.

Breakpoints

A breakpoint is used to mark a line on which the execution of the script should be temporarily halted, allowing the Test programmer to examine the values held in the program's variables and to step through the rest of the code, line by line if necessary.

The next grouping of buttons is for creating search queries or acting upon previous queries. The first button causes a Search dialog box to be displayed, as is shown in Figure 4-12.

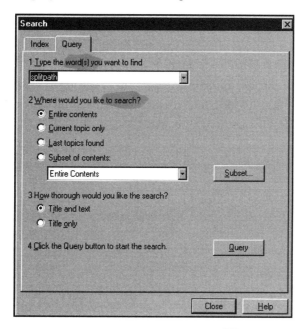

FIGURE 4-12
Use the Search dialog box to create queries for finding helpful information.

The second button causes the results from the previous query to be displayed in the Query Results window, as is shown in Figure 4-13. The next two buttons are used to navigate through the list of items found and displayed in the query results list, by moving to the next or previous query result.

Tip

When you're in the Query Results window, you can click on the pushpin to force the window to remain available.

FIGURE 4-13
After setting up a query in the Search dialog box, the Query Results window displays the results of the search.

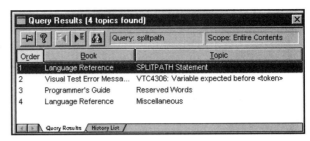

The last three buttons on this toolbar mark help topics once they've been found. The reality of online documentation is that it's sometimes difficult to track down the information needed to accomplish a particular task. In some cases, this information might need to be referenced multiple times. To help with this process, Microsoft has provided a bookmark feature that allows help topics to be marked for future reference.

The first of these last three buttons displays the InfoViewer Bookmarks dialog box, shown in Figure 4-14. It places the topic, currently being viewed in the InfoViewer Topic window (Figure 4-3), into the InfoViewer Bookmarks dialog box, so that it can be added to the existing list of bookmarks. The other two buttons on the InfoViewer toolbar navigate through these bookmarks.

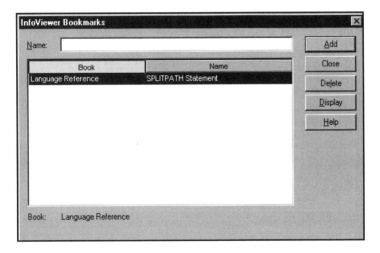

FIGURE 4-14 The InfoViewer Bookmarks dialog box shows bookmarks that have been put in place by the user for future reference.

InfoViewer Contents

The InfoViewer Contents toolbar (Figure 4-15) allows the user to specify subsets of the online help to speed queries and cut down on the amount of unrelated information that can be returned on broad queries. Once a subset has been defined the subset can be selected in the Search dialog box (Figure 4-12) to help focus the search.

FIGURE 4-15
Use the InfoViewer Contents toolbar to define subsets of the online help, so that only specific areas of the help are searched.

Making a Project

A *project* in the Developer Studio is a group of files that, together, make up a suite of tests. In the case of C/C++ developers, a project consists of the files that need to be compiled to create an executable or library file. A project is represented by a tree or hierarchical view of those files. When the number of files becomes unwieldy, placing them into subfolders helps organize those files.

It's not required for you to create a project in order to write test scripts. In the event that you don't, the Project Workspace window is still available, but it's missing the TestView tab. It only has the InfoView tab available, which shows the online documentation for Visual Test. If, however, a large automation project is undertaken, or you have other development tools installed that use the Developer Studio as an IDE, it's helpful to create a Project Workspace window, so your files are organized into one area and it's easy to find and edit them.

Creating a project is simple: Just select the New menu item found in the File menu. The dialog box shown in Figure 4-16 is displayed, giving you three file options. In this case, we want to create a Project Workspace.

After confirming that a Project Workspace will be created, you're prompted to specify where the project files will be placed, as shown in Figure 4-17.

FIGURE 4-16

Selecting the New menu item from the File menu provides the tester with three options.

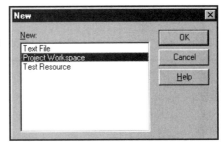

FIGURE 4-17

The New Project Work-space dialog box gives the programmer a choice of what type of project to create. Because Visual Test is the only programming language installed, it is the only choice available.

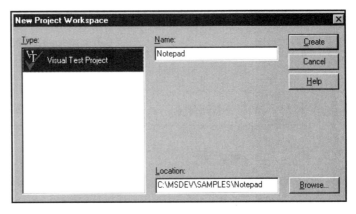

Note

If any other Visual tools are installed, the dialog boxes shown in Figure 4-16 and Figure 4-17 will offer more options. In these examples, only Visual Test is installed to clearly show the Visual Test components.

If you click the Create button, a directory is specified and created in the Location: edit control of Figure 4-17. It then places two files — notepad.vtp and template.tpl — into that directory. The first file, note-pad.vtp, is the Visual Test Project file and contains machine-independent information about the project hierarchy and its contents. It does not appear as a file in the Project Workspace, but is in the project directory and can be viewed by listing the contents of that directory. Because the *.vtp* file is machine independent, it is sharable with other team members.

The *.tpl* file is a template used whenever a new test case file is added to the project. If the template doesn't fit the testing team's needs, it can be replaced or modified and will automatically be used whenever new test case files are added.

After the project has been created, the Project Workspace looks like Figure 4-18. One more file is created after the initial workspace has been defined: notepad.mdp. The *.mdp* file holds machine-specific information and information about the user's workspace. Therefore, this file should not be shared with other team members. In the event that a new team member needs to pull over the project files, opening the *.vtp* file (in this case, notepad.vtp) will automatically create a *.mdp* file for that user's machine. The *.mdp* file doesn't appear in the Project Workspace tree, but it's in the same disk directory as the project files.

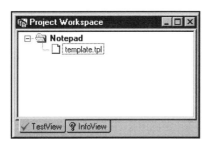

FIGURE 4-18
When a Visual Test project is first created, the only items in the Project Workspace window are the main project folder and a default template.

Adding to a Project

Now that the project has been created it is possible to add test cases to it. However, this is not done through the New menu item on the File menu. Going that route will only result in a separate text file being created that isn't a part of the project (and will require extra steps to add it to the project). Instead, a new test case file is created using the Insert menu shown in Figure 4-19.

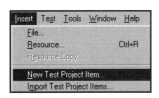

FIGURE 4-19
The Insert menu makes adding new or existing files to the project a simple task.

Note

If you want to import any existing files into the test project, the menu item to use is Import Test Project Items…, also shown in Figure 4-19. To add files to the project, click on the folder in which the existing file is to be placed, and then select this menu item.

Before selecting the New Test Project Item... menu item under the Insert menu, select a folder in the Project Workspace window, so the Developer Studio knows where to place the new file. In the case of the Notepad project we've just created, select the Notepad folder at the top of the tree. After selecting the folder and then New Test Project Item..., the dialog box shown in Figure 4-20 will appear.

FIGURE 4-20

Different types of files can be added to a project. Select the type of file to add, then type in the name. The three-letter file extension, if any, is added automatically.

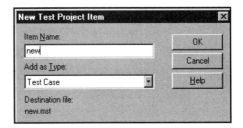

As you type in the name of the file, as shown in Figure 4-20, the Destination file: section of the dialog box shows the file name that will be created. It uses the extension associated with the type of file selected in the Add as Type: combo box (in this case a Test Case file).

Click on the OK button to place the new file into the project's directory and to show the file in the Project Workspace under the project tree. If it's a Test Case file, the *.mst* extension is automatically used. The contents of the editor for the new file are simply filled with the contents of the template file. This prompts the Test programmer in what to type and where to place specific source code.

When you add an existing file by using the Import Test Project Items... menu item in the Insert menu, the dialog box in Figure 4-21 comes up. It displays only those files in the directory associated with the folder in the project.

Unfortunately, there isn't a Browse button in the Import Test Project Items dialog box. Therefore, you have to copy existing files manually into the directory containing your project folder.

Tip

A quick way to add files is to right-click on the folder in the project you want to house the new file. When the pop-up menu appears, select New... to add a new file, or Import... to add an existing file to the selected folder.

Main Components of a Project

Throughout the first half of this book we'll build a test suite for the Windows Notepad application. This has been selected because it's available on everyone's system and most people are familiar with it and its functionality. The goal is to have a project that is similar to the one shown in Figure 4-22.

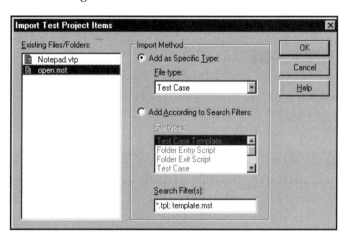

FIGURE 4-21
Files that already exist can be added to the project by using the Import Test Project Items dialog box.

FIGURE 4-22
This project is similar to the one we build in Part III.

When a new project is created, the name of the project is at the top of the project tree, and as each new item is added it falls in place underneath.

In Figure 4-22, initialize.mst is known as a *folder entry script* and appears as a green starting flag in the project window. This script is automatically run every time another script on the same level, or levels below, is executed. This only happens through the Suite Manager, however, so the entry script won't run when the test case files (*.mst* files) are executed in isolation, using the Developer Studio.

A folder entry script provides a place where initialization routines can be stored for tasks that need to be accomplished before each test case is executed. Entry scripts can also be placed in sub-folders. In this case, they will only run when scripts in those sub-folders, or in sub-folders of those sub-folders, are executed.

The folders in the project are known as *test folders* and hold test files related to a given area of the product (such as the File menu in Notepad) or to a particular task that needs to be performed (for example, benchmarking). One test folder can be placed within another, allowing for very structured projects. (In fact, an almost limitless number of folders can be placed inside another folder.)

A special folder appears in Figure 4-22 which isn't a test folder: It's an *include folder* and is identified by the lowercase *i* on its icon. This folder is searched by all test case files (*.mst* files) when they include a specific file as part of their requirement to execute correctly. It's searched by all *.mst* files at the level of the include folder and below.

Sub-include folders can be created at lower points in the project tree. These contain *.inc* files, which can only be accessed by files lower in the hierarchy. In the Notepad test suite example, only one include folder is used because of the suite's simple design.

An *include file*, delineated by the *.inc* extension in the file name, holds all the declarations for constants, user-defined types, global variables, and, sometimes, sharable subroutines and functions. Except for sharable subroutines and functions, an *.inc* file is comparable to a *.h* file in C, or an *.hpp* file in C++. *.inc* files will be discussed in more depth in Chapter 8.

Finally, the *test case* file type holds all tests that exercise the functionality of the product being automated. This file has a simple, dog-eared document icon with a letter *T* on it. An example can be seen in Figure 4-22 in the Help test folder: about.mst and topics.mst are two test case files holding one or more test scenarios. We create and dissect a simple test case file in Chapter 7. They also are discussed in more depth in Part III, when we build the initial structure for a test suite.

The Test Menu

You will use the Test menu the most when you're writing and debugging test scripts. These scripts can either be part of a project or separate, stand-alone scripts. The Test menu is shown in Figure 4-23.

FIGURE 4-23
The Test menu.

Compiling Scripts

Every time a script is executed, it must first be compiled to a form understandable by the test interpreter. You can save the compiled, interpretable form of a test script in a *p-code* or *pseudo-code* file, with a *.pcd* file extension. This feature has been available since the 2.0 version of Microsoft Test.

By saving a compiled script into a p-code file, as shown in Figure 4-24, the compilation step can be skipped for future executions of that script. While a p-code file doesn't run any faster than a script that must go through the compilation step, it does allow you to skip the compile time of the script. By doing this, the process is quicker, even though the actual execution time of the scripts is the same.

FIGURE 4-24
Save the compiled
form of a test case file
with the Compile...
menu item.

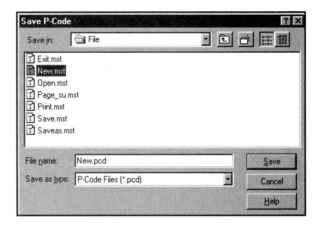

Another reason for compiling a script to p-code is so it can be distributed with the mtrun.exe run-time engine to other machines. The Visual Test license agreement says that only one copy of Visual Test can be installed on a single machine at any given time, but the mtrun.exe engine is freely distributable, as are any p-code files that you generate. Therefore, you could create a shipping product by using Visual Test as the development tool, compiling your product's source code into p-code, and distributing it with the mtrun.exe engine. Because p-code is machine independent, the process of distribution is that much easier.

Since p-code is a compiled or *tokenized* version of the source code text, comments and source code recognizable by humans are stripped out. As a result, a file can be distributed throughout your company without losing sleep about people making changes to it. This form of version control means you can ensure changes are only made with your knowledge.

Running a Test

If you select Go from the Test menu, or press the F5 key, the script in the active Source window will compile and run. The Output window will become active during the compilation process so that compilation errors can be reported back to the Test programmer (see Figure 4-25).

In the event that errors or warnings occur during compile time, the run of the script is terminated and the Test programmer is left to track down the root of the problem(s). Depending on how Visual Test is configured in its Options dialog box, you can ignore warnings that occur and allow the script to run. However, if an error does occur, it's because a fatal problem exists that will keep the script from running. Therefore, the script won't begin its execution step.

FIGURE 4-25 Errors and warnings that occur during the compilation of a script are displayed in the Output window.

Tracking Down Problems

When errors or warnings occur while compiling a script, the Output window reports information about them, as was shown in Figure 4-25.

The compiler does its best to not stop at the first error it encounters, so it can continue and report as many errors as possible in the compilation of the file. This is a great improvement over previous versions of Test, which would stop at the first error encountered.

When an error is encountered, the Test programmer can jump to the offending line by double-clicking on the error message in the Output window (under the Build tab). The line causing the problem is marked with an arrow on the left of the editor and it's up to the programmer to determine what the compiler is attempting to communicate.

Tip

Frequently, if you have a whole number of errors in a listing, they are based upon the first error. As a result, when you fix one specific problem, it might well result in all the other problems fixing themselves. Therefore, fix a couple of the obvious errors and recompile your script to get a fresh list of errors.

Tracking down compilation errors can be time-consuming and frustrating. There's no way around these errors other than becoming more familiar with Visual Test through using it more and more. Don't get too frustrated when an error is staring you in the face; just keep trying different things to track it down.

Tip

One thing I always do is create a temporary, untitled text file in the Developer Studio to try out different things, so that I can better understand how a feature works. Once I've got it figured out, I cut and paste the code into the main test case file.

Another way to understand what the compiler is trying to tell you is to press the F1 key, so it will bring up more information about the error that has occurred. When an error or warning is reported in the Output window, a number (such as "VTC4307") is given with the message. Click on that number to place the insertion cursor in the text of the Output window, then press F1. The context-sensitive help will search for information on it and provide a more thorough description of what's happening.

STEPPING THROUGH CODE

Even if a script is able to compile itself fully without errors or warnings, errors can still be encountered during the execution of the script. These types of errors are called *run-time errors*.

A simple example of a run-time error is when a script attempts to act upon a Windows control that doesn't exist. At compile time, the compiler checks to see if the Test programmer used the function, subroutine, or statement correctly. If so, the script is allowed to run. But if a line of code instructs Visual Test to click on a button that doesn't exist, the result is a run-time error.

Here is a script that will compile without any warnings or errors, but will generate a run-time error before completing its execution. It will generate the run-time error shown in Figure 4-26.

```
dim i as integer
dim j(5) as integer
    for i = 1 to 7
        j(i) = i
    next i
END
```

Another example of a run-time error is an *out-of-bounds error*. This type of error occurs when the program attempts to access an element of an array that doesn't exist. The compiler is unable to confirm this will happen, so the error doesn't occur until the script actually runs.

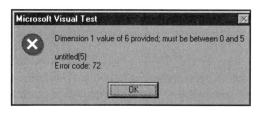

FIGURE 4-26
A run-time error has occurred. The compiler couldn't catch it because it couldn't determine that it would happen.

When these types of errors are encountered, it is sometimes necessary to track down what is going on by stepping through the source code line by line. This can be accomplished by setting a breakpoint on or around the line where the error is occurring. A breakpoint is a marker that tells the interpreter where to stop execution of the current script and turn control back over to the Test programmer. Figure 4-27 shows a script where a breakpoint has been set and execution has come to a halt.

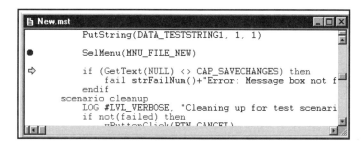

FIGURE 4-27 Execution of the script has been turned over to the programmer's control so that the script can be stepped through one line at a time.

There are two symbols on the left-hand side of Figure 4-27. The first is a large dot (actually, it appears on a color monitor as a small, red stop sign). The second item is an arrow that marks the line of code about to be executed. When the breakpoint was encountered, the script stopped before executing that line of code. (I had it execute that line of code so that the arrow and breakpoint symbol weren't overlapping.)

Now that the script is back under the programmer's control, Visual Test is in its debug mode and you can explore exactly what's going on with each variable as you execute the script one line at a time — as slow or fast as you want. (Just think how much fun it must have been tracking down problems in the days of punch cards and you'll appreciate this debugger even more.)

If you want to step through the source code, you can either use the Test toolbar, the Debug toolbar, or the keyboard equivalent of the menu items found under the Test menu. This is where the Step Into, Step Over, and Step Out menu items and toolbar buttons come into play.

Step Into will step into a function or subroutine for which source code is available. Step Over will allow a subroutine or function to perform its action and then move on to the next line of code. Step Out will allow you to get out of a function or subroutine you've stepped into.

Meanwhile, when you step through a script, Visual Test hides itself as each line of code gets executed, so that the application becomes active again. This allows you to step through a section of code without causing the Visual Test commands to act upon the Developer Studio instead of upon the application.

Note

If you find that Visual Test isn't hiding itself automatically, select the Options... menu item under the Tools menu, click on the Test tab to display the Visual Test settings, and make sure that both the Minimize on Start and Restore on End check boxes are checked.

WATCHING VARIABLES

Although stepping through a program one line at a time is helpful to make sure all the steps are being executed correctly, there's yet another detail that can be invoked to make tracking scripts even easier. These are windows for watching the values of a script's variables.

Visual Test supplies two types of these windows: the Test Watch window and the Test Locals window.

watch window

The Test Watch window is shown in Figure 4-28. It tracks only those variables it is told to track.

If you want to add a variable to the Test Watch window, click on an empty line and type in the name of the variable. Don't worry about using upper or lowercase characters, since Visual Test's compiler and interpreter aren't case-sensitive.

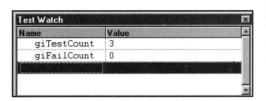

FIGURE 4-28
The Test Watch window shows the values held by variables it is told to track.

locals window

When working with variables in a function or subroutine, it isn't necessary to use the Test Watch window to track the values of those variables. This is because another window is provided, called the Test Locals window, which automatically displays the variables currently *in-scope* (available for use), with the exception of *global* variables. (You will find more details on global variables in Chapter 5.) Figure 4-29 shows the Test Locals window.

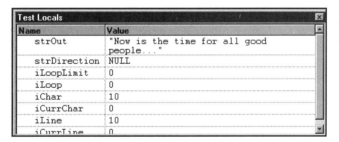

FIGURE 4-29
The Test Locals window automatically shows variables local to a section of code.

The Test Locals window will update itself automatically when moving in and out of functions and subroutines.

When leaving a routine, the window's variables are no longer used and are considered to be *out-of-scope* (no longer available). Therefore, the Test Locals window updates itself to show those variables that are still available. In the event that the Test Watch window is set to view the values of a variable that goes out of scope, it will put a message next to the variable that says, "<Error: Variable is not declared or is not in current scope>." Typically, the Test Watch window is used only to track global variables or local variables that can't be seen because the Test Locals window is so full.

BOOKMARKS

Bookmarks were mentioned briefly when the Edit toolbar was discussed earlier in this chapter. However, this feature is helpful enough to be mentioned again.

When working with source code, whether you're stepping through one line at a time or coding it for the first time, you may well want to move around the source code file to recall how something was written, declared, or used. The problem is that, when this happens, you lose your place and waste time trying to find where you were before you went on your search.

A bookmark allows tags to be set at specific lines of code so that the programmer can then search through those tags to return to a marked location (see Figure 4-30). To use a bookmark, either:

▶ Have the Edit toolbar up and available; or

▶ Use the Control+F2 keys to add/remove a bookmark and the F2 key to cycle through them.

FIGURE 4-30
Bookmarks make it easy for Test programmers to mark important sections of code, so they can be found and referenced more easily.

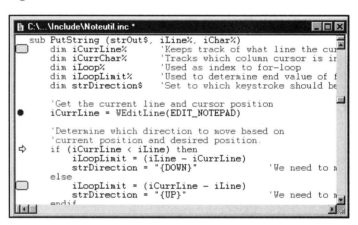

A bookmark appears as a blue, rounded rectangle on a color monitor.

Customizing the IDE

The development environment provided by the Developer Studio has gone through usability testing based on programmers' feedback and a number of new features have been added for each major release. However, you may well have specific requirements that have to be addressed if the tool is to be as helpful as possible. To help you with some of these personalized needs, Microsoft has made many features in the IDE customizable.

The Customize dialog box can be accessed in the Tools menu by selecting the Customize... menu item. This displays the dialog box shown in Figure 4-31 and makes available three customization areas:

▶ Toolbars

▶ Tools

▶ Keyboard

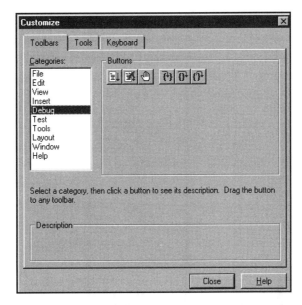

FIGURE 4-31
The Customize dialog box makes it possible for programmers to customize the development environment to their needs.

Toolbars

The Toolbars tab on the dialog box makes it easy for you to create your own toolbars with the features you need the most. Click on the category in the list box on the left. You'll see a number of buttons that act as shortcuts to many of the menu items. You can build a toolbar by clicking and dragging a button from the dialog box and dropping it anywhere on the screen where another toolbar does not exist. This creates a toolbar automatically for you. Then all you have to do is drag subsequent buttons into it. Easy! This new toolbar then becomes available in the list of toolbars shown in Figure 4-5.

Tools

As you can see in Figure 4-32, the Tools tab in the Customize dialog box allows the developer to add his own external tools to the Developer Studio's Tools menu. This way the tools are always within easy reach and are integrated into the development environment. Some programs, such as NuMega's BoundsChecker 3.0 and Software Testing Laboratories' *TestNow 2.0* automatically add themselves to the tools menu. These tools can be removed or modified via this customization dialog box.

FIGURE 4-32
The Tools tab in the Customize dialog box makes it easy to add your own tools to the Developer Studio's Tools menu.

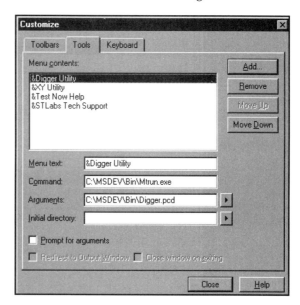

Keyboard

The Keyboard tab provides a means of adding accelerator or shortcut keys to commonly used menu items. Because Test programmers from previous versions of Visual Test are accustomed to specific keys for running and stepping through scripts, there are already some default keys carried over to make the transition to Visual Test a little smoother. For example, the F8 key shown in Figure 4-33 has been used in versions 2.0 and 3.0 as the Step Into shortcut key.

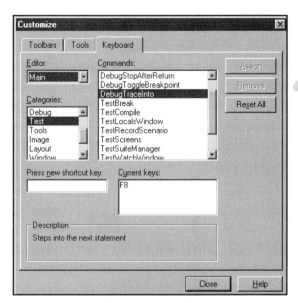

FIGURE 4-33
The Keyboard tab in the Customize dialog box makes it easy to add shortcut keys to commonly used menu items.

Options Dialog Box

Another form of customization is through the Options dialog box, which is also accessed via the Tools menu. Selecting the Options... menu item displays the dialog box shown in Figure 4-34. By stepping through the individual tabs in this dialog box, features of Visual Test can be tweaked for best performance, depending on your needs.

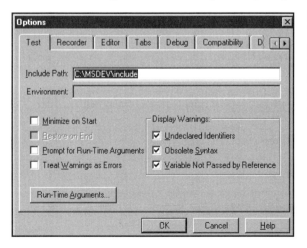

FIGURE 4-34
The Options dialog box gives you the flexibility to control how many Visual Test and Developer Studio features you want to have working.

Conclusion

A lot of time and effort was put in by the Microsoft Test group to bring Test up to this *visual* level, particularly by integrating it into the Developer Studio. As a result, Visual Test has shown that it truly is a development tool.

Because the Developer Studio is the main editing tool, those already familiar with the environment can focus on learning the Visual Test language and need to spend less time learning how to use the user interface. While there are a lot of features that make up this integrated development environment, they'll soon become second nature to you as you start using the features and developing scripts. Don't feel too overwhelmed, because you don't need to know all the features at once, and you should pick up on them as you need them.

In the next three chapters we look at the Visual Test language, the utilities found under the Test menu, and we dive into a simple scripting example designed especially for those new to programming in the Test language. The key is to push forward, not get too frustrated, and look back now and then to realize how much you've learned in such a short period of time.

Summary

There are four principal windows that appear in the Developer Studio's main window: Project WorkSpace; InfoViewer Topic; Output; and Source. These provide easy access to information about the script you're writing and testing. Also, there are seven main toolbars available: Standard; Resource; Edit; Debug; Test; InfoViewer; and InfoViewer Contents.

You can create and work with your own projects. A project is a group of files that, together, make up a suite of tests. It is represented by a tree or hierarchical view of sub-folders, such as test folders and include folders. You can also create a Project Workspace window, so your files are organized into one area. The Test menu allows you to write and debug scripts. The Test Watch window and Test Locals window allow you to watch variables and keep track of them. You can also use bookmarks.

Finally, it is possible to customize the IDE by adding or selecting the features you want, either on toolbars, tools, or the keyboard.

Visual Test Language

*V*isual Test's language is a robust version of BASIC that gives you enough flexibility to write complex scripts to meet your testing needs. The price to be paid for this flexibility, however, is the steep learning curve to understand all of the functions available. This learning curve is commonplace when learning any language, especially a language that works with a windowing environment. Don't get discouraged or overwhelmed by the amount of information, because you'll pick it up in time.

Fortunately, once you get the overall idea of the functions available to you, you'll know where and what to look for. The purpose of this chapter is not to step you through the Visual Test language piece by piece, but to give you an overview of what's available and tell you how to find more detailed information about those features. It isn't meant to replace the Visual Test online help documentation, but to provide a road map to what's available and where to look for information. As you write your scripts, knowledge of what statements and functions to use and which are available will come to you.

This chapter is a jump start on what the Test language has to offer. This way you can focus on what's important now—getting started in using Visual Test. As you get more comfortable with the language, move into the later chapters to discover some of the more advanced features. Some of the these are discussed in Chapter 13.

Note

If you are a programmer from the olden days of Applesoft BASIC, FORTRAN, or COBOL, or if you're new to programming altogether, I strongly recommend that you enroll in a local community college's *Introduction to Programming* class as soon as possible. These classes tend to be taught using the Pascal or C programming languages, structured languages after which the latest versions of BASIC are modeled.

Taking a class like this will give you the general introduction you need to pick up the Test language quickly. It's important to understand that Microsoft Visual Test is a programming language that has testing-centric utilities included to help simulate users' actions. This book does not teach basic programming methodology; it assumes you have some background in programming with a structured, procedural language like Visual BASIC, Pascal, or C. It points out how to do comparable tasks using the Test language.

The Basics of the Test Language

In this section, we shall go through the basic features of the Visual Test language. Some are extremely easy to use, some more complex. Let's start with a real easy nut to crack: *context-sensitive help*.

Context-Sensitive Help

I believe context-sensitive help to be one of the most important features of Visual Test. It's also the easiest to use. Therefore it's the first aspect of the language we're going to learn. It's extremely simple: Type in the keyword that you want to look up, making sure the flashing cursor is in or next to the word, and press the F1 key. That's it!

Declaring Variables

Unfortunately, it's all uphill from here. But declaring variables is also pretty straightforward.

There are three main *scopes*, or areas of visibility, that a variable can be declared as in the Test language:

▶ **Global variable:** The value of a *global* variable declaration can be referenced from any place within the source code, including other files (if they are included using the '$include metacommand), functions, subroutines, and error handlers. The scope of the variable is global, and therefore always available.

▶ **Local variable**: A *local* variable is accessible only by the function, subroutine, or main block of source code in which it is declared. The scope of a local variable is limited to the block of code in which it has been declared. If, for example, a variable has been declared within a function or subroutine, the main section of code cannot reference the variable within that subroutine or function. In the same way, a function or subroutine cannot access any variables outside themselves, unless those variables are globally declared.

▶ **Static variable:** A *static* variable is typically used only in functions and subroutines and causes those routines to save the value of a static variable, so that it is still available the next time the function or subroutine is called. A local variable in a routine is disposed of and reset to zero (0) when the routine terminates. This is not the case for a static variable, however.

A variable is declared in the Test language using the *dim* statement. In previous versions of BASIC, this statement was used only when working with arrays, but now applies to variables that hold only a single value as well. The format for declaring a variable is

```
dim variable[(subscripts)][AS type][,variable[(subscripts)][AS
type]]…
```

Items in square brackets are optional as part of the declaration. An example declaration that results in three variables of type *integer*, *string*, and *long*, is

```
dim A as integer, B as string, C as long
```

Variables can be declared anywhere in the test script. A common place to put declarations is at the top of the main script where the variables are being used, instead of interspersed throughout the script. This ensures the variables can be easily found.

An array of a given type can be declared by adding parentheses and the number of subscripts that make up that array:

```
dim D(10) as integer, E(5) as string
```

A global variable is declared using the "global" keyword and is the same as the local declaration, except that global is used in place of dim. The situation is the same for a static variable; the keyword "static" is used in place of dim. For example:

```
global F as integer
static G as string
```

SHORTHAND DECLARATIONS

Optionally, variables can be declared using shorthand notation instead of writing out the full name of the type. These abbreviated symbols, which represent the different types, are shown in Table 5-1.

TABLE 5-1 Single-Character Symbols Representing Variables.

Data Type	Shorthand
short	%
integer	%
long	&
single	!
double	#
string	$

An example of a variable declared using the shorthand notation is

```
dim MyVariable%, YourVariable$
```

where *MyVariable* is an *integer* type and *YourVariable* is a *string*.

Note

In Microsoft Test 3.0 the *short* data type was created to guarantee that a script executing under version 3.0 and that used a *short* type would continue to use a 16-bit form of an *integer*. This was done because an *integer*'s size will fluctuate between 16 bits (2 bytes) and 32 bits (4 bytes) when moving between the two environments such as Windows 3.1 (a 16-bit system) and Windows 95 or NT (32-bit systems). In Visual Test 4.0, however, the *integer* and *short* data types are both 32 bits, which is why they now both use the same shorthand notation (%).

Force Explicit Declarations

For better or worse, Test programmers can implicitly declare variables simply by using the shortcut character of a variable in the source code (for example, A$ = "Test"). By doing this, it is no longer necessary to use the dim statement. This is a poor practice to follow because it increases the chances for errors.

If, for example, you use the variable *iBook%*, but later accidentally referred to it as *iBooks%* (with an *s*), you now have two variables floating around when you think you only have one. Modifying the variable in one place and then referring to it (incorrectly) later will lead you to believe that somehow the variable didn't get set or was inadvertently modified somewhere else in the source code. Tracking down problems like this can be frustrating.

To force explicit declarations to be used, two check boxes need to be set in the Options dialog box. Those check boxes are Treat Warnings as Errors and Undeclared Identifiers, both of which are located under the Test tab. I suggest you turn these on to help you and your team avoid problems down the road.

The Main Section

When working in languages such as Pascal or C, there is always a main section of code that starts all the execution. In the C language there is a function named *main()* that is called by the operating system to get the program running. Pascal uses the *program* and *begin* statements, so that it's clear where execution begins.

The fact that Visual Test begins execution on the first line of code without a *main()* function or "begin" keyword throws most programmers who are familiar with other programming languages.

In the Test language, the first line *is* the beginning of the program. Any executable source code from the first line forward will be compiled and executed by Visual Test. Typically, a Visual Test script looks like this:

```
'Just for fun
dim i%, j%, k%
    viewport clear  'Clear the Output window
```

```
for i = 1 to 5
    for j = 1 to 20 step 5
        for k = 20 to 1 step -4
            print i,j,k
        next k
    next j
next i
end
```

If you type the following code into the Developer Studio's editor for a Visual Test file and then select Go from the Test menu, a bunch of numbers will print to the Output window.

Note

Comments to yourself or other programmers can be placed into the source code without being misunderstood by the compiler. Use the *rem* statement, or its shorthand notation, which is a single-quote mark ('), as used in the previous piece of code.

Writing Routines

Subroutines and functions provide a means of encapsulating code that is used multiple times, so it doesn't need to be replicated throughout the entire code base. By using a subroutine or function it's easier to change the behavior of the source code in one location. It also results in source code that is easier to read and to share with other testing teams.

Typically, subroutines and functions are placed after the *end* statement, outside the main section of source code. However, this is not a requirement, just a style that many programmers follow so that it resembles C's *main()* block of code. Separate routines are then referenced from that block of code to get everything running.

Others programmers will place all of the functions and subroutines at the top of the source code file and the main block of code that calls those routines at the bottom, which resembles the way a lot of beginner Pascal programmers were taught.

The fact is, it doesn't really matter, just as long as a style is chosen and adhered to. I advocate placing functions and subroutines after the end statement so that the first thing a programmer sees when opening up a test case file is the main section of code that gets everything started.

What it comes down to is that, no matter where a function or sub-routine is placed, its section of code isn't executed until it's called—either by the main program or indirectly from the main program by another function or subroutine originally called by the main program.

SUBROUTINES

A subroutine is the same as a function, with one significant difference: It doesn't return a value. C programmers can relate to a subroutine as a function with a *void* return type.

Subroutines and functions no longer need to be declared, as was the case in versions preceding Visual Test 4.0. There's no need for a forward pro-totype or declaration to be there to tell the compiler that the function or subroutine exists, except in the case of a function or subroutine that's in a dynamic linked library. (DLLs are discussed in Chapter 13.) The only part that needs attention is the actual definition of the function or sub-routine. This is a typical subroutine definition:

```
'****************************************************************
'* Subroutine:   ResetApp
'* Purpose:      Attempts to reset the application to a known
'*               state. This routine will likely grow in
'*               complexity as strange circumstances are
'*               discovered where it isn't able to reset the
'*               application.
'*
'****************************************************************

sub ResetApp()
    wMenuEnd
    wMenuSelect("FILE\NEW")

    if (GetText(NULL) = "Save changes?") then
        wButtonClick("No")
    endif
end sub 'ResetApp()
```

This subroutine performs a simple yet important task used when testing almost any application: It resets the application to a known state or con-dition. No local variables are used in this example, but if they were, they would be declared using the dim statement and be placed directly under the first line of the subroutine (*sub ResetApp()*). No parameters are required for this subroutine, either, which is why there are no variables listed inside its parentheses.

To activate the source code in the *sub ResetApp()* subroutine it must be called. This can be done by the main script, or another function or sub-routine.

FUNCTIONS

A function is similar to a subroutine, except that it returns a value when it has finished its task. Here is a typical function (it returns a string with a value representing how many times this function was called).

```
'****************************************************************
'* Function:    strFailNum
'* Purpose:     Keeps a counter of the total number of failures
'*              that have occurred using the fail command for
'*              the current test case file. For this to work,
'*              it must be called for each failure and is
'*              therefore designed to work with the fail
'*              statement.
'*
'* Parameters:  NONE
'*
'* Returns:     STRING  The string that is returned is formatted
'*                      to fit in front of the text being
'*                      included in the fail statement.
'*
'* Format
'* returned:    "Fail #<num>: "
'*
'* Use:         FAIL strFailNum()+"<descrip-of-failure>"
'*
'****************************************************************

function strFailNum() as string
    static iCount%

    iCount = iCount + 1
    strFailNum = "Fail #"+trim$(str$(iCount))+ _
                 ": "
end function 'strFailNum()
```

return value

Pay less attention to what this function does and more to how it is structured. The front part declares the name of the function to be *strFailNum*. The function doesn't take a parameter, either, but it does make use of a static variable. Recall that a static variable retains its value even after the function has been exited. Therefore, this function not only returns a nicely formatted string with error information, it also keeps a counter of how many times it was called. This function works by only being called when an error occurs so that the counter is updated only in those situations.

Note

A line of source code can be up to 256 characters long. Because it is difficult to read long lines of source code, especially in an editor at low resolution, it's preferable to break those single lines into multiple lines. This can be done by using the underscore character (_), as seen in the last piece of code.

As you may recall, a function must return a value when it terminates, and in this case the value must be an integer. A function returns a value by setting the name of the function equal to the value to be returned. This is not the same as the *return* statement used in the C language, which will immediately exit the function. Instead, the value isn't returned until the end of the function is reached or an *exit function* statement is used (use the exit statement sparingly, if at all, since common coding practices encourage routines exiting at a single point in the routine. In this case that single point would be at the *end function* statement). Assigning the name of the function to the value to be returned is the same way Pascal's functions return values.

MACROS

A *macro* is similar to a function in the way it operates: It can take parameters and returns a value to the section of code calling the macro. A macro takes a single expression instead of multiple lines of code, unlike functions and subroutines, which can take multiple lines of code:

```
MACRO ConvNum(theNum) = trim$(str$(theNum))
```

Another difference that macros bring to the table is that they don't allocate a chunk of memory to execute a task and then free that memory up, as do subroutines and functions. Instead, the compiler replaces every instance of where the macro is called with the expression that defines that macro. The result is a larger compiled-form of the code, but faster execution since the run-time engine doesn't need to take care of allocation and de-allocation of memory.

User-Defined Types

The term *type* refers to the kind of value held by a variable in the Test language. The standard types available in Visual Test are shown in Table 5-1. But there are times when it is helpful to encapsulate a number of variables that are related to each other. The way to do this is for you to create your own type. In Pascal this is known as a *record*, in C it's known as a *structure*, and in Visual Test it's known as a *user-defined type*. The following is an example of a user-defined type that might be created to help track information about a test:

```
type TESTINFO
    iTestID        as long
    strDescrip     as string
    strExpResult   as string
    strRecResult   as string
    fPassed        as integer
end type 'TESTINFO
```

Note

Notice that when declaring a *field* in a user-defined type, the longhand form of declaration is used. That is, a $ isn't used to declare a string, it is actually written out as "as string." This is a requirement of the compiler, I know not why.

Once a new type has been declared, it can be used like any other type by declaring a variable with either the dim, global, or static statements. An array of the type can also be created, if desired:

```
type TESTINFO
    iTestID        as long
    strDescrip     as string
    strExpResult   as string
    strRecResult   as string
    fPassed        as integer
end type 'TESTINFO

dim tiTestOne as TESTINFO
dim tiMenuTests(20) as TESTINFO
global tiAllTests(100) as TESTINFO
```

The first variable declaration creates a local variable called *tiTestOne* that is a single variable of type *TESTINFO*. The second declaration creates a local variable that is a 20 element array of type *TESTINFO*. The third declaration is a global variable that holds 100 array elements of type *TESTINFO*.

The fields or members of the user-defined type can be accessed by using the variable name along with the dot (.) operator:

```
'User-defined type declaration
type TESTINFO
    iTestID         as long
    strDescrip      as string
    strExpResult    as string
    strRecResult    as string
    fPassed         as integer
end type 'TESTINFO

'Variable declarations
dim tiTestOne as TESTINFO
dim tiMenuTests(20) as TESTINFO
global tiAllTests(100) as TESTINFO

    'Setting values to variables declared using a
    'user-defined type.
    tiTestOne.iTestID = 1
    tiTestOne.strDescrip = "Verify Open menu works"
    tiTestOne.strExpResult = "The Open dialog box"
    tiTestOne.fPassed = TRUE

    tiMenuTests(1).iTestID = 1
    tiMenuTests(1).strDescrip = "Verify Open menu works"
end
```

When a variable is declared in Visual Test it is automatically initialized to zero (0), or in the case of strings, set to an empty or *null* string. Therefore, it isn't necessary to set unused values to zero (0) yourself. You need only set those items in the user-defined type you wish to give a particular value to. Programming styles vary on this approach, however; some programmers still prefer to set each value to zero (0), to ensure it's initialized properly.

Conditional Branching

There are two types of statements in the Test language that allow for a situation to be assessed and acted upon, based on a true or false situation. They are known as *condition branches* and they allow you to control how the execution of the source code branches into other sections of source code depending on a given condition. They are

▶ if/then branching statements

▶ Select case branching statements

IF/THEN BRANCHING

The first type of branch is an if/then branch statement. The form this statement takes is very similar to C and Pascal programming languages. Listing 5-1 shows a couple of typical if/then statements. In them, the *PutString* subroutine takes a text string, line, and character position and places the provided string at the specified line and character positions in the active window. (The special w* functions will be discussed later in the "Working with Windows Controls" section of this chapter).

LISTING 5-1 A Couple Of Typical if/then Statements.

```
'****************************************************************
'* Subroutine:  PutString
'* Purpose:     Places a string into the Notepad editor at a
'*              specified line and character position.  If the
'*              line or character doesn't exist, this routine adds
'*              the necessary carriage returns and spaces.
'*
'* Parameters:  strOut$ String to be written to the editor
'*              iLine%  Line at which string is to be written
'*              iChar%  Character/column position to place string
'*
'****************************************************************

sub PutString (strOut$, iLine%, iChar%)
    dim iCurrLine%      'Keeps track of what line the cursor is on
    dim iCurrChar%      'Tracks which column the cursor is in
    dim iLoop%          'Used as an index to for-loop
    dim iLoopLimit%     'Used to determine end value of for-loop
    dim strDirection$   'Set to which keystroke should be used
```

```
'Get the current line and cursor position
iCurrLine = wEditLine("@1")

'Determine which direction to move based on
'current position and desired position.
if (iCurrLine < iLine) then
    iLoopLimit = (iLine - iCurrLine)
    strDirection = "{DOWN}"           'We need to move down
else
    iLoopLimit = (iCurrLine - iLine)
    strDirection = "{UP}"             'We need to move up
endif

'Move to the desired position, adding lines
'if necessary.
for iLoop = 1 to iLoopLimit
    if (wEditLine("@1") < wEditLines("@1")) then
        play strDirection
    elseif (strDirection = "{DOWN}") then
        play "{END}"
        play "{ENTER}"
    else
        play strDirection
    endif
next iLoop

'Get the current character position
iCurrChar = wEditPos("@1")

'Based on the current position, determine which
'direction to move.
if (iCurrChar < iChar) then
    iLoopLimit = (iChar - iCurrChar)
    strDirection = "{RIGHT}"
else
    iLoopLimit = (iCurrChar - iChar)
    strDirection = "{LEFT}"
endif

'Move to the desired position added spaces if needed.
for iLoop = 1 to iLoopLimit
    if (wEditPos("@1") < _
```

(continued)

LISTING 5-1 A Couple Of Typical if/then Statements. *(Continued)*

```
        wEditLineLen("@1",wEditLine("@1"))) then
        play strDirection
    elseif (strDirection = "{RIGHT}") then
        play " "
    else
        play strDirection
    endif
next iLoop

play strOut    'Type the string at the
               'current location
end sub 'PutString()
```

This subroutine will place a string at a specific line and character position in a text editor. The text string, line, and character positions are provided by the caller. The subroutine determines where the cursor is in the editor, whether or not spaces and carriage returns need to be added, and then types the string into the editor using the Test language's *play* statement. There are a number of conditions that need to be checked, which is why the if/then statement is so important.

The key to any conditional branch is that it must somehow evaluate to a true or false value (also known as a *boolean* value). If it evaluates to true, then the execution steps into the if statement. If it evaluates to false, then the code in the if statement isn't executed. In the situation where it evaluates to false and an else branch exists as part of the if statement, the else branch is executed.

Some of the if/then statements can get quite elaborate and hard to read. One way to cut down on this is to assign some of the values to individual variables and then test the conditions of those variables. Listing 5-2 shows both a convoluted if/then statement and then two other versions of it that are a little easier to read.

LISTING 5-2 An Example of a Complex-Looking if/then Statement, Broken Down Into Two More Readable Alternatives.

```
'*** original form of IF/THEN statement taken from Listing 5-1
    if (wEditPos("@1") < _
```

→ ordinary control see p.99

→ ordinary control see p.99

```
      wEditLineLen("@1",wEditLine("@1"))) then
      play strDirection
   elseif (strDirection = "{RIGHT}") then
      play " "
   else
      play strDirection
   endif


'*** alternate form of the above IF/THEN statement

'(Extra declarations that would be placed at the top of
'the subroutine)
dim iCurrPos%        'Current position of the cursor in the text line
dim iCurrLine%       'Current text line the cursor is in
dim iLineLen%        'Length of a given line of text

'(The modified IF/THEN statement requiring the new variables to
'be initialized first.)

   iCurrPos = wEditPos("@1")
   iCurrLine = wEditLine("@1")
   iLineLen = wEditLineLen("@1", iCurrLine)

   if (iCurrPos < iLineLen) then
      play strDirection
   elseif (strDirection = "{RIGHT}") then
      play " "
   else
      play strDirection
   endif


'*** alternate, alternate.
'(Going to extremes just for the sake of an example, the first
'line of the IF/THEN statement could be modified yet another
'way by adding a fourth variable)

dim fMoveCursor as integer

   fMoveCursor = (iCurrPos < iLineLen)

   if fMoveCursor then 'et cetera…
```

While the second version of the if/then statement in Listing 5-2 is easier to read, it requires three extra variables to be declared. The style to be used must be determined by the automation programming team and weighed against the experience of the users on that team.

In the third version, the first line of the if/then statement uses a fourth variable that is set to a boolean value (true or false). That variable can then be used as the sole expression. The last example goes to extremes, but can be helpful when a true/false value needs to be used multiple times, as it can be evaluated and stored once using a variable.

SELECT CASE

The second form of conditional branching is the Test language's *select case* statement. This is very similar to C's *switch* statement and Pascal's *case* statement and takes the form shown in Listing 5-3.

LISTING 5-3 A Select Case Statement.

```
'In this example we propose that a variable called
'iTestResult is used in a test script.  There are
'four different values it can be assigned to
'depending on the problem that may have resulted
'during the test execution: The test passed without
'problems; it failed; it was interrupted by the
'tester running the script; or an unknown error
'occurred causing the script to terminate un-
'expectedly. In this proposed example, the case
'statement might look something like this:

'Constants declared at the beginning of the script.
const RESULT_PASSED  = 1
const RESULT_FAILED  = 2
const RESULT_STOPPED = 3
const RESULT_UNKNOWN = 4

dim iTestResult as integer


'Select case statement encountered lower in the
'script and used to write out summary information.
select case iTestResult
    case RESULT_PASSED
```

```
        log "The test script passed."
    case RESULT_FAILED
        log "The test script failed."
    case RESULT_STOPPED, RESULT_UNKNOWN
        log "Test script terminated unexpectedly."
    case else
        log "Unknown value set to iTestResult!"
end select
```

The select case statement is easier to read in a situation like that shown in Listing 5-3 than is an if/then statement with a number of elseif branches.

Note

The *goto* statement is known as an *unconditional branch* and should be used sparingly. Heavy use of goto, especially when it jumps backward or up in a source code listing, leads to what programmers commonly call *spaghetti code,* since it's difficult to trace the path of the source code's execution. Using goto is commonly considered poor programming style. Avoid it or be prepared to face the wrath of fellow programmers.

Note also that the uses and abuses of unconditional branching are discussed in Chapter 8.

Loops

There are three different loops for controlling the execution of sections of code multiple times. These are the *for/next, while/wend,* and *do/while/until* loops. Refer to the documentation for complete details on each of these loops. We focus on brief introductions to each loop in this chapter.

FOR/NEXT LOOP

The for/next loop is the easiest of the three and is the most unlikely to get caught in a never-ending loop. A typical for/next loop takes the form shown in the following code:

```
'SYNTAX:
'for <counter> = <start> to <end> [step <increment>]
'   [<tasks to be carried out>]
```

```
'    [EXIT FOR]
'next [<counter>]
'
'Example:
dim iLoop%
    for iLoop = 2 to 20 step 2
        print "Counting by 2's: ";iLoop
    next iLoop
end
```

Here, the *iLoop* variable is initialized to the value 2, the *print* statement prints out the string and the value set to iLoop, and then it increments the iLoop counter by 2. If iLoop is still less than the <end> value, then the loop executes its contents again, using the new value of iLoop.

WHILE/WEND LOOP

The *while* statement requires the condition it evaluates to be true before it allows the script it encapsulates to be executed. Here is a very simple search algorithm using a while/wend loop:

```
'SYNTAX:
'while <condition>
'    [<tasks to be carried out>]
'    [EXIT WHILE]
'wend
'
'Example:
const MAX_NAMES = 100    'Max. # of names allowed

dim strNames(MAX_NAMES) as string   'Name array
dim iIndex as integer               'Index into array
dim strTheName as string            'Name to search for

    'Assume the array strNames gets filled with up to 100 random
    'names (index positions 0 to 99) taking the form
    '<FIRSTNAME>,<LASTNAME>, all in capital letters.  Now, search
    'for a name in that array and terminate when the name is found
    'or when the end of the array is reached.

    strTheName = "DAN,HODGE"
    iIndex = 0

    while (iIndex < MAX_NAMES) _
```

```
              AND (strNames(iIndex) <> strTheName)
            iIndex = iIndex + 1
    wend

      'source code continues ...
    end
```

Note

The conditional section of the while/wend statement does all of the work by determining if the name has been found or if the index has exceeded the total number of names in the list. When this statement is terminated, *iIndex* will either hold the location of the name in the array (a value between zero (0) and 99), or it will hold the value 100, signifying that the name wasn't found in the array.

DO/WHILE/UNTIL LOOP

This form of loop is used when the task needs to be done at least once, and possibly multiple times. If you use the do/while/until loop with the syntax shown in the following code, the statements will be executed and then it will determine whether or not the process needs to be repeated.

You can also use the *while* option. If you do, the execution will be repeated as long as a condition is true. Alternately, the *until* option will keep the execution going until a condition is met.

```
'Syntax:
'do
'    [<tasks to be carried out>]
'loop [ UNTIL | WHILE ] <condition>
'
'Example:
'Assume a function called RunTest that returns TRUE
'if the test has been executed successfully, and FALSE
'if an error occurred. Assume further that the tester
'wants execution of the tests to stop in the event any
'one of the tests fails. The code might look similar
'to the following:

dim fTestResult%    integer

    do
        fTestResult = RunTest()

        if (fTestResult) then
```

```
          print "This test passed."
     else
          print "This test failed."
     endif
   loop while fTestResult  —True
end
```

Working With Windows Controls

Visual Test's language is very similar to the Visual BASIC language. Most people assume that they're so similar because the two development teams at Microsoft work together and share the sections of the two languages that intersect. However, this isn't the case: They've gone down two separate paths, with notable divergence in the areas of pointers and Windows controls (that is, Windows 95 or Windows NT buttons, check boxes, menus, and so on), and other significant differences.

One of the key areas where Visual Test differs from Visual BASIC is in the functions and statements it provides for working with Windows controls. In previous versions of Test, these functions were kept in separate DLLs and linked to Test by the mstest.inc include file. But in the latest version of Test, this is no longer the case; the functions have been brought into the language and made intrinsic to it.

We'll start our introduction to working with Windows controls by taking a simple example of clicking on a button. This is the easiest statement for working with Windows controls and allows us to both demonstrate the basics and point generally to how all of the routines work with Windows controls.

Then we shall look at another example: working with controls that don't have a caption as part of their configuration.

Control With a Caption

Figure 5-1 shows the Open dialog box used by the Microsoft Notepad editor. This contains a number of Windows control types:

▶ Static

▶ Combo box

▶ Edit

▶ Toolbar

▶ Listview

▶ Button

q Win 95 (or WinNT 4.0)

FIGURE 5-1
The Open dialog box is a good example of a dialog box that contains a number of Windows controls that can be acted upon using Visual Test.

All these types can be worked with using the functions and statements provided in the Test language.

The easiest control to work with is a control that has a caption, or label, associated with it. A button, for example, has text on it that is considered a caption. To work with a button, the user need only use one of the many wButton* functions or statements. These are shown in Table 5-2.

TABLE 5-2 Functions and Statements for Working with a Windows Command Button.

Keyword	Type	Description
wButtonClassLen[1]	Function	Returns number of characters in button's class name.
wButtonClick	Statement	Clicks on a button given a caption.
wButtonDefault	Function	Determines whether a button is a default button or not.
wButtonDefaults	Function	Returns the number of default buttons in the active window.
wButtonEnabled	Function	Determines whether the specified button is enabled or grayed out.
wButtonExists	Function	Determines whether or not a button with a specific caption exists.
wButtonFind	Function	Returns the handle of a specified button.
wButtonFocus	Function	Returns true if the specified button has focus.
wButtonGetClass[1]	Statement	Fills a buffer with the names of classes associated with buttons.
wButtonMoveTo	Statement	Moves the mouse pointer to a specific location in the specified button.
wButtonSetClass	Statement	Informs the Test language what class names are associated with buttons.
wButtonSetFocus	Statement	Sets the input focus to the specified button.
ButtonGetClass[2]	Function	Returns the names of classes associated with buttons.

[1] Remains only for backward compatibility.
[2] Replaces the need for wButtonGetClass and wButtonClassLen.

The functions and statements shown in Table 5-2 are typical of all of Visual Test's routines that work with Windows controls. That is, there are some routines that are found for each control, and some specific to how each control works. An example of a common routine is the *wButtonSetFocus* statement. This is available for virtually every control, except that it varies in its name. So, for a check box control, instead of using wButtonSetFocus, it would use *WCheckSetFocus*.

When in doubt as to what routines are available for working with a particular Windows control:

1. Go into the Developer Studio and type a **W**, followed by the class name or type of control.

2. Highlight it.

3. Press the F1 key to get online help.

Note

Each control in Windows has a *class name* associated with it. For a command button, its class name is *button*. An edit control is *edit*, a check box control is *check*, and so on.

Because all controls in Windows are actually windows themselves, class names identify the type of control and the behavior associated with that control. For example, while a check box and a command button expect to be clicked on, it doesn't make sense for that to happen for a static control. All controls are simply windows and therefore need to have class names associated with them so that it can be determined what type of window they are and how they can be expected to act.

To find out the class name associated with a given control, use the Window Information utility (also known as *Winfo*) which is discussed in Chapter 6.

Returning to the Open dialog box, shown in Figure 5-1, we can click on the Open or Cancel buttons by using the following statements:

```
wButtonClick("Open")
wButtonClick("Cancel")
```

Pretty simple. If you look up *wButtonClick* in the online help you'll see there is a second, optional parameter that can be used as part of the statement. This tells the statement how long to look for the button it wants to click on, before giving up and generating an error saying the control can't be found. This *time-out* parameter is usually only provided in circumstances where a dialog box containing the button might take longer than usual to display. If the parameter isn't provided, the default wait time specified by the *SetDefaultWaitTimeout* function is used.

CONTROL WITHOUT A CAPTION

Working with controls that have captions is pretty easy and straightforward. Where things become more interesting is when working with controls that don't have a caption as part of their configuration.

Combo boxes, edit controls, and toolbars don't have captions. Instead, they usually have another Windows control sitting next to them, called a *static* control, that acts as a caption. A static control is simply a control whose only purpose is to provide text next to a captionless control, to help the user identify the purpose of the control.

In the case of Visual Test, the static control serves another purpose: to provide a place for the Test language's routines to begin searching for a particular control. In the case of the edit control in the Open dialog box, where the name of a file is typed in, the static control associated with it has the caption "File name:" as seen in Figure 5-2. The text of the static control is used to specify which edit control is to be typed into.

FIGURE 5-2
Notepad's Open dialog box with a file name typed into the edit control, and with the static control next to it.

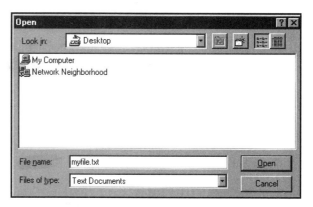

An example of using the edit control by using the static control is shown in the next line of code. It results in the Open dialog box appearing (as in Figure 5-2), with *myfile.txt* in the edit control:

```
wEditSetText("File name:","myfile.txt")
```

The first parameter of *wEditSetText()* is the name of the static control. The second argument is the text to be placed into that control. An optional third parameter is the amount of time to wait for the control to appear. As we discussed when we were working with a button, the time-out parameter can be typed in to do one of two things. Either it can explicitly control how long this specific line of code will wait for the control to appear, or the optional parameter can be excluded. This second option results in the wEditSetText statement waiting for the amount of time specified by the SetDefaultWaitTimeout function.

Note

The captions and labels used to identify a control are not case-sensitive. Therefore, the string supplied to the function or statement could be in capital letters, even though the label or caption might be lowercase. Also, to specify the underlined character in a label or caption, the ampersand (&) can be placed just before the letter to be underlined. This is not required, however, and if it isn't used, the control will still be found if the caption is spelled correctly. If the ampersand *is* used, it must be associated with the correct letter in the caption or label, otherwise the control will not be found. Also, remember to include any punctuation marks found in the caption such as single-quotes or ellipses (...).

Not Using a Caption or Label

In some cases there are controls that don't have a caption or static control label associated with them, making it impossible to type in a descriptive text string describing the control. In these situations, there are three good ways the control can be accessed:

▶ Ordinal value

▶ ID number

▶ Handle

ORDINALS

An *ordinal value* is most easily described as the tab-position of the control. This isn't really what the ordinal is, but does help you understand it.

When controls are added to a dialog box they are all on individual layers, commonly referred to as the *z-order*. These layers can be used to identify the control. With ordinals, the z-order is specifically relative to the number of the type of control in the dialog box. That is, if there are ten buttons and one edit control, the ordinal value associated with the edit control would have nothing to do with the ordinal values of the other ten buttons. Instead, in the case of a single edit control, its ordinal value would be 1.

Previously, an example was given using the wEditSetText statement to set the text of the edit control shown in Figure 5-2. Because this is the only edit control in the Open dialog box, the same goal could have been accomplished using an ordinal instead of the static control. An ordinal is identified by an @ symbol next to the number. If you pass this in place of a caption, the control's ordinal position will be used. Therefore, the following two statements, when working with the dialog box shown in Figure 5-2, accomplish exactly the same result:

```
wEditSetText("File name:","myfile.txt")
wEditSetText("@1","myfile.txt")
```

One benefit of using ordinals instead of captions is that, should the caption in the button ever change, as would be the case when localizing a product for another language, the script continues to function. This is because it's working with the ordinal value of the control instead of the text associated with it. The downfall is that ordinals change as controls of the same type are added or removed from a dialog box. Thus, using ordinals can be difficult when a product's user interface (UI) hasn't yet been frozen.

The ordinal position of a control can be determined through hit-and-miss testing, by typing in different values and seeing if the correct control is affected. Another way is to use the Window Information utility.

CONTROL ID NUMBER

Working with the *ID number* of a control is similar to working with the ordinal position of a control. Instead of using the @ symbol, the # symbol is used. This designates that you're passing the ID value of a control in place of a caption. Because I used the Winfo utility, I know that the ID number associated with the edit control in Figure 5-2 is 1152. I also know it can be used to place text into that same edit control with the following statement:

```
wEditSetText("#1152","myfile.txt")
```

The ID number of a control is assigned when the Windows programmer creates the control in the dialog box. These ID numbers are used by Windows programmers to affect a control or to determine which control is being acted upon by the user. This same ID number can be used by Visual Test programmers to identify a control, should the ordinal or caption value of the control not be a preferable means of identification.

The same perils are faced when using an ID number as when using an ordinal. Should a control be removed and then replaced, there is no guarantee that the ID number will be the same. As a matter of fact, much of the ID numbering is hidden from the Windows developer by placing those values into constants and then automatically changing those constants when the dialog box is modified.

The best way to work with a Windows control is to use its caption or associated label. Place the label into a constant and then use the constant every time that control is acted upon by one of the Test language's functions or statements. Then, should the product ever be localized for another language, the constant's value can be altered, effectively changing every place the caption was used throughout the script.

USING HANDLES

Every window and control in the Windows operating system has a *handle*. A handle is a value that is associated with an item that is created by Windows so that it can be referred to by its handle value.

Using a handle is very similar to using ordinals and ID numbers. The biggest difference is that a handle changes each time a program is run, whereas ID numbers and ordinals only differ if the program has been modified and recompiled. A handle to a control is used with the equal sign (=) in front of the value of the handle. For example:

```
hBtn = wEditFind("@1")
strhBtn = "=" + str$(hBtn)
wEditSetText(strhBtn, "myfile.txt")
```

Control Pitfalls

There are several pitfalls to using controls. You need to be aware of these, so we'll take a look at them here. We'll cover three problems, those associated with:

▶ Non-standard class names

▶ Labels not working

▶ Controls that aren't real

NON-STANDARD CLASS NAMES

There are situations where a control won't have the class name you expect. In Windows a programmer can modify the behavior of a standard control so that it inherits some or all of the standard behavior, but has some additional behavior added to it. When this is done, the correct thing for that Windows programmer to do is to give the control a non-standard name so that it will not be confused with standard controls used in Windows. This is common practice, especially when the control's behavior has been modified so that it no longer observes standard Windows behavior. It is known as *sub-classing* a control. In the case of Visual Basic buttons, they are known as *ThunderCommandButtons*, because the code name for Visual Basic when it first came out was Thunder. Therefore, Visual Basic's controls have "Thunder" as a prefix to their typical class name.

Visual Test is aware of the class names of Visual Basic's controls and will automatically recognize them. In the case of other applications, however, you'll have to inform Visual Test that a control isn't using a common class name. Use the Winfo utility to determine the control's class name and use the W*SetClass statement (where the asterisk (*) is replaced by the type of control). In the case of a button with the *MyButton* class name, the wButton* routines can be informed of it with the following line of source code: → any of these controls

```
wButtonSetClass("MyButton\Button\ThunderCommandButton")
```

Using any of the wButton* routines will now result in those routines looking for controls with class names of *ThunderCommandButton*, *Button*, and *MyButton*.

LABELS STOP WORKING

Static text controls, also known as *labels*, are typically placed next to a control that doesn't have a caption (such as an edit control). You can use these labels in different Test language routines to work with their associated controls.

Sometimes, you'll find that the labels don't work, even though they're next to the control they should act upon. In these situations, it's possible the label isn't in the layer or z-order preceding its associated control.

A Visual Test routine, when working with a label, looks for the control just after the label in the z-order. The z-order is controlled by the dialog box editor the Windows developer uses when he/she creates a dialog box. If the developer first created a label, then some other controls, followed by the control associated with the label, it's possible the Test language routines won't find the control next to the label.

There are two possible fixes for situations such as these. The first is to work with the control's ordinal or ID values instead of the label or caption. Alternatively, you can work closely with the developer, so that he or she can re-edit the dialog box and re-order the layering of the controls.

THE CONTROLS AREN'T REAL

There are some situations where an application appears to have buttons, edit controls, combo boxes, list boxes, and so on, but Visual Test isn't able to recognize them. Even when you attempt to determine their class name by using the Winfo utility, the utility doesn't show any information.

In situations like these it's probable that the controls really don't exist and are simply bitmaps being manipulated by the program to *look* like Windows controls. An example would be any program created with Asymetrix's ToolBook development product. These applications look like they were created using true Windows controls, but they're bogus. ToolBook fakes the controls by supplying and manipulating bitmaps, in order to make the development of products easier and to provide specialized handling of controls. Borland's Delphi product also has fake controls. And some of the controls created through the Microsoft Foundation Classes (MFCs) are fake (or *virtual*) as well.

The only solution in situations like these is to go to a very basic form of automation. You need to determine and use the specific coordinates of those controls on the screen, so that the mouse can be moved by Visual Test to those coordinates and told to click or drag.

Working with mouse and keyboard events is discussed later in this chapter, in the section on "Mouse and Keyboard Events."

Remaining Controls

The rest of the controls that can be manipulated through the Test language are shown in Table 5-3. The two main things to consider when working with any kinds of controls are

▶ Do the controls have a caption or label associated with them?

▶ Do they need to be accessed using ordinals and control IDs?

This table will tell you where to look for the specifics of functions and statements available for each control. Look up information on them via the online help for the specifics on each function or statement. Now that you understand the basics from the examples of working with buttons and edit controls, you're set for working with the other control types.

TABLE 5-3 Controls Used by Visual Test.

Type of Control	Beginning of Function Name
Check box button	wCheck*()
Column header	wHeader*()
Combo box	wCombo*()
Command button	wButton*()
Custom control	wCustom*()
Desktop items	wDesktop*()
Desktop taskbar	wTaskbar*()
Edit box	wEdit*()
List box	wList*()
Listview control	wView*()

Option (radio) button	*wOption*()*
Progress box	*wProgress*()*
Scroll bar	*wScroll*()*
Slider bar	*wSlider*()*
Spinner control	*wSpin*()*
Static label	*wLabel*()*
Static text	*wStatic*()*
Status bar	*wStatus*()*
Tab control	*wTab*()*
Toolbar control	*wToolbar*()*
Tooltips	*wTips*()*
Treeview control	*wTree*()*

Phasing Out Routines

Some of the routines you look up will give you the following warning when displayed in online help:

> **Important:** The **<old>** statement has been replaced by the **<new>** statement in Visual Test. Although **<old>** is still supported and test code containing it will still run, you should replace **<old>** with **<new>** in your older test case files. Doing this will extend the life expectancy of those test case files and make them run more efficiently.

(Where <old> and <new> represent the previous and newer versions of the statements, respectively.)

Many of these routines were subroutines that required an empty variable or *buffer* to be passed. The statement would fill it with the value the Test programmer wanted. Microsoft realized that the same thing could be done by using a function and assigning the return value to the variable that was once passed as a buffer. It cuts down on one argument in the parameter list and makes it one less function for the Visual Test team to maintain.

Working With Menus

Working with menus is very simple when working with Visual Test. There can be two types of menus available in an applications window:

▶ The first is a typical menu bar that goes across the top of the window, just under its caption.

▶ The second is the system menu in the upper left-hand corner of the window, on the caption bar.

The Menu Bar

When working with the menu bar, you have access to a number of functions and subroutines through the Test language, all of which start with wMenu*. The following is an example of how to pop down the File menu of an application is:

```
wMenuSelect("File")
```

The wMenuSelect statement works in a similar way to accessing files in a directory structure. A path to the menu item is specified in the string passed to the statement. So, to access the Open... menu item (usually found under the File menu), the following line of source code is used:

```
wMenuSelect("File\Open...")
```

In the event that the program has cascading or hierarchical menus, where a menu item has its own sub-menu items, the path simply continues by using backslashes (\) to instruct *wMenuSelect()* how to reach the menu item.

Note

The ellipsis (...) needs to be included since it's part of the actual text of the menu item. However, any accelerator keys (such as Ctrl+O) don't need to be included. Also, if you want to specify the underlined character, an ampersand is placed in front of the letter that's underlined in the menu listing. (For example, "&File\&Open..." could be passed as the string instead of simply "File\Open....")

If the direct-access method (DAM) keys are used, they must be used correctly. If the ampersand is included, it must be in the appropriate position. If it isn't in the correct location, then the wMenuSelect statement won't find the menu item and an error will be given.

System Menu

The system menu is very similar to the normal menu bar, except that the wSysMenu* functions and statements are used instead of wMenu*. The system menu sometimes doesn't appear on the window's caption bar: It depends on the style of window the programmer used. Typically, the system menu contains menu items to control the minimization, maximization, and restoration of a window. It also allows for moving and re-sizing the window.

Mouse and Keyboard Events

Even with all the different functions and statements in Visual Test that allow for the manipulation of Windows applications, there are certain situations where it's necessary to manipulate an application through less sophisticated methods.

Two examples are

▶ When working with fake, or virtual, controls that are simply bitmaps that act as Windows controls but go unrecognized by Visual Test.

▶ Occasions when it is necessary to emulate a user typing characters on the keyboard.

Fake Controls

In the first example, fake controls, I can site two companies that widely use them. The first is Asymetrix Corporation. It makes an excellent Windows development tool called ToolBook. All applications created with this product have bitmaps in place of actual Windows controls, which makes them more difficult to automate.

The other company is Microsoft Corporation, which has dialog boxes in Microsoft Excel, Microsoft Word, and other applications. These dialog boxes are referred to as SDM (Simple Dialog Manager) dialog boxes. They only have one or two actual controls; the rest are bitmap simulated controls.

There are other companies and situations where virtual controls exist, which is why the *play* statement has been provided in Visual Test (formerly *DoKeys()* and *QueMouse*()* in previous versions to Test 4.0).

The play statement allows for both keyboard and mouse simulation. When we designed the test suite for Notepad, *play()* had to be used to place text into the Notepad editor, instead of *wEditSetText()*. When *wEditSetText()* was used, sections of Notepad were unaware text had been placed in the editor. For example, it allowed you to exit the application without asking you to save changes. Using *play()*, however, provided the expected results.

Keyboard Events

The play statement is straightforward when it is used for keyboard events. It passes a string with the characters to be typed, and those characters are then sent to the active window. They generate the same windows messages as if someone were actually typing at the keyboard.

Note

Since no one is actually typing at the keyboard or using the mouse, no hardware interrupt is actually generated. As a result, screen savers often become active during the running of an automated test. It's a good idea to turn them off before running lengthy automated tests.

USING KEYSTROKES

The following code is an example of a script using the play statement. It pops down the File menu, clicks on the Open... menu item, types in a filename, then selects the Cancel button, all through keyboard strokes (based on Notepad's UI).

Use the play Statement Sparingly

Because functions and subroutines provide a level of error-trapping when dealing with specific Windows controls that the play statement cannot, *play()* should be used only as a last resort. An example is if you wanted to use the play statement to access menu items. If the following command is issued through the Test language and a menu doesn't exist, the play statement will send the keystrokes regardless:

```
play "%fo"
```

Whereas, if the wMenuSelect statement is used, and a menu doesn't exist, an error stating that the menu cannot be found is given, helping to avoid a runaway script.

```
play "%fo"          'Pop down the File menu and select Open
play "%n"           'Select the "File &name:" edit control
play "myfile.txt"   'Type in a filename
play "{TAB 3}"      'Tab three times to the Cancel button
play " "            'Press the spacebar to click the button
```

We see a number of things going on. The first line of code shows that, to select the Alt key, the percent sign (%) must be placed next to the key letter (for example, "%f" is like hitting Alt-F). This results in the File menu popping down. Type in the letter *O*, in the case of Notepad, to select the Open... menu item. So far, so good.

Assume the Open dialog box is displayed. As the DAM key for the "File Name" edit control in our piece of source code is the letter *N*, send an Alt-N by supplying the play statement with the string "%n".

Now, assume that the focus is in the correct edit control and the text *myfile.txt* has been typed. You need to use two separate statements: a special symbol ({TAB}), along with the number 3 (to specify that three tabs to be sent which positions the focus on the Cancel button). A single space simulates a use of the keyboard spacebar, which clicks on the Cancel button.

This shows how we can manipulate a dialog box without true Windows controls. Again, I can't stress enough how important it is to use control functions and statements such as wButton* and wEdit* before turning to the play statement. It's very easy for a script to get out of sync. Because you're only sending keyboard strokes, instead of looking for specific controls, the script will continue on its merry way, spewing keystrokes into whatever application or window happens to be active. The play statement is very much a *last* resort.

SPECIAL KEYS

While the play statement does fine with normal text, it requires special characters to designate specific keys. As we've already seen, an Alt key is specified by using the percent sign. The Control and Shift keys are also available with *play()* and are signified by the caret (^) and plus (+) signs, respectively. If you want to work with other types of keyboard keys, they can be simulated by placing braces ({ }) around specific keywords that map to those keys, as was done for the Tab key in our example. Refer to Table 5-4 for a list of these other keyboard keys.

TABLE 5-4 Special Strings Used With *play()* to Simulate Keyboard Keys.

Keyboard Key	*play()* equivalent
Enter key	"{ENTER}" or "~"
Escape key	"{ESC}"
Up arrow	"{UP}"
Down arrow	"{DOWN}"
Left arrow	"{LEFT}"
Right arrow	"{RIGHT}"
End key	"{END}"
Page-up key	"{PGUP}"
Page-down key	"{PGDN}"
Insert key	"{INSERT}"
Delete key	"{DELETE}"
Home key	"{HOME}"
Tab key	"{TAB}"
Backspace key	"{BS}"
F1 key	"{F1}", … on to …
F16 key	"{F16}"
Right Alt key	"{R_ALT}"

One situation that had me scratching my head for a good ten minutes when I first used Microsoft Test was working with the *DoKeys* statement in Test 1.0—this is the one the play statement now replaces. I was trying to test the accelerator keys to make sure they performed the appropriate menu actions. For example, Ctrl+O is in the File menu as the shortcut for displaying the Open dialog box. I knew I wanted to display the Open dialog box in Microsoft Word and so I used the following line of code, which has been converted to the play statement's equivalent:

```
play "^O"
```

The menu clearly shows Ctrl+O as the keystrokes to be used to activate the Open… menu item. What didn't occur to me until later was that, by using an uppercase *O*, I was actually sending a Ctrl+Shift+o. The play statement had to use the shift key in order to provide the uppercase *O*. Since Shift wasn't part of the keystroke that needed to be used, the accelerator wouldn't activate. When I changed the letter *O* to lowercase, it worked as expected.

Characters can be used in conjunction with one another to combine keystrokes. For example, I passed the following string to *play()* to send a Ctrl+Shift+O: "^+o." If I had wanted a key to act on multiple letters, I would have simply enclosed those letters in parentheses: "+(hello)" results in typing out "HELLO."

Mouse Events

The mouse events functionality of the play statement allows you to move the mouse, click onto specific coordinates, click and drag, and release the mouse button. If the optional first parameter of the play statement is provided with the handle to a window, the coordinates provided to the statement are relative to the upper left-hand corner of the specified window. Otherwise, the coordinates are relative to the upper left-hand corner of the desktop. Table 5-5 details the mouse action codes.

TABLE 5-5 Mouse Action Codes Recognized by the play Statement.

Action to Complete	Action Code
Click a mouse button down	BTNDOWN
Release a mouse button	BTNUP
Click at a specific location	CLICK
Double-click at a location	DBLCLICK
Drag to a location	DRAGTO
Move mouse to a location	MOVETO

These actions can also be affected by using the coordinate modifiers CURPOS and SCREEN. The CURPOS modifier causes the mouse to be moved, based on its current position. The SCREEN modifier overrides a window handle, if one's been provided, and bases the coordinates relative to the upper-left corner of the desktop. Listing 5-4 demonstrates some of these action codes and modifiers.

LISTING 5-4 Example of Controlling the Mouse With the play Statement.

```
'Screen-relative coordinates to the paintbrush
const TOOL_BRUSH = "SCREEN+44,SCREEN+130"
const MAX_WAIT   = 5     'Wait max. 5 seconds

dim hWnd as long

hWnd = wFndWnd("Paint",FW_PART OR FW_ALL, MAX_WAIT)
if (hWnd = 0) then
    if (RUN("pbrush.exe") <> 0) then
        pause "Error running Paintbrush."
        stop
    else
        hWnd = wGetActWnd(0)
    endif
endif

'Maximize that window
wSysMenu(hWnd)
wMenuSelect("Maximize")
```

```
'Maximize the canvas
wMenuSelect("Image\Attributes...")
wEditSetText("Width:","400")
wEditSetText("Height:","250")
wButtonClick("OK")

'Select the paintbrush tool
play "{CLICK "+TOOL_BRUSH+"}"

'Letter K
play hWnd,"{MOVETO 130,130}{DRAGTO 130,220,LEFT}"
play hWnd,"{MOVETO 170,130}{DRAGTO 130,175,LEFT}"
play hWnd,"{DRAGTO 170,220,LEFT}"

'Letter I
play hWnd,"{MOVETO 180,130}{DRAGTO 180,220,LEFT}"

'Letter L
play hWnd,"{MOVETO 190,130}{DRAGTO 190,220,LEFT}"
play hWnd,"{DRAGTO 230,220}"

'Letter R
play hWnd,"{MOVETO 240,130}{DRAGTO 260,130,LEFT}"
play hWnd,"{DRAGTO 280,150,LEFT}"
play hWnd,"{DRAGTO 280,170,LEFT}"
play hWnd,"{DRAGTO 260,190,LEFT}"
play hWnd,"{DRAGTO 240,190,LEFT}"
play hWnd,"{MOVETO 240,130}{DRAGTO 240,220,LEFT}"
play hWnd,"{MOVETO 250,190}{DRAGTO 280,220,LEFT}"

'Letter O
play hWnd,"{MOVETO 290,130}{DRAGTO 290,220,LEFT}"
play hWnd,"{DRAGTO 330,220,LEFT}"
play hWnd,"{DRAGTO 330,130,LEFT}"
play hWnd,"{DRAGTO 290,130,LEFT}"

'Letter Y
play hWnd,"{MOVETO 340,130}{DRAGTO 360,190,LEFT}"
play hWnd,"{DRAGTO 380,130,LEFT}"
play hWnd,"{MOVETO 360,190}{DRAGTO 360,220,LEFT}"
end
```

The Screen Utility

The Screen Utility is made up of capture and comparison routines that take and compare snapshots of a selected window. The comparisons are done through bitmap comparisons. This results in a highly effective process for detecting whether or not a screen exactly matches a previously captured version of it. The utility can detect any changes, even a single pixel, in a screen that has been captured. Therefore, it's very effective in verifying that a dialog box or window has not changed from the last time the tests were run.

However, this utility has shortcomings relating to:

▶ The amount of disk space

▶ The time it takes for a comparison

▶ The number of captures that may be required for a single application

The size of a single bitmap can be quite large, depending on the resolution and number of colors displayed on the screen. Because of this, comparisons can take a significant amount of time. And, if the comparisons are to be done at multiple screen resolutions, you need multiple capture files, since a captured bitmap at one resolution cannot be compared with a screen at another resolution.

The comparison and capture routines typically use a single capture file that can hold multiple bitmaps. These files, designated by a *.scn* file extension, allow for easy encapsulation of multiple screens, so there aren't too many files floating around on your machine.

Instead, you need to have a flexible approach to these routines. Make sure you have a subroutine that accepts

▶ The name of a screen being captured or compared

▶ The name of the *.scn* file to store the captured screen in, or from which to draw for a comparison

▶ The handle to the window which is being captured or compared

You can control whether a capture or comparison is performed by using a global variable or constant. This can be set prior to the test's execution. This will ensure the screen comparisons are done or, if the variable is set for capture mode, that the capture files are rebuilt automatically. The latter requires you to verify by hand that the captures were performed correctly, as is discussed in Chapter 6.

Here is an example of a capture/comparison routine you can use to flexibly handle captures and comparisons of windows and dialog boxes:

```
const NO_ERROR = 0   '0 means no error occurred
global gfCompare as integer

gfCompare = FALSE    'Results in window being captured

sub CompScreen(strScnName$, strScnFile$, hWnd&)
    dim ret as integer
    static iIndexErr as integer


    'If set to compare, then compare the screens
    if (gfCompare) then
        ret = ScnCompWindow(strScnFile, strScnName, hWnd,0,0)

        if (ret <> NO_ERROR) then
            iIndexErr = iIndexErr + 1
            ScnCaptureWindow("err.scn","err"+str$(iIndexErr),hWnd,0)
            log "Comparison error. Check err.scn file at "+ _
                "screen err"+str$(iIndexErr)+" for capture."
        endif

    else     'Otherwise, capture the screen
        ScnCaptureWindow(strScnFile,strScnName,hWnd,0)
    endif
end sub 'CompScreen
```

Note

In the event that a comparison fails, this example subroutine automatically writes out a capture of the problem screen, logs the error information, and allows the script to continue its execution. By doing this, you can return to the log files later and verify what exactly went wrong by looking at the captured window that was in error.

Simple Input/Output

There are a number of ways to allow you to read in and write out information through the Test language. The easiest are discussed here, to get you started quickly. The more advanced approaches are discussed in Chapter 13.

Visual Test 4.0 added a number of statements to make logging out information very easy for you. The first is the *log* statement. This writes information out to the Viewport—as a text file or database-compatible file, depending on how the test script is run. When executing the test script through the Developer Studio, all output from the log statement goes into the Viewport section of the Output window. If, however, the script is run using the Suite Manager, the user has some options as to where to place the output. The output is directed by settings in the Suite Manager's Options dialog box. This is an example of how the log statement can be used:

```
log "Now is the time for all good testers to come to"
log "the aid of their program manager."
log #10,"Extra information that can be printed out."
```

The first two lines are printed out at all times. The third line, however, is printed out only when the script is executed by the Suite Manager, and only if the Options dialog box has the detail level set to 10 or higher. The effect of this is that you can have log statements all over the place, but the level of detail is controllable through the Suite Manager.

Conclusion

This chapter covers what is available in the Test language in pretty broad strokes. There is much more to learn by looking through the online help, but this information will get you started on writing the simple scripts you need to start writing. Once you feel more comfortable with the language, explore what other options are available by working your way through the help file. Also, refer to the later chapters in this book for some more advanced examples.

The next chapter looks at the stand-alone utilities that accompany the Visual Test product. Then, Chapter 7 takes a look at a simple test case file and dissects it section by section.

Summary

This chapter takes you through the basics of the Visual Test language. It looks at context-sensitive help, declaring variables, compiling the main section of code, writing subroutines and functions, macros, user-defined types, conditional branching, and loops. It describes and discusses the use of Windows controls, with or without captions and labels. It deals with the two types of menus available: system menus and the more typical menu bars. Then it looks at mouse and keyboard events. Finally, it considers an approach to using the Screen Utility's capture and compare routines, and the language's simple I/O features.

Visual Test Utilities

There are four key utilities that come with Visual Test. These are as follows:

► The Scenario Recorder

► The Window Information utility

► The Screen Utility

► The Suite Manager

The purpose here is not to offer you an exhaustive description of these utilities. Instead, we'll be looking at each of them briefly, to understand when and how they might be used during the development of test scripts.

All of these utilities can be found at the bottom of Visual Test's Test menu. We shall start by looking at the utility that helps build test scripts by recording a tester's actions: the Scenario Recorder.

Scenario Recorder

The Scenario Recorder (also known as the Script Recorder in previous versions of Test) is one of the most misunderstood tools of Visual Test. As a matter of fact, while it most definitely helps sell the Visual Test product, it, and any automation tool that boasts a script recorder, does a disservice to the testers that use it because managers have misconceptions of its capabilities.

When activated, the Scenario Recorder tracks a user's actions and converts them to the Test language equivalent (see Figure 6-1). If the user clicks on a button or selects a menu item, the recorder will generate the appropriate source code to repeat those actions.

From the sounds of it, the recorder is a powerful tool in building test scripts. In reality, however, the code generated is sequential and sometimes won't execute properly without modification. This isn't to say that the recorder is useless; it's simply a tool that can play a small part in automating a project, and is not meant to be the main source for creating test scripts. The main source is still the test engineer who writes those scripts.

Recording a Script

Let's take an example of recording a simple situation where a user turns the recorder on, performs some actions, then turns the recorder off again. In this example, we're going to have Microsoft Notepad up and running already, type some text into the editor, then save the contents of the editor to a file called test1.txt.

We begin by displaying the Scenario Recorder. This is done by selecting the Scenario Recorder... menu item found under the Test menu, as shown in Figure 6-1.

FIGURE 6-1
Selecting the Scenario Recorder tool from the Developer Studio's Test menu.

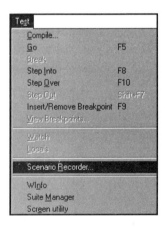

A simple dialog box is displayed offering the tester only a few options. These relate to how the script should be recorded. Figure 6-2 shows the settings used to generate the example script we'll be looking at in a moment.

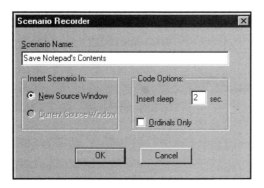

FIGURE 6-2
The dialog box displayed when selecting the Scenario Recorder tool from the Test menu.

The Ordinals Only check box makes the generated script more flexible, by not relying solely on the labels associated with individual controls. For example, instead of clicking on a button with the caption "Save" in the Save As dialog box, it would look for the tab order or *ordinal position* of the button in the dialog box. In our example, the "Save" button has an ordinal value of 1 (I'll show you how to determine this using the Window Information — Winfo — tool under "Window Information Utility," later in this chapter). If we had clicked on this check box, the recorder would have used WButtonClick("@1") instead of the wButtonClick("&Save") statement you see at the bottom of the listing in Figure 6-6.

Ordinals versus Captions

This brings up an interesting point. Why not use ordinals all the time, in place of literal strings that identify the buttons? There are pros and cons to both approaches and it's up to you to decide what your needs are. A reason for using an ordinal is when an application will be tested in a number of different languages. The caption of the button will change, but the ordinal position of the button will remain the same.

In other situations, such as when the user interface (UI) is still in a state of flux and has yet to be frozen, other controls may be added to the dialog box, possibly causing the ordinal position of a button to change. If you use a caption instead of an ordinal value, the button would still have been found by the Visual Test routines.

In both cases, either problem can be minimized by using proper programming techniques. In this case, the use of constants is warranted. We discuss them further in Chapter 8.

In this example we already have a blank, untitled instance of Notepad up and running. We've clicked on the OK button in the Scenario Recorder dialog box, so the recorder is active.

We begin by typing a simple string into the editor, so that we can see what type of code will be generated (see Figure 6-3). A recurring theme, I use my old stand-by, "Now is the time...", for lack of a better idea. Oh, the strain of the creative process!

FIGURE 6-3
Type some text into Notepad and save it to the file test1.txt.

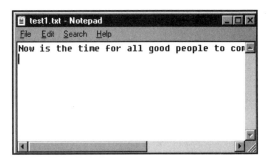

After typing in the text, we select the Save menu item from the File menu, which saves the text we've entered. Right about here some of you should have a warning bell going off in your heads. It's not obvious right away, but it becomes so, once the script is executed. The problem is one that I mentioned at the beginning of this section: about how generated scripts may not always work right away.

Once we finish recording this script and turn around to run it, a message box that wasn't displayed when the script was originally recorded will display "Replace existing file?" This is seen in Figure 6-4.

FIGURE 6-4
An example of how a script may not work when running it right after it was recorded.

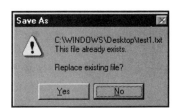

This is a simple example of how the recorder, while useful, isn't robust enough to catch events not encountered during the original recording. No script recorder is robust enough to catch things like this. Therefore, while the recorder offers a number of benefits, it's still necessary for you to go in and modify the scripts to handle the different events that can arise.

But we're a bit ahead of ourselves here. After completing the actions we wanted to record, we need to turn off the recorder. This is done by clicking on its icon or entry in the taskbar. When doing so, you are prompted with another dialog box, shown in Figure 6-5.

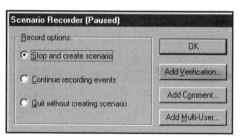

FIGURE 6-5
After deactivating the script recorder, this dialog box is displayed.

A feature new to the recorder for version 4.0 of Test is the Add Verification… button. This feature is pretty slick. It allows you to verify that the scenario or script you recorded ended up in the expected location of your application. That is, a particular dialog box that was supposed to be displayed at the end of the execution of the script is actually displayed. It allows you to verify that you are in a given window or that a particular control exists before testing continues. It also lets you verify that the position of the window is as expected.

When you use this button a *RecVerify** function call (found in the recorder.inc include file) is placed in the source code generated by the recorder. In the sample script that we generated, the Add Verification… button wasn't used.

Note

There are a number of different flavors of the *RecVerify** function which is why there is an asterisk (*) signifying that the last part of the function call will depend upon exactly what is being verified.

Another button in this dialog box is Add Multi-User, that allows for the script to synchronize itself with other machines on a network. In Chapter 15 we discuss synchronizing scripts more fully. This option causes the script to insert a command that will communicate back to the controlling or *host* computer and await its signal to proceed.

When the OK button in the Scenario Recorder (Paused) dialog box (Figure 6-5) is clicked on, the automatically-generated script is placed into a source window in the Microsoft Developer Studio.

The script we created is shown in Figure 6-6. (The script you see might vary slightly on your screen, because of other actions you may have taken during the recording, such as selecting other menus, clicking on text, working at a different screen resolution, and so on.)

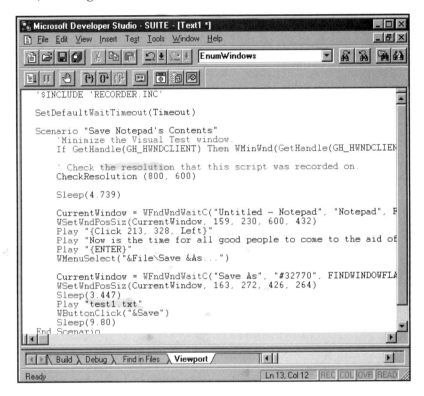

FIGURE 6-6 Sample script generated via the Scenario Recorder.

Realities of the Script Recorder

The Scenario Recorder is a helpful tool in automation but is not the only part of the automation equation. A common situation that testers new to automation encounter is similar to what happened to me when I first started using Microsoft Test: I was on a job where the Director of Development thought the recorder could do everything and that it didn't require any degree of intelligence to write automated scripts.

Microsoft has made great improvements in the recorder since it was first introduced in version 1.0, but it doesn't replace the need for an automation engineer who knows and understands the Test language. Nor is it Microsoft's intention to imply that this is the case. Unfortunately, many people new to automation hear about the Scenario Recorder and assume it's a simple matter of just turning it on, recording a section of the product to be tested, and turning it off again. Sorry.

It's up to you to help correct that misconception by explaining the pros and cons of the script recorder when the topic arises.

The Scenario Recorder is an excellent tool, especially when someone is first learning how to program in Visual Test. As a matter of fact, I strongly recommend using it to record the testing of a given area when you aren't sure what commands to use for individual controls. As you grow to know the Test language more, though, you'll find yourself using the recorder less and less.

The use of the recorder is implied in its name: Scenario Recorder. It's useful to record short, individual tests, not entire sections of an application. You can go in and cut out the sections of the code you find useful and dispose of the rest. By using the script recorder in this fashion you will quickly pick up on the syntax and common functions and statements that make up the Test language. Another good use of the recorder is to create a general skeleton of the area to be tested, allowing you to go in and fill in the more detailed sections of the test.

Window Information Utility

The Window Information (Winfo) utility, also found under the Test menu, is a very simple and straightforward tool. It's also a very necessary and valuable tool to have when automating scripts. It allows you to identify a control's type and how you can go about acting upon it through your test scripts. If you've done any Windows development, you'll find that the Winfo utility provides information similar to the Spy utility.

Fake/Virtual Windows Controls

As discussed in Chapter 5, the reality of Windows programs is that pro-grammers don't always use *true* Windows controls. Sometimes they are bitmaps: fake, or virtual, controls. Often, this is the only way for the pro-grammers to provide the end user with a cool-looking interface that helps sell the product. The result is a nightmare for the Test programmer because Visual Test's routines only recognize windows controls, or sub-classes of those controls; they don't recognize a bitmap that looks and acts like a Windows control, such as a stylish looking toolbar that was really drawn in a graphics editor.

Note

For details on subclassing in Windows, see the "Subclassed Windows Controls" sec-tion later in this chapter.

Let's look at Microsoft Paint as a simple example. When you have the main window of Paint up you'll notice a palette to the left of the win-dow that offers artists a number of tools with which to create their graphics. It looks like it's made up of a bunch of buttons with pictures of each individual tool (see Figure 6-7). It's really just a separate window, without a border, that contains a single bitmap or picture of controls instead of actual individual button controls. The developer who wrote the application simply checks the coordinates of where the user clicked the mouse to determine which tool becomes active. This is great for the end user, but how do you, as a tester, determine whether it's a grouping of controls or just a bitmap? This is where Winfo comes in handy.

FIGURE 6-7 Microsoft Paint's tool palette.

After selecting Winfo from the Test menu, the Window Information utility's window is displayed, as in Figure 6-8. With this utility you can determine what types of controls you're dealing with. In this case, the control is a small, borderless window that holds a bitmap. Well, bummer....

Now you know you can't use the wToolBar* or wButton* statements that are part of the Test language. Instead, you'll have to resort to using the wMoveToWnd statement by determining the pixel coordinates of each control, relative to the application's window. Not a fun way to do things, but a situation that can be worked through.

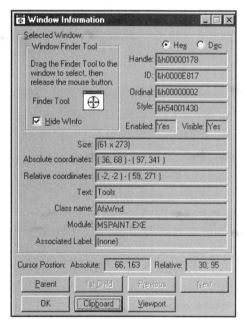

FIGURE 6-8
The Window Information (Winfo) utility window.

Another example is the Open dialog box in Microsoft Word. If you display it and then move Winfo's Finder tool over the controls of that window, you will notice that only some, not all, of the controls actually highlight. In any other Open dialog box, all the controls would highlight as the tool moved across them individually. So, why does nothing happen in Word? Once again, this is an unpleasant situation for testers who are writing scripts to test those types of dialog boxes, because true Windows controls don't exist, only bitmaps of those controls.

Fortunately, dialog boxes such as these aren't too common. I'm told that the reasons Microsoft Word has a dialog box like this are two-fold:

▶ It cuts down on the number of resources used by the application.

▶ It makes porting the application to other platforms easier, since the developer is dealing with a picture of a control and the coordinates of where the user can click. Using a bitmap this way saves time, as it doesn't require the programmer to redesign the dialog box for another platform (such as the Apple Macintosh).

Subclassed Windows Controls

Winfo also comes in handy when you're trying to act upon a Windows control and nothing is happening. Say, for example, that you try to click on a button named "OK". The statement you'd use in your script would be wButtonClick("OK"). But you find yourself pulling your hair out because the control is clearly a button, its label is "OK", yet for some reason Visual Test isn't clicking on it.

It could be that it is a button and not a bitmap, but the wButtonClick statement doesn't recognize it. The routines in Visual Test that allow you to act upon a control determine which control they're looking for by its class name. Everything in Windows has a class name associated with it. For a typical button, the class name is *Button*. For an edit control the class name is *Edit*. When you use the wButton* routines, the Test language looks for all of the objects in the active window that have *Button* as a class name. Then it searches through those objects, looking for the control that matches the caption you passed in that routine. If it doesn't find it, it reports an error back to you.

When a developer takes a Windows control and modifies its behavior to the point where it acts even a little different than Microsoft intended, it's called *subclassing* the control. And because that control is a little bit different, it is given a different class name.

Now, remember that those routines in the Test language which act upon a control use those class names to ensure they are affecting the appropriate control. Therefore, in the example of the wButtonClick statement, if for some reason the button isn't being clicked on, the Winfo utility can be used to determine the class name of that control.

Using the Finder tool (shaped like rifle scope's cross-hairs) in the Window Information window, the troublesome control can be selected to get information about it. In the Class Name section of the window, you'll see the class associated with that control. If the control is indeed subclassed, then the wButtonSetClass statement can be used to tell the rest of the wButton* routines that the subclassed control should be considered a button.

Note

An interesting side note is that, in previous versions of Test, the Winfo application was created using the Test language. The source code was included so that the utility could be modified and its source code studied to aid in the creation of other utilities. In Visual Test 4.0 the programmers have gone a different route and made the utility a part of the Test language. That is, you can display the utility using the command wDisplayInfo(0).

Visual Test Suite Manager

The Visual Test Suite Manager can be extremely useful, though you may well find yourself using it less as you become more familiar with Visual Test's language and tools. There are three main ways in which it is particularly useful:

▶ Managing multiple files

▶ Handling unexpected errors

▶ As an integrated tool

After examining each of these in detail, we shall briefly consider the developments in Test that led to the Suite Manager. The Suite Manager's main window can be seen in Figure 6-9.

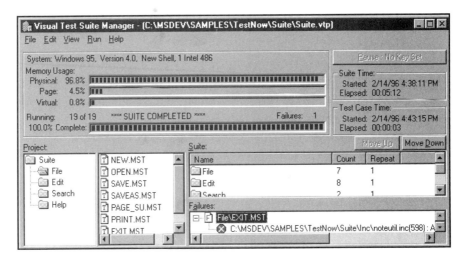

FIGURE 6-9 Visual Test Suite Manager's main window. Here, it is displaying the contents of a test suite that tests the Notepad application.

Managing Multiple Files

When writing automated tests for a product, the number of files you have to test can become unwieldy. In the case of the suite displayed in Figure 6-9, there are only 19 files, broken down into four folders. While this is not a huge number, they can grow quickly, especially on a large project with multiple automation engineers.

The Suite Manager is designed to help manage all the test case files in a test suite. However, while fully functional and very capable in what it does, this doesn't mean you *must* use it. As a matter of fact, Visual Test provides you with the tools to create a driver of your own if you wish. (We look at a simple driver in Chapter 14.)

Information Displayed

While it may look complex at first glance, the Suite Manager is a fairly straightforward utility. At the top of its main window (see Figure 6-9) it displays information about the type of computer the test is running on, the version of Windows, memory usage, and the percentage of tests executed by the driver. Because this information can be helpful, the default option is for this information to continue to be displayed, even during the running of the tests.

While the Suite Manager falls to the background, it continues to monitor memory usage, how many test case files have been completed, the number that remain to be executed, and how many test scenarios in those test case files failed their tests. Figure 6-10 shows the default form the Suite Manager takes when running through its lists of test case files.

FIGURE 6-10 An example of the information the Visual Test Suite Manager can display while executing automated test cases. In this example, a total of 19 test case files are going to be run by the Suite Manager.

Handling Unexpected Errors

One of the nice options of the Suite Manager is its ability to detect an *exception*, or system error. This is typically known as a *general protection fault* (under Windows 3.x it was known as an *unrecoverable application error*). An example of an exception is when one program illegally attempts to access memory being used by Windows or another application. Figure 6-11 shows the Options dialog that allows you to handle exceptions.

In Figure 6-11, you'll also notice that the manager can be configured to look for windows that contain a particular caption. If this option is active, the Suite Manager will dismiss the window automatically and continue running the test case file. Therefore, you won't need to supply any code to deal with a window that contains the caption specified in this dialog box.

FIGURE 6-11
The Options dialog box allows you to configure how the Suite Manager logs out testing information and handles run-time errors.

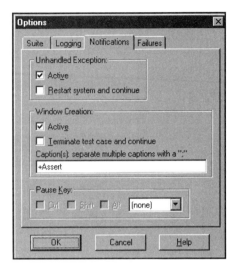

An Integrated Tool

The Suite Manager is an integrated tool. It is very capable and provides you with the engine you need to run all your test case files. It works with the Developer Studio application and the *.vtp* (Visual Test Project) file that is written to disk when a new Visual Test project is created. This integration makes picking and choosing files from the project extremely simple.

Remember that this utility was created using the Visual Test language and then compiled down to an executable form. This goes to show that if you don't care for the Suite Manager and would like to write your own, improved version of it, Visual Test's language and user interface editor make this a possibility.

No Source Code

The Visual Test Suite Manager has undergone a number of changes over the years, as Microsoft Test has evolved. Originally, it was a utility that came with Microsoft Test 2.0. As it included its own source code, it not only served as a place to organize and run test case files, but also created utilities with the User Interface Editor and wrote some Test BASIC code, to work with that interface and decipher the user's actions.

Now the Suite Manager has taken yet another step forward. It no longer includes the Test language source code. But if you look in the Visual Test installation directory, you'll see that it's of file type *.pcd*. This is a Visual Test pseudo-code file compiled using Visual Test, meaning it was written using the Test language.

I'm not sure why Microsoft chose not to include the source code for the driver in this version of Test. My guess is they either found it too difficult to support (in other words, they didn't like to give "Introduction to Programming" lessons over their support line) or they were behind schedule in shipping the product and didn't have enough time to clean up the code.

Whatever the reason, this utility demonstrates the true power of Visual Test. It now has the capability to write a Windows application with the aid of a run-time engine to interpret the pseudo-code file.

The Visual Test Screen Utility

The Visual Test Screen utility (see Figure 6-12) is used for capturing snapshots of anything that can be displayed on the Windows desktop. This can be either a complete window, the entire desktop, or a specific rectangular region specified by the Test programmer using *X* and *Y* coordinates.

FIGURE 6-12
The main window of the Visual Test Screen utility.

Dare to Compare

The Visual Test Screen utility provides a means for you to compare a screen with a snapshot of the same screen made previously, perhaps on a completely different build or version of the product. For example, if a tester takes a snapshot of a dialog box for which its UI design has been frozen, you can compare that snapshot with future releases of the product from the development team.

During the development of a product, communication is crucial, yet is not always as open between the programmers and testers as it should be. A decision might be made to move a particular dialog box control (such as a button) without alerting the testers to this decision. While this is usually a fairly harmless adjustment, nonetheless, it is necessary for the testing team to revisit this area of the product to verify that the dialog box still works as expected.

Three examples of what could happen when a dialog box is modified are

▶ The tab order could change, causing the dialog box to no longer follow the common user interface design guidelines.

▶ The internal ID number of the control could change if the control was removed and re-added (possibly causing the programmer's source code to break if it depended upon that ID number).

▶ The documentation team could miss out on the opportunity to take a final screenshot of the dialog box, causing the documentation to be out-of-date with the final product.

While documentation and quality assurance don't necessarily communicate on issues such as these, this is yet another opportunity for the documentation team to be alerted, since two teams—the development and testing teams—now know of the modification.

Capturing Screens

The Visual Test Screen utility doesn't usually create the bulk of the screen capture files used by the automated test cases. Because the UI of a product tends to evolve as the development for that product matures, it's not practical to manually recapture screenshots (see Figure 6-13).

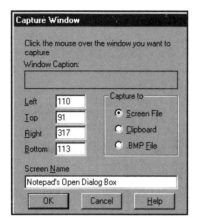

FIGURE 6-13
This dialog box is displayed when the user is capturing a window by hand.

The preferred method of capturing screens is programmatically. That is, to design the comparison routines you'll need to write to serve a dual purpose:

▶ To compare a window with a previously captured screenshot of that window

▶ To make a screenshot of that window (if a switch has been turned on in the code base of the test suite, to cause the capturing to occur)

Note

We look at the Test language routine that performs these two functions in Chapter 11.

The utility allows a test engineer to step through the auto-generated capture files to verify the captures were created as expected. This is known as creating a *gold capture file* or simply as *blessing* the capture files. It is necessary to bless them because, if an error in a dialog box exists during the capturing process (such as the misspelling of a label for a button), the later comparisons only serve to verify that the error still exists. Therefore, visually verifying the capture files is crucial each time they are regenerated.

The other use for the Visual Test Screen utility is to understand why a particular comparison failed. A good way to write the comparison function, which is discussed in Chapter 11, is to have it capture the window that fails the comparison and log out the fact that the comparison failed. The reason for this capture is so that, later, when you're running

135

through your log files to determine which tests failed, you can use the Screen utility to compare the blessed capture of the window with the failed capture of the window, generated during the test run.

Example of a Failed Comparison

Figure 6-14 shows an example of how a comparison might look. A picture of Notepad's Open dialog box has been saved in the blessed screen capture file.

FIGURE 6-14

The screen capture of Notepad's Open dialog box that will be the blessed capture, used for all present and future comparisons of Notepad's Open dialog box.

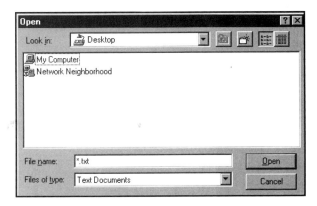

While the controls have maintained their positions and not changed as cited in a previous example of how the comparison utility can be helpful, something has changed and it will cause the comparison to fail.

Figure 6-15 is the same dialog box with one difference: Its list box is displaying a list of drives available to the user, instead of the top-level view shown in Figure 6-14. In this example, the comparison fails and the comparison function saves a copy of the dialog box for later examination, to help determine the cause of the failure.

Your tests have been run and you return to find that an error occurred during a comparison of one of the dialog boxes. Because you wrote your comparison function to make a capture of the dialog box in question, you can compare the failed dialog box against the approved capture of that dialog box.

Comparing the dialog boxes shown in Figures 6-14 and 6-15 using the Screen utility results in an XOR-ing of the two objects. That is, the Screen utility lays the two screenshots on top of each other, and any pixels that match up with each other or that have not changed will be canceled out. Those pixels that are different will show up in the comparison (see Figure 6-16).

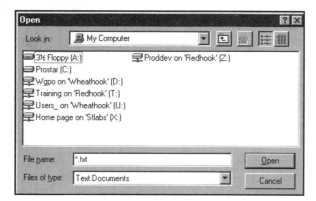

FIGURE 6-15
This is how Notepad's Open dialog box appeared during our supposed test run.

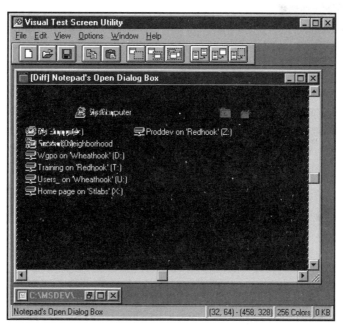

FIGURE 6-16
Comparing the dialog boxes shown in Figures 6-14 and 6-15, using the Screen utility.

In the instance of text that existed in the same location of both captures, but that has changed in some way, that text will appear as a more garbled or fuzzy image in the comparison window.

Drawbacks

There are some drawbacks to using the Screen utility, however. For example, when working with any screen that has a flashing cursor or a value that can change (as in the previous example, where the contents of the list box changed), the result can be a failed comparison. Even a single pixel changing will cause a comparison to fail.

Another drawback occurs when performing comparisons at different resolutions. Screens captured at one resolution can't be used for comparisons at another resolution. If the testing is being performed at 640x480, 800x600, 1024x768, and so on, there will need to be separate capture files for each resolution.

And there are more problems. If comparisons are being done at different color settings, such as 16 colors, 256 colors, and sixteen million colors, separate screen comparison files will need to be kept for each of these color settings as well.

And, in the worst-case situation of performing captures and comparisons at 1024x768 pixels (or at a higher resolution) and at 16 million colors, the size of the capture file can grow large, quickly. And because the comparisons are done at the level of pixel by pixel, the time to compare each screenshot can grow as the resolution and bits per pixel (number of colors) grow.

If at all possible, keep things simple by picking one resolution and one color setting to be used for captures and comparisons. And keep the use of the screen comparisons to a minimum. Don't go nuts and do a screen comparison of every piece of UI in the product. Pick key areas that need to be monitored and use the screen comparison utility just for those.

Masking

The Microsoft Test team introduced the ability to *mask* regions of a captured image in version 3.0 of Test. This feature is still available in version 4.0.

The general idea of the masking feature is to specify a region to be ignored during the comparison of the two images. This is done using the Screen utility. The user opens the blessed capture file and uses the mouse to draw a rectangle across the area to be ignored. This solves the problem mentioned previously, regarding values that can change between test runs. In Figure 6-17, we've masked out the areas shown in Figure 6-16 that changed and caused the comparison to fail.

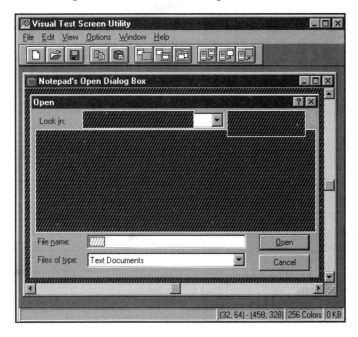

FIGURE 6-17 An example of masking out areas that can change between test runs.

In version 3.0 of Test there wasn't a way to set the exclude regions through the programming language. Fortunately, version 4.0 has a new function called *ScnSetExcludeRects* that allows for programmatically spec- / ifying such regions.

Conclusion

When I first sat down with Microsoft Test 1.0, I figured the product itself was an automated tool that built automated tests for me. How wrong I was! The tools that come with it can be helpful, but creating the test suite consists of a lot of script writing, learning how to deal with odd situations, maintenance as a product evolves, and patience as you move forward on tackling the task of automation.

There is no magic involved in Visual Test. It's simply a programming language that contains some routines and tools to help you work with the Windows user interface. Dive in, move forward, and you'll find that, in no time, you'll have a large test suite helping you test your product. And you'll find automation getting easier as you progress.

Summary

While Microsoft has provided a number of utilities to make the job of automation easier on us, the bulk of the job still involves writing scripts by hand. The Scenario Recorder helps. It generates some simple test scenarios by recording a user's actions. However, these often require modification and ongoing maintenance. Use the recorder only when you're uncertain how to go about automating an area, or if you're trying to automate a product that uses controls you aren't familiar with. It may show up some commands you didn't know about previously.

The Suite Manager is very helpful in managing multiple files on a project and aids in handling error conditions. It also allows you to control how the results of your tests are logged: whether they go to a simple *flat* text file, or into a database-compatible file format. It also allows you to control the number of times a test case file is run and tracks which of those files had failures.

The Winfo utility helps track down both fake, or virtual, controls so that you know how you need to work with them. In many cases you'll find it is simply a control that has been subclassed and requires the use of the W*SetClass statement. In other cases, you'll find that the control isn't recognized by Visual Test and will require you to provide *X* and *Y* coordinates to click on a specific pixel location.

And finally, the Screen utility is helpful in verifying that a dialog box, window, or the screen in general is exactly as it was when previously captured. It can become bulky, however, when working at high resolutions displaying a high number of colors. It can also be cumbersome when you need to keep screen comparisons of the product for multiple resolutions and color settings.

CHAPTER 7

Simple Coding Example

*N*ow that we've had a chance to get an overview of Visual Test's user interface (UI), Test language, and accompanying utilities, let's take a look at what a typical first test script might look like.

In our example, we're going to use Notepad, a simple text editor that ships with Windows NT and Windows 95. We're using it both because it's a simple application to automate, so our first automation script will be easy, and because almost everyone who's ever used Windows is familiar with Notepad.

In Chapter 9 we take a closer look at how to decide on an overall approach to take. But, as we're only automating a small piece of Notepad here, we won't be looking too closely at the overall approach just yet.

Note

Remember that the compiler for the Test language is not case-sensitive. Therefore, the capitalizing and lowercasing of characters in my source listings are based only on my style; and that style can change from time to time even though I've attempted to keep it consistent in this book.

Those of you who have a strong background in programming will notice we're not using a lot of structure. That is, we're not focusing on constants, functions, macros, subroutines, or include files. The reason is simply so that our first script is easier to follow. Listing 7-1 is an example of a typical first test script.

The Sample Script

LISTING 7-1 A Simple First Script That Tests Notepad's "New" Menu Item.

```
'*********************************************************************
'* This file contains a simple example of testing the "New"
'* menu item found under the File menu in the Windows Notepad
'* application.
'*********************************************************************

dim strText$, hwndApp&

    'Make sure the viewport is cleared
    VIEWPORT CLEAR

    'Check to see if Notepad is already running. If not, run it.
    hwndApp = wFndWnd("- Notepad", FW_ALL OR FW_EXIST OR FW_PART _
                                  OR FW_FOCUS OR FW_RESTORE)
    if (hwndApp = 0) then
        if (run("notepad.exe")) then
            print "Unable to run Notepad.exe"
            stop
        endif
        hwndApp = wGetActWnd(0)   takes a handle to the Notepad window
    endif

    print
    print "Tests begun on: "+DATETIME$+" for "+NAME$
    print


    '
    'Test the "New" menu item, respond "no".
    '

    'Write out information about test to be performed
    print "Test #1: 'New' with text. Select 'No'."

    'Make sure there's text in the Notepad window.
    WEditSetText("@1","")   'Clears out the contents of editor
    play "Now is the time for all good..."

    'Select the "New" menu item
    WMenuSelect("File\New")
```

```
If (GetText(NULL) = "Notepad") then  '"Save Changes" DB display?
    WButtonClick("No")                'No, don't save changes

    'Notepad's main window is a big edit control.
    'We can give it the focus and check text, put text, etc.
    'just like any other edit control. We use "@1" since it
    'is the first and only edit control.
    If (EditText("@1") <> "") then
        'Write out error information describing what went wrong.
        print "***Error: 'New' didn't clear window contents."
        print "Expected: <empty-window>"
        print "Received: "+EditText("@1")
        print
    EndIf
Else
    'Write out error information describing what went wrong.
    print "***Error: 'New' with text didn't display "+ _
            "the 'Are you sure?' message box."
    print "Expected: Notepad"
    print "Received: "+GetText(NULL)
    print
EndIf


'
'Test the "New" menu item, respond "Yes".
'
print "Test #2: 'New' with text. Select 'Yes'."
play "Now is the time for all good..."
strText = EditText("@1")    'Get editor's contents.
WMenuSelect("File\New")

'Because there is unsaved text, the 'Save changes/Are you sure?
'message box should be displayed.
If (GetText(NULL) = "Notepad") then
    WButtonClick("Yes")
    If (GetText(NULL) = "Save As") then
        WButtonClick("Cancel")
    Else
        print "***Error: 'New' with 'Yes, save changes' "+ _
                "didn't display SaveAs DB."
        print "Expected: Save As"
        print "Received: "+GetText(NULL)
```

(continued)

145

LISTING 7-1 A Simple First Script That Tests Notepad's "New" Menu Item. (*Continued*)

```
        print
    EndIf
Else
    print "***Error: 'New' with text didn't display "+ _
         "the 'Are you sure?' message box."
    print "Expected: Notepad"
    print "Received: "+GetText(NULL)
    print
EndIf


If (strText <> EditText("@1")) then
    print "***Error: Cancel out of SaveAs after 'New' "+ _
         "caused text change."
    print "Expected: "+strText
    print "Received: "+EditText("@1")
    print
EndIf


'
'Test the "New" menu item, respond "Cancel".
'
print "Test #3: 'New' with text. Select 'Cancel'."
strText = EditText("@1")
WMenuSelect("File\New")


'Because there is unsaved text, the Save changes/Are you sure?
'message box should be displayed.
If (GetText(NULL) = "Notepad") then
    WButtonClick("Cancel")
Else
    print "***Error: 'New' with text didn't display the "+ _
         "'Are you sure?' message box."
    print "Expected: Notepad"
    print "Received: "+GetText(NULL)
    print
EndIf


'If the text changed even though cancel was used,
'an error occurred.
If (strText <> EditText("@1")) then
    print "***Error: Cancel out of 'New' caused text change."
```

```
        print "Expected: "+strText
        print "Received: "+EditText("@1")
        print
    EndIf

    print
    print "*** Tests completed."

    WMenuSelect("File\Exit")      'Exit the Notepad application
    WButtonClick("No")            '"No" to "Save changes?" message box
END
```

The sample script can be broken up into four separate parts:

1) ▶ Declarations

2) ▶ Initialization

3) ▶ Tests

4) ▶ Clean-up

Each of these sections and the code that makes up those sections are discussed below.

Declarations

We begin our script by declaring the only two variables that are used:

```
'*****************************************************************
'* This file contains a simple example of testing the "New"
'* menu item found under the "File" menu in the Windows Notepad
'* application.
'*****************************************************************

dim strText$, hwndApp&
```

It is typical to have a declaration line shrink and grow as the script is first written and continues to evolve. As we discussed in Chapter 5, all variable declarations are made using the *dim* statement. *strText$* is a variable of type *string* that holds a string of characters. *HwndApp&* is a variable of type *long* that holds a handle to an application's main window. This handle is used by other functions and statements to ensure that the proper application window is acted upon.

147

Just Jump In

Even though a finished script may be well-organized and make sense upon examination, scripts don't start out that way. Don't look at this sample script as something that was written sequentially from start to finish. As in any program when it is first being written, the creative juices are flowing and the programmer is typically jumping back and forth between sections as the script unfolds. Only after a number of revisions have been made to a script does it start to resemble anything that looks somewhat organized.

The best way for you to create your own automated scripts is to jump in and start writing some automated tests. Don't worry if it's messy at first, you get better as you go along and you also get an idea of how you want to organize your overall automation task. As you continue to automate your tests, you find you do more planning—even if it's not on paper but just thinking something through in your head—before writing any actual code. If you're new to Visual Test, you're not at this stage, so just jump in. You'll get to where you can plan your automation with more forethought soon enough.

OR-ing

The *wFndWnd* function controls how it works by OR-ing together a number of constants known as *flags*. For those of you familiar with database queries, don't confuse this OR-ing with a typical database look-up. What is going on instead is a *bitwise-OR*, meaning it is taking the binary digits and adding them together. For this to work, the constant values are unique: They are all based on a power of 2, so that their binary representation is a single bit and unique from the other constants.

The main thing to understand is that the OR-ing going on in this function call has nothing to do with a "this or that" approach; it's more of a "this, and that, and that, and that" approach. By OR-ing the flags, we're actually adding the flags together, so that only one parameter needs to be passed to the *wFndWnd* function.

Getting Ready to Test — Initialization

The next few lines of code are used to initialize everything, so that the tests can begin:

```
'Make sure the viewport is cleared
VIEWPORT CLEAR

'Check to see if Notepad is already running. If not, run it.
hwndApp = wFndWnd("- Notepad", FW_ALL OR FW_EXIST OR FW_PART _
                        OR FW_FOCUS OR FW_RESTORE)
```

The first thing that occurs is a "VIEWPORT CLEAR" statement. This clears the window where all the output is placed. Any time the *print* statement is used, the output is placed in the Viewport (except in the situations when you are working with file input and output [I/O]).

After clearing the Viewport, the script uses the *wFndWnd* function to determine whether or not an application with the partial caption of "- Notepad" is up and running. Note that I said *partial caption*. *WFndWnd()* is configurable in how it works. This is controlled through OR-ing together a number of *flags* that are available to be used with this function.   *Find Window*

The flags I've chosen to use in this circumstance are: FW_ALL, FW_EXIST, FW_PART, FW_FOCUS and FW_RESTORE. These tell *wFndWnd()* to search all windows, return a handle to the window if it exists, search partial captions to see if any of them contain the caption passed as the first parameter of the function call, give the window the focus (activate it) once it is found, and restore the window so that it is in normal mode — neither minimized nor maximized.

In the event that the window isn't found, zero (0) is returned, letting us know that a valid window handle couldn't be supplied. In this situation, we know Notepad isn't up and running, so we need to take appropriate steps to make it so.

We can get Notepad running by using Visual Test's run statement. Now, this routine comes in two flavors: function or statement. If we use the statement form, it attempts to run the specified program. If it fails, however, we may not find out until we try to test the application later. So in this situation, I prefer to use the functional form:

→ *the window isn't found*

```
if (hwndApp = 0) then
    if (run("notepad.exe")) then
        print "Unable to run Notepad.exe"
        stop
    endif
    hwndApp = wGetActWnd(0)
endif
```

The functional form returns a number to us, letting us know whether or not it succeeded. Here's the counter-intuitive part of it, though. If it *does* succeed, it returns a zero (0) — a value commonly associated with *false*, or something failure-related.

Microsoft designed this function this way with good reason: Now they can communicate exactly why it failed to run by returning any number of values that are documented in the online help to explain the cause of the failure.

In this case, however, we don't care why it failed. We just want to know if Notepad successfully ran. If anything other than zero (0) is returned, we step into the next line of code that prints out an error message and stops the execution of the script.

Warning

This is important, because if a script ever gets into a situation where the application you're testing isn't up and running, it'll usually keep running — possibly causing unexpected results as it performs operations on whatever application does happen to be up and running.

If we successfully run the application, we can use *wGetActWnd()* to give us the handle to its window, so we can refer to it later:

```
hwndApp = wGetActWnd(0)
```

Finally, we print out the beginning information. This informs you, as you stare at the Viewport bleary-eyed, exactly when the tests commenced:

```
print
print "Tests begun on: "+DATETIME$+" for "+NAME$
print
```

It's arguable that the "Test started" line could be placed where the tests actually begin, but as you see in later chapters, we turn this initialization code into a re-usable module that all of our test cases will use. Therefore, we want the beginning test information printed in the initialization section, so if changes need to be made later, they can be done in this one module, rather than re-visiting each test case or test file in turn.

The Tests

In this example, there are only three separate situations we're looking for when testing the New menu item. In all three, we are testing that the Save changes? message box is being displayed. To do this, we need to make sure we have new, unsaved text in the editor. Then we select the New menu item.

TEST ONE

An interesting factoid about Notepad is that its main window is one large edit control. This makes testing it simpler, since we can use the *wEdit*()* routines to retrieve information about the text it is displaying. We start by making sure we have a clean slate and that no text exists in Notepad's main window. We do this with the *wEditSetText* function:

```
'
'Test the "New" menu item, respond "no".
'

'Write out information about test to be performed
print "Test #1: 'New' with text. Select 'No'."

'Make sure there's text in the Notepad window.
WEditSetText("@1","")   'Clears out the contents of editor
play "Now is the time for all good..."
```

WEditSetText() takes two parameters. The first identifies the edit control we're working with. In our example, we use an ordinal ("@1") to identify the first and only edit control found in the main window of Notepad. The second parameter identifies the text to be placed in the control. By passing a null string (such as ""), we effectively clear the contents of the window, allowing us to place our own sample text into the editor. In this case, our test string is "Now is the time for all good...." Figure 7-1 shows Notepad being tested.

FIGURE 7-1
Testing Notepad.

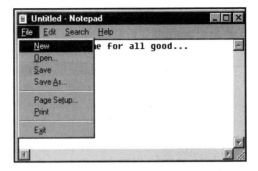

We begin the first test by selecting the New menu item from the File menu. It is to verify that when we say "No" to save changes, that the text is indeed cleared out of the editor's main window. We do it with the wMenuSelect statement. Because we've entered new text into Notepad, we're prompted to save changes:

```
'Select the "New" menu item
  WMenuSelect("File\New")

  If (GetText(NULL) = "Notepad") then '"Save Changes" DB display?
      WButtonClick("No")                'No, don't save changes

      'Notepad's main window is a big edit control.
      'We can give it the focus and check text, put text, etc.
      'just like any other edit control. We use "@1" since it
      'is the first and only edit control.
      If (EditText("@1") <> "") then       i i t still text, after we decided
          'Write out error information describing what went wrong.    not save.
          print "***Error: 'New' didn't clear window contents."
          print "Expected: <empty-window>"
          print "Received: "+EditText("@1")
          print
      EndIf
  Else
      'Write out error information describing what went wrong.
      print "***Error: 'New' with text didn't display "+ _
            "the 'Are you sure?' message box."
      print "Expected: Notepad"
      print "Received: "+GetText(NULL)
      print
  EndIf
```

We use the wButtonClick statement to click on the No button. Immediately afterwards, we employ the *EditText* function to determine exactly whether any text is in the main window. If there *is* still text in it, something has gone wrong. Clicking on No to save changes after selecting the New menu item should have cleared the contents of the window.

In the event that text is left over that shouldn't have been, the section of script that prints out an error message to the Viewport is executed.

If the Save changes? message box wasn't found in the first place, all the source code for this test would be skipped and an error message would be printed to inform us of the problem.

TEST TWO

The second test begins on the assumption that the first test finished cleanly and that whether the test passed or failed, the error was handled:

```
'
'Test the "New" menu item, respond "Yes".
'
print "Test #2: 'New' with text. Select 'Yes'."
play "Now is the time for all good..."
strText = EditText("@1")    'Get editor's contents.
WMenuSelect("File\New")
```

A new text string is added to Notepad to set the editor's "dirty-bit" so that, when the New menu item is selected, it verifies whether or not changes should be saved. For this test the contents of the editor are grabbed and saved in a variable called *strText*. This way, we can say "Yes" to the message box and verify later that the text remains unchanged:

```
'Because there is unsaved text, the 'Save changes/Are you sure?
'message box should be displayed.
If (GetText(NULL) = "Notepad") then
    WButtonClick("Yes")
    If (GetText(NULL) = "Save As") then
        WButtonClick("Cancel")
    Else
        print "***Error: 'New' with 'Yes, save changes' "+ _
            "didn't display SaveAs DB."
        print "Expected: Save As"
        print "Received: "+GetText(NULL)
```

determines caption of the currently active window

153

```
            print
        EndIf
    Else
        print "***Error: 'New' with text didn't display "+ _
             "the 'Are you sure?' message box."
        print "Expected: Notepad"
        print "Received: "+GetText(NULL)
        print
    EndIf
```

The *GetText* function is used to determine the caption of the currently active window. It turns out that the expected message box has the same caption as the main application: "Notepad" (without the leading hyphen, in this case). If the message box isn't displayed as expected, the *else* branch of the statement is exercised and an error message is printed to the Viewport.

Most likely, the message box will be displayed as expected and we can successfully click on the Yes button. The application will then display the Save As dialog box prompting the user to type in a file name (see Figure 7-2).

FIGURE 7-2
The Save As dialog box
is displayed.

Windows NT users not using version 4.0 of Windows NT will find that a script that does click on the Save button, shown in Figure 7-2, will need to be modified to click on the OK button instead. Windows NT 4.0 will eliminate this problem since it will have a UI similar to Windows 95.

Warning

Because our intent was only to see what happened when we selected New from the File menu and clicked on Yes as one of the three options in the Save changes? message box, it's not my intention to use the Save

As dialog box at this time. Therefore, I clicked the Cancel button in the dialog box instead.

Tip

If the Save As dialog box, shown in Figure 7-2, hadn't appeared in the last piece of code, the matching *else* branch of the *if* statement that checked to see whether the dialog appeared would be executed. This would cause an error message, telling us that the dialog box didn't appear as expected.

The last part of our program is designed to verify that, after doing everything — clicking on Yes to save changes, displaying the Save As dialog box, and then canceling out of that dialog box to return to the main window — our text remains unchanged:

```
If (strText <> EditText("@1")) then
    print "***Error: Cancel out of SaveAs after 'New' "+ _
        "caused text change."
    print "Expected: "+strText
    print "Received: "+EditText("@1")
    print
EndIf
```

So, it seems that a number of tests were actually going on in our second test. First, we checked to make sure the Save Changes? message box was displayed. It was, so we moved on from there to see whether or not the Save As dialog box appeared as expected. We chose to stop there and return to Notepad's main window and verify that the text in the editor when the test began was still there and unchanged.

The Reality of Automation

An unfortunate reality of test automation programming is that all error conditions need to be checked. That is, if you expect a dialog box to appear, you should enter the necessary code to verify whether or not it did appear. Otherwise, if an expected window or dialog box doesn't appear, the script will continue to execute, most likely on an unintended section of the program. This can result in many errors being reported that don't actually exist, simply because the script is trying to run itself in the wrong context. Remember that test automation is its own separate development project and it takes time to write, maintain, and constantly improve the scripts.

So why did Test Two only get counted as one test? Because that was the style I chose to follow. I had one main objective that I wanted to achieve: verifying that the Yes button worked and didn't change my editor's text. Some testers would have printed out the sub-tests that resulted (perhaps as Test 2.1, 2.2, and so on). It just depends on how you and your team choose to go about testing; there's no one way to do it. The trick is to pick a method and move forward.

TEST THREE

The final test is similar to Test Two. It too verifies that the text in the editor is unchanged after the tests have completed:

```
'
'Test the "New" menu item, respond "Cancel".
'
print "Test #3: 'New' with text. Select 'Cancel'."
strText = EditText("@1")
WMenuSelect("File\New")

'Because there is unsaved text, the Save changes/Are you sure?
'message box should be displayed.
If (GetText(NULL) = "Notepad") then
    WButtonClick("Cancel")
Else
    print "***Error: 'New' with text didn't display the "+ _
        "'Are you sure?' message box."
    print "Expected: Notepad"
    print "Received: "+GetText(NULL)
    print
EndIf
'If the text changed even though cancel was used,
'an error occurred.
If (strText <> EditText("@1")) then
    print "***Error: Cancel out of 'New' caused text change."
    print "Expected: "+strText
    print "Received: "+EditText("@1")
    print
EndIf
```

This test verifies that the last of the three buttons works when selecting New from the File menu, with unsaved text in the editor.

As a matter of style, one of the things I like to include in my error messages — you've probably noticed it already — is the *Expected* and *Received* information. In addition to the actual error, I like to print out what the expected results of the tests are, and then what the actual results were that caused the error to occur. The final output found in the Viewport at the completion of the test script can be seen in Figure 7-3.

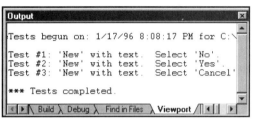

FIGURE 7-3
Output found in the Viewport at the completion of the test script.

The Clean-Up

The last section of the sample script focuses on printing out final information and returning the application that was being tested to a known state:

```
print
print "*** Tests completed."

WMenuSelect("File\Exit")     'Exit the Notepad application
WButtonClick("No")           '"No" to "Save changes?" message box
END
```

In this case, we shut down Notepad. In other situations you might choose to have Notepad stay up and the contents cleared from its main window, so that the next test case that runs starts from a clean state. Shutting down the application is one way of achieving this. Your team will need to decide which it prefers. If you really want to keep things flexible, then you might consider using a *.ini* file or a Registry setting to control how your scripts execute. We look at some examples of this later in this book.

Conclusion

This first script should have given you some ideas on how to begin your automation testing. The key message I want you to walk away with from this chapter is that you need to just go ahead, dive in, and start writing code. Follow this script as an example as you begin writing your tests; meanwhile, keep in mind that there isn't any one way to automate something, so be open to experimentation.

In the next chapters, we get into writing more flexible scripts so that when the inevitable need for changes arise, you'll take less of a hit when it comes to re-vamping your scripts.

Summary

In this chapter, we look at a simple, typical first test script, using Notepad. It consists of four parts: declarations, initialization, tests, and clean-up. Three tests are run, to show how to correct errors and make changes.

III

Building a Test Suite

8
Common Coding Guidelines

Whenever there exists a group of people on any given project, there are all kinds of styles that they bring to the table. These styles are anything from ways to manage people, to how to draft a document, to how to program a piece of code.

This chapter's purpose is to give you some suggestions on standards that you might want to consider having as a part of your automation project. They are only suggestions and a starting point for those new to writing any kind of code. They are part of my style and are in no way the definitive way to do things. If you don't have your own style yet, however, it's a very good place to start.

When working on a project where there is more than one person writing code, it is very important to define up front what types of standards or conventions are to be followed. You will appreciate the importance even more as common code is written that is shared between individuals on the team. It's also helpful to have a common style defined, so that when it becomes necessary to enter someone else's code you'll have an idea of which file to look in and in what section of that file to find whatever problem exists.

This is such an important concept that many companies have their own document on coding practices to be followed by all of the programmers on the development team. This type of document is just as important when writing test scripts because these are code and can be just as complex as the source code that makes up the product you are testing. I suggest you ask around to see if any such document exists at your company, so you can take it and tailor it to your automation team's needs.

By sitting down and building consensus amongst all of the testers who will be writing and maintaining the automated scripts, many problems can be avoided down the road. It is here that everyone's experiences and styles can come into play to help make a solid style that can be adhered to by everyone on the team. It's also key in getting new testers coming into a project up to speed quickly.

Coding Style

Let's take an example of a simple C program. I've been witness to a number of heated discussions between developers when it came to coding style. One such case was about where to place the curly braces ({}) in relation to a conditional branch. For example:

An opening brace on the same line as the *if* statement:

```
if (strX == "Hello") {
    printf("Hello World!");
}
```

An opening brace on a line by itself, lined up with the closing brace:

```
if (strX == "Hello")
{
    printf("Hello World!");
}
```

The (optional) opening or closing braces aren't used at all:

```
if (strX == "Hello")
    printf("Hello World!");
```

In the C programming language, all three of these examples do precisely the same thing. The first is typical of programmers who follow Brian W. Kernighan's and Dennis M. Ritchie's book, *"The C Programming Language,"* to the letter. This is characteristic of the true C programmers, who many times originate from the UNIX operating system world.

The second example is also used and defended because it is easy to count the opening and closing braces, especially in a particularly hairy piece of code that is made up of multiple conditional branches (such as if, else, and while); it's arguably easier to read that code when the braces are aligned. And the final example is legal because there is only one line of code relating to that conditional branch.

Many programmers tend to standardize on the second example, or a variation thereof, because of the increased readability of the code. Some people go so far as to advocate having the braces, even when it's a single line of code for that conditional branch. The reasoning for this is that, should it become necessary to add another line of code to that conditional branch, the braces are already in place and it lowers the odds that the developer will forget to add them, were they not already there. For example, if we add a line of code to the if statement (braces are forgotten):

```
if (strX == "Hello")
    printf("Hello World!");
    printf("How are you today?");
```

Here, the second printf is indented, but in fact it falls outside the if statement and will be executed every single time, which was not the intent of the programmer. To fix it, the braces would need to be added around both lines. The corrected code for the last example should be:

```
if (strX == "Hello")
{
    printf("Hello World!");
    printf("How are you today?");
}
```

When you're in a hurry to find an error in your code and you throw fatigue and stress into the mix, this is the type of error that will stare you in the face for a while, before you finally track it down.

Here's a list of some of the areas that are part of the topic of coding style. We discuss each of these in turn. They are

▶ Using comments for yourself and others

▶ Templates for defining a style for others to follow

▶ Variable and function naming conventions

▶ Uses and abuses of unconditional branching

▶ Source code file types and what source code goes where

▶ The idea of a file hierarchy for sharing source code

▶ Encapsulation of common sections of code

▶ Creation of *wrapper* functions for future flexibility

Comments

A *comment* is information found in a source code file that exists solely for the benefit of the programmer. When a piece of code is compiled into a form usable by the computer and unreadable to an average programmer, the comments are stripped, since they serve no purpose in the final form of that file (in other words, the file is in a form preferable to a computer, not a human).

The use of comments vary and depend on the style of each programmer. I've been through code that is completely uncommented, and I've been through other code that has a comment on each and every line of the source code file. Neither extreme is preferable; it's up to you and/or your team to decide to what degree a file should be commented.

There are two main reasons why anyone comments code. The first is for yourself, so that when you return to a section of code later, sometimes months or years after you wrote it originally, you can understand the code more quickly than you would had the comments not been included. I can recall situations in college where I was up all night banging out some final code on a project that was due the next day, taking a two-hour nap, and coming back later only to try to figure out what the heck I'd done. Sometimes my code would be really well thought out and I was impressed as to how much I was in the groove when I was writing it. Other times (more common) I'd come back and try to figure out why I'd written it a certain way when it was now obvious that there was a much easier way to do it. Had I included comments, which would have explained my reasoning at the time of writing the particular section of code, I would have saved myself time and realized what I was thinking at the time of writing.

The other reason for using comments is for other people. If you write routines that are useful to your team and therefore the company for which you work, most likely your routines will outlive the job position you're in. That is to say, you might move on to other groups or higher positions and your code will stay behind. When someone else is supposed to pick up where you left off, or see if they can cut and paste helpful sections of your code into their code, it's easier for them to do this if there are clear comments describing how things are set up and what they do.

Another time that others would be looking at your code is when you are on a team and sharing that code. For example, if you've created a utility that is helpful and generic enough for others to use, then you'll want to share it and cut down on the support time you'd otherwise have to provide, by having plenty of comments describing how to use the routine.

When I was at Asymetrix Corporation, I came across a section of code that had what some people refer to as a *magic number* or *magic cookie*. It's referred to this way because the number simply exists in the code but no one, sometimes not even the original programmer, remembers how they arrived at that number. Therefore, it's a magic number. When I went to the programmer to ask him how he came up with it, he couldn't remember. He had to sit down with pencil and paper again to figure out how he came up with it to make his routine work. This is an example of a perfect place where a comment would be added to the source code. Had the programmer placed a comment describing how the number was derived, I wouldn't have had to track him down and then get him to work through the formulas again.

In Microsoft Visual Test, a comment is any line that has, as the first item on that text line, the letters REM or the single quote ('). REM is short for Remark and the single quote is an abbreviation for the REM designator. The following code shows an example of a function that has some comments in it:

```
function tnSaveFile(tnstrDir$, tnstrFilter$) as string
  dim ofnFile as OPENFILENAME
  dim strFileChoice as STRING * TN_MAXPATH
  dim ret%

  tnCmnGetSaveOps (ofnFile, (tnstrDir), (tnstrFilter))
  ofnFile.lpstrFile = cptr(varptr(strFileChoice))   'Info buffer
  ofnFile.nMaxFile  = LEN(strFileChoice)            'Size of buffer
  ofnFile.Flags     = OFN_OVERWRITEPROMPT OR _       'Warn if exists
                      OFN_HIDEREADONLY  OR   _       'No Chkbox
```

165

```
                         OFN_PATHMUSTEXIST                      'Warn: bad path
      'Pass the struct on to the routine for final
      'processing and return a legal filename or
      'an empty string.

      if GetSaveFileName(ofnFile) then               'Get file info
         tnSaveFile = trim$(trim$(strFileChoice,0))   'Return file info
      else
         tnSaveFile = ""                              'Return empty string
      endif
   end function 'tnSaveFile
```

My style is to put my comment on the same line as the code, if it will fit. Otherwise, I put them just above the code, so that the person reading through the list understands what the next section of code is about to do.

I even go so far as to have a comment right after the end of the function block. That is, "end function 'tnSaveFile." I do this so that, if the function grows into something larger than it currently is, it'll be easier to tell when it ends. Otherwise, if my code has "end function" a bunch of times, you have to scroll back up through the code to find the beginning of the function to figure out which function block you're looking at.

I admit that I'm a commenting fool. I'd rather take the time to comment my stuff so that it helps others than to have them throw my old code away because it was uncommented. Don't worry about making it pretty by lining things up, just make sure you have some kind of comments in your code, so that others will have an easier time deciphering your work.

Templates

Templates play a big role in setting up the style you want everyone on the team to follow. A template takes much of what the team has agreed upon and lays it out in a format to be used by everyone. Much of a template is made up of commented information. (See Listing 8-1).

SAMPLE INCLUDE FILE TEMPLATE

There are two main source code file types in Visual Test. The first is the *include file*, and the second is the *test case file*. Include files and their uses are described more thoroughly when we look at the test case (*.mst*) files next. Below is a sample template that might be used by a test automation team.

LISTING 8-1 A Template for a Typical Include File.

```
'*********************** <filename.inc> **********************
'*
'* Purpose:
'*
'* Author:
'*
'* Revision History:
'*
'* [ 0]  da-mon-year   email  : action
'*
'****************************************************************

'$IFNDEF <AREA>_INCLUDED
'$DEFINE <AREA>_INCLUDED

'****************************************************************
'*********************** Constants **************************
'****************************************************************


'****************************************************************
'********************** User Def'd Types **********************
'****************************************************************


'****************************************************************
'********************** Global Variables ********************
'****************************************************************


'****************************************************************
'***************** Func/Proc Prototypes **********************
'****************************************************************


'$ENDIF <AREA>_INCLUDED
```

A sample template is shown in this listing. There are six sections that make up this template example.

main comment block

The first section is the front comment block that describes what the file is to be used for and provides any special instructions on how to use that file. For example: Does it rely on other files being included already? Is it a stand-alone file that doesn't need to be included with anything else? Are separate data files required to be in particular directories?

It also displays the name of the person who wrote the file. Having the name of the person handy makes it easier to track down whomever you need to answer any pressing questions about the use of the file.

And finally, the last section of the first block is the Revision section. This section's purpose is to provide information about the changes made to the file over its lifetime. Some people consider this "Big Brother"-ish, but the fact is that it makes it easier to resolve problems, should another person make changes to the file. What appears to be a simple change could in fact break other sections of the code base downstream. In the event that a situation like this occurs, the person who made the change can be contacted so that the situation can be resolved to everyone's benefit.

conditional compilation

The next section of the template is in place to help save time tracking down problems.

The '$ifndef statement checks to see if the file has already been included. Say, for example, there is a file that contains common declarations for the entire project — perhaps a constant that holds the caption of the main window of the application being tested. Instead of having that constant defined for every test file that exists in your suite, it would be moved up to a common include file that everyone can add to their test files by using the '$include metacommand. The result is, you only have to go to one file to make changes, instead of visiting multiple files.

In the event that there are more common files that rely on yet other common files, things can turn messy in a hurry. One common compilation error that occurs in any language is a *redeclaration error* which is the compiler's way of saying, "Hey, you've already got a variable, function, or whatever named this!" If an include file — sometimes referred to as a header file — is accidentally included multiple times, this is typically the error that is encountered.

The conditional compilation is a way to avoid this error. True, it allows the testing team to be a little sloppier in their programming (because it won't complain if a file is included multiple times), but it saves time and avoids the nightmare of having to track down exactly which file is including another file a second time.

Here's how it works: When a test file is run, it needs to compile all the source code into a form understandable by the Visual Test interpreter. Some of these files are "including" information from other files, for reasons mentioned above (that is, sharing common declarations instead of having multiple declarations for the same thing scattered throughout).

What's really going on underneath is that the pre-compiler is assembling all the files into one big file to be checked for syntax, and then compiled to its tokenized form (commonly referred to as *pseudo-code*). When an '$include metacommand is encountered, the contents of the file it references are inserted at the location of that '$include command. The result: one big file that the compiler can finally crunch into pseudo-code.

When a file is included a second time, the redeclaration error is usually encountered. This is where the conditional compilation comes in handy. The '$ifndef command checks to see if a particular *symbol* has already been defined. Now, in this case, a symbol can be any string or word. Visual Test's defined symbols don't hold an assigned value. Instead, the symbol is placed into a table letting the compiler know that it has been defined. The first time the pre-compiler brings in the file that contains the '$ifndef command, it checks to see if the symbol it refers to has been defined or not.

If it is the first time the file is being included, then most likely the symbol hasn't been defined (unless someone else is already using a symbol of the same name). The compiler then moves to the next line because the '$ifndef (if not defined) evaluates to true, since that particular symbol isn't yet defined.

So, referring back to the example listing, the next line is '$define. This is where the symbol is actually defined and then all the rest of the lines below it are included.

Let's look at this from another angle: the second time the file is included. The symbol has already been defined. When the '$ifndef metacommand is encountered, it finds that out. The result is just like any other *if not()* conditional branch: it doesn't enter that section of code. Instead, it drops out to the '$endif command at the bottom of the file. As a result, the declarations in that file are totally skipped and any redeclaration error messages are avoided.

It turns out that, in Visual Test 4.0, Microsoft put in a check to make things easier for us. It decided that, if the constant, variable, or whatever has already been declared, the compiler doesn't care if the file is included for a second time, as long as the type (for example, integer or string) or value haven't changed. The reason this is being brought up in this book is because the redeclaration errors can still be encountered, especially if your code is written to work with Microsoft Test 3.0 for 16-bit application testing (because Test 3.0 will still complain when a file is included more than once).

constants

The next section in the template is where constants are placed. Constants are basically variables that have values that never change and will cause an error to be generated if an attempt is made during the running of the script (*run-time*) to change a constant's value. This protects us as Test programmers from accidentally modifying a value that should never change (the example used previously is the caption of the main window of the application whose testing is being automated). In the event the value does need to change while the script is running, then it shouldn't be a constant.

Using a constant throughout an entire code base makes it easy to change a value without having to edit multiple files because of the change. Let's say we're testing a program and the caption being used is "Notepad." Then, one day, someone decides it needs to be "Notepad -" with a hyphen, so that the name of the file currently being viewed can be appended to that name. Consider having 20 test case files that test the application and having to search through each of those files looking for and replacing every instance of "Notepad" with "Notepad -"! That's why you want to use constants, and be comfortable in the knowledge that the value can't be changed, except at the one place in which that value is declared.

Declaration Placement

Placement of declarations is critical when declaring constants, variables and user-defined types. Visual Test uses what is known as a *one-pass compiler*. This means that it goes through a file one time as it does its compilation, usually from top to bottom. If it encounters a reference to something that has not yet been declared, a compiler error is encountered. If you used a constant when declaring a user-defined type, but it was declared lower in the file, an error similar to the following is encountered:

```
Error VTC4317: Constant expression expected before 'mytype'
Error VTC4308: '<end of line>' expected before 'type'
```

The above two errors were given simply because the declaration wasn't placed properly.

A rule of thumb for using constants is that, whenever a value is used more than once, and it's a value that shouldn't change during the running of the script, you should turn it into a constant. Not all constants necessarily go into one overall include file placed at the top of the shared file hierarchy (more on the hierarchy later). They might be placed down in the hierarchy near the test file that is using it, if that is the only place it is used. Otherwise, if there is a value that's being used only once, type that actual value into the program (this is known as a *literal*) and place comments next to it explaining how the value was derived, if it's not obvious already.

The names of constants usually appear in uppercase letters so that it is easy to determine what is a constant and what is a variable. The Visual Test editor and compiler are *not* case-sensitive, so even if the programmer declares a constant using uppercase letters, it can be referred to in lowercase. Thus, it's up to the Test programmers on the team to adhere to the style, even though Visual Test allows for sloppiness.

user-defined types

A user-defined type is a type not common enough to have already been defined in the programming language. An *integer* is a basic type that shows up in all languages. If it's preferable to have all of the information about a test kept in one variable, or in an array, for example, it is then that a user-defined type needs to be used. Once that type has been declared by a Test programmer, a variable of that type can be declared and used for tracking the information about a test or whatever that programmer has decided to track. (See Chapter 5 to learn how to declare a user-defined type.)

Because constants can be used to make up a user-defined type, the section where constants are declared is above the area for the declarations of user-defined types.

global variables

A global variable is a variable that is available, or *in scope*, every place in the test script. Unlike in the C language, where a global variable's scope can be limited to a particular file, in the Test language it is global no matter where you are in the overall code base, as long as the file is included directly or indirectly by the test case file. For example, when in a subroutine or function, the global variable can be referenced and changed. (This is the same for constants, except constants' values can't be changed).

Global variables should be used sparingly. It is usually considered poor programming style when they are overused. There are a number of reasons for this, one of the more important being that of dependencies. If a test suite is broken up into many parts to keep it modular, that modularity is undermined if it has to depend on a global variable declared someplace else. When possible, use variables that are *local* to the piece of code using that value.

The other reason not to use global variables is because they take up more memory. Local variables allocate memory only when they are being used. For example, memory is allocated for a local variable declared in a given function only when that function is being executed. At the end of its execution, its locally declared variable is freed from memory.

Sometimes, however, a global variable is the only way to go because the information stored in it is used by everyone. At other times, speed is a factor and by avoiding the (albeit small) amount of time for allowing the interpreter to allocate the memory for a local variable, crucial time is saved. This is more the exception than the norm, however.

An example of a variable that you might consider keeping as a global would be a running counter which keeps track of the number of errors that have occurred during the running of your tests.

function and subroutine prototypes

Known both as a *forward declaration* and *prototype*, declaring a function or subroutine and the values it uses is necessary when keeping your code compatible with version 3.0 of Test. Just like a constant or variable can't be used before it's declared, the same goes for a function or subroutine.

If the function FOO is declared first, and in that function it calls another function BAR, declared further down in the source code, compilation errors will result when compiled under versions of Test previous to 4.0. However, version 4.0 lets you get away with more and it is no longer necessary to prototype a function or subroutine, except when referring to functions stored in dynamic linked libraries (DLLs).

In Visual Test 4.0, if a function FOO is defined and calls a function BAR that occurs lower in the code base, it will find BAR and run as expected. This isn't the case for older versions of Microsoft Test.

A TYPICAL TEST CASE FILE TEMPLATE

A simple test case file was shown to you in Chapter 7. However, it didn't use some of the common coding guidelines (such as constants) so that a clear demonstration of a test case file could be given. Listing 8-2 is an example of a template that might be used by a test automation team.

LISTING 8-2   A Template for a Typical Test Case File.

```
'*****************************************************************
'* Filename:
'*
'* Purpose:
'*
'* Revision History:
'*
'*   [ 0]   da-mon-year      email   : action
'*
```

(continued)

LISTING 8-2   A Template for a Typical Test Case File.
(Continued)

```
'****************************************************************
'*********************** INCLUDES ******************************
'$include '<>.inc'  'Bring in your consts, prototypes, macros, …

'****************** GLOBALS INITIALIZED ************************

'********************** Main Tests ****************************

'************* Your functions & subroutines *******************

'****************************************************************
'* Subroutine:  <name>
'* Purpose:
'*
'* Parameters:
'*
'****************************************************************

'****************************************************************
'* Function:    <name>
'* Purpose:
'*
'* Parameters:
'*
'* Returns:
'*
'****************************************************************
```

Naming Conventions

My first programming experience was on my Apple II Plus computer,
back in 1982. I followed the tutorial that came with it and also bought a
couple of books that had some games for the TRS-80 computer, which I
had to convert to Applesoft BASIC.

The variable names used in those days, and even today, were simple and
didn't necessarily convey much information. For example, some programmers would start naming variables by working their way down the
alphabet. The result was single-character epithets that didn't mean any-

thing to someone looking through a printout of the program, unless they familiarized themselves with where they were declared and how they were used. Others would come up with slightly longer (two or three character) names for their variables that attempted to give some kind of hint as to their use. In the end, it became a detective game to track down where the variable was used, to determine what type of value it held, and its purpose.

Then, along came a Microsoft developer who wrote his thesis on a naming convention that was termed the *Hungarian Notation*. This naming convention is now used by Microsoft and almost all developers that write applications for Microsoft Windows. It's a convention you might want to add to your *Common Coding Guidelines* document.

It's a fairly simple concept that became necessary as more powerful programming languages became available. Imagine being able to look at a piece of code and, without searching for the place it was declared, knowing what type of value that variable held. This is the idea.

The best way to explain the Hungarian Notation is to show you some examples. Table 8-1 gives a list.

TABLE 8-1 Sample Variables Following the Hungarian Notation Naming Convention.

Variable	How Declared in Visual Test
strDescription	strDescription AS STRING
iDescription	iDescription AS INTEGER
iCount	iCount AS INTEGER
lTimer	lTimer AS LONG
pstrTestType	pstrTestType AS POINTER TO STRING * 10
rectWindow	rectWindow AS RECT
strfParse	FUNCTION strfParse (strX AS STRING) AS STRING

The first variable in Table 8-1 hints to the casual observer that it holds a description of some kind, and that the description is of type *string*. The second variable is also a description of some kind, but its type is an *integer*. Perhaps it is an index into an array of strings? Unfortunately, to figure this out we'd need to dig deeper into the code; we can't tell from the name alone, but at least we have an idea.

175

The next two variables, *iCount* and *lTimer*, are an *integer* and a *long*, respectively. iCount is most likely an index into a for-next loop or a counter used within a while loop. And, lTimer is perhaps used to keep track of a clock's time for benchmarking purposes. Since some functions dealing with a computer's clock return the number of seconds since the computer was turned on, this is typically a large number requiring a *long* (4 bytes) variable.

In the case of *rectWindow*, this is a situation where a standard type hasn't been used. Instead, a user-defined type has been created and a variable declared of that type. The *rect* type is standard to Visual Test and is used to define the boundaries of a rectangular region (such as a window). In this example, it's most likely used to track the dimensions of a window, perhaps to verify that it is displayed at the appropriate size.

When it comes to naming conventions for functions, some programmers go to the level of including the return type of that function as part of its name. In the case of *strfParse*, this is a function that supposedly performs some kind of parsing on a value passed to it. That function then returns a string to the line of code that called the function. In the example, the *f* implies it is a function and not a typical variable. The *str* implies that the value returned by the function is of type *string*.

These examples should give you an idea of how helpful naming conventions can be. Whether you use Hungarian Notation or not, always keep in mind that you need to create descriptive variable names both for yourself and for anyone who eventually inherits your source code.

Unconditional Branching

Computer Science classes downplay the idea of using a goto statement when programming. This is for a good reason; a goto is an unconditional branch that leads to "spaghetti" code and shows very poor programming practices. I stuck to this philosophy, and still do to this day. I avoid gotos like the plague. However, I know of at least one computer company that allows for them in their *Common Coding Guidelines* document, but only for certain situations. And it turns out that they are, in fact, reasonable situations.

IMMEDIATE EXITING

One situation that the company allows and even encourages the use of gotos is when you're working in a deeply embedded conditional structure and you need to exit that structure immediately (for example, if an unrecoverable error occurs).

In this case, there is a section of code at the end of the function that the programmer can jump to using a goto. But the company has strict rules for when you can do this:

1) The goto must always jump down/forward in the code. This helps avoid endless loops and spaghetti-type code.

2) The section of code jumped to should be at the end of the routine containing the goto.

3) It is preferable that this section of code is always passed through when exiting the routine, whether an error has occurred or not. This way, all clean-up code can be kept in one place for a given function.

4) Avoid gotos if at all possible.

ON ERROR GOTO

Other than this rare case, you normally avoid using this type of branching. However, Visual Test does have at least one circumstance where you have no choice, and that's when using the ON ERROR GOTO command. We get into this more when we discuss run-time errors in Chapter 13.

Test Language Source Code File Types

There are two main source code file types used in Microsoft Visual Test. These are standards, or conventions, that are encouraged, but don't necessarily have to be adhered to. The source code files are simple text files and the extension associated with these files is inconsequential—until you begin sharing code or working on a test automation team! This is where common guidelines need to be followed or hopeless confusion will result.

INCLUDE FILES

As explained in a previous chapter, an *include* or *header file* is a text file that contains source code depended upon by another file to make itself complete. It usually contains either generic, reusable information that is placed into a separate file so that other files can include it too, or contains a bunch of the up-front declarations for the main test case file that are moved into the separate include file to help cut down on clutter, making the test case file more readable.

In Microsoft Visual Test, include files have *.inc* as their file extension. It's worth noting that include files are only text and even though the standard is to use *.inc* as the file extension, any three-letter extension can be used.

Versions 1.0 to 3.0 of Microsoft Test used mstest.inc to include function and subroutine prototypes that linked into the DLLs that accompanied the product, constants to be used with the different functions, macros, and global variable declarations. It was included just like any other include file is incorporated into a test case file, by using the '$include metacommand:

```
'$include 'mstest.inc'
```

Customarily, declarations for constants, macros, and function and subroutine prototypes for linking in to DLLs go into an include file. Sometimes, reusable functions and subroutines (the actual definition code that controls the behavior of the routine, not just the declaration prototypes) are included as well.

Frequently, there is more than one include file in a test automation project. Listing 8-3 is an example of an include file that contains declarations common enough to be used by everyone on the testing team. Specifically, this file is for a test suite that tests sections of the Microsoft Windows Notepad program. Later we'll see include files specific to individual areas of the Notepad program that is being tested.

LISTING 8-3 "notemain.inc" — The Main Include File That Holds Common Declarations Used Throughout the Notepad Test Suite.

```
'************************ NOTEMAIN.INC ************************
'*
'* PURPOSE: All decls global to all Notepad tests and utils.
'*
'****************************************************************

'$ifndef NOTEMAIN_INCLUDED  'If NOTEMAIN.INC hasn't been included,
'$define NOTEMAIN_INCLUDED  'include it and define a symbol to make
                            'sure it doesn't get brought in again.
                            '(This avoids redeclaration errors)


'****************************************************************
'************************ CONSTANTS ************************
'****************************************************************

'*************** Name of Application Being Tested ***********
const APP_TARGET$   = "Notepad.exe"
const MAINWINDOW$   = "@1"  'Notepad editor window

'***************** Name of Temporary Files ******************
const TEMPFILE1$    = "TEMP1.TXT"
const TEMPFILE2$    = "TEMP2.TXT"

'******************** Test Data String ********************
const TEST_DATA1$   = "Now is the time for all good people."
const TEST_DATA2$   = "We, the people of the United States."

'Test_Data3 is a long string of text of word wrapping tests.
const TEST_DATA3$   = "Congress shall make no law respecting " + _
                      "an establishment of religion, or "      + _
                      "prohibiting the free exercise thereof;" + _
                      " or abridging the freedom of speech, "  + _
                      "or of the press..."

'*********************** Captions ************************
const CAP_TARGETAPP$ = "Notepad"  'Main title bar & gen. msg boxes

'********************* Button Captions ********************
const BTN_NO$       = "No"
const BTN_YES$      = "Yes"
```

(continued)

LISTING 8-3 "notemain.inc — The Main Include File That Holds Common Declarations Used Throughout the Notepad Test Suite. *(Continued)*

```
const BTN_OK$          = "Ok"
const BTN_CANCEL$      = "Cancel"
const BTN_SAVE$        = "Save"
const BTN_OPEN$        = "Open"

'********************** Menu Bar Constants ********************
'***** File Menu
const MNU_FILE_NEW$        = "File\New"
const MNU_FILE_OPEN$       = "File\Open..."
const MNU_FILE_SAVE$       = "File\Save"
const MNU_FILE_SAVEAS$     = "File\Save As..."
const MNU_FILE_PRINT$      = "File\Print"
const MNU_FILE_PAGESETUP$  = "File\Page Setup..."
const MNU_FILE_PRINTSETUP$ = "File\Print Setup..."
const MNU_FILE_EXIT$       = "File\Exit"

'***** Edit Menu
const MNU_EDIT_UNDO$       = "Edit\Undo"
const MNU_EDIT_CUT$        = "Edit\Cut"
const MNU_EDIT_COPY$       = "Edit\Copy"
const MNU_EDIT_PASTE$      = "Edit\Paste"
const MNU_EDIT_DELETE$     = "Edit\Delete"
const MNU_EDIT_SELECTALL$  = "Edit\Select All"
const MNU_EDIT_TIMEDATE$   = "Edit\Time/Date"
const MNU_EDIT_WORDWRAP$   = "Edit\Word Wrap"

'***** Search Menu
const MNU_SEARCH_FIND$     = "Search\Find..."
const MNU_SEARCH_FINDNEXT$ = "Search\Find Next"

'***** Help Menu
const MNU_HELP_TOPICS$     = "Help\Help Topics"
const MNU_HELP_ABOUT$      = "Help\About Notepad"


'*************************************************************
'********************** User Def'd Types ********************
'*************************************************************


'*************************************************************
'********************** Global Variables ********************
'*************************************************************
```

```
'************************************************************
'***************** Func/Proc Prototypes *********************
'************************************************************

'$endif NOTEMAIN_INCLUDED
```

When looking at Listing 8-3, you'll notice that the declarations are fairly high-level. That is, they are general enough to be used by almost any test case. If, for example, a test is written for the Find... menu item, the tester will most likely need to access the Search menu. In this case the test script should use the constant MNU_SEARCH_FIND for the Search menu and the Find... menu item. Listing 8-4 is an example of an include file that contains less common information.

Constant Affirmation

This section reaffirms the need for using constants. In it, I mention using a constant for a menu and one of its menu items. Now, suppose that other tests use that same menu and menu item, perhaps to set up a situation for yet another test. Perhaps there's a sample data file being used to test another feature, maybe the Delete key, but it needs to search to a particular section in the text file. The Find... menu item would be used. Since it's possible that other tests will need to use this menu item, the declaration statement for this constant should be placed in a common file accessed by all of the test case files, namely notemain.inc.

Now let's further suppose that later in the development cycle the development team decides that Locate... is a better name for that menu item. If constants were used, the testers on the automation project would only need to go to the one file, in this case notemain.inc, and change the value of that constant. Every place in the entire automation project where that menu item was used would change to the new value.

The only time this breaks down is when someone on the team doesn't use the constant and uses a literal string — that is, he or she types in a quoted string. Not every place would get updated and an error will occur when that tester's test file is run, because the name of the menu item had been changed. In short, use constants to make it easier to update your test scripts.

This next listing is an include file that holds less common information. Specifically, it's holding information relative to one area of the Notepad application that many test case files will rely upon. However, the rest of the files that make up the test suite for the product don't require this information.

LISTING 8-4 file.inc — The Include File for Test Cases That Test the File Menu in Notepad.

```
'*************************** FILE.INC ************************
'*
'* PURPOSE: Decls for the File menu tests.
'*
'**************************************************************


'$ifndef FILE_INCLUDED
'$define FILE_INCLUDED


'**************************************************************
'************************* CONSTANTS ***********************
'**************************************************************


'***** Dialog Control Names
const DCN_FILENAME$        = "File Name:"
const DCN_SPECIFICPRINTER$ = "Specific Printer:"
const DCN_OUTPUTFILENAME$  = "Output File Name:"


'***** Captions
const CAP_SAVEAS$          = "Save As"         'Save As Common DB
const CAP_OPEN$            = "Open"            'Open Common DB
const CAP_SAVE$            = "Save"            'Save Common DB
const CAP_PRINTTOFILE$     = "Print To File"   'print to file DB
const CAP_PAGESETUP$       = "Page Setup"      'page setup DB
const CAP_PRINTSETUP$      = "Print Setup"     'print setup DB


'***** Misc
const MAX_COUNT            = 15


'**************************************************************
'********************** User Def'd Types *******************
'**************************************************************
```

```
'****************************************************************
'********************* Global Variables **********************
'****************************************************************


'****************************************************************
'***************** Func/Proc Prototypes *********************
'****************************************************************

'$endif FILE_INCLUDED
```

Note

Notice that not necessarily all of the sections in the template for this include file are used. Yet, the comments are left in place so that if declarations need to be added to the template later in the project, an outline or template still exists which prompts you on where to place your declarations. For example, there aren't currently any user-defined types; however, a place holder remains in the event user-defined types are required later in the project.

Another strong reason for using include files is when working on a product that is to be internationalized. If separate include files exist that hold the strings or text associated with each menu, menu item, dialog box control, window caption, and so on, the international testing teams can make copies of the files created by the domestic testing team and localize them to the foreign language on which they're testing. The result is that the actual test code stays the same; only the include files are updated with the new foreign language values for captions, menu items, and so on.

TEST CASE FILES

A *test case file* is a file that contains individual testing tasks or scenarios. Each individual test is considered a scenario and a group of related scenarios is considered a test case. An example of a test case is given in Chapter 7, when we look at our first sample test script. That test case has three scenarios for testing the New menu item found under the File menu. Had we continued with that example and created test cases for the rest of the File menu and other menus in Notepad, we would have created a test suite comprised of those test cases.

Test case files have the *.mst* file extension, which is recognized by the Developer Studio editor and the Suite Manager, both tools discussed in Part II. These test case files merge in the include files (*.inc* files) to get the declarations, common functions, and subroutines needed to complete their testing tasks. As mentioned before, this merging or inserting is done by using the '$include metacommand.

To help clarify what goes into a *.mst* file and to demonstrate some of the common coding guidelines we've discussed so far, the sample test case file shown in Listing 7-1 in Chapter 7 has been placed into the template shown in Listing 8-2, shown earlier in this chapter. Look at the listing below and the differences between Listings 7-1 & 8-5 will then be explored.

LISTING 8-5 Sample Code From Listing 7-1 Placed Into the .mst Template. new.mst Tests the "New" Menu Item.

```
'***************************************************************
'* Filename: new.mst
'*
'* Purpose:  Test scenarios for the New menu item.
'*
'* Revision History:
'*
'*  [ 0]   da-mon-year     email    : action
'*  [ 1]   19-Mar-1996     TomA     : created first version
'*
'***************************************************************

'********************** INCLUDES ****************************
'$include 'notemain.inc'    'Common decls used by all test cases
'$include 'noteutil.inc'    'Common utils used by all test cases
'$include 'file.inc'        'Decls used by File menu test cases

'***************** GLOBALS INITIALIZED ********************

'********************** Main Tests ************************
TestsBegin
    dim strText$, hwndApp&

    '
    'Test the "New" menu item, respond "no".
    '
```

```
scenario "Test #1: 'New' with text.  Select 'No'."
   ResetApp

   'Make sure there's text in the Notepad window.
   PutString "Now is the time for all good...", 10, 10

   'Select the "New" menu item
   SelMenu(MNU_FILE_NEW)

   '"Save Changes" DB display?
   If (GetText(NULL) = "Notepad") then
       WButtonClick(BTN_NO)  'No, don't save changes

       'Notepad's main window is a big edit control.
       'We can give it the focus and check text, put text,
       'etc., just like any other edit control.  We use "@1"
       ' since it is the first and only edit control.
       If (EditText("@1") <> "") then
           'Write out error information describing problem.
           LogErr "'New' didn't clear window contents.", _
                   "", EditText("@1")
       EndIf
   Else
       'Write out error info describing what went wrong.
       LogErr "'New' with text didn't display the 'Are "+ _
               "you sure?' message box.", "Notepad", _
               GetText(NULL)
   EndIf
end scenario

'Only the first test from Listing 7-1 is used in this example
TestsEnd
```

Comparing this listing to the first version of this test in Listing 7-1 shows a number of marked differences. Let's take each of these one at a time.

include files

The first difference you notice is that we are now including a number of *.inc* files at the top of this *.mst* file. The first file, notemain.inc, provides a number of declarations for common constants that many of the test cases will be using to test Notepad. An example is the BTN_NO constant,

185

used to click on the No button in the Save changes? message box. This is a common button caption that will most likely be used by other test cases that make up the overall test suite, therefore it is placed in the main include file called notemain.inc. (A full listing of notemain.inc was shown in Listing 8-3).

The next include file is noteutil.inc. This file contains a number of utilities that were created during the development of the test suite. As functions and subroutines were written, if they were determined to be of use to the other test case files, they were moved into this separate *.inc* file, so that all *.mst* files had access to this common code. Some of the routines contained in noteutil.inc are used by the new.mst file, including *TestsBegin()*, *ResetApp()*, *PutString()*, *SelMenu()*, and *LogErr()*. Each of these is discussed in Chapter 11. *SelMenu()* is discussed in the "Encapsulation" section of this chapter.

The third include file is file.inc. This *.inc* file has declarations specific to the File menu, and was shown in Listing 8-4. Since the New menu item is in the File menu, new.mst needs to include file.inc. At first it might make sense that, as an example, the MNU_FILE_NEW constant would be placed into the file.inc include file. However, once more test cases are created, you'll find you need this menu item when testing other areas of the product. Therefore, the declaration of MNU_FILE_NEW is placed at the top of the file hierarchy into notemain.inc. This can be seen in Figure 8-1.

reusable routines

Another difference between Listings 7-1 & 8-5 is that the latter has some routines that don't exist in the standard Test language. These were helpful enough to make available to the other test cases, so they were placed in the test suite's noteutil.inc file, so they could be shared.

Although Chapter 11 goes into more detail about the routines included in our sample suite's noteutil.inc file, to help further demonstrate the differences between Listings 7-1 & 8-5, the functionality of *TestsBegin()*, *ResetApp()*, *PutString()*, *SelMenu()* and *TestsEnd()* — subroutines used in Listing 8-5 — are briefly described in this chapter.

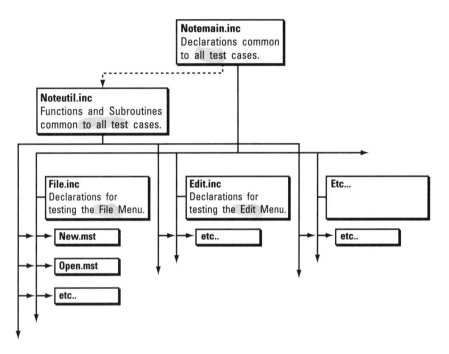

FIGURE 8-1 The file hierarchy used by the Notepad test suite.

As you'll recall from Chapter 7, there are four sections that make up a test case file: declarations, initialization, tests, and clean-up. The declarations were mostly taken care of by including the separate *.inc* files. Any remaining variables that needed to be declared were done locally in the *.mst* file itself.

The initialization is carried out by the *TestsBegin()* subroutine, whose source code can be found in noteutil.inc. *TestsBegin()* focuses on preparing Notepad to be tested and setting up dependencies relied upon by the rest of the test case. Examples of such dependencies include opening text files to be used as logs for tests executed and allocating memory required by the tests.

ResetApp(), *PutString()* and *SelMenu()* are routines that help with the third part of the test case file: test scenarios. *ResetApp()* was written to reset Notepad to a known state. It's a simple routine that selects the New menu item to clear the contents of Notepad and deals with any dialog boxes encountered during the resetting of the application (such as the

Save changes? message box). *PutString()* was constructed based on the assumption that the tester might want to be able to control the column and row position of the text placed in the editor. And finally, *SelMenu()* is a *wrapper* around the Test language's *wMenuSelect* statement, allowing for more flexibility in the future (more on this in the "Wrapper" section, later in this chapter).

So, Briefly, What Goes into a .mst File?

So what really goes into a *.mst* file? The answer is, "Whatever you and your team decide to put into it." As I've pointed out, they are only text files with extensions to help clarify what a particular file's purpose is. If your team decides to follow Microsoft's conventions, then an *.inc* file holds declarations and reusable functions and subroutines, and a *.mst* file holds local declarations to that file and specific test scenarios.

Many people don't follow Microsoft's lead on this, however. Some with C programming backgrounds look at the *.inc* file as a *.h* file, and the *.mst* file as a *.c* file. So, what about the shared libraries that C uses (*.lib*)? What's comparable to those in Visual Test?

Well, you could associate them with a *.dll* file, but if you're looking at them strictly from the Visual Test point of view, such a file type doesn't exist. Microsoft suggests you use the *.inc* file for holding reusable/library routines in addition to declarations.

The limit to two source code file types in Visual Test has prompted many people to come up with their own third type of source code file that holds the sharable and reusable routines. Some people use *.utl* (for utilities), others use *.lib* (for libraries, but this can be confusing, especially if a C compiler is installed on the same machine), and still others figure that all executing source code (in other words, non-declarations) should go into *.mst* files. As this can result in *.mst* files including other *.mst* files, it can get confusing.

As much as people may not agree with Microsoft's two-file-type approach to Test language source code, it's a style that has been suggested by the documentation for all four versions of its product and is being used by the majority of the Visual Test automators today. It comes back to keeping things simple, so that those who inherit your code can understand it without too much effort. While a third type of

Test language file called a *.utl* is tempting, to avoid confusion it's a good idea to use Microsoft's approach of putting reusable code into *.inc* files.

4) The last part of a test case file is clean-up. This is accomplished by the *TestsEnd()* subroutine. This returns Notepad to a known state, or perhaps even shuts the application down, depending on what the tester prefers. It also does other clean-up tasks, such as closing any text files that were opened for logging of tests and freeing up any memory that might have been allocated during testing.

constants

The last difference that you'll notice about Listing 8-5 is that it is now using constants. The value of these has already been mentioned a number of times. Remember the flexibility that constants provide, both for your team and potentially for the internationalization team, should your company choose to localize your product to foreign markets.

File Hierarchy

Figure 8-2 shows the file hierarchy that we briefly looked at in Figure 8-1. The idea of this hierarchy is simple: Move anything that is useful to other test case files up the hierarchy so that it can be easily shared. Anything specific to a particular area of the test suite that isn't used by all of the other test cases should be moved down the hierarchy.

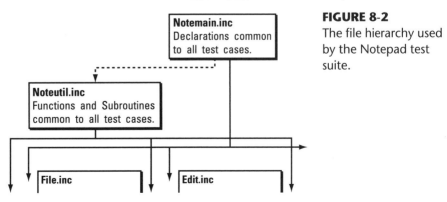

FIGURE 8-2
The file hierarchy used by the Notepad test suite.

The theory is, why force another test case to include source code it won't use? Sometimes, however, this can't be avoided, because not all of your routines will be used by every test case file. Weigh the costs and benefits at the time. On a small project, you'll typically have a single util.inc file (in this example, noteutil.inc), which is shared by all of the test cases.

In Figure 8-2, notemain.inc is the main include file for the entire test suite on the Notepad editor. Anything that will most likely be needed by the majority of the test cases should be placed in this include file. Then, all test case files should include notemain.inc to acquire all those macros, constants, function prototypes that link to DLLs, and global variables.

file.inc, edit.inc, and so on, are the declarations relating to the menu areas being tested. In our example, a menu-based approach has been taken to cover the functionality of the product. Each menu is considered an area and each area holds the common declarations for the test cases that test it.

Following this example, new.mst, open.mst, and the other files shown in Figure 8-1, would fall into the File menu area of testing and would need to include file.inc to get the declarations they require. You could take this as far as having an *.inc* file for each test case. But going to this degree probably isn't necessary and the declarations at the lower level of the hierarchy can be placed into the *.mst* file.

Notice that in this diagram notemain.inc gets included twice. The first time is by noteutil.inc. noteutil includes notemain because there are constants its utilities need to use. But then, all of the test cases include notemain.inc and noteutil.inc, so it appears that notemain.inc is being brought in multiple times.

The automation engineer could look at this and surmise that notemain.inc will always be included, since noteutil.inc is always included by each test case. So why have the test case include notemain, too? This is done so that a file's dependencies can be determined simply by looking at the files it includes. If it ever became necessary to move one of the test case files, it would be easier to determine which files, or copies of those files, needed to go with it. If this explicit approach isn't taken, the tester would need to look through each separate include file to make sure the files it relies upon are being included. This can get really messy and confusing. Therefore, I suggest going ahead and letting files be included multiple times, just to make it easier down the line to determine which files rely upon which other files.

Refer to the "Conditional Compilation" section discussed earlier in this chapter on how to avoid errors that can be generated when including a file multiple times.

Note

Even though we're referring to this as a file hierarchy, it doesn't necessarily mean that we're using a hierarchical directory structure. All these files can be in a single directory yet still maintain a hierarchical association with each other, as shown in Figures 8-1 and 8-2.

Encapsulation

The idea of encapsulation was broached when we briefly looked at the subroutines *TestsBegin()*, *TestsEnd()*, *ResetApp()*, *SelMenu()*, and *PutString()*. If you've already been through a C or Pascal programming class, or you've done any programming in Visual BASIC or any other structured programming language, you are already aware of the importance of encapsulating source code.

This topic is being discussed only because there have been many occasions when I've gone into a company using Microsoft Test and the person writing the scripts is writing one long sequential piece of code. When he or she finds a section of code that acts as it should, and wants the same thing to happen in another section of the automation scripts, they copied and pasted that code into that other area.

Whenever you have a piece of code that needs to be used more than once, it needs to be placed into either a function or a subroutine. These are blocks of code or sub-programs that can be executed simply by placing the name of the routine where you want its code to execute.

Subroutines and functions are very much like constants. You should create them when a piece of code is used in more than one place, so that all you need to do to modify it is to alter the function or subroutine in question.

If working with functions and subroutines is completely new to you, I strongly suggest you take a beginning programming class in C, Pascal, or any other structured programming language, including Visual BASIC.

Wrapper

A *wrapper* function or subroutine is a routine that's been created around another function, statement, or subroutine. This is done so that extra features can be added to how the standard routine operates. Often, they contribute to the flexibility of the test suite when it becomes necessary to add new features to the tests' capabilities.

The example I'll use for a wrapper is the *SelMenu()* subroutine mentioned earlier in this chapter. *SelMenu()* is a routine that I created and placed into the noteutil.inc file, to be used by all test cases when selecting a menu. If you are familiar with the wMenuSelect statement, then you're scratching your head wondering why I would try to recreate functionality that already exists.

The reason for doing this is based on my past experience of requests from my clients. On one project I used the wMenuSelect statement to select menus throughout all my test scripts. After writing hundreds of tests, I had a client come back to me and ask me to have Visual Test print out each menu as it was selected.

Unfortunately, wMenuSelect doesn't have this capability, so I had to revisit each test script and find where wMenuSelect was used and put a print statement after it. Either that or get fancy and write some kind of Windows utility that would look for a message telling me a menu had popped up or a menu item had been selected.

In fact, I chose to do neither. Instead, I created a new function that I placed in my util file (in this case noteutil.inc), called *SelMenu()*. *SelMenu()* did exactly the same thing that wMenuSelect did.

I went through all my scripts and replaced wMenuSelect with *SelMenu()*, then I went into *SelMenu()* and placed a print statement right after the wMenuSelect statement. Did it pay off? Yes, it most certainly did, because later that week the client requested a way to turn printing the menu information on and off. Instead of revisiting a couple hundred test files, I was able to instead update my *SelMenu()* subroutine to check whether a global variable had been set to true or false. It took me less than two minutes to implement the new functionality, instead of a couple of hours.

This is a simple yet effective example of how helpful wrappers can be. As you are writing your tests, think of other wrappers you can create to save yourself time. If you find yourself always putting a print statement after performing a particular action, this is a prime place to create a wrapper of some kind.

Conclusion

This chapter focused on common coding guidelines that should be created and followed by a single automation programmer or a team of programmers. By achieving consensus on styles and guidelines up front, many problems can be avoided as a project matures. The common coding guidelines should continue to grow throughout the project, so that a well-polished document is available when the next project begins.

As utilities are created on a project, you'll find that some are generic and helpful enough to be sharable with other teams. I encourage you or your team to follow Microsoft's example of sharing common utilities by making others in your company or others in your QA community aware of what utilities you've created in Visual Test. By sharing this information, teams can see what others who are using Visual Test have accomplished, which will help them support the direction they are headed in, or get ideas on other directions to explore. It's also an opportunity to swap these utilities so that each programmer's test automation arsenal grows stronger and more capable. Find time at the end of your project to document your creation — both in the code and in a separate document — so that it's easier for others to pick up and understand.

Summary

Testing requires consensus in the testing team. This should cover coding style, such as comments, templates, naming conventions, unconditional branching, and test language source code file types. It should also apply to your test hierarchy and encapsulation. This chapter takes you through each of these in turn.

9
Defining an Approach

When given a product to automate, the first thing you need to do is define the approach you're going to take. You do this by taking time out to explore and understand the application fully.

Looking through the user interface will give you an idea as to whether or not the product relies heavily on menus, dialog boxes, toolbars, floating palettes, or other, perhaps specially designed, user interface (UI) elements.

A clear understanding from the customer, or person requesting the automation, is necessary to ensure you don't spike too deeply into any given area, especially if it's of little or no interest to the overall automation of the product or portions of a product. Clear goals need to be set and understood, through constant communication, to verify that the automation effort is on track.

Once goals are set, you'll have a better idea of how to approach and lay out the design of your automated tests, such as how many test cases and suites will need to be created, the directory structure you'll use, and how files will relate to each other.

Exploring the Application

While looking through the product, have Visual Test's Window Information (Winfo) utility up and running, so you can check to see if the controls are standard Windows controls, or if they are controls Visual Test might not recognize. This will give you an idea of the difficulty of the automation to be carried out. (See Figure 9-1).

FIGURE 9-1

The Window Information (Winfo) utility.

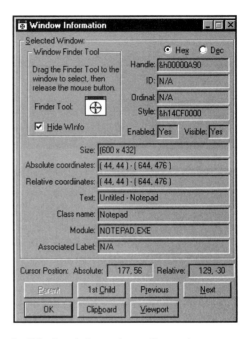

Tip

See Chapter 6 for more information on the Window Information utility and non-standard control types.

Continuing with Notepad as our sample application, we find it is an application with a user interface made up solely of menus and dialog boxes that are accessed through its menus. This makes our job as Test programmers easier, since Visual Test can work with menus by using its *wMenuSelect* statement. But what about the dialog boxes that are displayed?

It turns out that, as we bring up each dialog box and select a few controls in each of them using Winfo, we find that Notepad uses standard Windows controls. Even if it had subclassed controls, we'd still be able to work with them by using the *w*SetClass* statement that is available for every control type recognized by the Test language (for example: *wButtonSetClass*, *wEditSetClass*, *wCheckSetClass*, and so on).

Our attention then turns to Notepad's main window and the editor where the user will be typing in the text. By once again using Winfo, we find that Notepad's editing area is actually a separate window of class *Edit*. This means that Notepad's editor is actually a large edit control, which allows us to use Visual Test's *wEdit** commands. Thus, Notepad doesn't have any nasty surprises. As we can see in Figure 9-2, its dialog box controls are standard and the text area is a large edit control which will allow us greater control over the manipulation of the text.

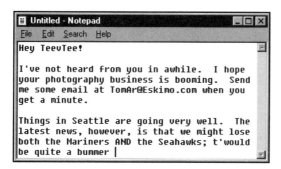

FIGURE 9-2
Notepad doesn't hold any surprises.

After taking this tour through Notepad, we have an idea of the level of difficulty we will run into when writing scripts. Because Notepad uses common Windows controls, the automation process won't be too daunting.

Types of Approach

There isn't any one approach to take when it comes to automation. It depends on the type of UI the application makes available to the user. In the case of Notepad, most of its functionality is available via the menus, as shown in Figure 9-3. Therefore, we'll structure our tests around those menus and menu items.

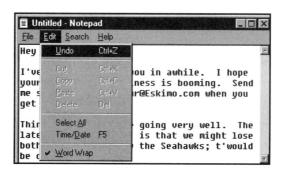

FIGURE 9-3
Most of Notepad's functionality is available through its menus.

In the case of Notepad, since everything is accessible through its menus, the approach we'll be taking is a *menu-based* approach. This means our test case files will be organized around Notepad's menus and that our file and directory structure will follow this same type of organizational approach.

Another approach we could take with Notepad is a *dialog-centric* one. The idea of this is to have all testing originate from individual dialog boxes and for testing of the product to spread from that starting point. The menu-based approach is more straightforward in the case of Notepad, so it's the method we'll follow throughout this book when using the Notepad example. An example of Notepad's Find dialog box is shown in Figure 9-4.

FIGURE 9-4
While Notepad definitely has its dialog boxes, they are simple instead of complex.

In the event that an application consists of a number of toolbars and not as many menus or dialog boxes, or that the center of attention for the application is its toolbars, a *toolbar-based* approach can be taken. This approach is similar to the menu-based and dialog-centric approaches, in that all testing centers around that aspect of the product and originates from this UI component.

What's more likely to happen, especially in a complex application that employs all of these and other types of user interfaces, is to have a combination of all three approaches. The tests that focus on the menus will go so far as to display the dialog boxes and test that each dialog box's controls perform some action, but will then stop testing at that point.

The testing of the effect of using a dialog box control would then be handled by the dialog-centric test case files, to verify that each control is acting as expected. The test case files would then follow the toolbar-based approach to verify that each toolbar is functional. This is known as taking a *component and functionality approach* to automation. Although following this combination method involves some overlap, an effort is made to keep this to a minimum. Figure 9-5 gives an example of an application that has menus, dialog boxes and a toolbar/tool palette. In the case of Paint, a combination of approaches would be taken to fully automate the product.

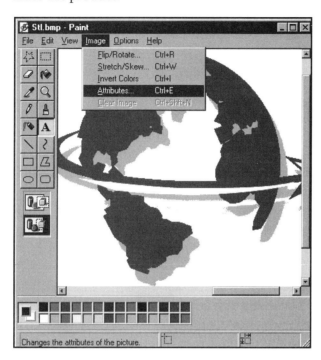

FIGURE 9-5
Microsoft Paint is an example of an application that has menus, dialog boxes, and a toolbar/tool palette.

Whatever approach you decide to take, don't concern yourself too greatly if you find later that it seems to make more sense taking a different approach. It's difficult to plan out exactly how to approach the task of automation. The only sound advice anyone can give is to pick an approach, move forward, and make adjustments along the way.

Defining What's To Be Tested

It's not uncommon to be on a project where the person running it comes in and says, "We want to automate the testing on our product so that it will be released with higher quality in a shorter period of time." A great sentiment, but when it comes down to the bottom line (time and money) the attitude can quickly change to, "This is costing us a fortune and the end is nowhere in sight!"

A realistic understanding and commitment to supplying whatever resources are needed must meet the requirements set for the automation team. Visual Test and other automation tools don't replace a mature and methodical approach to software quality assurance. If the company's goal is to increase the quality of the product with test automation as one of the tools to help in this effort, clear definitions need to be made and understood up front, so that larger frustrations can be avoided down the road.

When finding yourself in this situation, where the management team has heard wonderful things about test automation but doesn't necessarily understand the true commitment it requires of people and time, it's important to be as up-front and factual about the situation as possible. This is especially important if the testing team is new to automation and doesn't have previous war stories or metrics to help anecdotally explain or demonstrate automation.

Work Together

Begin by working with your manager to help define exactly what is to be automated. A typical response that I've received from clients is, "Automate everything!" You, too, might run into this response. In these situations, I explain how test automation is a tool to help software test engineers in their work, not to replace testers on a project.

A simple example I use is the Open dialog box that almost every Windows program has. Would the manager prefer the programmer spend a day writing exhaustive test scenarios to test for all the possibilities they can think of for the Open dialog box (such as legal filenames, illegal filenames, names for files that don't exist, long paths to reach a file, opening network files, opening an illegal file type, and opening a file under low memory)? Or, would he or she prefer that the programmer focus on a few key tests to make sure that, for the most part, the dialog box is functioning as expected (that it can open an existing file, and give an error message if the file is not found), leaving the exhaustive testing for later, when it can be done quickly at key milestones in the project cycle?

Simply put, you don't want to spend time automating something that will take less time to test by hand.

By taking an exhaustive approach, tests will be written that go deep into the functionality of a specific area of the product, but the testing team will run out of time in automating the entire product. That is, unless there is a very large team of automation programmers. Simply put, you don't want to spend time automating something that will take less time to test by hand.

Break down your automation into a couple of steps:

1. Pick an area of the product that you would like to have automated.

2. Set up a broad automation of the entire product.

PICK ONE AREA

First and foremost, pick an area of the product that you and your manager would like to have automated. (Refer to Chapters 10 and 11 for coding examples). Spend a day or two automating that area to give yourself an idea of what's involved in putting a script together. Two things are happening when you do this:

▶ First, you're getting an idea of how long it takes to automate a feature of the product. This will help in future educated guesses on how long it will take to automate other features.

▶ Second, this will be an education for your manager on exactly what is involved in automating a feature of the product. Show her your source code, so she can see how much programming is required to test a simple feature of the product.

This is a great exercise because you are working with your manager instead of against her. You're explaining in a factual manner what the realities of automation are and helping her understand the time that will be needed to automate an entire product. This will help both of you estimate your time and resource requirements to complete your goals.

DESIGN A SKELETON

The next step is to set up a broad automation of the entire product. Determine the approach you're going to take and write some simple tests that basically touch each top-level feature of the product.

I always start with the menus, because they are simple to access and it's clear what I need to write code-wise to touch each menu item. This is known as a *breadth-first* layout: it stretches widely across the top level of the product instead of diving deep into individual areas or features. A *depth-first* layout focuses on one area at a time, going as deep as it can into that area before moving on to the next one. On a short timeline with only one or two critical features to automate, the depth-first layout is the way to go. However, the breadth-first method offers more flexibility and room to grow. In the case of testing Notepad, following the menu-based approach and setting up a project in Visual Test results in the project Tree shown in Figure 9-6.

FIGURE 9-6

The Project Tree resulting from a menu-based approach.

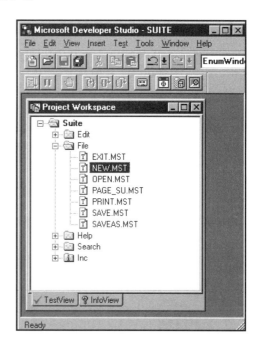

The result of the breadth-first method is a broad outline or skeleton of the automation project you are putting together. Once you have this set up you can return to your manager with a list of each of the top-level areas you are touching through your automated scripts. Use this list to get direction from your manager on what features he or she feels are most important to focus on first. As these features are automated, you can work your way out to the less-critical features.

Avoid a False Sense of Security

As your test cases grow in number, guard against being lulled into the assumption that all test cases are thorough and complete. Just because a test case exists for a given feature of the product doesn't mean that it has been completed by an experienced tester or that the tester involved in writing the test case file had the necessary amount of time to complete a thorough list of scenarios. Keep records of which areas are being thoroughly tested through manual and automated tests so that future testing teams have a clear picture of the status of the testing effort. Having a lot of tests doesn't mean that they are relevant or that holes don't exist. Avoid getting a false sense of security just because some of your tests are automated.

Another benefit in setting up a skeleton as one of the first steps in your automation project is that your team now has a structure to follow for their test scenarios and regression tests. There is a file for each area, which your teammates can access and modify with their test scripts.

It also serves as a *smoke test* or quick verification that can be used whenever a new build is received from the development team. By running this framework, you can quickly and effectively determine which areas of the product have become unstable between builds.

If you want to be really fancy, you can set up your tests to check for a global variable's setting. This would determine whether or not you need to run the scenarios that will eventually be placed into a given file, or to simply touch the feature and then drop out of the test case file. This way, when your test case files grow, you can run smoke tests by simply setting a global value.

Once the skeleton has been set up, the team can then prioritize the areas that are to be automated. Once these goals are established, the team has a clear understanding of how much time should be spent on any given area and how deep it should go into automating a feature of the product.

Set Clear Goals

Goals are important. They enable the status of the project to be determined more easily. Also, by identifying areas of concern up front, timelines can be adjusted to be more accurate.

Goals need to be adjusted throughout the automation test development cycle, to reflect where the team is and whether or not it's falling behind or getting ahead of schedule. Reassessing these goals will help determine whether the focus is too deep or too shallow and whether more people need to be added to the automation project (see Figure 9-7).

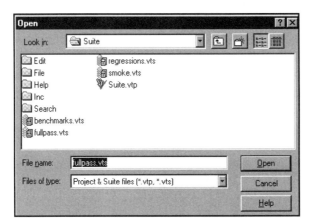

FIGURE 9-7 The goals of writing benchmark, full pass, smoke and regression tests are all attainable. It's important to figure out where to focus attention first, however, otherwise the testing team might try to tackle all of the goals at once, resulting in a lot of work being done on a little of each goal. Once created, though, the test suite files (*.vts* file extension) can then be run one at a time or in combination by using the Visual Test Suite Manager.

Make sure you understand exactly what it is your manager would like you to accomplish. Don't let her get away with simply saying that she wants the product to be tested quickly, while assuring higher quality through test automation. It's clear from what I've said before that there's so much more to automation than taking a "just do it and I'll be back later to check on you" approach. Taking a lax approach leads to all parties making assumptions that will most likely be wrong.

Here are a couple of goals, my comments about those goals, and the requirements I see to help the testing team reach them. They are just a few to get you started in the many discussions your team will need to have regarding the project you're embarking upon.

Goal 1: Use automated tests every time a new release of the product is given to the testing team by development.

Comments: This is a very good use of automated tests, because it allows testers to get a feel of whether anything has broken or not. A break in a key feature may make it impossible to write any further automation for a new build of the product.

Requirements: The development group will need to fix the problems and compile another version for the testers. Management will need to support the testing team's decision to refuse a build, even in time-critical situations. Otherwise, the risk is that more time will be lost when the automation group modifies its scripts to skip testing on unstable areas.

Goal 2: Use the automated tests for regressing known or reported bugs in the product.

Comments: Another excellent use of test automation. The testers can take the bugs found in the bug list and write automated tests that verify that they don't return in future builds. It will not be possible to automate 100 percent of the reported bugs because often they are found in special machine configurations or low memory situations. Sometimes it is easier and more efficient to attempt to reproduce a bug by hand than to attempt to automate it.

Regarding where to put regression tests, some people intermingle them with their existing test scenarios, while others keep them in separate test case files. I prefer a separate test case file so that, should a number of bugs that are being regressed still exist, the regression tests can be skipped, allowing the rest of the tests to run. It also allows me to pick what types of tests I'll be running: smoke, regression, full pass, benchmark, or whatever.

Requirements: Enough testers need to be available to write the automated regression tests. In the event that not enough are available, it must be understood that, while testing focuses on writing automated tests — for regressing bugs or testing features in general — the number of bugs reported by the testing team will drop. Sometimes the number of bugs filed is used as a measure to determine the stability of the product. In this situation, it's a false indicator because testing is focused on writing scripts instead of manually testing the product.

Tip

I suggest having at least one person who focuses solely on test automation who can drive the effort and direct other automators as they are brought in at peak times.

Goal 3: The entire product is to be automated, taking a breadth-first approach.

Comments: It sounds all well and good to tell you about setting up the breadth-first, or skeleton, layout but the problem you're going to face, especially early in the development cycle, is the stability of the product. This instability, both in the fatal errors encountered in the product and the unfrozen nature of the user interface, makes automation challenging, to say the least. Many times you will find yourself having to rewrite sections of code because a decision has been made to redesign all of the dialog boxes, for whatever reason. Your time is best spent creating a general framework of common utilities. Pick one or two features to automate and take your time by building common utilities, such as the ones discussed in Chapter 11, that these beginning tests will use, and that future test case files will most likely use.

Requirements: Management needs to keep in mind these issues so that, when design changes are made, it is understood that the testing team will take a hit in productivity. However, this should not be the deciding factor as to whether or not a feature should be changed in the product. It is only to say that managers should understand that these changes will break test scripts and require a maintenance pass to fix the test scripts.

Something very helpful is to create a mock application, specifically in Visual BASIC, because of Test's ability to work with VB controls. Once the UI design is frozen based on this mock-up, the mock application can be handed over to testing for them to set up their testing structure. Or, if the product is beyond a 1.0 version, the testing team should have access to the previous version of the product for writing its scripts. Then, when the actual product becomes stable, the scripts will be further along and can be moved off the mock-up and onto the true build of the product.

Goal 4: Visual Test is to be used to benchmark critical areas of the product.

Comments: I would suggest creating a totally separate test suite, simply because of the nature of benchmarking. To arrive at accurate results, it's typical for actions to be run multiple times so that an average time can be calculated. This necessary repetition of tests makes the timing of events more accurate, but can result in the tests taking a very long time to complete.

Requirement: The area to be benchmarked should be code complete and in a stable state.

In conclusion, the benefit you gain from involving your manager in the definition and goal-setting process is your manager's support and understanding of the process. This helps her explain the realities of automation to her managers as well.

Although it may seem strange to you to have company politics discussed in this book, it really is a necessary part of the automation process, because of the hype given to automating tests and general misconceptions held by those who have never been involved in the process. By setting clear goals, including them in your overall *test plan* for the project you're on, and educating your manager along the way, you will greatly reduce the frustrations experienced by others new to automation that don't take this approach.

Determine a Layout

You need to determine a layout to:

▶ Organize the files that make up your test suite

▶ Set the directory structure that will house your files

Suite Organization

Just because we've decided to take a menu-based approach with Notepad doesn't mean we need to break up our files and directory structure to follow that approach. I've suggested you break up your files, but that isn't mandatory. The approach we're taking with Notepad is to step methodically through each menu item under each of Notepad's menus.

Now that we know how we'll step through and test Notepad, let's look at our options for creating our test case files. We have several.

SINGLE FILE

One approach to a test case file is to use a single file to house all of Notepad's test scenarios. The benefit in doing this is that the Test program need only work with one file. Everything is in one place and it doesn't need to go searching high and low to find the source code it wants to edit.

You can do this by placing each scenario into a separate function that returns a boolean (true or false) value, letting the main program know whether or not the test scenario passed.

There are a number of downsides to this approach. The first is that, because everything is kept in one file, sharing common routines with other testing teams becomes difficult. Sure, the other teams can cut and paste the code they want to use out of the single file, but then there'll be two copies of those routines floating around, causing the source code to instantly be out of sync. Any advances the other team makes with the source code taken from the single automation file will need to be re-integrated, if there is any benefit to be gained.

Another problem is that, if there are a number of Test programmers on the team, it becomes very difficult to merge everyone's changes and modifications into a single file. If one team member modifies a common utility, such as a logging routine, and another member modifies that same routine, merging those changes quickly gets ugly.

In the event of a feature in the product breaking from one build to the next, resulting in a general protection fault (GPF), the tester running the automated suite will need to go into the source code and comment out the problem area, so that the rest of the tests can execute. Then that tester will need to remember to uncomment the test for future passes on the product.

Using a single test suite file is an approach I've seen many companies take when they first start automating. This is usually because there is only one test automation programmer on the project and they're new to automation. After they get further into the details of automating the product, they soon break the single file into multiple files for the reasons mentioned above.

While you can start out with a single file, keep these problems in the back of your mind and be ready to move to multiple files once you have a handle on exactly how you want to approach the automation.

AREA TEST CASE FILES

Another approach that many first-time Test programmers take is to break their tests up into multiple files based on the areas of the product being tested. In the case of Notepad, this would mean having a single test case file for the File menu, another one for the Edit menu, and so on. This isn't a bad approach to take, but you can still run into the problems mentioned above. If, in the example of Notepad, selecting the New menu item under the File menu caused a GPF, the rest of the test scenarios in that file would go un-executed unless the tester went in and placed comments around the line of code causing the error.

FUNCTIONALITY TEST CASE FILES

This last approach follows the method of breaking the test case files up into specific features of a product. An example would be to have a test case file for the New menu item under the File menu. So, basically, we've taken things one step further by breaking them down into their most basic form and representing them as test case files.

According to this method, the File menu in Notepad would have seven test case files — a file for each menu item — made up of a number of scenarios. Figure 9-8 shows how a separate *.mst* file, or test case file, exists for each menu item under the File menu.

Note

Visual Test's defaults assume the approach shown in Figure 9-8, where multiple scenarios are placed into a test case file.

FIGURE 9-8
A separate test case file exists for each menu item under the File menu.

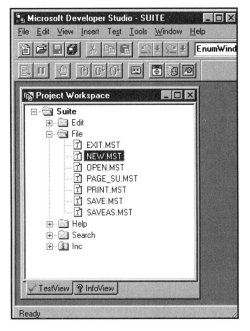

This is the approach I like to take because I can easily control which feature of a product I want to test. There is yet another level, however, that one can go to in organizing their test files: into test scenarios.

TEST SCENARIO FILES

I've seen some companies, some (but not all) groups in Microsoft in particular, take the organization of their files one step further; and that is, to have a separate file for each test scenario.

To refresh your memory, a test scenario is a specific test on a feature. For example, testing that the appropriate error message is given when an illegal file name is supplied in the Open dialog box is a scenario. Testing that an error is given when you attempt to read the wrong type of file into the program is another scenario. A test case is a grouping of scenarios for a particular area.

By breaking down a test program into tests by scenarios, the result is hundreds, and very possibly thousands of files to deal with. However, it allows individuals on a testing team to add their own, individual scenarios to the hopper for testing. A driver like the Visual Test Suite Manager can be used to run those test files, or a separate driver can be written that pulls in all files from a specific directory and runs those tests individually.

In my opinion, this approach leads to too much structure. Each test scenario file needs to set up the application to a known state, so that it doesn't rely on the test scenario file that ran before it. Each file is also expected to clean up after itself when it completes its testing task.

The result will mean you have a project structure resembling that in Figure 9-9.

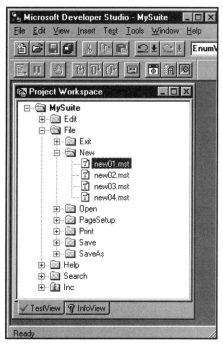

FIGURE 9-9
This is an example of putting one individual test scenario into a test case file.

Note As a project's structure is constructed using Visual Test, a directory structure is built to map directly to the structure represented in the TestView (as shown in the TestView window in Figure 9-9).

File Sharing

As test scenarios are written, you'll create functions and subroutines common enough to be used by other test scenarios and test case files. These common routines usually find their way into separate files, so that sharing those routines is a simpler process.

Visual Test provides a special folder for those files that need to be included by test case files in different sections of the project. This is an *include folder* and shows up at the bottom of both Figures 9-8 and 9-9.

Files common to other areas of the project are placed in this folder. Examples include the main include file and the main utility file. The main include file holds common declarations, such as constants for menu items and captions of windows, that are broad enough to be made available to all test scenarios. The main utility include file holds function and subroutine utilities, such as log file routines, test initialization, and clean-up, that are likely to be used by test scenarios.

Conclusion

When we come to build our first scenarios in Chapter 10, the creation of common utilities and moving them into a sharable file and location will become much clearer, especially in our first scenario. We'll build the functionality that we need and later find that it's useful enough to move into a higher section of the project hierarchy, thereby making it available to everyone.

As has been a common message throughout this book, I encourage you to dive in on the first couple of test case files and scenarios to get your feet wet and better understand what's available in the Test language. By jumping in and learning first, you will be able to write a more thorough description of how you are going to approach the automated testing on your project when it comes time to write your overall test plan, or to add information about the automation process to an existing test plan.

Summary

It is essential to take the time to define your approach to testing a product. You should first explore the product, checking to see what it is comprised of, how it functions, and what its features are. Then you need to decide on the approach to take, though this can change as you go along. It can be either menu-based, dialog-centric, toolbar-based, or based on functionality. Then you and your manager need to define what is to be tested and set clear goals.

Once your goals are defined, you need to determine a layout: How will you organize the files that make up your test suite and set the directory structure that will house your files? You can take one of four possible approaches: single file, area test files, functionality test files, or test scenario files. But always bear in mind the need to share your files and update them.

Writing Simple Test Cases

A test case is a group of tests, or test scenarios, that focus on a particular area or feature of a product that is being tested. A test scenario is a specific test that is performed on an area or feature of a product. This chapter focuses on creating the first simple test cases. To be able to create these test cases, however, we must first create the scenarios that make them up.

In Chapter 9, we talked about picking an approach to take with our automation on the product we're testing. Throughout this book we've been looking at Notepad as our test subject, and shall continue to use it in this chapter. We determined in Chapter 9 that the basis of our approach with testing Notepad would be menu-based, because Notepad's functionality is all reachable through its menus: There aren't any toolbars, tool palettes, or separate windows that add to Notepad's functionality.

We also discussed in Chapter 9 how to determine which layout to use. Visual Test supports the concept of functionality test case files, where each automated test case file is for a specific feature of the product and contains a number of scenarios for that feature. This is opposed to a single test suite file that holds all tests, or a separate file for each test scenario, both extremes.

Following the menu-based approach and organizing our testing into test case files that contain scenarios for one feature of the product at a time means we need to create a *.mst* file (test case file) for each menu item.

The First Test Scenario

We'll start off with the New menu item found under the File menu (see Figure 10-1). Our goal with writing our first, simple test cases is just to get something down "on paper," so that we have some content to the overall structure we're building. We can add to it later, it's just there to give us a feel and provide others with examples, so that it's easier to add content to each test case file later.

FIGURE 10-1
The New menu item found under Notepad's File menu is the first feature we're going to test.

As we walk through the Notepad application and use the New menu item, we find there are three beginning situations relating to it that we could set up for our initial test scenarios. All of them center around Notepad having text in its window that has not yet been saved, which results in the Save Changes? message box, shown in Figure 10-2, being displayed. It contains three options: Yes, No, and Cancel.

Our first test case is going to center around these three options. Again, these three initial test scenarios are tests that will eventually need to be created, and since they're the most obvious, we choose to create them now, so they can provide some substance to the overall structure we're creating.

FIGURE 10-2
This message box is displayed when the New menu item is selected and unsaved text is in the Notepad editor. It has three options: Yes, No, and Cancel.

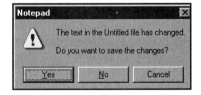

As we create these three key scenarios, we'll find that other scenarios come to mind. It's common to have other ideas for tests come to us as we move toward our set of goals. Because of this, we'll end up with

more than just the three scenarios we mention here by the time we get
to writing the first test case.

Version One

Because these are the very first lines of code, we're going to write a very
simple beginning script to:

▶ Run Notepad

▶ Put some text into the window

▶ Select the New menu item

Here is our first script: → gives Notepad -[Untitled]

```
run "notepad.exe", nowait
play "Now is the time for all good people..."
wMenuSelect("File\New")
```
→ puts this text on the screen

→ open New item

If the script runs as expected, when the script completes, Notepad
should be up and running, "Now is the time for all good people..."
should be in its main window, and the message box shown in Figure
10-2 should be displayed.

The *run* statement in the first line is a simple Test language statement
that runs another program. The *nowait* parameter, which is the second
argument, tells the statement to run the program and not wait for the
program to terminate before continuing with the script. Without the
nowait option, Visual Test would run Notepad and then wait until
Notepad was exited before continuing with the script.

The second line, which contains the *play* statement, causes Visual Test
to type text into a window that has focus. This is a helpful command,
but can be a nuisance if it's not used cautiously. For example, if
Notepad didn't run because of low memory or because the program
wasn't found, the play command would continue on its merry way and
just spew text into whatever window had the focus.

The wMenuSelect statement on the third line causes Visual Test to
select the New menu item found under the File menu. Note that if the
New menu item had three dots or ellipses as part of its name, those

would need to be included in the text (for example, wMenuSelect "File\New…"). If it had an *accelerator* or *short cut key*, such as Ctrl+N, this would *not* be included as part of the text used by wMenuSelect.

Continuing with this first version of our script, we now need to verify that the message box was displayed as expected. If it wasn't, we need to report an error somehow, so we can track what error occurred. And, as our last task, we'll go ahead and dismiss the message box by clicking on the Cancel button. The continuation of our script is shown in the next piece of code:

```
run "notepad.exe", nowait
play "Now is the time for all good people..."
wMenuSelect("File\New")

if GetText(NULL) <> "Notepad" then
    print "Error: Message box not found."
else
    wButtonClick("Cancel")
endif
```

How Could I Know?

One of the first and most common frustrations about any programming language is the question: How would I know to use a particular statement, for example, the *GetText* and *wButtonClick* statements we used in the first and second versions of this beginning test case file? I didn't even know they existed until a few minutes ago!

By reading this book you will pick up on the most common statements and functions you'll need to write automated tests. What you need to do, though, is explore the online help that comes with Visual Test, to pick up on the more obscure routines available. There's really no other way to do it. As you write your automated scripts and look at other's scripts, you'll begin to pick it up. No matter how good you get, however, you'll always be referring back to the online help to make sure that you're using many of the commands correctly. Don't get too frustrated; it's all a part of programming!

The *GetText()* function returns the text in the window's *caption* specified by the parameter passed to it. In this case, *null* is passed which, according to the online help, tells the function to grab the text out of the active window. In this case, the message box should be the active window. And, as shown in Figure 10-2, its caption is "Notepad."

(handwritten margin note: in this situation this is message box title.)

If the caption of Notepad's main window was also "Notepad," we'd have to find another way to verify that the message box was displayed, since we couldn't determine which window's caption we were receiving from the call to *GetText()*. Fortunately, the caption in Notepad's main window includes the name of the file that it is viewing, or "Untitled" if no file is being viewed.

The print statement is employed to communicate that the message box wasn't found. Whenever this statement is used, and is not in conjunction with writing out to a file, the output is placed into the Output window, viewable when the Viewport tab is selected, as shown in Figure 10-3.

FIGURE 10-3
The print statement places text into the Output window, specifically under the Viewport tab.

The wButtonClick statement looks for a button control with the specified caption as the first parameter for this statement. If it finds the button, it clicks on it. If it doesn't find the button, it gives a *run-time error* message saying that it couldn't find it. (We'll discuss run-time errors in the "Advanced Topics" section later in this book).

In a nutshell, that's our first scenario. We ran the Notepad application, put some text into its main window so that we could set Notepad's *dirty-bit* (letting it know there was something in the main window that had not yet been saved), selected the New menu item to display the message box, which then prompted us to save changes, and then clicked on the Cancel button to dismiss the message box.

We could and probably should add some code to this script so that it verifies that the text remains unchanged. We can do this easily by using an edit control function to return the contents of Notepad's main window. (Remember that in Chapter 9 we discovered, by using the Window Information utility, that the text entry portion of Notepad's main window is really an edit control). This results in the final first version of our script, shown here:

```
run "notepad.exe", nowait
play "Now is the time for all good people..."
wMenuSelect "File\New"

if GetText(NULL) <> "Notepad" then
    print "Error: Message box not found."
else
    wButtonClick "Cancel"
endif

if EditText("@1") = "Now is the time for all good people..." then
    print "Test passed."
endif

END
```

We mentioned the use of ordinals back in Chapter 5 when working with controls. Because Notepad's text entry area is one big edit control, and because it doesn't have a caption associated with it, we can refer to it by using the "@1", since it is the only edit control available.

This first version works well and is a good outline with which to move forward. We can take this scenario and refine it, so it is even more flexible and capable, as you'll see in the second version of this script.

Version Two

The second version of our first script for the New menu item uses the Scenario statement which is new to Visual Test 4.0. This statement allows us to break up our scripts into distinct sections for each test that is to be executed. Within the block of the test, or scenario, we are also able to control cleaning up any effects of the test, allowing us to return the application being tested to a known state.

This script accomplishes the same results as the last script except that it now has more structure to it by using the *scenario* and *end scenario* statements:

```
'** Initialize the test case **

viewport clear        'Clean the contents of the Viewport
                      'tab in the Output window.


'Get test application up and running. If it can't be run
'for whatever reason, print an error message and stop
'the execution of the script.

if run("notepad.exe") then
    print "Error: Unable to run notepad.exe"
    stop  → terminates execution of the test case.
endif


'** Beginning of the test scenarios **

scenario "Test that 'Save changes' message box is displayed."
    play "Now is the time for all good people..."
    wMenuSelect("File\New")

    if GetText(NULL) <> "Notepad" then
        fail "Error: Message box not found."
    endif

scenario cleanup                    → Click on Cancel button
    if not(failed) then                only if scenario not
        wButtonClick("Cancel")            failed
    endif
end scenario

scenario "Verify that the original text remains unchanged."
    if EditText("@1")<>"Now is the time for all good people..."
then
        fail "Original test text changed."
    endif
end scenario
```

```
'** Clean-up before the test case file ends **
wMenuSelect("File\Exit")      'Shut down Notepad application

if GetText(NULL) = "Notepad" then
    wButtonClick("No")         'Click 'No' to "Save changes?"
endif
```

```
END
```

In this second version you'll notice a new command called VIEWPORT CLEAR. This command causes the contents of the Viewport in the Output window to be cleared so that running a script again won't add to the contents. I use this option especially when designing new scripts because it is less confusing since you then need only deal with the output from the latest run.

The stop statement terminates the execution of the test case and is used in this script only in the event Notepad isn't able to be run. Optionally, the end statement could have been used in place of stop, but what happens in that situation is that any ON END commands that have been set up will then be executed before terminating the test case.

Note

Many compilers for other languages, such as C, Fortran, and Pascal, are *case-sensitive,* meaning that lowercase characters and uppercase characters, are treated as separate entities. In these situations it would be possible, although confusing, to have an *a* variable and an *A* variable, having no relation to one another.

In Visual Test, however, the Test language *isn't* case-insensitive. For all the compiler cares, your scripts could be typed all in uppercase or all in lowercase. My style varies in capitalization and I've been asked many times in class whether or not capitalization matters. It doesn't, as far as the compiler is concerned. It may matter in terms of how your team defines its programming style (for example, whether constants are usually declared and used with all capital letters).

This case-insensitivity does not apply, however, to literal strings. That is, text that appears in quotes. A quoted string of "ABCD" is not equal to "abcd."

Another difference between this script and the first version is that the *fail* statement is now used in place of the print statement. It is to be used only in a scenario block, otherwise an error is generated when encountered during script execution (run-time). The fail statement causes the current scenario block to mark itself as a failed test scenario. The result is that script execution jumps to the *end scenario* statement, except in the situation where a *scenario cleanup* section of a test scenario exists.

In the scenario cleanup section of the first test scenario, you may have noticed the following *if* statement:

```
if not(failed) then
```

The *failed* identifier in that if statement is actually a function call. It determines the state of the current test scenario and returns true if the test scenario is considered to have *failed*, and false if it is considered to have *passed*. This function is used in this script to determine whether or not it should click on the Cancel button. If the scenario failed, then the message box can't have been displayed, and therefore it should not attempt to click on the message box's Cancel button in the clean-up portion of the test scenario.

The last section of the latest version of this script has some final clean-up and shutdown code that wasn't in the first version. This clean-up code, shown in the next piece of code, is used to shut down the Notepad application. It's up to you whether or not you want to have something like this in your test case files. The reason I put it in mine is so that the application is more easily placed back into a known state for the next test case. If it's shut down and then re-run by the next test case file, it's back to a known condition.

```
'** Clean-up before the test case file ends **

wMenuSelect("File\Exit")      'Shut down Notepad application

if GetText(NULL) = "Notepad" then
    wButtonClick("No")        'Click 'No' to "Save changes?"
endif

END
```

The other reason I include shutdown code in my test case files is so that, if I'm using the Visual Test Suite Manager to run my test case files, and I pick and choose the files in no particular order, I'm certain Notepad is being closed down and multiple instances of Notepad won't be up and running. Because each test case file "shuts the lights off before it leaves," you ensure the entire test suite is cleaning up after itself.

Final Version

After starting with a very simple script in Version One and moving to a more structured script in Version Two, we move to the final version of this script. This removes the code from this test case file that will be needed by other test case files and places it into a noteutil.inc file that can be included if needed. Constants are put into place as well, for some of the values that are sharable between other tests. Those constants and other declarations are placed into a notemain.inc file.

Not only does moving this code make things more sharable, it also makes the code less cluttered. The sections of code you need can be brought in with the '$include' statement, which causes it to be placed at the same location as the '$include statement during compilation. So, finally, we have our full testing version. It is presented in Listing 10-1.

LISTING 10-1 This is a Final Version of new.mst.

```
'****************************************************************
'* Filename:     NEW.MST
'*
'* Purpose:      Tests the New menu item for the File menu in
'*               Notepad's main window.
'*
'* Revision History:
'*
'*  [ 0]   da-mon-year   email    : action
'*  [ 1]   28-FEB-1996   TomAr    First few scenarios for the "New"
'*                                menu item to give some
'*                                structure.
'*  [ 2]   29-FEB-1996   TVT      Created common constants, etc.
'*                                and moved to notemain.inc. Made
'*                                common subs and funcs and moved
'*                                to noteutil.inc.
'*
'****************************************************************
```

```
'*********************** INCLUDES ****************************
'$include 'notemain.inc'
'$include 'noteutil.inc'

'****************** GLOBALS INITIALIZED *********************

'******************** LOCALS DECLARED **********************
                    → procedure
TestBegin()                'Initialize the test case

    '** Beginning of the test scenarios **
    scenario strTestNum()+"Test that 'Save changes' message box"+ _
                         " is displayed."
        play DATA_TESTSTRING1

        SelMenu(MNU_FILE_NEW)

        if (GetText(NULL) <> CAP_SAVECHANGES) then
            fail strFailNum()+"Error: Message box not found."
        endif

    scenario cleanup
        if not(failed) then
            wButtonClick(BTN_CANCEL)
        endif
    end scenario


    scenario strTestNum()+"Verify that the original text remains"+ _
                        " unchanged."
        if EditText(EDIT_NOTEPAD) <> DATA_TESTSTRING1 then
            fail strFailNum()+"Original test string changed."
        endif
    end scenario

TestEnd()
END
```

Subroutine
see p 261

TEMPLATE

A number of things have changed between Version Two and this latest
version. Looking through this listing, the first thing you'll notice is that

comments have been added to make the code more informed and readable. These were taken from the templates mentioned in Chapter 8.

INCLUDE FILES

The '*$include* metacommand is used in the last version to bring in two separate files that contain source code needed by this test case file. The order in which these files are brought in can be important, especially if the second file relies upon another file being included first.

It turns out that I've set up these include files so they will include any files that they rely upon. In the event that a Test programmer doesn't realize what other files are needed, the file they bring in will include what it needs. The include files have also been set up with *conditional compilation* commands to avoid any kind of recompilation errors should a file accidentally be included multiple times (such as, if they were included once explicitly by the test case file that needs a particular file, then included again by another include file used by the test case).

Note

Remember that when you use the '$include command, it is basically inserting the contents of the file at the location of the '$include line. Depending on how your team sets up its include files, it might be important which order these files are included.

NEW FUNCTIONS

A number of new subroutines and functions have been added to this latest version. The first one is *TestBegin(),* which replaces the initialization code for starting up the application. That initialization code was moved to the noteutil.inc file and placed into the new *TestBegin()* subroutine. Our code looks cleaner and it's a function that all the other test cases can use.

The next routine added to this script is *strTestNum()*. When called, it increments a counter and returns a text string with that counter in it. You'll notice that *strTestNum()* is being used with the scenario statement. By using it in this way, the output for each of our scenarios not only contains a description of the scenario, but also of the current test number. Furthermore, if other test scenarios are added later, also using *strTestNum()* alongside the text in the scenario statement, the test count will be bumped up without requiring you to step through the code and change the numbers by hand. This is especially the case where a new test scenario is inserted between other scenarios. The exact same idea follows for the *strFailNum()* function that gets called with the fail statement.

this is ✸

The *SelMenu()* subroutine was created to replace the *wMenuSelect* statement. It functions exactly like the wMenuSelect statement we used in the previous versions of this script, except it is now more flexible. *SelMenu()* takes the extra step of making sure no other menus are already displayed, before using the wMenuSelect statement. It also uses the *log* statement to write out information about which menus are selected during the test run. Coolest of all, the logging of this menu information is controllable through the Visual Test Suite Manager. You can turn it on and off, depending on the level of detail you want in your log files.

this is *wrapper*

The last new subroutine is *TestEnd()*, which is placed at the very end of the test case file. *TestEnd()* replaces the clean-up and shutdown source code that was added in the second version of this script. It, too, can be found in the noteutil.inc file, making it available to all other test case files.

As the test automation project evolves, other needs will become apparent, and because many of these routines have been encapsulated and made sharable between test case files, there is less likelihood that small adjustments will require you to revisit every test case file to make those adjustments uniform. Instead, these common routines can be tweaked for any special needs that arise.

For example, if it later became apparent that it was necessary to log out memory information consistently, the Test programmer could either go and place print or log statements that provide this information throughout each test case file, or you could go to one or two of the commonly used routines and add the code there. A prime place for such a modification would be in the *SelMenu()* subroutine. You might also modify the *TestBegin()* and *TestEnd()* subroutines to log out beginning and ending memory information.

GLOBAL VARIABLE

A global variable was also added to make the handle to the Notepad application available to anyone who includes the notemain.inc and noteutil.inc files. The variable is called *ghWndNotepad*. It is declared in the notemain.inc file and initialized by the *TestBegin()* subroutine found in noteutil.inc. There are enough functions and statements in Visual Test that require the handle to the main window that this is the easiest way to make it available.

There is a danger with using this global variable, especially on large teams. What happens if the variable gets modified somewhere deep in the source code? It's a variable, just like any other variable, except that it's global and many test case files will rely upon it.

This could easily happen if a Test programmer isn't aware of how the global variable should be used and simply employs it any way he or she sees fit. One way around this dilemma is to make the variable accessible only through a function call. That is, create the global variable but don't make mention of it anywhere in any documentation. Instead, create a function that simply returns that value of that variable. This approach is what's known as *data hiding*, which is something that can't be completely done in Visual Test. However, setting up a mechanism such as the function just mentioned helps to some degree.

See p. 247
ghWndNotepad

CONSTANTS

The last change you may notice in the final version of the script is that it now uses constants where once there were text strings and numbers. These constants are declared in the notemain.inc file and are generic enough that other test case files will make use of them. A common style to follow with constants is to capitalize them. This makes it obvious that they are values that cannot be changed during run-time. Creating these constants and using them in all the test case files has one particular advantage. Should it later be necessary to change the name of a menu, the text of the test string, or the caption of a button from "Yes" to "Oui," it can be done in one place, resulting in all the test case files automatically being updated, since they include the notemain.inc file and use the constants.

Preliminary Results

The preliminary results from running the final version of this test case file are shown in Figure 10-4. I say "preliminary" because our work is not yet done. All the subroutines, functions, constants, and files that have been created came from the one scenario we wrote. It did end up breaking into two scenarios because it seemed to make most sense, but we've still only tested one situation when we set out at the beginning of this chapter to test three: Yes, No, and Cancel. The Cancel button has undergone its first tests. Now it's the turn of the Yes and No buttons.

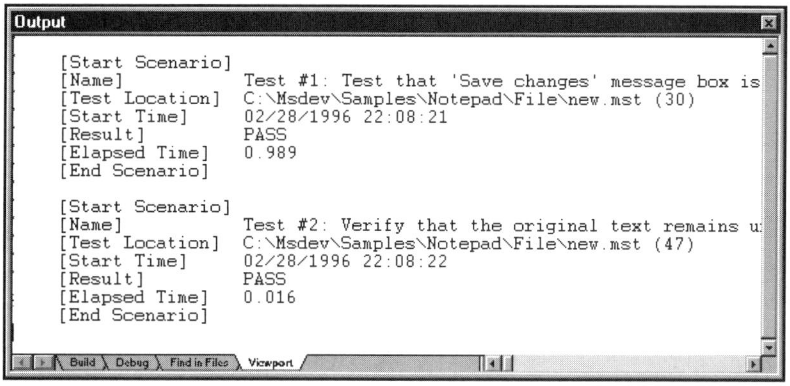

```
Output                                                                    ⊠
    [Start Scenario]
    [Name]            Test #1: Test that 'Save changes' message box is
    [Test Location]   C:\Msdev\Samples\Notepad\File\new.mst (30)
    [Start Time]      02/28/1996 22:08:21
    [Result]          PASS
    [Elapsed Time]    0.989
    [End Scenario]

    [Start Scenario]
    [Name]            Test #2: Verify that the original text remains u:
    [Test Location]   C:\Msdev\Samples\Notepad\File\new.mst (47)
    [Start Time]      02/28/1996 22:08:22
    [Result]          PASS
    [Elapsed Time]    0.016
    [End Scenario]

  ◄ ► ▌ Build ╲ Debug ╲ Find in Files ╲ Viewport ╱            ◄►
```

FIGURE 10-4 The Output window as it appears after running the final version of the new.mst test case file.

Again, the goal is to get a few simple test scenarios written and placed into the test case file. After this has been done, focus can shift to the next menu item and its test scenarios. After all the menus have had at least one or two tests, a structure exists that can be modified from there, depending on the goals of the automation team. Our file structure can be seen in Figure 10-5. It shows what Visual Test's Project Workspace looks like with the current test case and its associated files. As the number of test case files grows, so will the project and its structure.

FIGURE 10-5
Visual Test's representation of the files that have been created so far.

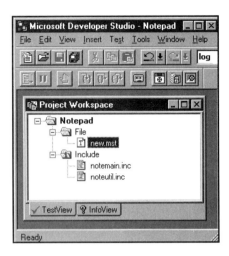

Resulting Test Case

The last two scenarios took no time at all to write because the bulk of the support routines, which are discussed more fully in Chapter 11, were written with the first test scenario. The result is a total of four test scenarios. They test the three buttons on the Save Changes? message box and whether or not the text remains unchanged when the Cancel button is selected. The code for this is in Listing 10-2.

LISTING 10-2 Our Initial Task of Creating at Least Three Tests for the Save Changes Message Box is Complete.

```
'*****************************************************************
'* Filename:    NEW.MST
'*
'* Purpose:     Tests the New menu item for the File menu in
'*              Notepad's main window.
'*
'* Revision History:
'*
'* [ 0]   da-mon-year   email    : action
'* [ 1]   28-FEB-1996   TomAr    First few scenarios for the "New"
'*                                menu item to give some
'*                                structure.
'* [ 2]   29-FEB-1996   TVT      Created common constants, etc.
'*                                and moved to notemain.inc. Made
'*                                common subs and funcs and moved
'*                                to noteutil.inc.
```

```
'*  [ 3]   01-MAR-1996  TomAr   Added some final test scenarios
'*                               to fill in this first test case.
'*
'*****************************************************************


'********************** INCLUDES *****************************
'$include 'notemain.inc'
'$include 'noteutil.inc'

'***************** GLOBALS INITIALIZED ***********************

'******************** LOCALS DECLARED ***********************

TestBegin()            'Initialize the test case

    '** Beginning of the test scenarios **
    scenario strTestNum()+"Test that 'Save changes' message box"+ _
                       " is displayed."
        play DATA_TESTSTRING1

        SelMenu(MNU_FILE_NEW)

        if (GetText(NULL) <> CAP_SAVECHANGES) then
            fail strFailNum()+"Error: Message box not found."
        endif

    scenario cleanup
        if not(failed) then
            wButtonClick(BTN_CANCEL)
        endif

    end scenario


    scenario strTestNum()+"Verify that the original text remains"+ _
                       " unchanged after clicking Cancel."
        if EditText(EDIT_NOTEPAD) <> DATA_TESTSTRING1 then
            fail strFailNum()+"Original test string changed."
        endif
    end scenario

    ResetApp     'Clear contents of Notepad to get to known state
```

(continued)

LISTING 10-2 Our Initial Task of Creating at Least Three Tests for the Save Changes Message Box is Complete. *(Continued)*

```
scenario strTestNum()+"Click 'No' to 'Save Changes?' msg"
        play DATA_TESTSTRING1
        SelMenu(MNU_FILE_NEW)
        wButtonClick(BTN_NO)
        if EditText(EDIT_NOTEPAD) <> "" then
            fail strFailNum()+"Text was not cleared as expected."
        endif
    scenario cleanup
        ResetApp
    end scenario


    scenario strTestNum()+"Click 'Yes' to 'Save changes?' msg"
        play DATA_TESTSTRING1

        SelMenu(MNU_FILE_NEW)
        wButtonClick(BTN_YES)    'Yes to save changes

        if (GetText(NULL) <> CAP_SAVEAS) then
            fail strFailNum()+"Save As dialog box not displayed."
        else
            'We don't want to test the Save As dialog box,
            'just make sure it displays. We can determine
            'how we want to test it later.
            wButtonClick(BTN_CANCEL)
        endif
    scenario cleanup
        ResetApp
    end scenario

TestEnd()
END
```

Only three new constants were created and one subroutine. The three constants are BTN_YES, BTN_NO, and CAP_SAVEAS. This gives us support for clicking on the Yes and No buttons, and for verifying the caption of the Save As dialog box. The one subroutine that was created is *ResetApp()*. The purpose of this subroutine is to place Notepad back into a known condition or *base state* by clearing the contents of its editor.

Note

Notice that in these last scenarios we're not checking for the existence of the message box before attempting to click on the Yes or No buttons. In the event that the message box isn't displayed and the script attempts to click on a button that won't be there without the message box, the scenario encounters a run-time error, marks the test scenario as a failure, and then moves on to the next test scenario (unless there is a scenario cleanup statement, when it runs through the clean-up code before moving on).

Conclusion

When focusing on an area to automate, the toughest part is writing that first line of code. The trick to it is to write something, anything, and move forward with more and more revisions to the work you've done. It's very similar to a writer with writer's block; you're not sure what to write, and perhaps you're overwhelmed with the task ahead. But if you sit down and start typing you'll eventually hit upon something that looks like it's worth keeping. So, you keep it, move forward, refine, adjust, and eventually you have something that looks like it will work.

This chapter covered the development of one single test case file but demonstrates how a number of utilities fall out of the beginning development. As more test cases are created, more utilities become necessary and are written to help support the testing on a product. Keep adding them to the separate utilities file, in our case noteutil.inc, and you'll soon have an admirable arsenal available to you and perhaps other teams at your company.

The remaining test case files that test the rest of the menu items in Notepad can be found in Appendix F, "Listing of All Test Cases." The final version of notemain.inc is in Appendix D, " Listing for notemain.inc " and the final version of the noteutil.inc file is in Appendix E, " Listing for noteutil.inc." Look them over, take what you find useful and keep the rest for later, in the event that you might need them. The source code is also available on disk in the back of this book.

Summary

This chapter runs through a simple group of test scenarios using Notepad. It walks through three versions of the test, gradually getting more complex. It deals with the problems you might encounter and how to deal with them. It discusses include files, new functions, the global variable, and constants. Finally, it looks at the results of the test examples.

Common Utilities and Routines

*W*hile developing the test case file in Chapter 10, we ended up creating a couple of extra files that now accompany the test case file and will be used by future test case files. These two files are notemain.inc and noteutil.inc and are the subject of discussion in this chapter.

notemain.inc

One of the two files we found that we needed to create when writing the test case file in Chapter 10 was the notemain.inc file. This file holds all the declarations most likely needed by other test case files. It will constantly change as the project grows and you'll find yourself moving pieces of notemain.inc to other include files specific to a given area of the product, and other pieces of code from files lower in the hierarchy up to notemain.inc. This file is written out in Listing 11-1.

LISTING 11-1 The Main Include File: notemain.inc.

```
'*********************** NOTEMAIN.INC ************************
'*
'* Purpose: Holds common declarations to be used by all test
'*          case files. Anything not common enough to be
'*          used by the majority of the test case files should
'*          be moved to an include file lower in the hierarchy
'*          specific to the area it concerns.
'*
'* Author:  Tom Arnold
'*
'* Revision History:
```

(continued)

235

LISTING 11-1 The Main Include File: notemain.inc.
(Continued)

```
'*
'* [ 0]   da-mon-year    email    action
'* [ 1]   29-FEB-1996    TomAr    Created notemain.inc to hold
'*                                common declarations.
'* [ 2]   29-FEB-1996    TVT      Moved in some common constants.
'*************************************************************

'$IFNDEF NOTEMAIN_INCLUDED
'$DEFINE NOTEMAIN_INCLUDED


'*************************************************************
'*********************** Constants ***************************
'*************************************************************


'********** General Application Info
const TEST_APP$          = "NOTEPAD.EXE" 'Exe file name

'********** Window captions/class names
const CAP_NOTEPAD$       = "- Notepad"   'Partial capt.: main window
const CAP_SAVECHANGES$   = "Notepad"     'Caption of SaveChngs msgbox
const CAP_SAVEAS         = "Save As"     'Caption of SaveAs dialog
const TEST_APP_CLASS$    = "Notepad"     'Classname of app's main win

'********** Logging Detail Settings
const LVL_MENUINFO%      = 10            'Menu info if Detail > 10
const LVL_VERBOSE%       = 100           'All calls to LOG enabled

'********** Edit control captions
const EDIT_NOTEPAD$      = "@1"          'Notepad's main edit window

'********** Button control captions
const BTN_NO$            = "No"          'Caption for No button
const BTN_YES$           = "Yes"         'Caption for Yes button
const BTN_CANCEL$        = "Cancel"      'Caption for Cancel button

'********** Menu Bar and Menu Item captions
'***** Menu items for the File menu
const MNU_FILE_NEW$      = "File\New"
const MNU_FILE_OPEN$     = "File\Open..."
```

```
const MNU_FILE_SAVE$    = "File\Save"
const MNU_FILE_SAVEAS$  = "File\Save As..."
const MNU_FILE_PGSETUP$ = "File\Page Setup..."
const MNU_FILE_PRINT$   = "File\Print"
const MNU_FILE_EXIT$    = "File\Exit"

'***** Menu items for the Edit menu
const MNU_EDIT_UNDO$    = "Edit\Undo"
const MNU_EDIT_CUT$     = "Edit\Cut"
const MNU_EDIT_COPY$    = "Edit\Copy"
const MNU_EDIT_PASTE$   = "Edit\Paste"
const MNU_EDIT_DELETE$  = "Edit\Delete"
const MNU_EDIT_SELALL$  = "Edit\Select All"
const MNU_EDIT_TIMEDATE$= "Edit\Time/Date"
const MNU_EDIT_WRDWRAP$ = "Edit\Word Wrap"

'***** Menu items for the Search menu
const MNU_SEARCH_FIND$  = "Search\Find..."
const MNU_SEARCH_FNEXT$ = "Search\Find Next"

'***** Menu items for the Help menu
const MNU_HELP_TOPICS   = "Help\Help Topics"
const MNU_HELP_ABOUT    = "Help\About Notepad"

'********** Other constants
const MAX_WAIT%          = 5 '# of secs to search for window
const DATA_TESTSTRING1$ = "Now is the time for all good people..."
const FW_NOTEPAD&        = FW_PART OR FW_ALL OR FW_FOCUS OR _
                          FW_RESTORE OR FW_EXIST
                          'Search criteria for Notepad


'*************************************************************
'******************** User Def'd Types *********************
'*************************************************************


'*************************************************************
'******************** Global Variables *********************
'*************************************************************


global ghWndNotepad&     'Global handle to Notepad's main window
```

(continued)

LISTING 11-1 The Main Include File: notemain.inc.
(Continued)

```
'****************************************************************
'****************** Func/Proc Prototypes ********************
'****************************************************************


'$ENDIF NOTEMAIN_INCLUDED
```

Let's dissect this listing.

Conditional Compilation

A technique that can be used, which is especially helpful for large teams, is the *conditional compilation* commands. These commands are referred to as *metacommands* in Visual Test and they provide instructions to the Test pre-compiler, telling it to perform certain actions before actually trying to compile the code.

This is the conditional compilation portion of notemain.inc. Use this to avoid including source code multiple times.

```
'$IFNDEF NOTEMAIN_INCLUDED
'$DEFINE NOTEMAIN_INCLUDED
  :
… more code …
  :
'$ENDIF NOTEMAIN_INCLUDED
```

The first two lines appear before any actual source code in the notemain.inc file. The '*$IFNDEF* command checks to see if the NOTEMAIN_INCLUDED symbol has already been defined. If it has not, as in the case where the file is being included for the first time, it continues to the next line of code, where it then defines the symbol NOTEMAIN_INCLUDED. The rest of the source code in the notemain.inc file is then included for compilation.

Note

In the case of Visual Test, a *symbol* declared using the '$DEFINE metacommand has no value. It is simply placed into a table internal to the Test language. Other metacommands can be used to determine whether or not a particular symbol has been defined, such as '$IFNDEF (if not defined), '$IFDEF (if defined), and so on.

If other source code files also include the notemain.inc file, the '$IFNDEF metacommand will determine that NOTEMAIN_INCLUDED is already defined the second time the file is included, perhaps by a utility *.inc* file or the test case file itself. The compiler will jump down to the last line shown in the code fragment above and thereby not include any of the source code for a second time.

If source code is included more than once, a *redeclaration error* can occur, as shown in Figure 11-1. In the event of such an error, it is up to the Test programmer to determine how a variable is being reused or redeclared. Sometimes this is simply because someone else is already using the same variable name, which will require the Test programmer to change the name of their variable. At other times, it's because some source code from a file is being included multiple times, requiring the programmer to determine which file is being included multiple times and how that's happening.

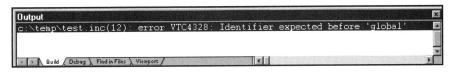

FIGURE 11-1 An error occurs because a declaration for a global variable is causing a compilation error the second time the file is included.

Note

Note that in the case demonstrated in the figure, the error shows itself as something other than a redeclaration error, but the error is indeed being generated because the global declaration is being encountered a second time.

In a small source code base it isn't difficult to find out why a file is being included multiple times, because the programmer can simply search through the files in the project one at a time.

On a larger code base there might exist a multi-tiered hierarchy to make code sharing easier, but this makes tracking down redeclaration errors more complex. Searching through a large number of files to determine which ones are being included and by which files can be time-consuming and frustrating. This is why the conditional compilation is so important. While it does lead to laxness in regulating how files are shared and included, on a time-critical project where frustrations are already high, it can pay off to set up the code base with this type of conditional compilation.

Figure 11-2 shows another type of redeclaration error. One of the frustrations of redeclaration errors is that they can be caused by including a file more than once without using conditional compilation to protect against the errors. The error won't be as exact as saying that you've included the file twice. Instead it will give you a symptom of the problem, relying on you to figure out what's causing it.

FIGURE 11-2
Another example of a redeclaration error.

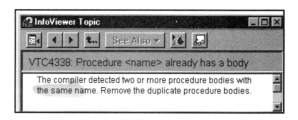

Visual Test 4.0 has somewhat simplified the problem of redeclaration errors. If a declaration for a constant is encountered multiple times, for example, and its value or declaration hasn't changed, the 4.0 compiler will not report the error. However, if you are writing your scripts to work with previous versions of Test for testing in a 16-bit environment, you will need to use previous versions of Test that aren't as forgiving as version 4.0. Save yourself time by building in the conditional compilation up front.

Tip

CONSTANTS

The largest section of the notemain.inc file is the Constants section. This holds values that will be used more than once and by multiple test case and utility files. If it becomes necessary to change any of the values, it can be done by editing this file. As a result, anywhere those constants were used, they're always updated to use the latest value. Listing 11-2 shows the section of code containing the constants.

LISTING 11-2 The Constants Section of notemain.inc Makes Up the Lion's Share of the File.

```
'****************************************************************
'************************* Constants *************************
'****************************************************************


'********** General Application Info
const TEST_APP$          = "NOTEPAD.EXE" 'Exe file name

'********** Window captions/class names
const CAP_NOTEPAD$       = "- Notepad"   'Partial capt.: main window
const CAP_SAVECHANGES$   = "Notepad"     'Caption of SaveChngs msgbox
const CAP_SAVEAS         = "Save As"     'Caption of SaveAs dialog
const TEST_APP_CLASS$    = "Notepad"     'Classname of app's main win

'********** Logging Detail Settings
const LVL_MENUINFO%      = 10            'Menu info if Detail > 10
const LVL_VERBOSE%       = 100           'All calls to LOG enabled

'********** Edit control captions
const EDIT_NOTEPAD$      = "@1"          'Notepad's main edit window

'********** Button control captions
const BTN_NO$            = "No"          'Caption for No button
const BTN_YES$           = "Yes"         'Caption for Yes button
const BTN_CANCEL$        = "Cancel"      'Caption for Cancel button

'********** Menu Bar and Menu Item captions
'***** Menu items for the File menu
const MNU_FILE_NEW$      = "File\New"
const MNU_FILE_OPEN$     = "File\Open..."
const MNU_FILE_SAVE$     = "File\Save"
const MNU_FILE_SAVEAS$   = "File\Save As..."
const MNU_FILE_PGSETUP$  = "File\Page Setup..."
const MNU_FILE_PRINT$    = "File\Print"
const MNU_FILE_EXIT$     = "File\Exit"

'***** Menu items for the Edit menu
const MNU_EDIT_UNDO$     = "Edit\Undo"
const MNU_EDIT_CUT$      = "Edit\Cut"
const MNU_EDIT_COPY$     = "Edit\Copy"
const MNU_EDIT_PASTE$    = "Edit\Paste"
```

(continued)

LISTING 11-2 The Constants Section of notemain.inc Makes Up the Lion's Share of the File.
(Continued)

```
const MNU_EDIT_DELETE$  = "Edit\Delete"
const MNU_EDIT_SELALL$  = "Edit\Select All"
const MNU_EDIT_TIMEDATE$= "Edit\Time/Date"
const MNU_EDIT_WRDWRAP$ = "Edit\Word Wrap"

'***** Menu items for the Search menu
const MNU_SEARCH_FIND$  = "Search\Find..."
const MNU_SEARCH_FNEXT$ = "Search\Find Next"

'***** Menu items for the Help menu
const MNU_HELP_TOPICS   = "Help\Help Topics"
const MNU_HELP_ABOUT    = "Help\About Notepad"

'********** Other constants
const MAX_WAIT%          = 5 '# of secs to search for window
const DATA_TESTSTRING1$ = "Now is the time for all good people..."
const FW_NOTEPAD&        = FW_PART OR FW_ALL OR FW_FOCUS OR _
                          FW_RESTORE OR FW_EXIST
                             'Search criteria for Notepad
```

GENERAL CONSTANTS

The first grouping of constants in notemain.inc is the General and Window Captions constants. This grouping provides the test case files with information on the application that is being tested. This includes the name of the application and the captions of the main windows, dialog boxes, and message boxes that make up this application.

The naming conventions used for these constants roughly follow the idea of *Hungarian Notation* (see the "Naming Conventions" section of Chapter 8 for more information on Hungarian Notation). I've chosen to use CAP_ as the prefix to any constant that refers to a window caption, whether it's a top-level window, message box, or dialog box window. The TEST_APP_CLASS constant is a special case where it isn't actually a caption, it's the class name of Notepad's main window. It seemed to fit best in the caption section of this file.

LOGGING DETAIL

The Logging Detail Settings section of the include file, shown in the next code excerpt, was created specifically for use with the Visual Test Suite Manager. The Suite Manager has a dialog box, shown in Figure 11-3, that allows the tester to control the level at which the Test language's *log* statement will write out information. By setting up our tests to use the log statement with the constants we've created, we can have a number of levels at which information is logged out.

```
'********** Logging Detail Settings

    const LVL_MENUINFO%      = 10         'Menu info if Detail > 10
    const LVL_VERBOSE%       = 100        'All calls to LOG enabled
```

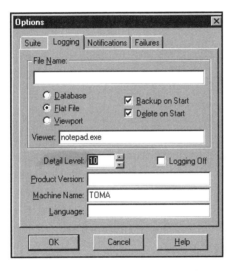

Figure 11-3
The Visual Test Suite Manager's dialog box. It allows the tester to specify at what level of detail information should be logged.

The log statement has a number associated with it which tells that statement only to log out information when the details setting is higher than the number used by a given log line of code.

These levels are defined and controlled by the Test programmer. The levels shown in the last piece of code were created as a starting point. It is certain that more LVL_-type constants will be created as the project matures, and possibly it will become necessary to change the actual values of those constants. This is simply a place to start. LVL_VERBOSE was defined as 100 because it's assumed that other levels will fall in the range of 0 to 99. The verbose setting is meant to be a catchall way of getting as much detail out of the overall test suite as possible.

The log statement will be discussed and demonstrated more thoroughly when we look at the contents of noteutil.inc later in this chapter.

CONTROL CAPTIONS

The next section in this initial version of notemain.inc declares constants that hold the values for commonly encountered captions in Windows controls. The first captions used by new.mst, in Chapter 10, are moved into the notemain.inc file and made constants. The naming conventions for these constants use the type of control as the prefix to the name:

```
'********** Edit control captions
const EDIT_NOTEPAD$     = "@1"              'Notepad's main edit window

'********** Button control captions
const BTN_NO$           = "No"             'Caption for No button
const BTN_YES$          = "Yes"            'Caption for Yes button
const BTN_CANCEL$       = "Cancel"         'Caption for Cancel button
```

Remember that Notepad's main window, where text is typed in, is actually a large edit control. Because there is no label or caption visibly associated with it, it's necessary to use the ordinal value to identify the control when using the *wEdit** routines. Because this is the only edit control on the main window, the ordinal position is 1. This translates to "@1", so that the *wEdit** routines know they are dealing with an ordinal and not a caption of "1."

Buttons with captions of "Yes," "No," and "Cancel" will be encountered throughout Notepad. Therefore, the constants for these controls are kept in notemain.inc, the top-most portion of the file-sharing hierarchy. If this product is localized to the French or German markets, these commonly used button captions can be changed at this level. If this weren't the process followed when tests were written for different sections of Notepad, then other constants, or worse yet no constants and just literal strings, would be used for these values. This would mean the testing team having to visit multiple files to make a single caption change.

MENU CONSTANTS

Even though new.mst, the first test case file created for this automation project, only used the New and Exit menu items found under the File menu, I took it upon myself to declare the rest of the constants that we'll eventually need to use as we continue setting up our overall automation structure for Notepad:

```
'********** Menu Bar and Menu Item captions
'***** Menu items for the File menu
const MNU_FILE_NEW$      = "File\New"
const MNU_FILE_OPEN$     = "File\Open..."
const MNU_FILE_SAVE$     = "File\Save"
const MNU_FILE_SAVEAS$   = "File\Save As..."
const MNU_FILE_PGSETUP$  = "File\Page Setup..."
const MNU_FILE_PRINT$    = "File\Print"
const MNU_FILE_EXIT$     = "File\Exit"

'***** Menu items for the Edit menu
const MNU_EDIT_UNDO$     = "Edit\Undo"
const MNU_EDIT_CUT$      = "Edit\Cut"
const MNU_EDIT_COPY$     = "Edit\Copy"
const MNU_EDIT_PASTE$    = "Edit\Paste"
const MNU_EDIT_DELETE$   = "Edit\Delete"
const MNU_EDIT_SELALL$   = "Edit\Select All"
const MNU_EDIT_TIMEDATE$ = "Edit\Time/Date"
const MNU_EDIT_WRDWRAP$  = "Edit\Word Wrap"

'***** Menu items for the Search menu
const MNU_SEARCH_FIND$   = "Search\Find..."
const MNU_SEARCH_FNEXT$  = "Search\Find Next"

'***** Menu items for the Help menu
const MNU_HELP_TOPICS    = "Help\Help Topics"
const MNU_HELP_ABOUT     = "Help\About Notepad"
```

The MNU_ prefix was used for the menus. It's important to note that this is only the naming convention that I chose and that it could have been anything, as long as it was a unique and legal name that the compiler would understand, and preferably something that showed a sense of organization. You'll also notice that the equal signs line up in this listing. This is the degree to which I go so that the code is a little more readable. There's no reason for you to go to this degree, unless you want your scripts to appear ordered, maintained, and easy to read.

OTHER CONSTANTS

The last section for the constants declared in notemain.inc is for the three constants that don't yet fit into their own category. Therefore, they've been moved into a generic category. As the project matures this will most likely change and they will be moved around into more clearly defined declaration blocks.

```
'********** Other constants
const MAX_WAIT%        = 5 '# of secs to search for window
const DATA_TESTSTRING1$ = "Now is the time for all good people..."
const FW_NOTEPAD&       = FW_PART OR FW_ALL OR FW_FOCUS OR _
                          FW_RESTORE OR FW_EXIST
                         'Search criteria for Notepad
```

The first two constants are easily enough understood. The first is a default time used by a number of the Test language routines to determine how long the routine should wait for a control to appear before giving an error message or continuing on. The second is a generic test string that gets typed into the Notepad window for testing purposes.

The third and final constant is FW_NOTEPAD. This is unique in that it doesn't appear to be assigned one value. Instead, it uses other constants that are defined intrinsically to Visual Test (in other words, they aren't declared any place, they are already a part of the Test language). These values are being OR-ed together and assigned back to the FW_NOTEPAD constant.

The FW_ prefix stands for Find Window and was used in the FW_NOTEPAD name because it is basically a subset or specific definition of the other FW_ constants. These constants are used by the *wFndWnd()* and *wFndWndC()* functions to find a window or control. I wanted to control exactly how I search for a window and didn't want to have to type in all the other FW_ constants every time I performed such a search. Therefore, the FW_NOTEPAD constant was created.

Note

Even though the FW_ constants are being OR-ed together, this is not the same as a database type of OR-ing. In a database language this would be communicating that the search was looking for <this> value OR <that> value OR <this other> value. This isn't the case in this situation. What is actually going on is a bitwise OR-ing causing the binary digit values of each FW_ constant to be merged or added together. It is done this way so that a single value can be passed to the *wFndWnd** routine that contains the OR-ed results, instead of requiring *wFndWnd()* to take many more parameters that would need to be passed. This keeps the parameter list small, by requiring that only one value be passed to tell the *wFndWnd()* routine how to work.

Other Sections of notemain.inc

The other sections of the notemain.inc file are for the declarations of user-defined types, global variables, and function prototypes. The user-defined types section is placed after the constant declarations, since constants can be used as part of the declaration of a user-defined type.

The Visual Test compiler requires constants, types, and variable declarations to be declared prior to where they're used. Therefore, if a constant is used as part of a user-defined type declaration, that constant must appear before the type declaration in the source code listing.

```
'***************************************************************
'********************* User Def'd Types *********************
'***************************************************************


'***************************************************************
'********************* Global Variables *********************
'***************************************************************

  global ghWndNotepad&    'Global handle to Notepad's main window

'***************************************************************
'***************** Func/Proc Prototypes *****************
'***************************************************************
```

At this stage, there aren't any user-defined types for the automation project. There is, however, a global variable declaration: *ghWndNotepad*. This variable is assigned the value of Notepad's main window handle by the *TestBegin()* subroutine found in the noteutil.inc include file. By making this variable global, any time that the handle to Notepad's main window needs to be used as part of a function call (a common occurrence), the Test programmer has access to it.

In addition, the function prototype section is not yet being used. This section is meant for linking into libraries outside Microsoft Visual Test. An example would be linking into a dynamic linked library (DLL) that you or someone else may have written using Visual C/C++. Another example is linking into one of Windows' main libraries to use a windows routine, such as a common dialog box or something to help track memory usage. Linking into external libraries is discussed later in this book in the "Advanced Topics" section of Chapter 13.

noteutil.inc

The term *utilities* is not referring to actual stand-alone applications in the case of our automated test suite. Instead, it is referring to functions and subroutines that provide the test cases in our test suite with useful code, encapsulated into a function or subroutine, and made available by sharing it through a common include file; in this case, it's shared through noteutil.inc., as shown in Listing 11-3.

LISTING 11-3 The Version of noteutil.inc We Created to Write a Single Test Case to Test the File Menu's "New" Menu Item.

```
'*********************** NOTEUTIL.INC ************************
'*
'* Purpose: Common functions and subroutines useful to other
'*          test case files are placed into this file for
'*          our Notepad project. As this file grows other
'*          testing teams might be interested in using this
'*          file to get a head start on their automation.
'*
'* Author:  Tom Arnold
'*
'* Revision History:
'*
'* [ 0]  da-mon-year    email    action
'* [ 1]  28-FEB-1996    TomAr    Created NOTEUTIL.INC to hold
```

```
'*                            common functions & subroutines.
'* [ 2]  29-FEB-1996    TVT    Moved in some common funcs.
'***************************************************************

'$IFNDEF NOTEUTIL_INCLUDED
'$DEFINE NOTEUTIL_INCLUDED

'*********************** INCLUDES ****************************
'$include 'notemain.inc'

'***************************************************************
'* Subroutine:  PutString
'* Purpose:     Places a string into the Notepad editor at a
'*              specified line and character position. If the
'*              line or character doesn't exist, this routine adds
'*              the necessary carriage returns and spaces.
'*
'* Parameters:  strOut$ String to be written to the editor
'*              iLine%  Line at which string is to be written
'*              iChar%  Character/column position to place string
'*
'***************************************************************

sub PutString (strOut$, iLine%, iChar%)
    dim iCurrLine%      'Keeps track of what line the cursor is on
    dim iCurrChar%      'Tracks which column the cursor is in
    dim iLoop%          'Used as index to for loop
    dim iLoopLimit%     'Used to determine end value of for loop
    dim strDirection$   'Set to which keystroke should be used

    'Get the current line and cursor position
    iCurrLine = wEditLine(EDIT_NOTEPAD)

    'Determine which direction to move based on
    'current position and desired position.
    if (iCurrLine < iLine) then
        iLoopLimit = (iLine - iCurrLine)
        strDirection = "{DOWN}"              'We need to move down
    else
        iLoopLimit = (iCurrLine - iLine)
        strDirection = "{UP}"                'We need to move up
    endif
```

See p. 257

(continued)

LISTING 11-3 The Version of noteutil.inc We Created to Write a Single Test Case to Test the File Menu's "New" Menu Item.
(Continued)

```
'Move to the desired position, adding lines if necessary.
    for iLoop = 1 to iLoopLimit
        if (wEditLine(EDIT_NOTEPAD) < wEditLines(EDIT_NOTEPAD)) then
            Play strDirection
        elseif (strDirection = "{DOWN}") then
            Play "{END}"
            Play "{ENTER}"
        else
            Play strDirection
        endif
    next iLoop

    'Get the current character position
    iCurrChar = wEditPos(EDIT_NOTEPAD)

    'Based on the current position, determine which
    'direction to move.
    if (iCurrChar < iChar) then
        iLoopLimit = (iChar - iCurrChar)
        strDirection = "{RIGHT}"
    else
        iLoopLimit = (iCurrChar - iChar)
        strDirection = "{LEFT}"
    endif

    'Move to the desired position added spaces if needed.
    for iLoop - 1 to iLoopLimit
        if (wEditPos(EDIT_NOTEPAD) < _
            wEditLineLen(EDIT_NOTEPAD,wEditLine(EDIT_NOTEPAD))) then
            Play strDirection
        elseif (strDirection = "{RIGHT}") then
            Play " "
        else
            Play strDirection
        endif
    next iLoop

    Play strOut    'Type the string at the
                   'current location
end sub 'PutString()
```

Sle p.259

```
'*****************************************************************
'* Subroutine:    ResetApp
'* Purpose:       Attempts to reset the application to a known
'*                state. This routine will likely grow in
'*                complexity as strange circumstances are
'*                discovered where it isn't able to reset the
'*                application.
'*
'*****************************************************************

sub ResetApp()
    WMenuEnd
    SelMenu(MNU_FILE_NEW)

    if (GetText(NULL) = CAP_SAVECHANGES) then
        wButtonClick(BTN_NO)
    endif
end sub 'ResetApp()


'*****************************************************************
'* Subroutine:    SelMenu
'* Purpose:       This is a wrapper around the wMenuSelect
'*                statement, allowing us a level of detailed
'*                information if requested.
'*
'* Parameters:    STRING  A wMenuSelect-compatible string.
'*
'*****************************************************************

sub SelMenu(strMenu$)
    WMenuEnd                   'Verify a menu isn't already popped down
    wMenuSelect(strMenu)       'Select the menu item

    'The detail level represented by the LVL_MENUINFO constant is
    'controlled from the Options dialog box in the Suite Manager.
    'If the level specified in the Suite Manager is greater than
    'the level specified by LVL_MENUINFO (below) then the info
    'will be logged out. Otherwise, the information isn't logged.
    'This is a way to control the level/detail of information
    'provided.
```

(continued)

LISTING 11-3 The Version of noteutil.inc We Created to Write a Single Test Case to Test the File Menu's "New" Menu Item. *(Continued)*

```
     Log #LVL_MENUINFO, "Selected menu: "+strMenu$
end sub 'SelMenu()



'*****************************************************************
'* Function:    strFailNum
'* Purpose:     Keeps a counter of the total number of failures
'*              that have occurred using the fail command for
'*              the current test case file. For this to work,
'*              it must be called for each failure and is
'*              therefore designed to work with the fail
'*              statement.
'*
'* Parameters:  NONE
'*
'* Returns:     STRING  The string that is returned is formatted
'*                      to fit in front of the text being
'*                      included in the fail statement.
'*
'* Format
'* returned:    "Fail #<num>: "
'*
'* Use:         FAIL strFailNum()+"<descrip-of-failure>"
'*
'*****************************************************************

function strFailNum() as string
    static iCount%

    iCount = iCount + 1
    strFailNum = "Fail #"+trim$(str$(iCount))+": "
end function 'strFailNum()



'*****************************************************************
'* Function:    strTestNum
'* Purpose:     Keeps a counter of the total number of tests
'*              that have been executed for the current test
'*              case file. For this to work, it must be
'*              called for each test. It is designed to work
```

```
'*               with the scenario statement. This is why it
'*               returns a string.
'*
'* Parameters:   NONE
'*
'* Returns:      STRING  The string that is returned is formatted
'*                       to fit in front of the text being
'*                       included in the scenario statement.
'*
'* Format
'* returned:     "Test #<num>: "
'*
'* Use:          SCENARIO strTestNum()+"<descrip-of-test>"
'*
'****************************************************************

function strTestNum() as string
    static iCount%

    iCount = iCount + 1
    strTestNum = "Test #"+trim$(str$(iCount))+": "
end function 'strTestNum()


'****************************************************************
'* Subroutine:   TestBegin
'* Purpose:      All initialization code that needs to be run
'*               before the scenarios of a test case are
'*               executed should be placed in this subroutine.
'*               This subroutine needs to be called first by
'*               each test case.
'*
'* Parameters:   NONE
'*
'****************************************************************

sub TestBegin()
    log #LVL_VERBOSE, "Initializing Test Case and attempting to"
    log #LVL_VERBOSE, "find or run ";TEST_APP;" application."

    viewport clear      'Clean the contents of the Viewport tab
                        'in the Output window.

    'Get test application up and running. If it can be run
```

(continued)

LISTING 11-3 The Version of noteutil.inc We Created to Write a Single Test Case to Test the File Menu's "New" Menu Item.
(Continued)

```
    'for whatever reason, print an error message and stop
    'the execution of the script.

    ghWndNotepad = wFndWndC(CAP_NOTEPAD, TEST_APP_CLASS, _
                            FW_NOTEPAD, MAX_WAIT)

    if (ghWndNotepad = 0) then
        log #LVL_VERBOSE, "Unable to find ";TEST_APP;"."
        if run(TEST_APP) then
            fail "Error: Unable to run notepad.exe"
        else
            ghWndNotepad = wFndWnd(CAP_NOTEPAD, FW_NOTEPAD, _
                                   MAX_WAIT)
            log #LVL_VERBOSE, "Successfully ran ";TEST_APP
        endif
    else
        log #LVL_VERBOSE, "Found ";TEST_APP;" already running."
        ResetApp()
    endif

    'Note: A call to the fail statement will generate
    'a run-time error, since it is not in a scenario block.
    'The result is an error message box, if you are in
    'Microsoft Developer Studio. If you are in the Visual
    'Test Suite Manager the Suite Manager will move on to the
    'next test case file. This, which is what you would want, since
    'it doesn't make sense for the rest of the tests to run,
    'because the test application can't be brought up.
end sub 'TestBegin()


'******************************************************************
'* Subroutine:   TestEnd
'* Purpose:      Clean-up code that needs to be executed after
'*                all scenarios for a given test case file have
'*                been executed.
'*
'* Parameters:   NONE
'*
```

```
'****************************************************************

sub TestEnd()
    '** Clean-up before the test case file ends **

    wMenuSelect(MNU_FILE_EXIT)      'Shut down Notepad application

    if (GetText(NULL) = CAP_SAVECHANGES) then
        wButtonClick(BTN_NO)        'Click 'No' to "Save changes?"
    endif
end sub 'TestEnd()


'****************************************************************
'* Subroutine:  <name>
'* Purpose:
'*
'* Parameters:
'*
'****************************************************************


'****************************************************************
'* Function:    <name>
'* Purpose:
'*
'* Parameters:
'*
'* Returns:
'*
'****************************************************************


'$ENDIF NOTEUTIL_INCLUDED
```

The noteutil.inc include file consists of seven functions and subroutines. They range from counters, to keep track of the number of tests and failures that occur, to test initialization and clean-up routines. Because this is the first version of this file, and it will grow as more test cases are added to the project, we'll take the opportunity to step through these first functions.

Why noteutil.inc Includes notemain.inc

noteutil.inc includes notemain.inc, the overall header file for the project, even though it's likely that a test case file would have already included notemain.inc.

By having every file in the automation project include the files it needs, even in cases where it might cause a file to be included multiple times, determining file dependencies later is a much simpler task. If someone should come along in a year or so and wish to remove sections of the automation project for use on another project, having these explicit declarations means the person knows exactly what files are needed for his test to run correctly.

One of the first lines of the noteutil.inc file is the metacommand to include our project's main header file. This command, shown in the following code, is in the noteutil.inc file because the noteutil.inc file relies upon declarations found in notemain.inc. This is purely a matter of style and it's arguable whether this style should be followed or not. I do it this way because I've set up my include files so they don't cause a redeclaration error by using conditional compilation commands. This way, each file can include exactly what it needs to function correctly.

```
'*********************** INCLUDES *****************************
'$include 'notemain.inc'
```

A New Level of Retentiveness? You'd Think So... At First

You may or may not have noticed that the functions and subroutines in this file have been arranged into alphabetical order. A friend showed me this one time and I thought it was a good idea. (I made fun of him at first, then saw the value in it, when he explained the idea further.)

The idea of organizing your routines like this doesn't make sense when working within an editor, and even less if the number of routines is low. However, as the file gets bigger in size, and one day you'll find yourself working from a printout of the utility file, you'll then see the benefit of this approach, since you'll know in which direction to search through your reams of paper. Just something to keep in mind.

PutString()

The *PutString()* subroutine was written because there might come a time when you need a test scenario to check whether certain text exists at a particular location. Perhaps this might occur when testing cut and paste functionality, or when typing text in the middle of a string and verifying that the word wrapping is working as expected. Whatever the case, this routine was written to provide everyone on our fictitious testing team a way to insert text at a specific line and character position. As Listing 11-4 shows, the *PutString()* subroutine takes three arguments. The first argument is the string to be placed into Notepad's editor, the second is the line position, and the third is the character position at which to place the string.

LISTING 11-4 The *PutString()* Subroutine Takes Three Arguments.

```
'*****************************************************************
'* Subroutine:   PutString
'* Purpose:      Places a string into the Notepad editor at a
'*               specified line and character position. If the
'*               line or character doesn't exist, this routine adds
'*               the necessary carriage returns and spaces.
'*
'* Parameters:   strOut$ String to be written to the editor
'*               iLine%  Line at which string is to be written
'*               iChar%  Character/column position to place string
'*
'*****************************************************************
  sub PutString (strOut$, iLine%, iChar%)
        dim iCurrLine%        'Keeps track of what line the cursor is on
        dim iCurrChar%        'Tracks which column cursor is in
        dim iLoop%            'Used as index to for loop
        dim iLoopLimit%       'Used to determine end value of for loop
        dim strDirection$     'Set to which keystroke should be used

        'Get the current line and cursor position
        iCurrLine = wEditLine(EDIT_NOTEPAD)

        'Determine which direction to move based on
        'current position and desired position.
        if (iCurrLine < iLine) then
            iLoopLimit = (iLine - iCurrLine)
```

(continued)

LISTING 11-4 The PutString() Subroutine Takes Three Arguments.
(Continued)

```
        strDirection = "{DOWN}"                'We need to move down
    else
        iLoopLimit = (iCurrLine - iLine)
        strDirection = "{UP}"                  'We need to move up
    endif

    'Move to the desired position, adding lines if necessary.
    for iLoop = 1 to iLoopLimit
        if (wEditLine(EDIT_NOTEPAD) < wEditLines(EDIT_NOTEPAD)) then
            Play strDirection
        elseif (strDirection = "{DOWN}") then
            Play "{END}"
            Play "{ENTER}"
        else
            Play strDirection
        endif
    next iLoop

    'Get the current character position
    iCurrChar = wEditPos(EDIT_NOTEPAD)

    'Based on the current position, determine which
    'direction to move.
    if (iCurrChar < iChar) then
        iLoopLimit = (iChar - iCurrChar)
        strDirection = "{RIGHT}"
    else
        iLoopLimit = (iCurrChar - iChar)
        strDirection = "{LEFT}"
    endif

    'Move to the desired position added spaces if needed.
    for iLoop = 1 to iLoopLimit
        if (wEditPos(EDIT_NOTEPAD) < _
            wEditLineLen(EDIT_NOTEPAD,wEditLine(EDIT_NOTEPAD))) then
            Play strDirection
        elseif (strDirection = "{RIGHT}") then
            Play " "
        else
```

```
            Play strDirection
        endif
    next iLoop

    Play strOut      'Type the string at the
                     'current location
end sub 'PutString()
```

Instead of stepping through each of these functions line by line, I'll just point out key things about each one. The main feature of *PutString()* is that it's basically an improved version of the play statement, when it comes to working with keystrokes and Notepad. The user can easily specify where to place a line of text and the routine will automatically add carriage returns and spaces to get to the appropriate line and character position in the editor.

ResetApp()

The *ResetApp()* routine was written so that the state of Notepad can be returned to a known starting point at any time during the running of an automated test (see the next piece of code). This routine is just a starting point and only considers the situations where a menu might already be displayed and how to deal with the Save Changes? message box, if displayed. Notice also that *ResetApp()* is using another routine we've written called *SelMenu()* to select a menu item. Not only should the routines that you write be used by your test cases, they should be used by the utility routines themselves.

```
'***************************************************************
'* Subroutine:   ResetApp
'* Purpose:      Attempts to reset the application to a known
'*               state. This routine will likely grow in
'*               complexity as strange circumstances are
'*               discovered where this routine isn't able to
'*               reset the application.
'*
'***************************************************************

sub ResetApp()
    WMenuEnd
    SelMenu(MNU_FILE_NEW)
```

```
        if (GetText(NULL) = CAP_SAVECHANGES) then
            wButtonClick(BTN_NO)
        endif
    end sub 'ResetApp()
```

There's always room for improvement when it comes to routines like this. The most obvious addition would be to deal with any dialog box that might be displayed when it is called. Other helpful clean-up tasks could be added to this and other commonly called routines. An example in the case of *ResetApp()* would be a routine to back up the current log file every time the routine is called. Another would be to dump out the current state of memory available.

Not only do routines like *ResetApp()* serve their obvious purpose, but they also provide hooks into the automated scripts, so you can include other special routines for housekeeping and other reasons.

SelMenu()

SelMenu() is another simple subroutine whose true purpose is to provide an easy place for us to insert other routines. It provides a structure from which we can hang or insert status tracking routines. In its current form it verifies that a menu isn't already displayed, then selects the menu item passed to it by using Visual Test's wMenuSelect statement. This can be seen in the following:

```
'*****************************************************************

'* Subroutine:   SelMenu
'* Purpose:      This is a wrapper around the wMenuSelect
'*               statement, allowing us a level of detailed
'*               information if requested.
'*
'* Parameters:   STRING  A wMenuSelect-compatible string.
'*
'*****************************************************************

sub SelMenu(strMenu$)
    WMenuEnd                        'Verify a menu isn't already popped
down
    wMenuSelect(strMenu)       'Select the menu item
```

```
'The detail level represented by the LVL_MENUINFO constant is
'controlled from the Options dialog box in the Suite Manager.
'If the level specified in the Suite Manager is greater than
'the level specified by LVL_MENUINFO (below) then the info
'will be logged out. Otherwise, the information isn't logged.
'This is a way to control the level/detail of information
'provided.

    Log #LVL_MENUINFO, "Selected menu: "+strMenu$
end sub 'SelMenu()
```

The log statement was mentioned earlier in this chapter when we looked at the constants defined for the Visual Test Suite Manager. The last line before the end of the *SelMenu()* subroutine shows how this statement is used with one of the constants declared in notemain.inc. If the level of detail set in the Suite Manager is greater than the level represented by the LVL_MENUINFO constant, then the information provided with this log statement will be written to the Viewport or log file, whichever is specified in the Suite Manager.

strFailNum() and *strTestNum()*

The scenario and fail statements provided in the Test language are great for writing out information about the tests and any errors encountered by them. However, they lack a counter to keep track of the number of tests and errors that occur.

One of the things that managers like to see is numbers, so they have a feel for the status of a project. A typical figure that supervisors like to have available to them is the number of tests being run on a given area of the product. While this is somewhat silly, since the number of tests doesn't communicate the quality of those tests, it's a metric that people nonetheless like to hear. The same goes for the number of errors encountered for a given test case.

This is where *strFailNum()* and *strTestNum()* come in. Their source code is virtually the same. *StrFailNum()* returns the number of times it has been called and is meant to be used with the fail statement. *StrTestNum()* is similar, except that it is used with the scenario statement:

```
'*****************************************************************
'* Function:     strFailNum
'* Purpose:      Keeps a counter of the total number of failures
'*               that have occurred using the fail command for
'*               the current test case file. For this to work,
'*               it must be called for each failure and is
'*               therefore designed to work with the fail
'*               statement.
'*
'* Parameters:   NONE
'*
'* Returns:      STRING  The string that is returned is formatted
'*                       to fit in front of the text being
'*                       included in the fail statement.
'*
'* Format
'* returned:     "Fail #<num>: "
'*
'* Use:          FAIL strFailNum()+"<descrip-of-failure>"
'*
'*****************************************************************

function strFailNum() as string
    static iCount%
                                        → convrts data
    iCount = iCount + 1
    strFailNum = "Fail #"+trim$(str$(iCount))+": "
end function 'strFailNum()
```

These two routines are different than those we've already looked at. Instead of being subroutines, they're functions. They return a value back to the place where the function call was placed.

The first thing you'll notice is that the comment block is somewhat different because it contains information about the return value. Also included is an example of how the function is to be used. This is so that, when my teammates go to use the function, they'll use it correctly the first time.

The next thing you'll notice is that a *static* variable is used. This is similar to a global variable in that it retains its value from function call to function call. However, static variables can only be accessed by the function. This way, the value can't be accidentally changed by another

Test programmer. If you later decide to check how many failures have occurred without bumping the counter, the variable may need to be changed to a global variable.

Every time these functions are called they bump their static counter variables by one and then return a string with the number in it. Because a *string* and an *integer* are two different types, the number needs to be changed with a call to *STR$()*—a function built into the Test language.

The *TRIM$()* function trims off any leading or trailing spaces that might be a part of the number conversion. For example, a leading space is left when converting a number to a string. The *STR$()* function leaves room for a minus sign in the event that the number is negative.

TestBegin()

TestBegin() is the first subroutine called by every test case file in the entire test suite. This happens because our imaginary testing team has decided it's the way everyone will write their code. When a decision like this is made, it's a good idea to include it in the template used by the testing team, so that everyone remembers to start putting their code after the *TestBegin()* call.

The purpose of *TestBegin()* is to do whatever is necessary to set up the application to make it ready for testing. This includes locating an instance of Notepad that is already up and running, or running the application if it can't be found. Another thing that needs to be done is to assign the handle of the application's main window to a variable, so it can be used later.

```
'***************************************************************
'* Subroutine:   TestBegin
'* Purpose:      All initialization code that needs to be run
'*               before the scenarios of a test case are
'*               executed should be placed in this subroutine.
'*               This subroutine needs to be called first by
'*               each test case.
'*
'* Parameters:   NONE
'*
'***************************************************************
```

```
sub TestBegin()
    log #LVL_VERBOSE, "Initializing Test Case and attempting to"
    log #LVL_VERBOSE, "find or run ";TEST_APP;" application."

    viewport clear        'Clean the contents of the Viewport tab
                          'in the Output window.

    'Get test application up and running. If it can be run
    'for whatever reason, print an error message and stop
    'the execution of the script.

    ghWndNotepad = wFndWndC(CAP_NOTEPAD, TEST_APP_CLASS, _
                            FW_NOTEPAD, MAX_WAIT)

    if (ghWndNotepad = 0) then
        log #LVL_VERBOSE, "Unable to find ";TEST_APP;"."
        if run(TEST_APP) then
            fail "Error: Unable to run notepad.exe"
        else
            ghWndNotepad = wFndWnd(CAP_NOTEPAD, FW_NOTEPAD, _
                                   MAX_WAIT)
            log #LVL_VERBOSE, "Successfully ran ";TEST_APP
        endif
    else
        log #LVL_VERBOSE, "Found ";TEST_APP;" already running."
        ResetApp()
    endif

    'Note: Having a call to the Fail statement will generate
    'a run-time error since it is not in a SCENARIO block.
    'The result is an error message box being given if you
    'are in Microsoft Developer Studio. If you are in the
    'Visual Test Suite Manager the result will be the Suite
    'Manager moving on to the next test case file, which is
    'what you would want since it doesn't make sense for the
    'rest of the tests to run since the test application
    'can't be brought up.

end sub 'TestBegin()
```

If the tests are being run by the Suite Manager and the level of detail is set to a value higher than LVL_VERBOSE, some initial information will be logged out at the beginning of the test suite.

Some of the initial setup is also handled by the Suite Manager. For example, I used to put code in this routine to delete or back up my log files. Since the Suite Manager in Visual Test 4.0 now does this for me, the code is no longer included in my routines.

The *wFndWndC()* function is used to find an instance of Notepad that is already up and running. If one isn't found then zero (0) is returned instead of a handle to a window.

Now here's something quirky about Visual Test that catches everyone at some point. It concerns the *not* operator. In the section of code after attempting to find an instance of Notepad is this line:

```
if (ghWndNotepad = 0) then
```

Most of you are looking at this and asking why it doesn't look like the line of code shown in the next fragment. The reason is because the *not* operator is a *bitwise* operator, not a *logical* operator. Therefore, it flips each digit in the binary representation of a number to its opposite value (1 goes to 0, 0 goes to 1).

```
if not(ghWndNotepad) then
```

Theoretically, at least in C and Pascal, these two pieces of code should behave exactly the same. Not so in Visual Test's language.

The intent of the line is to cause the code in the if statement to execute in the event *ghWndNotepad* is equal to zero (0). In this case, both lines will behave in exactly the same way. In the situation where ghWndNotepad is set to a window handle, however, the first example will skip the code in the if statement, as intended, while the second will move into the if statement, which is not the desired behavior.

The reason is because the not operator flips the bits of the value stored in the ghWndNotepad variable, resulting in a value that still isn't zero (0) (false). If the value is non-zero, then it is considered true and will continue into the if statement. In the case where the value is -1, however, it won't step into the if statement. The binary representation of -1 in Visual Test is all of the binary digits set to 1, meaning that they all flip to 0 when the not operator is used. So, stick to the explicit version when checking if a variable is zero (0) or not, unless you're truly dealing with false and true values, as defined by the Test language.

The rest of the routine is self-explanatory. The comment about the fail statement at the end of the subroutine points out that if it is used outside a scenario block it will generate a run-time error. If the Suite Manager is running, it stops execution on the current test case file and the Suite Manager moves on to the next test case file.

TestEnd()

TestEnd() is the same idea as *TestBegin()*, except that it cleans up after the testing is done. In its current form, it doesn't do much, but it will grow in complexity as more test cases are added to the suite:

```
'****************************************************************
'* Subroutine:  TestEnd
'* Purpose:     Clean-up code that needs to be executed after
'*              all scenarios for a given test case file have
'*              been executed.
'*
'* Parameters:  NONE
'*
'****************************************************************

sub TestEnd()
    '** Clean-up before the test case file ends **
    wMenuSelect(MNU_FILE_EXIT)    'Shut down Notepad application

    if (GetText(NULL) = CAP_SAVECHANGES) then
        wButtonClick(BTN_NO)      'Click 'No' to "Save changes?"
    endif
end sub 'TestEnd()
```

A different way to write this script is to have it call the *ResetApp()* subroutine and then call *SelMenu()* to select the Exit menu item. Don't be surprised if this is the case in the final version of this subroutine.

Conclusion

It's incredible the amount of support code that can be written after setting up the first test case. The trick is to write that first test case and then cut out the sections of code that look like they'll be needed by other test case files. Throw that code into subroutines and put them into a separate file, so they're easy to share.

As your list of utilities grows, share them with other testing teams if you work at a big company. Or share them at discussion groups with others who are writing test automation. I know it's hard to share your code because you might be worried about other's opinions, but you'd be surprised how many beginners are out there who don't have a clue as to where to start. You can help both them and those who are more experienced — and who are often good enough to share their routines with you, so you can assimilate them into your existing code base.

One of the main themes of this section of the book, if you've not picked up on it already, is to keep your scripts as clean and as flexible as possible. Make your job and your teammates' jobs easy by using constants for common values and placing reusable code into files where they're accessible.

Summary

This chapter discusses two files: notemain.inc and noteutil.inc.

notemain.inc holds all the declarations most likely needed by other test case files. It deals with conditional compilation commands (also known as metacommands), constants, logging, control captions, declarations of user-defined types, global variables, and function prototypes.

noteutil.inc contains all the functions and subroutines that provide the test cases in our test suite with useful code, encapsulated into a function or subroutine, and made available by sharing it through a common include file — including notemain.inc. These functions and subroutines are discussed in detail.

Overview of the Final Test Suite

12

*T*he previous two chapters, Chapters 10 and 11, have focused on building a test case file for Notepad's New menu item. The idea behind that exercise was to demonstrate exactly how much initial coding goes into creating the first couple of tests. Now that we have an understanding of what it took to write a single test case file, I've gone ahead and written the rest of the test cases to create a skeleton or structure that can be added to by other testers. The purpose of this chapter is to explore what effect the addition of these test cases has on the original files created in chapters 10 and 11. Additionally, we'll explore how to run all of the test cases that have been created.

Developing a Structure

Before sitting down to write this chapter, I developed the structure that will be used as more tests are added to automate the testing of the Notepad application. I created a few tests for each feature of the product, so that they are all at least touched upon, albeit briefly. This was done based on the same idea followed for writing the tests for the New menu item found under the File menu. Figure 12-1 shows what the project looks like when viewed in the Microsoft Developer Studio.

Now that the rest of the structure is in place, along with a few tests for each of Notepad's features, we can see what additional utilities have been created and placed into the noteutil.inc file (the main function and subroutine utilities shared by all test case files).

After looking briefly at the new utilities we added as the structure filled out, we'll see how the test case files work with the Microsoft Visual Test Suite Manager. This includes seeing how logging is controlled using the Suite Manager's different settings.

FIGURE 12-1
The Project Workspace window for the Notepad test suite, as it appears in the Microsoft Developer Studio.

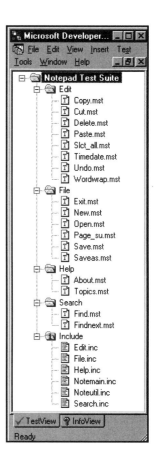

Additional Utilities

The noteutil.inc file is a living and breathing component of the Notepad test suite. As tests are added to the suite, other utilities that are useful and generic enough to be used by other test case files become apparent and migrate to the noteutil.inc file.

iFailCount() and *iTestCount()*

Two other functions that were added to make a Test programmer's life easier are *iFailCount()* and *iTestCount()*. These are very simple, but critical to protect a variable from being changed. *iFailCount()* returns the total number of failures that have occurred during the running of a test case file:

```
'******************************************************************
'* Function:    iFailCount
'* Purpose:     Returns current number of failures for the current
'*              test case file. This only works if the test
'*              scenarios are using strFailNum() in conjunction
'*              with calls to the fail statement. It is done this
'*              way to avoid Test programmers directly accessing
'*              the giFailCount global variable.
'*
'* Parameters:  NONE
'*
'* Returns:     INTEGER Current value of giFailCount, which is
'*                      a global value incremented every time
'*                      strFailNum is called.
'*
'******************************************************************

function iFailCount() as integer
    iFailCount = giFailCount
end function 'iFailCount
```

Note

Because *iFailCount()* and *iTestCount()* are very similar, only the function *iFailCount()* is shown.

The source code that makes up *iFailCount()* is extremely simple. All it does is return the value currently held in the giFailCount global integer variable by assigning it to the function's name. As mentioned briefly in Chapter 8, this is a simple form of data hiding. The idea is to get the entire Test programming team to use the function instead of the actual variable when retrieving information about how many tests have been executed and how many of them have failed.

If Test programmers new to the team want to retrieve the current number of tests or failures, they need only refer to *iTestCount()* or *iFailCount()*. As a result, the odds of someone accidentally modifying the global variables that hold this information decrease.

The idea of data hiding isn't meant as a security measure, at least not in this situation. It's intended to cut down on the number of logical bugs that can be created because someone on the programming team modified a variable they shouldn't have. The goal in our example is to modify the value of *giFailCount* through the use of the *strFailNum()* function, which will be discussed shortly. To retrieve that value, *iFailCount()* is used, resulting in the global variable being modified indirectly at all times.

strFailNum() & *strTestNum()*

The Visual Test language provides a means to log out information as a test case is running. What it lacks, however, is a counter so that a running total of the number of tests and failures that have occurred can be tracked. *StrFailNum()* and *strTestNum()* are my attempt to fill in this missing functionality and to provide more helpful information:

```
'*****************************************************************
'* Function:     strFailNum
'* Purpose:      Keeps a counter of the total number of failures
'*               that have occurred using the FAIL command for
'*               the current test case file.  For this to work,
'*               it must be called for each FAILure and is
'*               therefore designed to work with the FAIL
'*               statement.
'*
'* Parameters:   NONE
'*
'* Returns:      STRING  The string that is returned is formatted
'*                       to fit in front of the text being
'*                       included in the FAIL statement.
'*
'* Format
'* returned:     "Fail #<num>: "
'*
'* Use:          FAIL strFailNum()+"<descrip-of-failure>"
'*
'*****************************************************************

function strFailNum() as string
    giFailCount = giFailCount + 1
    strFailNum = "Fail #"+trim$(str$(giFailCount))+": "
end function 'strFailNum()
```

strFailNum() is yet another simple function, but powerful in what it contributes to the overall test suite. When it is called it increments a global counter variable, *giFailCount*, that keeps track of how many times *strFailNum()* is called. It is designed to work specifically with the Test language's fail statement. It returns a string that can be prepended to the text outputted by the fail statement.

This function is very similar to the one created in Chapter 11. It has since evolved, however, which is why it is being shown again. Now, instead of using a static variable, it is using a global variable so that the current number of failures and tests can be retrieved more easily. The giFailCount global variable is the same one used by *iFailCount()*. The object is to get information about a test case file without adding to the potential for other bugs. Therefore, the *iFailCount()* function is provided so you never need to interact directly with the global variable. Also, should the requirements change for how the global variable gets incremented, it's much easier to modify the guts of a function than to search through all existing scripts for a global variable and then change how it is used.

Tracking the Numbers of Tests and Failures

All four functions—*strFailNum()*, *strTestNum()*, *iFailCount()*, and *iTestCount()*—work together to provide information about how many tests and failures have occurred for a given test case file.

Some people take a different approach, however, by hard coding the test and fail numbers so they don't change when new tests are added. On one project I was on, it was critical to cross-verify the automated tests with those described in the overall test plan. In this case, it was necessary to type in a unique test number of each test, thereby hard coding that information into each test case file.

Usually this isn't required, at least not for most software companies. Therefore, the typical approach is to create functions similar to these four, so that when a test is moved, or placed in front of another test, it isn't necessary to go through and renumber the hard-coded test information by hand. When the test case file completes, you have a count as to how many tests passed and how many failed.

TestEnd()

The *TestEnd()* subroutine isn't a new routine added as the test suite grew. It did evolve, however, into a routine that provides more information at the end of the execution of each test case. *TestEnd()* now prints out summary information about how many tests were executed and how many failures were encountered. This listing provides more information than the original version shown in Chapter 11:

```
'******************************************************************
'* Subroutine:  TestEnd
'* Purpose:     Clean-up code that needs to be executed after
'*              all scenarios for a given test case file have
'*              been executed.
'*
'* Parameters:  NONE
'*
'******************************************************************

sub TestEnd()
    dim iPPass%          'Percent passed
    dim strMetrix$       'Misc metrics

    '** Clean-up before the test case file ends **

    wMenuSelect(MNU_FILE_EXIT)      'Shut down Notepad application

    if GetText(NULL) = CAP_SAVECHANGES then
        wButtonClick(BTN_NO)        'Click 'No' to "Save changes?"
    endif

    'Set up info to be logged out
    iPPass = ((iTestCount - iFailCount) / iTestCount) * 100
    strMetrix = "Scenarios: "+trim$(str$(iTestCount)) + _
            SPACE$(MAX_GAP) + "Errors: "+trim$(str$(iFailCount)) _
            +SPACE$(MAX_GAP) + "Passed: "+trim$(str$(iPPass))+"%"

    'Log out final information for the test case file
    'When doing the LEFT$() stuff a bunch of spaces are added
    'for padding and then are cropped off so that the max size
    'of the line being written out is 70 characters. By cropping
    'like this the info can adjust its size and still have the
    'right-hand border of the box remain in line.
```

```
        log #LVL_SUMMARY,"*************************** Test Case "+ _
                        "Results ************************"
        log #LVL_SUMMARY,"*"+space$(68)+"*"
        log #LVL_SUMMARY,"* Test Case: "+(left$(NAME$(0)+ _
                        space$(70),56))+"*"
        log #LVL_SUMMARY,"*"+space$(68)+"*"
        log #LVL_SUMMARY,"* "+left$(strMetrix+space$(70),67)+"*"
        log #LVL_SUMMARY,"*"+space$(68)+"*"
        log #LVL_SUMMARY,"* Test case completed testing at "+ _
                        left$(datetime$+space$(70),36)+"*"
        log #LVL_SUMMARY,"*"+space$(68)+"*"
        log #LVL_SUMMARY,STRING$(70,"*")
    end sub 'TestEnd()
```

TestBegin() and *TestEnd()* both assume that each test case calls them, respectively, before running any test scenarios, and after all the test scenarios have been completed for a given test case file. By operating on these assumptions, by building these subroutines into our Test templates, and by educating new programmers as they come onto the scene allows us the flexibility to provide initialization and clean-up code for each test case file.

TestEnd() has evolved from the first version shown in Chapter 11. It now provides summary information about how many tests were run and how many failures were encountered. It also takes those numbers and comes up with a percentage of how many of the tests passed for the given test case file. As the project matures, so will the noteutil.inc file, and all the functions and subroutines it contains.

Documenting noteutil.inc

Because we created a template for subroutine and function comment blocks early on, as described in Chapter 8, the project is now at a state where documentation can be constructed so that newcomers can come up to speed quickly.

Each comment block in the noteutil.inc file can be copied and pasted into a document to be used when writing test scripts. By doing this, we're creating our own documentation that is not only helpful to new Test programmers, but to existing Test programmers. After all, they need to remember which parameters have to be passed to a function or subroutine, and what value will be returned by a given function.

If you really want to be cool, you can copy and paste the information into an online help document and compile it down to a *.hlp* file similar to the Help files provided with almost any Windows application. On one project, my teammates and I went so far as to write a script in Visual Test to step through the *.inc* file and copy all pertinent comment blocks over to a separate file, so that it was easy to paste them into a separate document.

Note

The entire listing for noteutil.inc can be found on the disk included at the back of this book. It is also in hard copy form, so you can easily view it now. The hard copy printout can be found in Appendix E, "Listing for noteutil.inc."

Running the Test Suite

The overall structure or skeleton is now in place, since there exists a test case file for each of Notepad's features (for this test suite, each of Notepad's menu items was considered a feature).

Microsoft thought things through well in this latest version of Test, when it comes to how the project file for a given test suite, in this case notepad.vtp, is shared between the Developer Studio and the Suite Manager. As Figure 12-2 shows, the *.vtp* file type is used by both the Developer Studio and the Suite Manager.

FIGURE 12-2
The .vtp file type is a Visual Test Project file and is used by both the Developer Studio and the Suite Manager.

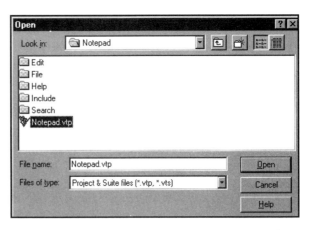

The *.vtp* file is created automatically whenever a new test suite is started. When selecting the Suite Manager menu item from the Test menu in the Developer Studio, the project that is currently open in the Developer Studio is also opened in the Suite Manager, as shown in Figure 12-3. Although the Suite Manager is a separate utility, they integrate seamlessly with each other, which makes the Test programmer's job that much less painstaking.

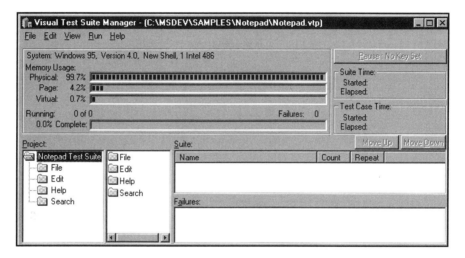

FIGURE 12-3   Selecting the Suite Manager menu item runs the separate driver utility, which results in opening the project currently being viewed in the Developer Studio.

Here's where all of the programming pays off. The test suite is now under the control of the Suite Manager and the tests can be run all at once, one at a time, or even repeatedly. The Suite Manager is a *driver* that runs each script that shows up in its suite list.

Running the Tests

The first thing to do to get your tests up and running is to select which of the test cases you'd like to execute. To keep it simple, I'm going to have our example run all the tests in the Notepad project. By clicking on each folder and dragging it over to the Suite: list box, I gradually build a suite of tests to run. Compare Figure 12-3 to Figure 12-4, to see the difference between a Suite Manager that has nothing to run, and a Suite Manager that has been configured to run all the tests found in the File, Edit, Search, and Help folders.

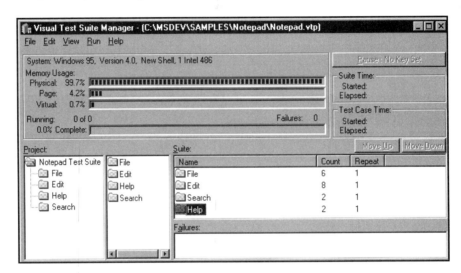

FIGURE 12-4 Folders have been dragged over from the Project: area to the Suite: area of the Suite Manager. Notice that the Count column shows how many test case files are in the folder and that the Repeat column can be used to cause a test case, or test cases, to be run multiple times.

The Suite Manager is now ready to run each of the test cases in turn. By pressing the F5 key or selecting the Run All menu item from the Run menu, the tests will begin.

Before we do this, however, I'd like to remind you of the log statements that we used throughout our test case files and utilities found in noteutil.inc. Recall that for each log statement, there was an associated level at which it would activate and write its information out to the Viewport, text file, or database-compatible file. The following code shows the section of constants declared in the notemain.inc file: the main include file for the entire test suite. These constants were declared based on levels I defined and allow anyone running the test suite to adjust to what degree or level of detail he or she would like to see output.

```
'********** Logging Detail Settings
const LVL_SUMMARY%      = 5   'Summary info after each test case
const LVL_MENUINFO%     = 10  'Give menu info if Detail > 10
```

```
const LVL_STATUSINFO    = 20  'General status info
const LVL_VERBOSE%      = 100 'Have all calls to LOG enabled
```

These levels used in the test case files by the log statement can now be
controlled via the Logging section of the Options dialog box in the Suite
Manager. (See Figure 12-5).

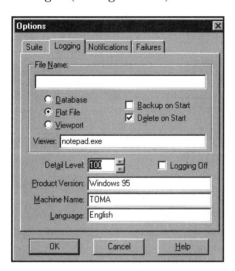

FIGURE 12-5
The Logging section of the Options
dialog box. The highest level of detail
has been selected (100).

If the name of the log file isn't selected, a default file name will be created, based on the name of the suite (in this case it would be notepad.log).

Now that the final settings have been selected the test suite is ready to be
run. When the Run All menu item found under the Run menu is
selected, the Suite Manager hides the lower portion of its window and
keeps the upper portion active, behind the scenes. This is so that a quick
glance will give the tester an idea as to where the test suite is in its execution (see Figure 12-6). Through the Options dialog box, shown in
Figure 12-5, this behavior can be modified so that the Suite Manager's
window disappears entirely if the test so desires.

Note

For more information on the Visual Test Suite Manager, refer to Chapter 6."

When the test suite has finished, any errors that were encountered during the run are shown in the Failures: section of the manager. In our
example, an error didn't occur, so the Suite Manager returns to its previ-

ous full size. It shows the final results for the test suite just executed in the top portion of its window, as shown in Figure 12-7.

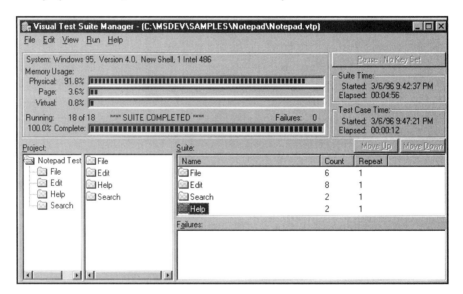

FIGURE 12-6 The upper portion of the Suite Manager stays visible and continuously updates itself, so that its status can be easily determined.

FIGURE 12-7 The summary results of the run for a test suite are shown in the top portion of the Suite Manager's window.

One of the key reasons to use the Suite Manager is that it takes care of many of the problems that can arise while running test case files. For example, if a compilation error occurs because someone didn't check their source code for typos, or a run-time error occurs because a control can't be found, or a memory access violation occurs, the Suite Manager will handle the situation and act accordingly.

Creating Other Test Suites

When we dragged the folders containing the test case files into the Suite: section of the Suite Manager, they defined a test suite. To avoid having to drag them around in the future, this suite can be saved to a separate file known as a *suite file* that has a *.vts* extension (Visual Test Suite).

Even though there exists one project file for Notepad's test cases, multiple suite files can be defined, depending on what exactly it is that the tester wishes to accomplish. For example, this test suite could be saved under the name of "Fullpass.vts," since it runs all of the tests that make up the Notepad project.

Another example is setting the numbers in the Repeat column to greater than 1, so that each test case is run multiple times. In this example, the test suite could be saved under the name of "Stress.vts," signifying a stress test, since each test is run many times instead of just once.

There is a setting available in the Options dialog box that allows you to specify that any test case files with a test scenario fail should be placed into a separate test suite file, constructed automatically by the Suite Manager. (See Figure 12-8). This way you can easily re-run the test case files that found problems. This can be very helpful and less time-consuming when tracking down the specific failures.

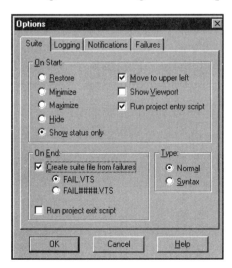

FIGURE 12-8
The Suite Manager can be configured to automatically create a test suite based on test case files that contain test scenarios that failed during the execution of the test suite.

Test Results

After the test suite has completed its run, if the logging setting wasn't turned off, then a log file exists in the same directory as your project. The entire log file for the run of the all of Notepad's test case files is available in Appendix G, "Log File Generated from Run of Notepad Test Suite."

Conclusion

The key to getting a structure for a test suite designed is to jump in, try out some ideas, make some mistakes, and adjust your approach from there. By focusing on one area of the product first, and automating it, you will end up writing many of the key support utilities that will be relied upon by the rest of the test case files.

Do your best to keep things as flexible as possible. It's not easy to look forward and predict what requests your manager will have for output from the test cases. Nor to predict what might change in the product as a result of changes to the test suite.

By staying as flexible as possible, through using common coding guidelines, sharable utilities, and common sense, your test suite will make maintenance less of a daunting task. Keep moving forward, don't concern yourself so much with whether you're doing things right, so that you are constantly second-guessing yourself. You'll find the automation will get easier with time as you continue to practice this fine art.

Summary

In this chapter, we review the structure for our beginning test suite. We then look at those utilities that were modified or added to the noteutil.inc file: *iFailCount()*, *iTestCount()*, *strFailNum()*, *strTestNum()*,and *TestEnd()* functions, as well as at documenting noteutil.inc. We then consider how to run a test suite, using the Suite Manager and the Project Workspace window. Before we run the tests, we configure the Suite Manager to run all our tests, and include a log statement. Finally, all the errors encountered are returned by the Suite Manager. Rather than having to create a new test suite each time, we can save them in a suite file for a later test program.

IV

Advanced Topics

Beyond the Basics

*A*ll the previous chapters in this book have looked at the information needed to get started quickly on automating the testing of a product. In this chapter, we'll take a closer look at some of the features you'll find yourself needing as you get deeper into the building of your test suite.

We'll start by looking at how to work with files, so you can write and retrieve information using any of three separate access methods. These are

▶ Sequential

▶ Binary

▶ Random

Moving on to performance issues, we will focus on writing benchmarks for an application using Visual Test. Then we'll take a brief look at how pointers work in Visual Test, along with how to allocate and free up memory through the Test language. Next, we'll discuss how to link into the dynamic linked libraries (DLLs) available to us in Windows. Finally, we will address the issue of trapping special run-time information using the tools built into Visual Test, including NuMega Technologies' BoundsChecker 3.0 functionality.

File Input/Output

Even though the Visual Test product has routines new to version 4.0 which help you write information out to database files and text files through the use of the *scenario*, *log*, and *fail* statements, sometimes there is a need to control exactly how the information is written out to or read in from a particular file.

An example of how capable Visual Test is in its file input/output (I/O) support is the Digger 1.0 utility, which is part of Software Testing Laboratories' (STLabs) Test Now 2.0 product. Digger, included on the disk in the back of this book, has the ability to read in the resources from a 16-bit executable file, so that a template can be created with that resource information. It steps through the binary *.exe* file, finds the table that holds the information about the application's menus and dialog boxes, and pulls that information into Digger so it can be converted to Test-compatible code. This entire utility was written using the Visual Test language; no special C or C++ had to be written or DLLs created to help with Digger's file I/O.

Note

Even though the Digger 1.0 utility only reads in 16-bit file formats, the Window Grabber tool in the main window of Digger supplies the same functionality by allowing you to click on a window from which you to extract resources. That is, for an executable file that is in the 32-bit file format, use Digger's Window Grabber tool to get resource information.

There are three types of file access that can be done through Visual Test, other than using the scenario, log, and fail statements. These types of access are sequential, binary, and random. Each of these types of access are controlled using the Test language's open statement.

The open Statement

Microsoft Visual Test's syntax for the open statement is

```
OPEN filename$ [FOR mode] AS [#] filenumber% [LEN = reclength%]
```

The square brackets show which sections of the open statement are either optional or are dependent on the *mode* that's being used.

A *file number* must be used when opening a file with the open statement. Subsequent lines of code that work with the file use that file number when identifying which file to write to or read from. Only 20 file numbers are available, so this limited resource must be used in a flexible manner if you're not to step on other team members' use of file I/O through Visual Test.

Most programmers new to the open statement just type any number between 1 and 20 in the place where the file number is required. While this works in the short term, if the routine that performs the I/O operations is placed into a location where it can be used and shared with others, problems can occur when another section of code attempts to use the same file number.

To avoid this problem, Visual Test has a function called *freefile*, the purpose of which is to return the next available file number. When a file's I/O is terminated using the *close* statement, the file number associated with that file is placed back into the pool of free file numbers.

Before opening a file, make sure a variable is set to the return value of a freefile function call and that the variable is then used to open the file and write to or read from it. Also use the variable to close the file. By taking this simple approach to working with files, tracking down error messages like the one shown in Figure 13-1 is no longer necessary.

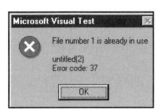

FIGURE 13-1
This error occurs when the same file number is used by two separate files. It can be avoided using the freefile statement.

The individual modes that a file can be opened with are *append*, *binary*, *input*, *output*, and *random*. We'll start by looking at the input, output, and append modes. They are associated with accessing a sequential file.

Sequential Access

A sequential file is typically the same thing as a text file and is used in situations such as keeping track of a test case file's status by writing out information as each test case is performed. While this use has been replaced by the *log* statement, it's still useful when you need to write any other kind of information out to a text file. It's also the easiest of the three file I/O access methods to use.

There are three different modes that can be used with the open statement when working with sequential files:

▶ **append:** Using the *append* mode will cause the file pointer (an internal variable managed by the operating system that keeps track of where we are in the text file) to move to the end of the file, so that any information written to the file using the *print* statement will be placed at the end of that file.

▶ **input:** Using the *input* mode causes the file to be opened and ready for reading in information using the input statement.

▶ **output:** The *output* mode is similar to the append mode, except that it begins writing information out at the beginning of the file, effectively writing over the top of any information previously stored in that file.

Here is an example of writing out to a text file, then reading information back in from that file and printing it to the Output window's Viewport tab:

```
CONST FILENAME$ = "test.txt"
dim iFileNum%, strLineIn$

    viewport clear  'Clear contents of the Output window

    'Get Visual Test to give us an available file number
    iFileNum = FREEFILE

    'Open the file for output so we can write information
    open FILENAME$ for output as #iFileNum

    'Use the #<file-number> to write to the file
    print #iFileNum, "This is an example of writing text to"
    print #iFileNum, "a sequential file. This text was"
    print #iFileNum, "written on ";DATETIME$

    'Close the file and free the file number for
    'others to use.
    close #iFileNum

    'Prove that it wrote something out by reading it
    'back in and printing it to the Output window
    iFileNum = FREEFILE

    open FILENAME$ for input as #iFileNum
```

```
    print "Output of file ";FILENAME$;":"
    while not(EOF(iFileNum))
        line input #iFileNum, strLineIn
        print strLineIn
    wend
    close #iFileNum
end
```

The print and line input statements are used to place or get text to or from a sequential (text) file. The *print* command, along with a # symbol and the number of the file, places the text associated with the print command into the file. A *line input* command, which also uses the # symbol and the file number, pulls text from the sequential file one line at a time.

Note

As implied by its name, a sequential file can only be read from or written to in a sequential manner. That is, you can't jump around in the file to write out or read in information. Also, a file cannot be opened both for reading and for writing at the same time, it must be one or the other.

Because each file has a unique file number associated with it, there can be up to 20 files open at any one time. They can all be read from or written to through the Test language.

Tip

The *freefile()* function doesn't consider a file number to be in use until the file is actually opened. Therefore, if you plan on having multiple files open at the same time, get a freefile number to a file, open it, then get the next freefile number. Otherwise, if you do all of the freefiles at one time, it will result in the same number being returned.

Also note that the close statement can either be used by itself, closing all files at once, or it can be used with specific file numbers to close individual files. I recommend taking the extra time to close each file individually. That way, if the code is ever shared with others, it won't end up closing other programmers' open files which may be lurking behind the scenes in the same code base.

The *EOF()* function was also used. This function returns a true value if the end of the file has been reached. Reading past the end of a file will generate a run-time error with the error message: "Input past end of file." This error is easily avoided by using the *EOF()* function before attempting to read in anything from the data file.

Binary Files

Accessing a binary file isn't any more difficult than working with a sequential text file. The only difference is that more effort is required to keep track of where you are in the file and you must know the file format.

Here is an example of reading in the header of a Windows executable file:

```
type EXEHEADER
    exSignature     as short
    exExtraBytes    as short
    exPages         as short
    exRelocItems    as short
    exHeaderSize    as short
    exMinAlloc      as short
    exMaxAlloc      as short
    exInitSS        as short
    exInitSP        as short
    exCheckSum      as short
    exInitIP        as short
    exInitCS        as short
    exRelocTable    as short 'if val >= &h40 then it's a Win app.
    exOverlay       as short
    reserved        as long
end type 'EXEHEADER

type OLDHEADER
    msdosHeader     as EXEHEADER
    breserved       as string * 28
    winInfoOffset   as short
    wreserved       as short
    msdosStub       as string * 1
end type 'OLDHEADER

dim ohHeader as OLDHEADER
dim strApp$, hFile%

    strApp = inputbox("Enter the full path name of an EXE file:")

if EXISTS(strApp) then
        hFile = FREEFILE                    'get a file number
        open strApp for BINARY as #hFile    'open the file
        get #hFile, 1, ohHeader             'read from byte 1 into
                                            'the variable ohHeader
```

```
        close hFile                          'close the file
    endif
end
```

Admittedly, this looks a little hairy at first, but really it's not. It's made up of everything you've already learned about Visual Test. The first part consists of user-defined types based on the file formats I found in a book called *Inside Windows File Formats* by Tom Swan.

All I did was convert the C structures that he listed in his book to Visual Test-compatible structures. And again, that was just experimentation to figure out what seemed to work best. The most important part of the conversion was making sure I had the right number of bytes for each element in the user-defined types. While it's simple to provide a variable of a particular type for Visual Test to fill with information from a given file, it's another matter to make sure you're getting what you really intended.

According to Tom Swan's book, and as is commented in the code we've used, if the *exRelocTab* field has a value equal to or greater than hex 40 (which is decimal 64), then the executable file is, by definition, a Windows program (as opposed to a DOS executable file).

By checking a couple of other key values to make sure I've read everything in correctly, such as looking at the contents of the variable in the Developer Studio's Test Locals window, as shown in Figure 13-2, I can move on and read in the rest of the information I need. The previous section of code is just a simple example of reading in the first few bytes of information, but it demonstrates the process we need to go through. A structure is created, a variable of that structure or user-defined type is declared, and then that variable is passed to the *get* command associated with the *binary* mode of input. The Test programmer then needs to verify through the Test Locals window in the Developer Studio that the values are as expected.

This form of I/O is the most painstaking because you're not dealing with a single user-defined type, you're dealing with many user-defined types that are reading in information from a file. And you also need access to documentation or books like Tom Swan's *Inside Windows File Formats*.

FIGURE 13-2

The Test Locals window shows the values read into the ohHeader variable by the get statement.

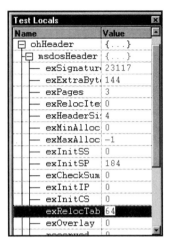

Random Access I/O

The sequential access method is the easiest one to work with, while the binary mode is at the other extreme, because it requires attention to detail and access to file format information. The random mode, for working with random access files, is in between in regards to ease of use.

A random access file is constructed using a specific file structure used throughout that file. By using a single structure (user-defined type), or record, it's easy to randomly pick a record in the file and quickly read it in. This is because the location of a record can be determined simply by looking at the size of a single record and multiplying it by the position of the record you want to get out of the file, minus one record. Also, keep in mind that unlike a standard array in Visual Test, a random access file's contents are 1-based instead of 0-based. That is, to access the first record in a file, you don't access record 0, you access record 1.

In this next example, a type has been created with the intent of tracking statistics on test scenarios. Only test data used in this example is to show how to write to a file and read information back out of it.

```
const MAX_STRING = 40
const FILENAME$  = "test.tst"

type SCENARIOINFO
    iTestID    as integer
    strTestDesc as string * MAX_STRING
```

```
        strResExp    as string * MAX_STRING
        strResRec    as string * MAX_STRING
        fPassed      as integer
    end type 'SCENARIOINFO

    dim iLoop%, iFileNum%, iRecSize%
    dim siRecord as SCENARIOINFO

        viewport clear

        'LEN() isn't just for lengths of strings, it
        'returns how many bytes types take up in memory.
        iRecSize = len(SCENARIOINFO)

        'Notice that LEN= is now used with the open
        'statement. Only for RANDOM mode, though.
        iFileNum = FREEFILE
        open FILENAME for random as iFileNum len=iRecSize

        'Write out some sample records just so we have
        'something to play with. fPassed will flip between
        'TRUE and FALSE just for fun.
        for iLoop = 1 to 10
            'Fill with test info
            siRecord.iTestID    = iLoop
            siRecord.strTestDesc= "Desc for test #"+str$(iLoop)
            siRecord.strResExp  = "Results for #"+str$(iLoop)
            siRecord.strResRec  = "Received for #"+str$(iLoop)
            siRecord.fPassed    = ((iLoop mod 2) = 0)

            put #iFileNum, iLoop, siRecord
        next iLoop

        'Let's grab the 5th record from the file and
        'print it to the Output window's Viewport tab.
        get #iFileNum, 5, siRecord
        print siRecord.iTestID
        print siRecord.strTestDesc
        print siRecord.strResExp
        print siRecord.strResRec

        close #iFileNum
    end
```

Because a single record is used for each random access file, when a section of code requests a specific record out of the file, the access time is quick and the retrieval simple, since the location of the record can be calculated by the size of the records.

Notice that in the user-defined type SCENARIOINFO a fixed-length string was used. Because records can't stray from a fixed size when working with a random mode file, the only way to guarantee that the strings will be the correct size is to use fixed-length strings. Attempting to use a variable-length string will result in this error message: "error VTC4456: Illegal variable type for random file I/O."

Even though much of the information in each record is text, it can't be cleanly viewed using a text editor because not all the values are text values. Take, for example, the *iTestID* field in the SCENARIOINFO type. When it has the value of 1 that's not the same as a string with the number 1 in it. Instead, it's written out as a 1 which, when read into a text editor, is interpreted as Ctrl-A (a CHR$(1)). This is why you see garbage (unprintable characters) mixed in with text when you attempt to open a binary file.

And lastly, notice that the *LEN()* function is used to determine the size of the SCENARIOINFO structure. Many Test programmers only think of using *LEN()* to determine the length of a string. By using it instead of calculating the size of a structure by hand, you're saving yourself time and making your code flexible should the fields in the user-defined type ever be modified or removed.

Benchmark Testing

Benchmark tests for software are created to assess the performance of key sections of source code or user interface components. By running benchmarks for this type of verification the testing team can track whether or not a given feature or features are remaining within the guidelines set by the product specification for performance.

A typical example of using benchmarks is in intensive operations such as searches and sorts, whether they're performed in the computer's memory or on a disk drive. One of the more difficult goals of benchmarking is keeping the results as precise and error-free as possible. If, for example, you were tracking the performance of a search or sort that is disk-drive intensive, the results can have a high degree of error because the disk drive's performance is affected by a number of variables: disk fragmentation; amount of data on the disk; and position of the drive head when the tests began. Seek time and disk latency are timing averages made by the drive manufacturer and also add to the range of the error that can occur in the test results.

Part of the job of benchmarking is to make sure that results reported on performance are accurate and relevant. If a task is reported to have taken 5.4723 seconds, perhaps a second faster than previously reported, and the error is plus or minus 1.35 seconds, it should not necessarily be reported as a performance increase. Such a favorable gain might turn out to be lost the following week when a new build comes out from the development group. Given a +or-1.35 second error, you are setting yourself up for a thumping by the development staff for drawing unnecessary attention from upper management for a supposed performance loss.

Therefore, it's critical to cut down on the *noise*, or errors, that creep into a benchmark's results by measuring only the precise section of code or user interface component that is of concern.

One way to help cut back on these errors is to run a test multiple times, so that an average time can be taken and a more accurate set of numbers communicated to others. Both favorable and unfavorable information must be communicated, but some thought must be put into it, otherwise there is an increased risk of losing faith in the results of the benchmarks.

Here is a simple example of a benchmark test that calculates the average time it takes the Open dialog box to display:

```
'$include 'notemain.inc'
'$include 'noteutil.inc'
'$include 'file.inc'
'$include 'winapi.inc'
```

```
const BENCH_ITERS = 20   'Number of bench iterations

TestBegin
    dim lTimeStart as long, lTimeStop as long
    dim lAvgTime as long, iLoop as integer

    viewport clear

    wMenuSelect(MNU_FILE_OPEN)
    wButtonClick(BTN_CANCEL)

    dTimeStart = GetTickCount()
    for iLoop = 1 to BENCH_ITERS
        wMenuSelect(MNU_FILE_OPEN)

        if (GetText(NULL) = CAP_OPEN) then
            wButtonClick(BTN_CANCEL)
        endif
    next iLoop
    dTimeStop = GetTickCount()

    dAvgTime = (dTimeStop - dTimeStart) / BENCH_ITERS

    log "Average time to display the "+CAP_OPEN
    log "dialog box = ";dAvgTime;" seconds."
TestEnd
```

There are a number of things going on here that need to be pointed out. As this continues the testing of Notepad, we've created a new folder in the Project Workspace named *Benchmark* (see Figure 13-3*)*. Because it's in the same hierarchy as the rest of the test case files, it has access to the following four files:

▶ **notemain.inc:** This has all the main declarations for the Notepad application; it was included so that the MNU_FILE_OPEN and BTN_CANCEL constants could be used.

▶ **noteutil.inc:** This has all of the common utilities; it was included so that the *TestBegin()* and *TestEnd()* subroutines could be used.

▶ **file.inc:** This has the File menu-specific declarations; it was included so that the CAP_OPEN constant could be used.

▶ **winapi.inc:** This is a file we've not yet explored; it has declarations for working with the Windows libraries and was included so that the *GetTickCount()* function could be used to track how many milliseconds it took to open and close the dialog box (accurate to increments of 55 milliseconds).

FIGURE 13-3
A new folder has been added to the Project Workspace that holds benchmark tests. Because this folder is a part of the project it has access to the same include files that the rest of the test case files have.

The *Timer* function, which is intrinsic to the Test language could also have been used. It would have required the use of variables declared as *doubles* instead of *longs*. There isn't any noticeable difference between the two, other than that the Timer function returns the results in seconds instead of milliseconds. (Subtracting the two values of *GetTickCount()* returned 955 milliseconds, whereas the use of the Timer function resulted in .955031967 seconds). By using *Timer()*, however, the need to include winapi.inc is no longer valid, and a good deal of compile time is saved by not including it.

Note

Benchmark times are dependent on the machine and its configuration. You could even go so far as to have the SIMMs (Single In-line Memory Modules which serve as the computer's RAM or main memory) in the machine the same speed to cut back on error in accuracy. If benchmarks are important to your company's product, take care to use the same machine in the same configuration each time benchmarks are generated.

Notice also that before the benchmarks were executed, the dialog box was brought up and dismissed once. The reason for this is because the first time a dialog box is displayed, Windows needs to load in the resources for it.

Assuming that the results sought for displaying the dialog box are based on subsequent accesses to the dialog box, a good deal of error is reduced in the timing calculations by getting the loading of resources out of the way before the benchmarks began. This way the tests are measuring only the time to display the dialog box instead of timing how long it takes to load in the resources as well.

Working with Pointers

Simply put, a *pointer* is a variable that holds a memory address. Sometimes it's the memory location of another variable and at other times it's the address of the first chunk of memory in a block of allocated memory. Everyone has a hard time when they first start working with pointers, so don't feel like it's beyond you if you're new to them. They are crucial when working beyond the basics of Visual Test, however, especially when working with Windows APIs (discussed in the section "Linking to Windows APIs" later in this chapter). If you are new to pointers, I strongly suggest you purchase a book on beginning to advanced programming, because this book assumes you have a general knowledge of programming, including programming with pointers. Even so, we'll take some simple examples of pointers.

Pointers in Visual Test can be of almost any type. You can have a pointer to an integer, long, string, and even other pointers. You can also have pointers to user-defined types. To get the address of a variable, so that it can be assigned to a pointer, the *VarPtr()* function is used. The variable whose address needs to be obtained is placed as the parameter in the *VarPtr()* call, with the return value assigned to the pointer variable. *VarPtr()* plays the equivalent role as the C language's ampersand (&) operator in getting a variable's address. To dereference a pointer so that the value it is pointing to can be determined, the square brackets are used with a zero (0) as an index. For example, ptrX[0] is a dereference of the pointer variable called ptrX. Here is an example of using *VarPtr()* to get the address of a variable:

```
dim ptrX as pointer to integer
dim y as integer
```

```
    y = 7
    ptrX = VarPtr(y)    'Get address of y
    print ptrX          'Address of y is printed
    print ptrX[0]       '7 is printed
end
```

Dereferencing a pointer in the Test language is similar to other languages, but uses its own notation, as shown in Table 13-1.

TABLE 13-1   Examples of how the Test, C and Pascal Languages Dereference a Pointer.

Language	Dereference
Visual Test	ptrX[0]
C	*ptrX
Pascal	ptrX^

When using pointers with user-defined types with fields, the comparisons shown in Table 13-2 can be made.

TABLE 13-2   Examples of how the Test, C and Pascal Languages Dereference a Variable Pointing to a User-Defined Type.

Language	Dereference
Visual Test	ptrX[0].
C language #1:	(*ptrX).
C language #2:	ptrX->
Pascal	ptrX^.

Dynamic Memory

In addition to variables that point to other variables' memory addresses, you can allocate blocks of memory for whatever use you might have.

To do this, use the *allocate* statement. When you've finished using the block of memory, free it up with the *deallocate* statement. Here is an example:

```
dim iLoop as integer
dim ptrA as pointer to long
```

```
        allocate ptrA, 10      'Because ptrA is pointing to a LONG,
                               '40 bytes are allocated because each
                               'LONG value takes up 4 bytes.

        for iLoop = 0 to 9
            ptrA[iLoop] = iLoop * iLoop
        next iLoop

        for iLoop = 0 to 9
            print ptrA[iLoop]
        next iLoop

        deallocate ptrA
    end
```

This source code could have been written using an array, so it seems kind of silly to go through the extra steps of allocating and deallocating memory. But this was just a simple example to get us started. Now, the next example is a little more fun and demonstrates how a linked list can be created using the Test language. It allocates memory one node at a time, then uses a recursive subroutine to free up the allocated memory:

```
'Simple example of a singly-linked list
const MAX_NODES = 20

type CTRLNODE
    strDesc as string
    pcnNext as pointer to CTRLNODE
end type 'CTRLNODE

dim cnHead as CTRLNODE
dim pcnTemp as pointer to CTRLNODE
dim iLoop as integer

    viewport clear
    iLoop = 0
    cnHead.strDesc = "Node # 0"

    'pcnTemp is a temporary pointer that steps through
    'the list of all of the records, setting the values
    'of each one's strDesc field.
    pcnTemp = varptr(cnHead)
```

```
    'Allocate one node at a time
    do
        iLoop = iLoop + 1
        allocate pcnTemp[0].pcnNext, 1
        pcnTemp = pcnTemp[0].pcnNext
        pcnTemp[0].strDesc = "Node #"+str$(iLoop)
    loop until  (iLoop >= MAX_NODES)

    'Print the nodes out
    pcnTemp = varptr(cnHead)
    while (pcnTemp <> NULL)
        print pcnTemp[0].strDesc
        pcnTemp = pcnTemp[0].pcnNext
    wend

    FreeNodes(varptr(cnHead))
end

'Easiest way to free up a singly-linked list
'is recursively.
sub FreeNodes(pcnNode as pointer to CTRLNODE)
    if (pcnNode <> NULL) then
        FreeNodes(pcnNode[0].pcnNext)
        deallocate pcnNode
    endif
end sub 'FreeNodes
```

Visual Test's language really is a very capable and fully functional programming language. I've wondered why Visual BASIC doesn't follow the Visual Test team's lead and make pointers available so that linked lists, open-ended hash tables, binary trees, directed graphs, and other basic data structures can be created. This could be especially useful in automated testing when tracking paths that have been taken.

A Short Story

On one project I had a feature that I had to test each time I progressed another level deeper in the product. That feature allowed me to escape back to the very top of the menu hierarchy, no matter how deep I was into the program's menu tree. No big deal, right? Well, the trick was being able to work my way back down to where I was, so that I could

(continued)

> **A Short Story** (Continued)
>
> continue where I left off. The only way to do this cleanly, without a lot of repeated code, was to build a linked list that kept track of my menu selections as I stepped deeper into the program. When I popped back to the top of the structure, all I had to do was walk the linked list using the menu selections it had recorded on my way down, to return to where I was. By using a linked list that allocated memory only as it was needed, I didn't need to use an array that would sit around taking up memory even when it wasn't being used. The linked list grew and shrank depending on how deep I was in the menu structure.

Linking to Windows APIs

One of the great features of Visual Test is its ability to link into Windows APIs and other dynamic linked libraries (DLLs). This functionality makes the Visual Test language extensible; if you have a DLL that has functionality you want to access from Visual Test, odds are you'll be able to link into it without any trouble.

A Simple Example

To link into a DLL, you must type in a declaration or *prototype* for linking into that library. The easiest way to explain this is with an example:

```
declare function MessageBox lib "user32.dll" _
        alias "MessageBoxA" (hWnd&, lpText$, lpCaption$, uType&) _
        as long

MessageBox(NULL, "This is our test message box", _
        "Test Caption", MB_OK OR MB ICONSTOP)
```

This is yet another piece of source code that looks kind of hairy, right? Again, it's not as bad as it looks. It looks especially weird because the lines were so long that continuation marks (_) were used to make the code more easy to read.

The first line declares that a function called *MessageBox()* is going to be based upon a function in the user32.dll called *MessageBoxA()*. Because linking into a DLL is case-sensitive, even though Visual Test's compiler is case-insensitive, the *alias* option was provided so that the correct upper and lowercase characters can be used for establishing the link with the DLL. It also provides a way for the Test programmer to use a function name different than the one used in the actual DLL.

Our example goes one step further in that *MessageBox()* is no longer available, as was the case in the 16-bit version of the DLLs. It is now called *MessageBoxA()*. Through this same aliasing technique, it's also possible to declare a function with a name to be used through the Test language that is different from the name of the actual function in the dynamic link library. In our example, we linked to *MessageBoxA()* but will use the name *MessageBox()* when accessing the function through the Test language.

That's all there is to establishing a link with a function in a DLL. Now, depending on the function itself, it can get a little more challenging and therefore a little more fun.

Another Example

Let's take an example that's a little more involved and requires a little more attention to what's going on. Windows 3.1 introduced the concept of *common dialogs boxes* that made frequently used dialog boxes available to developers at a fraction of the time it would take to write comparable dialog boxes. At the same time, if developers used these common dialog boxes they got a free ride whenever Microsoft made changes to those dialog boxes in future versions of Windows.

An example of a common dialog box is the Open dialog box. If a program is written and run under Windows 3.1x, the Open dialog box is an old style dialog box associated with Windows 3.1x. When running that same program under Windows 95, without any changes to that program's source code, the dialog box that appears is the new and improved Windows 95 dialog box, shown in Figure 13-4.

FIGURE 13-4
The Windows common
Open dialog box.

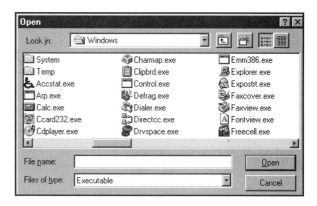

This is the power of the common dialog box. The code that manages the user's actions — clicking on a button, filling the contents of a list box, verifying that a file exists, navigating up and down the directory tree, and so on — has been programmed and tested by Microsoft already. The only thing a Windows programmer needs to do is supply the initialization information so that the dialog box can display itself appropriately and then return information back to the program that invoked it.

Here is an example of a more challenging API call using the common Open dialog box. The API to display the Open dialog box is *GetOpenFilename()*.

```
'*** Include file ***
'$include 'winapi.inc'

'*** My constants ***
const MAXPATH   = 128        'Max size path
const FILTDELIM = ","        'Filter delimeter
const NUL       = CHR$(0)    'A string NULL   specific to Visual Test
                                              see p. 312

'*** Main program ***
dim strFilter as string
                                        → Files of type
    viewport clear
    strFilter = "Executable,*.exe,Text,*.txt,Word,*.doc"
    print strGetFile("C:\WINDOWS",strFilter)
END

'*** Function def ***
function strGetFile(strDir$, strFilter$) AS STRING
```

```
dim iRet          AS INTEGER
dim ofnFile       AS OPENFILENAME
dim strFileChoice AS STRING * MAXPATH
dim strStartDir   AS STRING * MAXPATH
dim strFileFilter AS STRING * MAXPATH
```

adds null to the string directory

```
strStartDir = strDir+NUL  'Ensure this is null terminated

'Replace all FILTDELIM characters with CHR$(0). Make sure
'string is terminated with two nulls as required by
'GetOpenFileName() API.
iRet = INSTR(strFilter, FILTDELIM)
while (iRet)
    MID$(strFilter, iRet, 1) = NUL
    iRet = INSTR(strFilter, FILTDELIM)
wend
strFileFilter = trim$(strFilter) + NUL + NUL

'Initialize the structure before passing it
ofnFile.lStructSize      = LEN(OPENFILENAME)
ofnFile.hwndOwner        = wGetActWnd(0)
ofnFile.lpstrFilter      = cptr(varptr(strFileFilter))
ofnFile.nFilterIndex     = 1
ofnFile.lpstrInitialDir  = cptr(varptr(strStartDir))
ofnFile.lpstrFile        = cptr(varptr(strFileChoice))
ofnFile.nMaxFile         = LEN(strFileChoice)
ofnFile.Flags            = OFN_FILEMUSTEXIST OR _
                           OFN_HIDEREADONLY  OR _
                           OFN_PATHMUSTEXIST

if GetOpenFileName(ofnFile) then
    strGetFile = trim$(trim$(strFileChoice,0))
else
    strGetFile = ""
endif
end function 'strGetFile
```

See p.310

Yet another gross-looking piece of code, you say? While there are a number of things going on that we need to look at, it's not all that bad, especially as it's broken down and explained step by step. In most cases, it takes a lot of experimentation with a function until it works correctly, and then it takes some hands-on testing to make sure it's working as expected.

The first part of coming up with a piece of code like this is to determine which API you'd like to use. This requires some hunting through the Win32 Software Development Kit's (SDK's) online help. I found it when I was looking at the new features available in Windows 3.1 from the previous version of Windows 3.0. It's under the heading of Common Dialog Box Functions (see Figure 13-5).

FIGURE 13-5
Tracking down a function that does what you want takes a lot of searching and persistence.

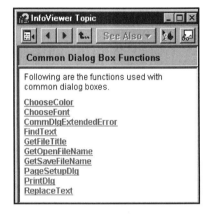

The only way you're going to know what's in the SDK's online help is to take some time to scroll through it to familiarize yourself with what's available. This is the same action you should take with the Visual Test online help.

Note

Use the InfoViewer toolbar to tell the editor which online help file to search when performing keyword lookups. That is, if you use the toolbar to select the Win32 Software Development Kit, then search on the function name GetOpenFileName, the Win32 SDK help file will be searched. An even better shortcut is to select the help file as just described, then type the function name into the Developer Studio editor, click on the function name, and press the F1 key to invoke the context-sensitive help.

Once you've found the function you want to work with, read through the online documentation to see how it works. The first thing you'll notice is that it's all assuming that you're going to access the libraries through C or C++. Therefore, you're going to notice C and C++ types being used that you may not be familiar with. Again, sweat it out. C and C++ have the same base types as the Test language does. What Microsoft has done with the SDK is to add some more types created from those base types.

In some cases, even though the online help for the main routine is found, deeper digging is required. In the case of *GetOpenFileName()*, as shown in Figure 13-6, a structure called OPENFILENAME is passed to the function.

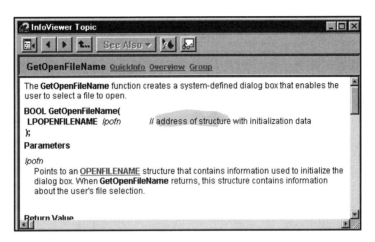

FIGURE 13-6   The *GetOpenFileName()* function's documentation is available in the Win32 SDK's online help.

Clicking on the highlighted structure in the help file shows exactly what it looks like, as shown in Figure 13-7.

By jumping to the openfilename topic in the online help, we've finally reached the meat of working with the *GetOpenFileName* function. Remember, though, that this help topic is based on the C language and therefore some of the types are foreign to us as Test programmers. Fortunately, the Visual Test team created an include file for us called winapi.inc. The C structure shown in Figure 13-7 has a counterpart in the winapi.inc file with the same user-defined type name. The Test version of this structure, or user-defined type, is shown here:

```
type OPENFILENAME
    lStructSize         as long
    hwndOwner           as long
    hInstance           as long
    lpstrFilter         as pointer to string * 1
    lpstrCustomFilter   as pointer to string * 1
    nMaxCustFilter      as long
    nFilterIndex        as long
```

```
          lpstrFile        as pointer to string * 1
          nMaxFile         as long
          lpstrFileTitle   as pointer to string * 1
          nMaxFileTitle    as long
          lpstrInitialDir  as pointer to string * 1
          lpstrTitle       as pointer to string * 1
          Flags            as long
          nFileOffset      as short
          nFileExtension   as short
          lpstrDefExt      as pointer to string * 1
          lCustData        as long
          lpfnHook         as dlgproc
          lpTemplateName   as pointer to string * 1
      end type
```

FIGURE 13-7

The OPENFILENAME structure is used by the *GetOpenFileName()* function. It needs to be initialized with data based on how you want it to be displayed.

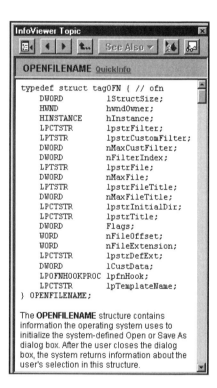

The winapi.inc file provides function prototypes, sometimes referred to as *links*, for the same APIs used by Windows developers working in the C language. winapi.inc also provides the Test language user-defined types that match the C structures used by many of the APIs.

Note

Referring to Table 13-3, you'll notice that anytime a C type has anything to do with a *word*, it is a *short* in the Test language. A *long* is a *long*, any kind of handle (such as *hwnd* or *hdc*) is a *long*, and any pointer to a string in a user-defined type is a *pointer to string* * 1 in the Test language.

TABLE 13-3   Summary of Some of the Declarations Used By C Programmers Who Write Windows Applications and the Test Language Equivalent.

Description	C language	Visual Test equivalent
16-bit Integer	*word*	*short*
32-bit Integer (long)	*dword*	*long*
Handle to a window	*hwnd*	*long*
Handle to an instance	*hinstance*	*long*
Long pointer to constant string	*lpctstr*	*pointer to string * 1*
Long pointer to a string	*lptstr*	*pointer to string * 1*
Pointer to a function	*lpfnhookproc*	*dlgproc*
RGB color reference	*colorref*	*long*
Long parameter	*lparam*	*long*
Word parameter	*wparam*	*short*
Generic handle	*handle*	*long*
Handle to a device context	*hdc*	*long*

If you feel overwhelmed at first, don't worry about it, it'll make more sense as you use them more and more. Fortunately the winapi.inc file already has the Visual Test equivalents for most of the Windows APIs, with their structures and constants already defined for you. You'll really be tested on how well you understand this when you're working with someone else's DLLs. And even then, it's usually trial and error, so just press on until it falls into place.

Here again is the first part of the code that brings in the winapi.inc file and tests our function (*strGetFile()*), written to wrap around the *GetOpenFileName* API.

```
'*** Include file ***
'$include 'winapi.inc'

'*** My constants ***
const MAXPATH   = 128        'Max size path
```

```
const FILTDELIM = ","        'Filter delimeter
const NUL       = CHR$(0)    'A string NULL

'*** Main program ***
dim strFilter as string

    viewport clear
    strFilter = "Executable,*.exe,Text,*.txt,Word,*.doc"
    print strGetFile("C:\WINDOWS",strFilter)
END
```

This first section includes the winapi.inc file, making all of the declarations relating to the APIs available to use, and linking into those APIs. Next, it defines some constants that we'll be needing in our function to make it easier to adjust things later, should it become necessary. And finally, because we created a function of our own to call the Windows API that displays the Open dialog box (our function is called *strGetFile*), we need to call that function with some test data to get it to display the dialog box.

Note

When reading through the online help about the GetOpenFileName API it commented on what fields in the user-defined type needed to be filled and with what information. To make it simple, our function only requires two parameters — the starting directory and the filter used by the dialog box — to display the Open dialog box. The rest of the parameters are set within the function.

In the next piece of code, we've taken the front portion of the *strGetFile* function, to show you what the first steps of the function are. In the C language, most all of the functions that deal with strings expect a byte at the end of the string with a zero value.

This is called a *null* character and is represented in C by a "\0". In Visual Test, however, it is represented by a CHR$(0) (*not* the null value, which is used with pointers). This is known as a *zero-terminated* or *null-terminated* string and is used by the C libraries to determine when they've reached the end of a string.

If the null termination is forgotten, many times the result is a General Protection Fault, because the function read past the end of the string into a section of memory that might be allocated by someone else. Therefore, you'll notice that a null (which, as you'll notice in the next-to-last piece of code, is a constant we created and set to CHR$(0)) is appended to the *strDir* parameter that specifies that directory to be used by the Open dialog box.

These are the first few lines of our function, which add the required null characters to the strings that were passed and also step through the filter string, formatting it to be compatible with the *GetOpenFileName* API's requirements.

```
'*** Function def ***
function strGetFile(strDir$, strFilter$) AS STRING
    dim iRet            AS INTEGER
    dim ofnFile         AS OPENFILENAME
    dim strFileChoice   AS STRING * MAXPATH
    dim strStartDir     AS STRING * MAXPATH
    dim strFileFilter   AS STRING * MAXPATH

    strStartDir = strDir+NUL   'Ensure this is null terminated

    'Replace all FILTDELIM characters with CHR$(0). Make sure
    'string is terminated with two nulls as required by
    'GetOpenFileName() API.
    iRet = INSTR(strFilter, FILTDELIM)
    while (iRet)
        MID$(strFilter, iRet, 1) = NUL
        iRet = INSTR(strFilter, FILTDELIM)
    wend
    strFileFilter = trim$(strFilter) + NUL + NUL
```

required by API

Also in this piece of code, you'll notice that *strFilter* is being stepped through, so that the commas, specified by the FILTDELIM constant, can be removed and replaced with null characters. This is done because it's what the online documentation for the OPENFILENAME structure has told us to do. The filter string must be a description of the filter, a null character, and then the actual filter to be used, another null, then another filter description, a null, and the filter, and so on.

After all filter descriptions and filters have been supplied, two null characters must be placed at the end of the string. Again, this is according to the documentation on the API and how it wants the information to be provided to it. For example:

```
"Executable file<NULL>*.EXE<NULL>Text file<NULL>*.TXT<NULL><NULL>"
```

where <NULL> is a CHR$(0).

This step could have been avoided by requiring the user of our function to pass a string like this to our function:

```
"Executable file"+CHR$(0)+"*.EXE"+CHR$(0)+"Text
file"+CHR$(0)+"*.TXT"+CHR$(0)+CHR$(0).
```

Instead, to make a friendlier function, we only require a comma-separated string and then have our function replace the commas with the null characters.

The last part of our function simply assigns values to the variable ofnFile, which was declared of the type OPENFILENAME. A variable of OPENFILENAME is required by the *GetOpenFileName* API and is defined in the winapi.inc file provided by Visual Test:

```
      'Initialize the structure before passing it
      ofnFile.lStructSize    = LEN(OPENFILENAME)
      ofnFile.hwndOwner      = wGetActWnd(0)
      ofnFile.lpstrFilter    = cptr(varptr(strFileFilter))
      ofnFile.nFilterIndex   = 1
      ofnFile.lpstrInitialDir = cptr(varptr(strStartDir))
      ofnFile.lpstrFile      = cptr(varptr(strFileChoice))
      ofnFile.nMaxFile       = LEN(strFileChoice)
      ofnFile.Flags          = OFN_FILEMUSTEXIST OR _
                               OFN_HIDEREADONLY  OR _
                               OFN_PATHMUSTEXIST

      if GetOpenFileName(ofnFile) then
          strGetFile = trim$(trim$(strFileChoice,0))
      else
          strGetFile = ""
      endif
  end function 'strGetFile
```

All that's left is to fill in the OPENFILENAME structure using the ofnFile variable, which was declared at the top of this function. The first field in the structure is *lStructSize* and needs to be set to the size of the structure. Instead of counting up how many bytes the structure uses, the quicker method is to use the LEN function, which is intrinsic to the Test language.

The hwndOwner field is set to wGetActWnd(0), which is also an intrinsic function of the Test language. By passing zero (0) to wGetActWnd(), it returns the handle to the currently active window and assigns it to hwndOwner. This tells the GetOpenFileName function who the *parent* of the Open dialog box is and won't allow the dialog box to fall behind its parent window, even when you click on that parent.

Here's where things get a bit strange. The lpstrFilter field requires a pointer to a string that contains the list of filters to be used by the Open dialog box. Looking back three pieces of code, to the one that shows the Test language version of the OPENFILENAME structure, you'll see that this field is declared as *pointer to a string * 1*.

The problem is the *strFileFilter*, which is what lpstrFilter (actually ofnFile.lpstrFilter) is being set to, is a fixed-length string of size MAX-PATH (our previously defined constant of 128 characters). We can get a pointer to our strFileFilter string by using the Test language's VARPTR(), but it will be a pointer to a string of size 128 and lpstrFilter only wants a string of size 1.

The way around this is to change the pointer returned by VARPTR() into an un-typed, or *void*, pointer. This is done using the CPTR function, which is also part of the Test language. *CPTR()* makes the pointer generic, so that the Test compiler won't complain about a type mismatch. (Attempting to assign a 128 character string to a 1 character string).

Why did the Visual Test team members declare it as a pointer to a string of size 1 instead of 128? Because they didn't know what size string would be passed to it. Size 1 is the smallest string pointer they can create and therefore that is what was used.

The rest of the fields are initialized based on the requirements specified by the online help. This includes strFileChoice, which serves as a buffer that is filled when the call to *GetOpenFileName()* returns. Therefore, the last part of the code, where the API is called and the structure passed, if you select a legal file from the Open dialog box, the API returns a non-zero value (interpreted as true) and your function is assigned the value that was placed in the strFileChoice field before the API returned.

If you select the Cancel button in the dialog box or the API fails in some way, a false (0) value is returned and we assign an empty string to be returned by our function.

Callback Functions

A callback function is simply a function that passes a pointer to itself, so that others can dereference that pointer to call back that function whenever it's needed. An example of a callback function is a window procedure, or *winproc*. A winproc is a function associated with a window that processes all messages sent to that window. Every single window in Windows has a winproc associated with it, so that it can deal with things like mouse movements or clicks on the window. A *dialogproc* is the same idea as a winproc, except that it focuses specifically on handling messages for dialog boxes.

A simple example of a callback function is working with the *SetTimer* API, which is declared in the Win32 SDK as:

```
UINT SetTimer(HWND hwnd, UINT idTimer, UINT uTimeout, TIMERPROC
tmprc);
```

A *UINT* is an unsigned-integer, meaning that the last bit in that integer isn't used to signify whether the number is positive or negative. Therefore, since that sign-bit is now ignored, it can allow for large positive integers. In Visual Test there's no such thing as an unsigned integer and so really big numbers will still appear to Visual Test as negative numbers. This doesn't hurt anything, other than confuse the Test programmer now and then. There will be times when you are expecting a large positive number, but find a negative number showing up in the Test Locals window. The *hwnd* we already know from Table 13-3 to be a *long*.

Well, what about that *timerproc* type then? As we look further down into the online help for the SetTimer API we find that *timerproc* is declared as:

```
VOID CALLBACK TimerProc(HWND hwnd, UINT uMsg, UINT idEvent, DWORD
dwTime);
```

So TimerProc is actually a pointer to a type of function that needs to be supplied by the programmer.

The SetTimer API is a nifty little function that creates what is known as a *timer* which, after a certain amount of time (specified when the timer was created), dereferences a pointer to a function and calls it with the parameters shown in the TimerProc declaration. It's up to the programmer to fill in the details of what TimerProc does when it's called: to define the *TimerProc()* function.

Here is an example of a callback function using the SetTimer API. By providing a pointer to a function we've written called aTest to the SetTimer API, aTest() will be called whenever 1 second elapses:

```
'$include 'winapi.inc'

global giCount%
dim iTimerID%
dim pfnaTest as TIMERPROC

    viewport clear
    pfnaTest = varptr(aTest)
    iTimerID = SetTimer(0,0,1000,pfnaTest)

    giCount = 0
    while (giCount < 10)
        sleep .1
        print "Waiting for timer"
    wend

    KillTimer(0,iTimerID)
end

sub aTest(hWnd&, iMsg&, iEvent&, dwTime&)
    giCount = giCount + 1
    print "Callback #";giCount
end sub 'aTest
```

When you look at this code, you'll probably do a double-take when you see the *while* statement. That statement loops until the variable giCount is equal to or greater than 10; yet nowhere in the loop does it increment that counter. It appears to be an endless loop.

Because a timer was created using the SetTimer API, a timer delay of 1000 milliseconds (1 second) was specified, and a pointer to the function aTest() was passed, even though the program was looping. When the timer calls back aTest() it's as if a function call to aTest() were inserted at the next line of code to execute. The function completes its task and control returns back to where the execution left off before the interruption.

Tip

One problem with Visual Test that previous versions didn't have is that it doesn't yield often enough to allow the timer to perform the callback. Therefore, it's necessary to put in a delay, albeit a small one (such as sleep .1).

Capturing Information

The Visual Test language provides a number of ways to trap information during the execution of a test suite. The way these traps work is very similar to how a callback function works, except these are built into the language.

Trapping Run-time Errors

A run-time error is an error that is generated through some action of the Test language that is illegal and occurs while the script is executing. The error isn't a syntax error or an error that could have been caught by the compiler, it's an error that could not have been determined to have existed until the script actually executed.

An example of a run-time error is having the script attempt to access an element of an array that doesn't exist, resulting in an out-of-bounds error. Another example of a run-time error is attempting to access a file that doesn't exist. In both of these examples, the compiler could not have determined that an error condition existed until the scripts were actually executed.

The following script starts by setting up a run-time error trap using the *on error goto* statement and then purposely causes an error by attempting to delete a nonexistent file, to demonstrate how error handling works.

```
on error goto MyErrorHandler
dim i$

    viewport clear
    i$ = "thisisanerrorwaitingtohappen.txt"
    print i$
    kill(i$)     'The KILL statement deletes a file
end

MyErrorHandler:
    print "An error occurred."
```

The actual code for a *run-time error handler* is typically placed after the main code's final *end* statement. If it were placed before the end of the main code block, the error handler's code would be executed, since *MyErrorHandler* is only a label used by the goto statement and not a subroutine or function that only executes when called.

OPTIONS IN AN ERROR HANDLER

Once an error occurs, and execution jumps down into the error handling code, there are a number of options available to the Test programmer. The first is to simply *resume* from the same line on which the error occurred. Perhaps the error handler fixes whatever the error condition is and allows the interpreter another shot at the same line of code.

Another option is to simply continue on with the next line of code in the test script. This can be done using the *resume next* statement. Many people who want their scripts to continue no matter what, use this as their only form of error handling. The result is a script that trips along and, sometimes, recovers from the error. Other times the script just keeps tripping until the end of the script is reached. If at all possible, it's preferable to handle each error in some way, so that execution can continue as cleanly as possible.

Another option is to resume operation but at a different section of code. This can be accomplished using the *resume <label>* statement where <label> is a goto label that exists some place in the code base. Execution then moves to that section of code.

The final option is new to Visual Test and allows for multiple error handlers in the same script. The *resume error* statement communicates that it doesn't want to deal with the error, and that the error handler the next level up can deal with the problem. If no other error handler exists, the script's execution terminates and a message box describing the error is presented to the Test programmer.

Note

There can be only one global error handler to which local errors can be escalated. If a local error handler ignores an error using the resume error statement it is passed on to the global error handler. While there can only be one global error handler, it can be changed as the script is executing should the situation merit that a different catchall error trap be used.

LOCAL ERROR HANDLERS

Visual Test has provided Test programmers with another level of run-time error handling. This is known as the *local handler* and is specified by using the keyword "local" in the *on error goto* statement.

This type of error handling allows the user to create error handlers within functions and subroutines that are specific only to those routines. Something of a hierarchy is set up by doing this, which is especially noticeable when the main section of code that has an error handler calls a function that has an error handler, which in turn calls another function or subroutine, which also has an error handler. (!!)

Each function or subroutine can attempt to process its own errors by using the *on local error goto* statement and if things get too out of hand, the routine can use the resume error statement, which bumps error handling up one level. The statement for setting up a local error trap must be inside the function or subroutine for which it is trapping errors.

A local error handler remains active as long as execution continues in the subroutine or function that contains it. Once the subroutine or function finishes execution, the error handler for that routine goes out of scope and is turned off.

To turn off an on error goto statement, you need only supply a zero (0) in place of a label (*on error goto 0*).

INFORMATION IN AN ERROR HANDLER

There are a few functions and a global variable that are available to you specifically for getting information about the run-time error that occurred. The first function is *ERF()*, which returns the name of the file in which the error occurred. *ERL()* is similar to *ERF()*, except that it returns the line number on which the error was generated. And the *ERR* global variable has the error number associated with the error that most recently occurred. Used in conjunction with the *ERROR$* function, passing ERR to *ERROR$()* will return an error string associated with the specified error.

With access to this type of information, you can write out the same information that would have otherwise been displayed in a message box had the error trap not been activated. And, by writing code to handle specific error conditions that occur, you have a better chance of getting the script back on track by fixing the problem in the error handler.

Trapping BoundsChecker Information

NuMega Technologies, Inc. and the Microsoft Visual Test team put their heads together to add an additional way to gather as much information as possible during the running of a test suite. This was by using the BoundsChecker technology.

There are two ways this technology can be invoked in Visual Test. The first is to use BOUNDSCHECKER as a parameter on the *run* statement (in other words, RUN "NOTEPAD.EXE",BOUNDSCHECKER). This generates a run-time error when BoundsChecker detects any errors in the Notepad application. Or, if a *BoundsCheckerNotify* statement has been put in place prior to running the Notepad application, that handler will be called should an error occur.

You can create a BoundsCheckerNotify notification if you want to use BoundsChecker without including it as part of the run statement. This notification is very similar to the on error goto statement except that, instead of giving it a label to go to in the code base, it's given the name of a subroutine to be called when the error or notification occurs.

The next piece of code gives an example of a BoundsChecker notification trap. Just like an on error goto statement, the BoundsChecker notification can be invoked at the beginning of the script so that the entire script can make use of the BoundsChecker information:

```
on BoundsCheckerNotify (NULL) call MyErrorHandler

    viewport clear
    run "notepad.exe", BOUNDSCHECKER     'In lieu of NOWAIT parameter

    'run all test scenarios

    wMenuSelect("File\Exit")
end

sub MyErrorHandler(vInfo as variant)
    print "A BoundsChecker error occurred: ";vInfo
end sub
```

The vInfo parameter is a *variant* type, meaning that any kind of value can be passed to it.

Flexible Error Handling

The error handling code needs to be placed in the upper hierarchy of the shared files so that it is automatically invoked when a test case file includes the main *.inc* files it needs. This is one method of making sure that the same error handling information is shared throughout the code base.

Another approach is to create a generic error handler that is at the top of the hierarchy for handling any error conditions that are ignored by the test case files. Then the error handling can be handled by the test case itself or ignored, so that the handler for the test suite can take a crack at it.

An approach that I used before this multi-tiered error handling was introduced was to create an include file called *err_hdr.inc* (error header) that held the front, initialization portion of the on error handler and notifications. This was included with the rest of the include files.

Another file called *err_ftr.inc* (error footer) was created and included right after the test case file's end statement. It held the meat of the error handling code that actually attempted to deal with the error.

The reasoning behind this approach was that the test case template—and therefore all test case files—would automatically include the error handling source code. Should modifications need to be made, only the err_hdr.inc and err_ftr.inc files themselves need be updated, since they are automatically brought in by the test case files. This is a simple approach and is still valid, but not as flexible as using multiple levels of error handling.

Conclusion

This chapter focused on topics that weren't covered in Chapter 5, so that some advanced topics in using Visual Test could be addressed. Because many of the topics quickly approach the area of Windows programming, discussion can quickly leave the scope of this book and move into how to program Windows applications.

Visual Test is a very capable programming language and can actually be used to create a Windows application if one wishes to use it as that kind of tool. That's not the true purpose of the language, however. It is an attempt to provide as much flexibility as possible so that a Test programmer is not hindered by the tool. Microsoft's Visual Test team has succeeded in creating a power automation tool but should the reader wish to proceed into the topics of Windows programming, there are books on the market focused specifically on that topic.

Summary

This chapter looks at how to work with files, then at performance issues, such as writing benchmarks, pointers, allocating and freeing up memory, dynamic linked libraries (DLLs), how to link into Windows application programmer interfaces (APIs), and trapping special run-time information using the tools built into Visual Test, including NuMega Technologies' BoundsChecker 3.0 functionality.

CHAPTER 14

Working with Resources

*V*ersions 2.0 and 3.0 of Microsoft Test offered the ability to add menus, dialog boxes, and a special icon bar to test scripts. The same capability is available in Visual Test 4.0, except that it now uses the User Interface Editor that comes with the Developer Studio. The icon bar and sysMenu functionalities, however, have been removed. The abilities to work with string tables, bitmaps, icons, and cursors, however, have been added.

Visual Test Resource Files

Visual Test scripts can make use of resources — an interface element providing a means of communication between the program and the user — through the use of a Visual Test Resource (*.vtr*) file. All the different types of resources that can be created for use by Visual Test can be stored in one file so as to avoid multiple files laying around on the Test programmer's machine.

In previous versions of Test, a separate include (*.inc*) file was needed to keep track of the information needed to work with the resources stored in a *.res* file. In Visual Test 4.0, however, these two files have been combined into the single *.vtr* file to make things less complex. And the Visual Test team went one step further. Now the *.vtr* file can be combined with a pseudo-code (*.pcd*) file that is created when compiling and saving a Test language source code file. No longer is it necessary to track multiple files when distributing compiled test cases to other machines. Now the *.vtr* file is a part of the compiled script file.

Creating a Resource File

A Visual Test Resource file can be created in the Developer Studio by selecting the New menu item under the File menu, and then selecting the Test Resource item from the dialog box, as shown in Figure 14-1.

FIGURE 14-1

The Test programmer is given the option of what type of new item to create. To create a *.vtr* file, the Test Resource item in the New dialog box's list box should be selected.

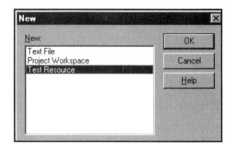

When a new resource file is first created, it looks similar to the screen shown in Figure 14-2. No resources yet exist, but can be easily added by selecting the Resource... menu item from the Developer Studio's Insert menu.

FIGURE 14-2

A new resource file has been created showing nothing more than a folder named *TestRes1*.

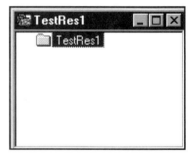

When creating a new resource via the Insert menu, or through the appropriate toolbar icon, the Test programmer has nine types of resources from which to choose, as shown in Figure 14-3. The main types of resources that Test programmers find themselves creating are Menus, String Tables, and Dialog boxes. The remainder of the resources can be used individually, or as part of the design for menus and dialog boxes (for example, icons and bitmaps can be added to a dialog box, and accelerator tables can work with menus).

As an optional shortcut, you may also right-click on the TestRes1 folder to insert items much like you can when creating items in a Test project.

Tip

FIGURE 14-3
Nine kinds of resources can be created in the Developer Studio and saved into a Visual Test Resource (*.vtr*) file.

Each type of resource has a folder associated with it. As more resources are created for a *.vtr* file they are automatically placed into the appropriate folder. For a large project that is using a number of different types of resources, the Test programmer might find that the resource file is using many or all of the different types of resources. Figure 14-4 shows what a typical resource file might look like in this situation.

FIGURE 14-4
As more of the nine types of resources are added, the *.vtr* file's graphical depiction will look similar to this.

One of the nine types of resources that can be created is the Toolbar resource. As of this writing, it has not been determined exactly how this resource is used in relation to Visual Test. Speculation is that it is a carryover from what is a part of the Developer Studio when working with Visual C++.

Note

The Resource Editors

When creating any kind of resource for a Visual Test Resource file, the *properties* (or settings) associated with each resource are accessible via the Properties dialog box. The contents of this dialog box change depending on the individual resource whose settings are being modified.

Tip

Use the *pushpin* button in the upper-left corner of the Properties dialog box (see Figure 14-5) to force the dialog box to remain visible while working with any of the editors.

FIGURE 14-5 The Properties dialog box for the Accelerator Editor shows the simplicity of this type of resource. It allows the Test programmer to determine which key and modifier to use to invoke an action. Also, the ID setting is used to associate an accelerator with a menu item.

Accelerator Editor

The Accelerator Editor allows for associating a *shortcut* or *accelerator key* with a menu item or specific action. This editor is used to create an accelerator key associated with a given menu item. By creating a new resource for an accelerator key or keys, and by typing the key for which an accelerator is to be created, the Test programmer is prompted with the Properties dialog box associated with accelerator keys. The Test programmer then defines exactly which keystrokes are to be used to invoke the action and to which menu item it is associated. (When we look at creating a menu later in this chapter, we will use the Accelerator Editor to create shortcuts.)

Binary Editor

The Binary Editor is what the Developer Studio uses when it is asked to open a non-text file that is not recognized as any of the resource types supported by the Developer Studio (for example: bitmap, icon, cursor). It is an editor that is not for the faint of heart. Specifically, it allows for the manipulation of data at the binary level so that individual bytes can be modified. Changing these types of values can result in a file being interpreted as corrupt, and may cause the file to act unexpectedly. Only use this editor if you know what you're doing at the byte level in a binary file. Figure 14-6 shows what a wave file looks like when opened in the Developer Studio.

```
32dohs.wav                                                           _ □ X
000000  52 49 46 46 B3 B6 02 00   57 41 56 45 66 6D 74 20   RIFF....WAVEfmt
000010  10 00 00 00 01 00 01 00   E0 2E 00 00 E0 2E 00 00   ................
000020  01 00 08 00 64 61 74 61   8F B6 02 00 80 7E 7E 7E   ....data....~~~
000030  7F 7F 7E 7F 7E 7E 7E 7F   7E 7E 7E 7F 7F 7E 7F 7F   .. ~~~.~~~..~
000040  7F 80 80 7E 7F 81 81 81   81 80 7F 80 80 80 7F 7E   ...~........~
000050  7F 7F 7F 81 80 80 7E 7F 81   81 81 81 80 7F 80 80 80   ....~...~......
000060  7F 7F 7E 7F 80 80 7F 7F   7F 7E 7D 7F 80 80 80 7F   .~.....~}....
000070  82 81 80 81 82 81 7F 82   82 81 80 82 82 82 81 83   ................
000080  82 82 81 81 82 81 82 82   82 81 82 82 82 83 84 84   ................
000090  82 82 82 82 82 80 81 81   82 81 81 81 82 82 82 82   ................
0000A0  82 82 82 82 82 82 82 82   84 84 82 82 82 82 82 82
```

FIGURE 14-6   This is an example of a binary file that was opened by the Developer Studio, but not recognized as a resource it supports. It is a wave file, as can be seen in the right-hand column where the ASCII representation of the data is displayed. The left side is the hexadecimal values of the bytes in the file.

Graphic Editor

The Graphic Editor (see Figure 14-7) is used for creating bitmaps, cursors, and icons, which are all resource types supported by the Developer Studio and available to Visual Test. This editor closely resembles a painting program, but is integrated into the studio and saves out to the different resource types.

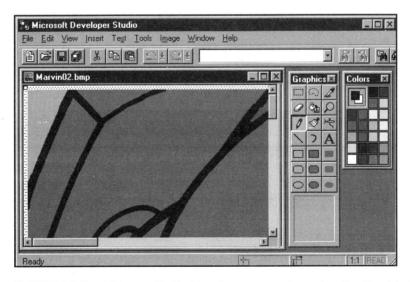

FIGURE 14-7   A bitmap file that has been opened, causing the Graphic Editor and its associated toolbars to be displayed.

Dialog Editor

The Dialog Editor (see Figure 14-8) resembles a drawing program and has two toolbars (*Dialog* and *Controls)* that appear when the editor is active. The Dialog palette allows for aligning, re-sizing, and testing the current state of the dialog box and its controls. The Controls palette allows the Test programmer to place different types of controls onto the dialog box for designing the dialog.

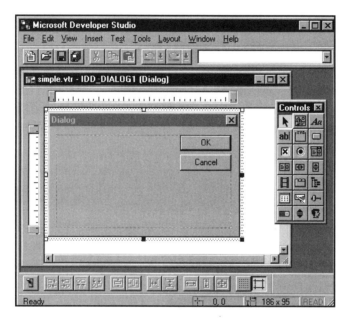

FIGURE 14-8   The Dialog Editor allows the Test programmer to design a dialog box by simply drawing the controls onto the dialog box window.

Menu Editor

The Menu Editor is created simply by typing the names of the menus and their menu items. The Properties dialog box (shown in Figure 14-9 along with the Menu Editor) allows for controlling the name of the menus, their menu items, the IDs associated with the menus and menu items, and the way that each item should appear.

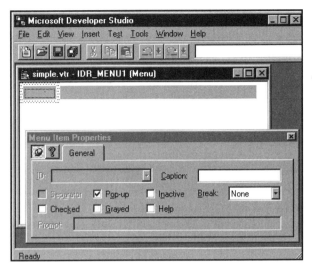

FIGURE 14-9
The Menu Editor and its Properties dialog box are used to create a menu bar by typing the name of the menu and its menu items.

String Editor

The String Editor (see Figure 14-10) allows for the creation of string tables that can be accessed from the Test language using the *RES$* function. The editor can be used to create commonly used strings that must be loaded during the running of a test case file. While some Test programmers use constants to hold values, in the event Visual Test's memory space runs low, a string table can be used instead, thus allowing only required strings to be loaded individually.

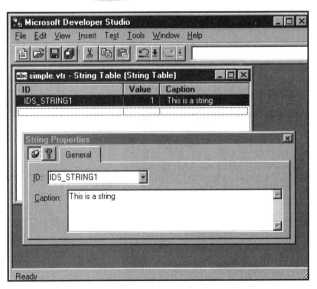

FIGURE 14-10 The String Editor (which looks similar to the Accelerator Editor) is added to and edited by simply typing directly into the editor.

The result is that instead of having separate *.inc* files (depending on for which language the tests are running), a separate *.vtr* file can be used. This separate file holds menus, dialog boxes, string tables, and so on, that are for a specific language, should the Test programmer choose to take that approach.

Version Resource

The version resource is meant to be viewable from the resource editor so that other programmers can determine the version of the resource file, or the file in which the resource has been imbedded. It holds the version number, copyright, and other miscellaneous information.

Working with Dialog Boxes

The new way to work with dialog boxes in Visual Test 4.0 isn't always the most intuitive approach. However, it does result in a number of files being encapsulated and is, therefore, a little cleaner in its implementation.

Dialog boxes in Visual Test can take two forms: *simple* and *complex*. In the 2.0 and 3.0 versions of Test, these two styles of dialog boxes were invoked by using the *DlgBox* and *DlgBoxEx* functions. Things have been simplified with the use of a single function called *Dialog*.

Creating a Dialog Box

Before discussing the two separate types of dialog boxes, let's first create a dialog box that is to be used by the Test language. In this example, we will create a resource file called simple.vtr that will allow us to create and work with a beginning dialog box.

The resource file is created by selecting New from the File menu and selecting the Test Resource item displayed in the subsequent dialog box (see Figure 14-1). By then selecting the Resource… menu item from the Developer Studio's Insert menu, a Test programmer can select Dialog from the Insert Resource dialog box. Selecting Save from the File menu and typing **simple.vtr,** the newly created resource file appears as shown in Figure 14-11.

see 14-3

FIGURE 14-11
After creating a new resource file, inserting a dialog box resource, and saving the file, the resource window appears as shown here.

As mentioned earlier in this chapter, the editor used to create a dialog box is very similar to a drawing program. Instead of having lines, rectangles, ellipses, and other shapes on a toolbar, controls can be placed directly on the mock dialog box that appears in the editor. A simple dialog box is shown in Figure 14-12.

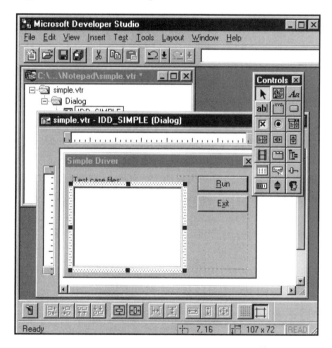

FIGURE 14-12
A dialog box is created by drawing the desired controls onto the dialog box shown in the editor.

As each control is created on the dialog box, its properties can be set to help manage how each control appears or behaves. To access the Properties dialog box, right-click on the object and select Properties from the pop-up menu. Or, double-click on the object and the Properties dialog box will appear. As an example, Figure 14-13 shows the properties associated with a list box control. Remember that you can press the F1 key to obtain specific descriptions of each option in a dialog box, including each of the controls in the Properties dialog box.

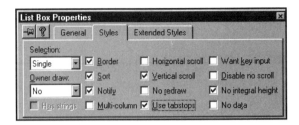

FIGURE 14-13 The properties for a control can be viewed by double-clicking on the control. This is also where the names of the constants that are associated with a control and used by the Test language can be modified.

Double-clicking on the dialog box itself also allows for adjusting how the dialog box appears and behaves. In each of these properties dialog boxes for each control, the constant associated with the control can be modified. It is this constant that is used in the Test language to identify the dialog box and its controls.

After drawing the desired controls onto the dialog box, it can be tested and modified within the editor. To test the dialog box, either click on the toolbar item that looks like a light switch, or select the Test menu item under the Layout menu (see Figure 14-14).

FIGURE 14-14
The Layout menu appears when working with the Dialog Editor. Many of the menu items on this menu are available through the toolbars that appear when the editor appears.

Also available in the Layout menu is the Tab Order menu item that allows the Test programmer to specify which control has the focus when the dialog box first appears, and in what order the controls are cycled through when the Tab key is pressed. Selecting the Tab Order menu item shown in Figure 14-14 causes the dialog box in the editor to have numbers placed by each control, indicating their tab positions (see Figure 14-15). Clicking on each control, one at a time, in the order in which the tabbing should occur, results in those numbers adjusting themselves.

334

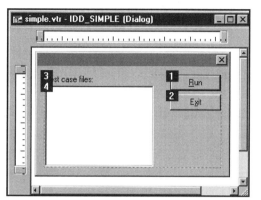

FIGURE 14-15
When the Tab Order menu item is selected from the Layout menu, numbers appear next to each control in the dialog box that is being edited. Clicking on the controls in the order in which they should be tabbed to adjusts those tab values.

Simple Dialog Box

A simple dialog box is employed when the dialog box used to communicate between the program and the user doesn't need to interact with the user by updating items in its list box, process the selection of menu items, or activate and gray controls, depending on settings in the dialog box. A simple dialog box, as implied by its name, is an easy-to-construct-and-implement interface that allows simple communication between the user and the program that is executing. When a simple dialog box is displayed, however, the script controlling the dialog box comes to a halt until the user dismisses the dialog box, or performs some action to cause the dialog box to dismiss itself.

We're now going to put to use the dialog box that we just created. The purpose is to provide an easy interface to a tester, allowing the tester to see a list of test case files and choose whether to run each of them in turn, or to exit the program that is driving the running of the test cases one by one.

Three steps must be followed to make the newly created dialog resource available to the script we are about to create. The first step is to include the *.vtr* file, previously named simple.vtr, into the project we've been working on throughout this book. The resource is added to the project just as any other file (for example: test case, include file, test case folder, and so on) was previously added — via the Insert menu.

The second step is to create a script that will use the resource file. In this case, we will create our own simple driver that runs the test case files in the Notepad test suite one at a time. We'll create a new test case file that won't necessarily hold any test cases, but will contain a script to act as a driver. Keeping it simple, we'll name it driver.mst.

3) The third and final step is to include the Visual Test Resource (*.vtr*) file into the source code file itself. This is the same idea as including an include (*.inc*) file, except that, in this case, it is a file holding resources. Instead of using the '$INCLUDE metacommand, the '$RESOURCE metacommand will be used.

The Notepad project window and the resulting driver.mst script appear as shown in Figure 14-16 after the simple.vtr resource file has been added to the project and the new .mst file has been created.

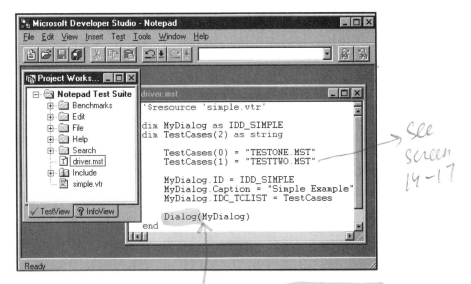

FIGURE 14-16 Script called driver.mst that includes the resource file, initializes the structure associated with the dialog box, and then displays the dialog box by passing the structure to the *dialog* function.

When a dialog box is created and saved into a *.vtr* file, an internal *type* is created that is associated with that dialog box and its controls. The *simple* form of working with a dialog box (see Figure 14-16) is done by creating a variable of that internal type, initializing the members or elements of that type, and then passing the variable to the *dialog* function. The result of running the script shown in Figure 14-16 is the dialog box shown in Figure 14-17. No actual guts to the driver have been provided yet; this is simply an example of how to get the dialog box to display itself.

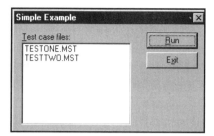

FIGURE 14-17 This dialog box, created earlier in this chapter, is accessed by saving it as part of a *.vtr* file and including it into a Test Project. Including the *.vtr* file into the script, initializing a variable of a type created when the dialog box was created, and passing that variable to the *dialog* function causes the dialog box to appear when the script is executed.

In most cases, when dealing with the simple form of a dialog box, the constant values won't be used, other than the one that identifies the ID number of the dialog box to be displayed. The only thing the user must do is determine which user-defined type to use, declare a variable of that type, initialize the fields in the type that are of interest to the Test programmer, and then pass that type to the *dialog* function along with the ID number or constant for the dialog box to be displayed.

When the *dialog* function completes its task (which is when the user clicks on one of the command buttons), the variable that was initialized and passed to *dialog()* has been reset to reflect any changes to the controls of the dialog box made by the user. In the example shown in Figure 14-16, the return value for the *dialog* function is ignored. If it weren't ignored, the function would have returned the ID number of the button that was used to dismiss the dialog box. This way, the user can determine which button caused the dialog box to be dismissed.

Determining Types and Constants

In Microsoft Test 2.0 and 3.0, determining the type was a simple exercise. When the dialog box was saved, it was placed into a *.res* file. An *.inc* file that held the type and constant declarations associated with the dialog box and its controls was created at the same time the *.res* file was created. It was a matter of including the *.inc* file to get access to the user-defined type and then specifying the name of the *.res* file in the call to *DlgBox()*.

In Visual Test 4.0, however, the *.inc* and *.res* files are combined into the single *.vtr* file and the *dialog* function is used instead of *DlgBox()*. While I think this is a very cool way to handle the problem of multiple files, my concern is that the user-defined type and its constants are now somewhat hidden from the Test programmer unless the programmer knows the secret to finding those types. Trying to track down this information for the first time can be frustrating when stepping through all of the online documentation.

To display the type and constants associated with the dialog box, the *.vtr* file must be included into a project. Once included in the project, the Test programmer can then right-click on the *.vtr* file (in this case, simple.vtr), and select a menu item that wasn't available previously: Display declarations. Selecting this pop-up menu item causes all of the constants and types associated with dialog boxes, bitmaps, icons, and every other kind of resource stored in the *.vtr* file to be dumped to the Output window under the Viewport tab, as shown in Figure 14-18.

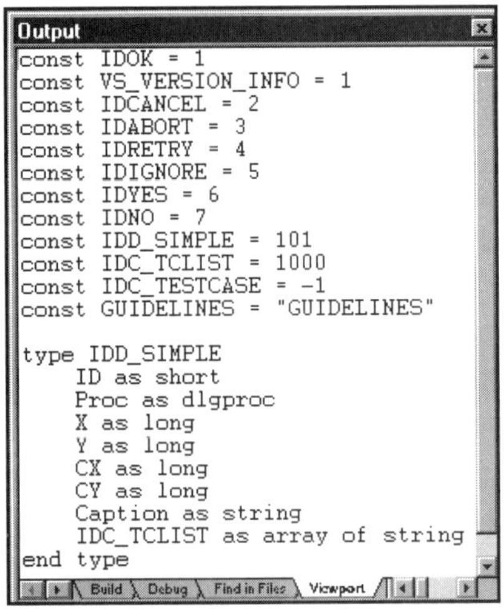

```
Output                                              ×
const IDOK = 1
const VS_VERSION_INFO = 1
const IDCANCEL = 2
const IDABORT = 3
const IDRETRY = 4
const IDIGNORE = 5
const IDYES = 6
const IDNO = 7
const IDD_SIMPLE = 101
const IDC_TCLIST = 1000
const IDC_TESTCASE = -1
const GUIDELINES = "GUIDELINES"

type IDD_SIMPLE
    ID as short
    Proc as dlgproc
    X as long
    Y as long
    CX as long
    CY as long
    Caption as string
    IDC_TCLIST as array of string
end type
  ◄ ► \ Build \ Debug \ Find in Files \ Viewport / ◄    ►
```

FIGURE 14-18
The constant and type declarations for a given *.vtr* file can be dumped to the Output window. Unlike Test 2.0 and 3.0, where a separate *.inc* file was automatically generated that held this kind of information, this information is now all kept in a single *.vtr* file. Using the Output window is now the preferred way to access information about the declarations.

Complex Dialog Box

The *complex* dialog box, which we'll use to complete the driver described earlier in this chapter, is a bit more challenging than the *simple* dialog box. It approaches programming very similar to straight Windows programming using the C language. Because of this, there is a fine line between discussing the complex dialog box and moving into Windows programming topics. We'll end up blurring that line a little bit to get advanced Test programmers started, but will then need to allow them to continue learning on their own by looking through the Windows APIs.

When it becomes necessary to be able to process events that occur while a dialog box is up and displayed to a user, it is then necessary to use a complex dialog box. The simple dialog box works by filling a structure and getting the user's selections returned in that structure when the dialog box is dismissed. The complex dialog box, which also gets the final settings of the controls in the dialog box, allows another level of control such that the Test program can interact with the dialog box while it is displayed.

For this example, the driver.mst file has been updated to work with a complex dialog box. Also, the simple.vtr file has been removed from the Notepad project and replaced with another resource file called driver.vtr that has the newly created dialog box shown in Figure 14-19.

FIGURE 14-19

This dialog box is a new and improved version over the simple dialog box we looked at previously. It is in a file called driver.vtr and replaces the simple.vtr resource file. (The two types of dialog boxes could co-exist in the same resource file if the Test programmer so chooses).

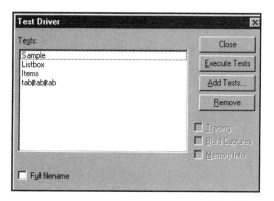

When working with a complex dialog box, a variable must be declared of the type that was automatically created when the dialog box was saved into the .vtr file. The only element of the type that must be initialized, however, is the proc field, as shown in Listing 14-1. (The full listing can be found in the file DRIVER.MST on the included disk.)

LISTING 14-1   A Partial Listing of DRIVER.MST.

```
'(Some initial comments and code removed

    dlgTestDriver.proc = VARPTR(DriverProc)
```

(continued)

LISTING 14-1 A partial listing of DRIVER.MST.
(Continued)

```
    Dialog(dlgTestDriver)
end

'*********************************************************************
'* Function:    DriverProc
'* Purpose:
'*              Main procedure for the driver.
'*
'* Parameters:
'*              hWnd&
'*                      Handle to the parent window
'*              msg&
'*                      Message that's being sent to the dialog box
'*              wParam&
'*                      Word parameter associated with msg%
'*              lParam&
'*                      Long parameter associated with msg%
'*
'* Returns:
'*              INTEGER
'*                      TRUE if this proc handled the msg.
'*                      FALSE if windows default should occur.
'*
'*********************************************************************

function DriverProc (hWnd&, msg&, wParam&, lParam&) as long
    dim ret%
    dim strTemp as string * MAX_FILENAME
    dim iSel%
    dim index%

    select case msg
        case WM_INITDIALOG
            InitDriver(hWnd)    'Init dialog box w/ .INI settings
            LoadList (hWnd)     'Load in list of test suites

            'execScripts = 0 we know we are ready to execute
            'execScripts = 1 we know we are executing scripts
            'execScripts = 2 we just clicked the stop button

            execScripts = 0 'Initialize execScripts
        case WM_COMMAND
```

→ holds ID number of control

```
select case wParam
    case IDCANCEL
        if execScripts = 0 then
            SaveDriver (hWnd)          'Save settings
            EndDialog (hWnd, wParam)'Close dialog
            DriverProc = TRUE
        else
            execScripts = 2
        end if

    case BTN_ADD
        strTemp=strGetFile("", FILTERSTRING)

        if (strTemp <> "") then
            '* increment the tail
            TestListTail  = TestListTail + 1
            '* write the new one.
            TestList(TestListTail) = strTemp

            if fDisplayPath then
                ret=SendMessage(GetDlgItem(hwnd, _
                    LB_TESTS),LB_ADDSTRING,0,strTemp)
            else
                ret=SendMessage(GetDlgItem(hwnd, _
                    LB_TESTS),LB_ADDSTRING,0, _
                    strGetFilename(strTemp))
            end if
        endif
        DriverProc = TRUE

    case BTN_REMOVE
        iSel = SendMessage(GetDlgItem(hwnd, LB_TESTS), _
            LB_GETCURSEL,0,0)
        if (iSel <> LB_ERR) then
            ret=SendMessage(GetDlgItem(hwnd,LB_TESTS), _
                LB_DELETESTRING, iSel, 0)

            'Keep selection when removing items
            ret=SendMessage(GetDlgItem(hwnd,LB_TESTS), _
                LB_GETCOUNT, 0, 0)
            if (iSel > (ret-1)) then
                ret=SendMessage(GetDlgItem(hwnd, _
```

(continued)

LISTING 14-1   A partial listing of DRIVER.MST.
(Continued)

```
                            LB_TESTS), LB_SETCURSEL, (ret-1), 0)
                    else
                        ret=SendMessage(GetDlgItem(hwnd, _
                            LB_TESTS), LB_SETCURSEL, iSel, 0)
                    endif

                    '*** Synch the listbox with TestList array.
                    for index = iSel to TestListTail - 1
                        '* bump everything up 1.
                        TestList(index) = TestList(index + 1)
                    next index
                    TestListTail = TestListTail -1
                endif
                DriverProc = TRUE

            case BTN_EXEC
                SaveDriver(hWnd) 'Save settings before running
                execScripts = 1
                enableWindow(GetDlgItem(hwnd,BTN_EXEC),FALSE)
                enableWindow(GetDlgItem(hwnd,BTN_ADD),FALSE)
                enableWindow(GetDlgItem(hwnd,BTN_REMOVE),FALSE)
                SetDlgItemText (hwnd,IDCANCEL,"Stop")
                RunTests(hWnd) 'Run tests
                ret = ShowWindow(hwnd, SW_SHOW)
                DriverProc = TRUE

            case CB_FULLNAME
                ret = SendMessage(GetDlgItem(hwnd, _
                    LB_TESTS),LB_RESETCONTENT, 0,0)
                if wCheckState("Full Filename") = CHECKED then
                    '* TestList array is 0 based, thus ...
                    for index = 0 to TestListTail
                        ret = SendMessage(GetDlgItem(hwnd, _
                            LB_TESTS),LB_ADDSTRING, _
                            0,trim$(TestList(index)))
                    next index
                    fDisplayPath = TRUE
                else
                    for index = 0 to TestListTail
                        ret = SendMessage(GetDlgItem(hWnd, _
                            LB_TESTS),LB_ADDSTRING, _
```

```
                            0,strGetFilename(TestList(index)))
                  next index
                  fDisplayPath = FALSE
              end if
          case else
              DriverProc = FALSE
        end select

    case else
        DriverProc = FALSE
    end select
end function 'DriverProc
```

A number of the functions that *DriverProc()* calls are in the remainder of the driver.mst file. Many of the others, however, are Windows API calls that are the same calls that Windows programmers use when writing Windows applications.

A *proc* (pronounced "prock") is a procedure that handles all the messages for a window in the Windows 95 or Windows NT operating system. When a mouse is moved across a window, the proc is called with a message letting it know something is happening. When a control is clicked on, the proc is called with the message, ID number of the control, and other information. When a dialog box is about to be displayed, the proc is called letting it know by sending a WM_INITDIALOG message.

Windows messages begin with the *WM_* prefix and all procs are sent four arguments when they're called. Those arguments are a handle to the window receiving the message, the message that is being sent, and two parameters (*wParam* and *lParam*) whose values depend on the type of message being sent. Looking up a message in the Win32 SDK online help will explain what information is passed to the wParam and lParam parameters depending on the Windows message.

When a message is sent to a proc, it can either be processed or ignored. If it is processed by the proc, the proc must return a non-zero value, letting Windows know that the message was not ignored. If the message is ignored, returning a 0 (FALSE) informs Windows that it should go ahead and handle the message in the default manner (in many cases, Windows' default response is to do nothing).

When a control is clicked on, a WM_COMMAND message is sent. All messages in a proc are typically handled in a case statement structure. It is up to yet another case statement to deal with determining which control was clicked on and what to do for that control. In the case of a WM_COMMAND, the wParam parameter holds the ID number of the control that was clicked on. This secondary case statement can then respond, based on which control was selected.

Something to keep in mind when dealing with a proc is that tons of messages are being sent over and over again to the proc. It is necessary to keep track of the state which the dialog box is in. In our proc, we have a global variable called *execScripts* that tracks whether the driver is in the process of stepping through and running each test case one at a time, the dialog box is idling, awaiting the user's command, or the STOP button has been clicked on to cause the execution of the scripts to halt. Because the proc is called by Windows itself, extra parameters cannot be added to the parameter list for the proc. Therefore, many times it is necessary to use global variables to make data available to the proc, which is not necessarily the preferable way to pass data around in a program.

Note

Missing from the top of Listing 14-1 is the statement for including the winapi.inc file discussed in Chapter 13. When working with Windows APIs, including the winapi.inc file automatically links into a number of the APIs and provides declarations for constants and user-defined types associated with those APIs. For more information on working with Windows APIs or the winapi.inc file, refer to Chapter 13.

Working with Menus

An example of a menu that has been created for the example test case driver shown earlier in this chapter is found in Figure 14-20. This figure shows the Menu Editor and its property dialog box. Again, it is here, in the property dialog box, where the names of the constants can be set.

Note

To add a *direct access method* (DAM) key to a menu item, use the ampersand in front of the letter to be underlined. Do not confuse a DAM key with an accelerator or shortcut key. The DAM key is for use with the Alt key.

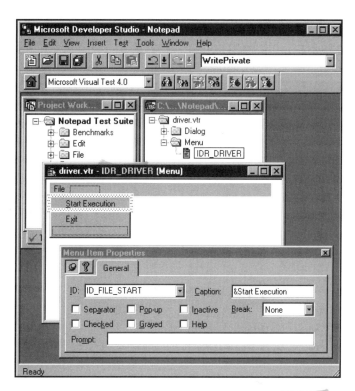

FIGURE 14-20   IDR_DRIVER is the name of the constant that represents the menu for the sample driver stored in the driver.vtr resource file. Adding menus and menu items is as simple as typing the names directly into the editor.

Once a menu has been added to a resource file, that menu can be used through the Test language's *SetMenu* statement. The online help information for the SetMenu function needs some major help. First of all, the function says that it takes three parameters (an ID, handle, and the name of the resource file in which the menu is stored). This is incorrect. It takes only two. The second place where it is incorrect is in the order of the parameters. It says that it takes a menu ID, then the handle to a window. Actually, it's reversed, and it takes the handle to the window as the first parameter and the menu ID as the second.

The SetMenu function call can be placed in the WM_INITDIALOG section of the proc, and the IDs associated with the menu items can be intermingled with the existing IDs found in the case statement under the WM_COMMAND section. Excerpts of the modified dialog proc are shown in Listing 14-2. Adding a menu requires a call to SetMenu() with the handle of the window to add the menu to, the ID number of the resource, and then modifications to the proc so that selecting menu items results in something happening.

LISTING 14-2   Excerpts of the Modified Dialog Proc

```
(... code above this section is not shown ...)
select case msg
    case WM_INITDIALOG
        SetMenu(hWnd,IDR_DRIVER) 'Add menu to the dialog window
        InitDriver(hWnd)          'Init dialog box w/ .INI settings
        LoadList (hWnd)           'Load in list of test suites

(... some code removed ...)

case WM_COMMAND
    select case wParam
        case IDCANCEL,ID_FILE_EXIT
            if execScripts = 0 then
                SaveDriver (hWnd)        'Save settings
                EndDialog (hWnd, wParam)'Close dialog
                DriverProc = TRUE
            else
                execScripts = 2
            end if

        case BTN_EXEC, ID_FILE_START
            SaveDriver (hWnd)      'Save settings before running
            execScripts = 1
            enableWindow (GetDlgItem(hwnd, BTN_EXEC),FALSE)
            enableWindow (GetDlgItem(hwnd, BTN_ADD),FALSE)
            enableWindow (GetDlgItem(hwnd, BTN_REMOVE),FALSE)
            SetDlgItemText (hwnd,IDCANCEL,"Stop")
            RunTests (hWnd)        'Run tests
            ret = ShowWindow(hwnd, SW_SHOW)
            DriverProc = TRUE

(... code continues ...)
```

The menu is successfully integrated by adding the SetMenu function call to the WM_INITDIALOG section of the case statement. Also, the constants associated with the menu IDs (ID_FILE_EXIT and ID_FILE_START) are added to the same section of the case statement as the IDCANCEL for the Close button, and BTN_EXEC for the Execute Tests button, as shown in Listing 14-2. Another way to attach a menu to a dialog box is via the Properties dialog box in the dialog box editor. Through this UI approach you can select the menu to associate with the dialog box.

Accelerator Keys

Adding an accelerator key is as simple as typing the key into the Accelerator Editor and selecting which modifier (that is, Ctrl, Alt, or Shift) key to use with the chosen letter. Once this has been done, the accelerator can then be associated with the ID of a menu item that should already have been created.

The documentation states that the description of the accelerator key will automatically be added to the menu, but I couldn't get this to work. Therefore, if it does not work for you either, you can type the accelerator key in next to the name of the menu item and separate the two descriptions with a tab. To separate with a tab, the \t escape sequence must be used as part of the string. For example, to create a menu item named "Exit" that has its letter x marked as the DAM key and Ctrl+X identified as the accelerator key, the string you would type into the menu item's property dialog box would be "E&xit\tCtrl+X" (without the quotation marks, of course).

Note Accelerator keys do not work with menus that have been attached to dialog boxes. I couldn't find this mentioned in the Visual Test 4.0 online help, but this was the case and was stated in the Test 2.0 and 3.0 documentation.

The Remaining Resources

The remaining resources are easy and straightforward to use. These resources are the icon, bitmap, cursor, and string table.

Icon Resource

Icons are basically 32 x 32 pixel-sized bitmaps that can be used in dialog boxes or painted into windows (or *device contexts*). Icons can also be used with list view controls. To load an icon out of a resource file, the *.vtr* file must first be included (as it was in the listings shown earlier in this chapter) by using the $RESOURCE metacommand. The *Icon* function loads the icon in the resource file by specifying the ID number or name of the icon. A handle is returned that can later be used with other functions and statements.

To draw an icon to a window or device context, the *DrawIcon* statement is used. Once an icon has been loaded by using the Icon function, it remains in memory until the script either terminates, or the *DestroyIcon* statement is called.

One of the more interesting uses of icons is with the *list view* control in a dialog box. While we didn't look at a list view control, it is very similar to a list box control. To load an icon and associate it with the text being displayed in a list view control, the Test programmer can use the *ImageIcon* function. By prepending the return value of the ImageIcon function to the text that is to be displayed in the list view control, the icon appears in that control with the text.

Bitmap Resource

Working with a bitmap resource is also straightforward. Its only function is to be used as an object in a dialog box or to be drawn to a window using the *DrawBitmap* statement.

Like the icon resource, the bitmap resource can be manipulated by using the Bitmap function to load a bitmap, the DrawBitmap statement to display a bitmap in a given window, and the *DestroyBitmap* statement to remove the resource from memory.

Referring to the DrawBitmap section of the online help, the Test programmer will find that the bitmap can be drawn in a number of ways, including drawing the bitmap as expected, or merging it with the graphics that already exist at the specified location.

Cursor Resource

Similar to the other resources, a cursor can be loaded into memory (*Cursor* function), drawn to a window (*DrawCursor* statement), and destroyed or removed from memory (*DestroyCursor* statement). It can also change the current mouse pointer by using the *SetCursor* command.

String Table Resource

The string table resource is a nice addition to Visual Test because it allows for the use of text strings to be implemented in a flexible fashion.

An approach to keeping several strings around to be used as a part of testing is to place those strings into constants. When only a few strings are used this is not a concern. However, when a large number of strings is needed to refer to all text in an application (including text strings that must be used to provide test data to the application), the amount of memory used in Visual Test's stack can grow quite high.

The trade-off in these situations is to opt for using disk space to store strings instead of using Visual Test's limited stack segment of memory. This is accomplished by placing strings into a string table, and then loading the individual strings as they are needed. With this solution, however, comes the price of speed since the string must be loaded in from the disk and placed into a variable. This isn't a huge amount of time, but it is slower than when working with conventional random-access memory.

As with any resource, the items defined in the resource are accessed by IDs. By calling the RES$ function with an ID, the function returns the string associated with that ID. Because the same variable can be used again for another string, the value previously stored in the variable is freed from memory. There is no need to worry about freeing strings loaded in from a string table.

Summary

By providing access to resources from the Visual Test language, Microsoft has made Visual Test a very capable tool for testing and adding UI components to those tests to make them easier to use. Simple dialog boxes provide an easy way to communicate with the user of the test script, while a complex dialog box approaches the level of Windows development by working with the Windows APIs.

Although this is an area of Visual Test that isn't used as often as other sections of the product, it is nice to know that it has these capabilities allowing for future modifications to automated tests.

Testing Across a Network

*O*ne of the more interesting aspects of Visual Test is its support for distributing tests across a NetBIOS-compatible network. NetBIOS is an application programmer interface (API) that activates network operations on IBM PC compatibles running under a Microsoft operating system. NetBIOS is the main protocol on which Microsoft applications depend.

With this support for distributing tests, a number of possibilities are opened to the Test programmer when automating testing on an application. Two possibilities, for example, are running the same tests on different computer configurations, and running tests to test database access from multiple stations. When it comes to running tests on multiple machines, there are, of course, other possibilities that are too numerous to list here. Because of the support that Visual Test provides, many of these scenarios can be accomplished through the use of the *Visual Test Network Distribution Procedures*.

Note

The network functionality has been changed from the support that was provided in previous versions of Test. However, these changes help simplify the entire process, thus making it easier to learn, use, and understand. Any scripts that were written previous to Visual Test 4.0 must be updated to follow the new Test language functions.

Roles and Responsibilities

Two roles must be filled in order for Test's network routines to work. The first role is that of the *host,* whose duty it is to find available stations, pass tasks to those stations and then collect data from those stations.

The second role is that of the *station,* whose job it is to contact a host, notify the host that it is willing to take on tasks, run those tasks, and then report the results back to the host.

For a station to be able to work on a network, there must first be a host. For a host to be effective, it must have a station or stations with which to work. While the host generally manages the stations by assigning tasks and collecting results, it is not in control of the station. The station, depending on how its script has been written, can disconnect from the host at any time. Therefore, it is a cooperative effort and the scripts must be written in a particular way to allow the communication and cooperation to occur.

Figure 15-1 shows a common model of working with a host and station. In this example, a single host exists in which it is working with one or more stations. The host first establishes itself as a host, and then checks the network for any stations that have declared themselves as available to a host. Tasks are distributed to the station (or stations) and results collected.

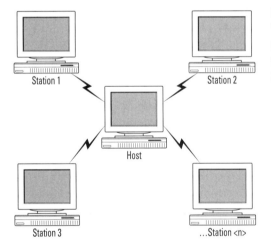

FIGURE 15-1
Typical host/station relationship model used when working with the Visual Test Network Distribution Procedures.

Capabilities of the Host

A computer that acts as a host is any computer running Visual Test that declares itself to be a host on the network. Therefore, a computer that acted as a station in one situation can be a host in another.

The host has specific duties for which it is responsible when acting in the role as a host. The first is to establish itself on the network as a host, so any available stations can locate it and make themselves known as being available for processing tasks. The second is to locate available stations and initiate a session with one or more of the available stations. Next, the host must monitor the status of the station so that it knows if it is idling, passing back information, or no longer available to the host. The next duty is to assign tasks to the stations (based on the host's needs). Receiving data back from the stations is the fifth responsibility of the host machine. The host is also responsible for handling any special situations that arise on the host's side (such as run-time errors). Finally, the host is responsible for cleaning up after itself and terminating the sessions with the stations. These responsibilities are shown in Figure 15-2.

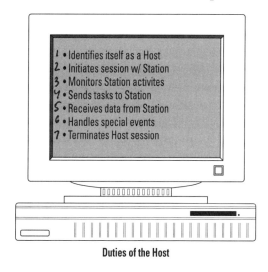

Duties of the Host

FIGURE 15-2
The host is responsible for identifying itself as a host, managing the selected stations and itself, and terminating any sessions that were established when the tasks have been completed.

Identifying a Host

To avoid the "chicken-and-the-egg" scenario, the host is obligated to start the host/station relationship by identifying itself on the network as a host. This is done by using the *TalkCreateHost* function. This function requires a name to be passed to it, which will be used to identify the host, along with a pointer to a subroutine which will process all messages sent to the host. This function takes the following form:

```
TalkCreateHost(strHostName$, varptr(AHostMsgHandler))
```

In the documentation, it looks confusing and it's difficult to understand how the second parameter (in this case, *AHostMsgHandler*) is supposed to be used. This is yet another situation where things look weird at first, but really are not too bad once you've had a chance to read through everything. The unfortunate reality of online help is that it makes it difficult to locate information because it is many times necessary to jump to multiple topics instead of having all information in one place. Once the general concepts are understood, however, the online help is an excellent tool.

The first parameter to *TalkCreateHost()* is a 15-character, alphanumeric string that uniquely identifies the host on the network. So, type in any name that you know isn't in use. Use only letters and numbers to identify your host on the network. The second parameter is a pointer to a subroutine. This pointer is being passed to *TalkCreateHost()* so that when an event occurs of which the host should be aware, the host can be notified automatically no matter what it is otherwise doing. This is known as a *callback* routine. As discussed in Chapter 13, a callback routine is used for events that can occur at any time (also known as *asynchronous events*).

It is up to you, the Test programmer, to create the routine that will be called automatically by Visual Test when an event occurs that affects the host. I used *AHostMsgHandler* in the previous example just to show how the name of the callback routine isn't important. The values that it takes are important, however. When the callback is made by Visual Test, it expects to be able to pass a certain number and types of parameters to the callback routine. These parameters are defined in the online help. They result in the Test programmer having to define a subroutine similar to the following:

```
sub AHostMsgHandler(iMsg%, hHost&, iStation%, lType&, _
                    vData as VARIANT)

    … guts of the subroutine go here …

end sub 'AHostMsgHandler
```

The result is a subroutine that takes five parameters of type SHORT, LONG, SHORT, LONG, and VARIANT, where VARIANT is a type new to Visual Test 4.0 that allows for any type of value to be passed.

Note

The online help uses the SHORT data type instead of the INTEGER type when speaking about the callback function that works with a host script. Because the SHORT and INTEGER data types are virtually the same, I'm using the shorthand notation for an INTEGER declaration (%) instead of SHORT. This will work without any ill effects.

By calling *TalkCreateHost()*, a handler has been established for all messages sent to the host by the station (or by Visual Test) because of an action taken by a station. No matter which line of code the host is currently executing when a message comes in, the host will act as if a call to *AHostMsgHandler()* has been placed on the very next line of code to be executed. Execution will jump into the message handler and, upon completion, return control back to the host where it was interrupted.

Warning

Because a callback can occur at any time, no matter what the host script is doing, it is important to not have any code in the callback routine that adjusts or affects the state of an application that is potentially being manipulated by the host. For example, if the host is clicking on items in a dialog box and a callback occurs, the callback routine should not dismiss the dialog box, because, when control returns to the main script, the dialog box will no longer be available and will result in errors since the script tries to continue from where it was interrupted. This same situation applies to adjusting the current directory or active disk drive.

The return value of *TalkCreateHost()* is a number or handle that identifies the host. Because multiple host sessions can be running on the network, and even multiple host sessions can be running in a single script, the handle to the host is very important in identifying exactly which host is making requests to the stations on the network.

Assuming a host script with a callback routine called AHostMsgHandler, the identification process required by a host script would look something like the following:

```
dim hHost&
    hHost = TalkCreateHost("MainHost",varptr(AHostMsgHandler))
    '…more source code follows…
end
```

✓ handle to host machine

THE HOST'S CALLBACK ROUTINE

When a host is identified by using the TalkCreateHost function, a pointer to a callback function must be provided. A typical callback function that processes messages sent to the host would take a form similar to this:

```
Sub AHostMsgHandler(iMsg%, hHost&, iStation%, lType&, _
                    vData AS VARIANT)
    Dim strStationName AS STRING          → gets the station name

    strStationName = TalkGetStationName(hHost, iStation)
                                           ↓ station ID
    Print "Station ["+strStationName+"] has ";   number
    Select Case(iMsg)                      from Talk Get Station Count
        Case TALK_CONNECT
            Print "connected."

        Case TALK_HUNGUP
            Print "disconnected."

        Case TALK_DATA
            Print "sent data."
            'Use another SELECT CASE statement to
            'determine the data type and what to do
            'with the data that has been passed.

        Case TALK_SYNC
            Print "notified it is ready to synchronize."

        Case Else
            'Unexpected message has been sent
    End Select
end sub 'AHostMsgHandler
```

This script is only a beginning shell to a typical handler for processing a host's messages. It is up to the Test programmer to provide the reactions to the different messages that can be sent using the network procedures.

As you will see later in this chapter, the callback routine used by the station is nearly the same. Both a host and a station must have a callback routine, so that they can process incoming messages as they occur. The callback routine provides for working with these asynchronous events.

Locating Stations

A host locates stations that are available on the network by using the *TalkGetStationCount* function. The host passes its handle to this function along with a boolean (TRUE or FALSE) value that determines whether the number of active stations (or active and inactive stations) is returned. Typically, the second parameter will be set to TRUE, so that *TalkGetStationCount()* returns the number of active stations on the network.

As the host finds stations on the network via its call to *TalkGetStationCount()*, it assigns values to each station it encounters, beginning with 1. If a station deactivates or disconnects itself from the host, it is considered inactive, and the host maintains its unique identifying number should the station reactivate. As new stations become available, they are given the next highest number in the existing list of stations. The number returned by *TalkGetStationCount()* is considered the last ID number of the available stations. Therefore, the numbers from 1 to whatever value was returned by *TalkGetStationCount()* are all ID numbers of available stations on the network. The numbers correspond to an internal station list that was built by Visual Test when stations identified themselves on the network and the TalkGetStationCount function was called. This list is automatically maintained by Visual Test and accessible only by using the ID numbers associated with each station.

Monitoring a Station

Once the host has ascertained how many connections exist for stations on the network through the use of *TalkGetStationCount()*, the host can then begin querying information about those stations. The first function available to the host for extracting information is *TalkGetStationName()*. By passing one of the station ID numbers to this function, a string is returned that is the network name of the computer. This information can be helpful in logging information about tests run on a specific machine. Because the ID number of a station depends on the order in which stations registered themselves on the network as being available to a host, the ID number changes from session to session, making the station name the only static information available (unless the owner of the station changes the network name of the computer).

As a host hands out tasks to the available stations, it should first verify that each station is still active. This can be done through the use of the *TalkStationActive* function, which returns a TRUE or a FALSE value depending on the status of the station. If a station is inactive and the host attempts to send information, an error will result, notifying the host that the station is no longer available.

The last way of monitoring a station's activity is an inactive approach on the side of the host. That is, a callback function was established when the host first identified itself to the network. Should the stations take any actions that could affect the host, the host will be notified. The two previously mentioned functions are an active approach to gathering information on and monitoring a station. The latter form of using the callback function helps to monitor the station, but is more of an involuntary reflex than a voluntary one.

The following is an example of pulling together what I've shown you so far. This script identifies the computer it is running on as a host on the network. It will then look for any computers that are running a script that identifies those computers as stations. Then, it will step through the list of stations, one by one, and print out the name of each of those stations. (**Note:** This is assuming that a station script is running on a computer somewhere on the network.)

```
dim hHost&, iStationCount%, iLoop%

    hHost = TalkCreateHost("MainHost",varptr(AHostMsgHandler))
    iStationCount = TalkGetStationCount(hHost, TRUE)

    for iLoop = 1 to iStationCount
        print "Station #";iLoop;" = [" + _
            TalkGetStationName(hllost,iLoop) + "]"
    next iLoop
end

'***
'* Simple message handler for messages sent to the Host
'***
```

```
Sub AHostMsgHandler(iMsg%, hHost&, iStation%, lType&, _
                    vData AS VARIANT)
    dim strStationName AS STRING

    strStationName = TalkGetStationName(hHost, iStation)

    print "Station ["+strStationName+"] has ";
    select case(iMsg)
        case TALK_CONNECT
            print "connected."

        case TALK_HUNGUP
            print "disconnected."

        case TALK_DATA
            print "sent data."
            'Place another select case statement here based on
            'the lType parameter to determine the type of data
            'sent and how to deal with it.

        case TALK_SYNC
            print "notified it is ready to synchronize testing."

        case else
            'Unexpected message has been sent. Print an error
            'message or just ignore it.
    end select
end sub 'AHostMsgHandler
```

Sending and Receiving Data

Once the host has identified itself, has set up a callback function for processing messages sent by the station, and has set up a session with available stations on the network, it can then begin sending tasks to a station
or stations. This is done through the use of the *TalkSendData* function,
which takes the following form:

```
TalkSendData (hHost&, iStation%, lDataType&, vData AS VARIANT)
```

The *hHost* parameter is the handle of the host sending the data. This is
the value that is returned by *TalkCreateHost()* and is used to identify
which host session is sending the information. The *iStation* parameter is

the ID number of the station that is to receive the data. If 0 is sent instead of a specific ID number, then the data is sent to all the stations currently active. The *lDataType* parameter is a value that informs the station what kind of data is being sent in the *vData* parameter. This can be any string or number, and the lDataType value is defined by the Test programmer, depending on the different types of data being sent.

A piece of functionality that was lost when moving to Visual Test 4.0 is the ability to copy a file across the network from one machine to another. In Test 2.0 and 3.0, a function called *GetDataFile* would pull a file across the network to the station. Because this is no longer available, it is up to the testers who are running the host and station scripts to define how they will provide access to different types of files. One example is to use a common, shared directory on the network. By passing the path to that file in that directory, the host or station can then use the Test language's *copy* statement to bring the file across. Another (less appealing) method would be to read in a text file one line at a time and pass it across to the station, allowing it to reassemble the file on the other side by writing the lines back out one at a time. Two examples of situations in which it is necessary to pass files back and forth across the network are when a script file must be executed on another machine and when a log file must be sent back to a host.

The *TalkSendData* statement is used both by the host and the station whenever information must be sent back and forth. The station, however, provides a 0 for the iStation parameter. I'll go into this a little further when I introduce you to the station side of the network routines.

Terminating a Session

The final responsibility of a host script is to terminate the session it has with the other stations. Fortunately, this is a simple task accomplished by using the *TalkHangUp* statement. By calling this statement and providing the handle to the host that is hanging up, all of the stations are automatically notified that the host has severed connections. An example of what this might look like is

```
TalkHangUp(hHost)   'Where hHost is a handle to the host
```

Note

Hosts and stations are responsible for handling unexpected events. What is specifically being referred to in this sense is dealing with run-time errors (a station or host that has disconnected, among other things). This is no different than any other test script. It should do its best to robustly handle unexpected situations.

The Station's Role

The station uses much of the same functionality as the host. Figure 15-3 shows some of the duties of the station.

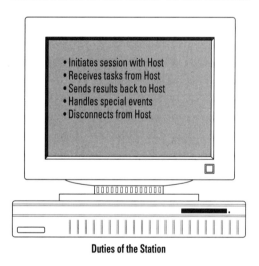

Duties of the Station

FIGURE 15-3
The station is responsible for contacting the host, receiving tasks from the host and carrying out those tasks, and returning results back to the host. It must also cleanly disconnect and terminate when the host severs the connection.

In order for a station session to begin on a network, there must first be a host script running somewhere on that same network. If there is a host session available, the station can connect by using the *TalkCallHost* function. The station must know the name of the host session that is running, and pass that as the first parameter to *TalkCallHost()*. Like the host session, the station must also provide a pointer to a callback function so that messages sent to the station by the host (or because of actions taken by the host) can be processed by the station:

```
dim hHost&
    hHost = TalkCallHost("MainHost",varptr(AStationMsgHandler))
```

The TalkCallHost function returns a LONG value that is the handle to the host session. This handle is used when the station is working with the host (by sending it information), or when disconnecting from a host session.

The Station's Callback Routine

The station's callback routine is very similar to the style of routine used by the host. It takes the same parameters and processes the messages in the same fashion. However, the station can only receive two types of messages from the host: TALK_DATA and TALK_HUNGUP. A simple station script might look like this:

```
sub AStationMsgHandler(iMsg%, hHost&, iStation%, lType&, _
                       vData AS VARIANT)
    print "Host #";hHost;" has ";
    select case(iMsg)
        case TALK_HUNGUP
            print "disconnected."
        case TALK_DATA
            print "sent data."
            'Extra code should be added here to determine the
            'type of data being sent and how to process that data.
        case else
            'Unexpected message has been sent
    end select
end sub 'AStationMsgHandler
```

The *iMsg* parameter is one of the TALK_ messages. The *hHost* parameter identifies from which host the information is coming (a station can connect to multiple hosts if it wants to). The *iStation* parameter is unused in this situation, since it is the station that is receiving the information. The *lType* parameter is a value defined and agreed upon by the host and station scripts. It identifies the type of data being sent. The *vData* parameter is the actual data that was sent by the host.

Some examples of constants that one might create for the lType variable are:

```
const DT_DISPLAY = 1    'Print the data sent in vData
const DT_TYPE    = 2    'Use the PLAY statement to type
```

```
const DT_FNAME   = 3    'vData contains a filename
const DT_NETLOC  = 4    'vData holds a network path
const DT_SENDLOG = 5    'Send current log file. (vData unused)
```

I used *DT_* to stand for data type, and also because Visual Test already
has at least one constant relating to this that is defined in the language:
DT_NO_DATA (which is equal to 0). The last constant in the example
could be used as a request to the station by the host asking for the current log file to be sent to it. In this example, vData isn't used. However,
it might make sense to use vData to hold the network location where the
host would like the log file placed. The point is that this is a flexible situation, where it is necessary for the host and station script writers to work
together and agree upon a standard set of messages. Typically, a second
select case statement is used to process these different types of data, just
as the *select case* statement is used to process the different messages that
can be sent.

Hanging Up

When a station has completed its tasks, or is in a situation where it is
decided that it should sever communications with the host, the
TalkHangUp statement is used. When this statement is called by the station and the handle to a host is passed as the first and only parameter,
the host with which the station was communicating receives a
TALK_HUNGUP message, and the station is marked as inactive in the
internal list kept by Visual Test. Any calls to the TalkStationActive function made by the host for a station that has hung up results in FALSE
being returned, signifying that the station is no longer available.

The station can reconnect with a host session whenever it wants. When
this happens, the station is assigned the same ID number it was using
before, and the host can continue working with that station. Reconnect-
ing with the station is accomplished through the same process as when
originally connecting. The host will receive a TALK_CONNECT message,
letting it know that a station is sending it a message, and the message is
that it is available for processing tasks.

Waiting for Messages

Even though a station or host can be working on other tasks while it is awaiting messages from its counterpart, oftentimes the scripts for a station or host are much simpler — simpler in the sense that all they want to do is sit there and process messages from one another, assigning tasks when they can, and sending results back from those tasks.

In this situation, a method that can be used is putting the script to sleep until a message is received. This can be done using the SLEEP statement. Using this statement without a number after it will put the script to sleep indefinitely, awaking only when it receives a message. The result is that the only functioning portion of the host or station script is in the call-back function. In the case of the station script, it might remain asleep or performing tasks until it receives a TALK_HUNGUP message. Upon receiving this message it understands that the host is no longer available and that it can terminate its execution by using the END statement.

The host is less likely to be a script that will sleep. It will most likely be sending tasks off to any station that will make itself available, and then processing the results of those tasks as they come back. However, in the event of times when there is nothing for the host to do, it too can make use of the SLEEP statement.

Tip

Some programmers prefer to check for other things while awaiting a call to the call-back function. In these cases, they typically use a WHILE statement and simply loop, looking for whatever situation it is that they're looking for and awaiting a callback. In some situations the while loop is executing so fast that a callback can't occur or interrupt the script. Therefore, in these situations it is a good idea to use a SLEEP .1 in the loop, so that it at least pauses for a fraction of a second. This was done in Chapter 13, when the SetTimer function was demonstrated for callback functions.

Synchronizing Scripts

One option available through the *Talk* routines is the ability for the stations to be synchronized by a host so that the tasks passed to the stations begin execution at roughly the same time. An example of when this might be useful in testing is in verifying database access and verifying that critical sections (such as record locking) are working as expected.

For synchronizing to work, the host must be informed by each station as to when it is ready and waiting for the signal from the host. This is done by each station calling the *TalkWaitSync* function. The result is the host receiving a TALK_SYNC message informing it as each station is awaiting the signal from the host. Another way for the host to determine how many stations are ready is for it to call the *TalkGetSyncCount* function. This function returns the number of stations that are awaiting the signal to begin the processing of the task.

Once the stations are all awaiting the signal, the host releases the stations from waiting, allowing each station to begin processing the tasks, by calling *TalkReleaseSync()*. The TalkReleaseSync function causes the TalkWaitSync function, which was called by each station, to return from the function call. If the result of the function call is TRUE, the station knows to move forward. If FALSE is returned, then the synchronization most likely timed-out or the host passed a FALSE to the TalkReleaseSync function notifying the station to abort. The station is free to attempt a re-synchronization with the host if it so chooses.

Network Protocols

Windows 95 and Windows NT support NetBEUI as its main NetBIOS-compatible protocol. NetBEUI (which stands for NetBios Extended User Interface) is the standard Windows protocol and is basically a superset of NetBIOS.

Another protocol available in Windows (and also considered the de facto standard in the UNIX world) is TCP/IP (Transmission Control Protocol over Internet Protocol), two protocols at different layers working together across a network.

For information on installing these protocols and others that support NetBIOS, refer to your Windows documentation. Visual Test does support these protocols.

Note

The network routines that were available in previous versions of Test were somewhat flaky and difficult to get to work when moving from network to network. Scripts that friends and I wrote worked perfectly on our standard Windows 3.1 network, but failed when moving to a classroom that had the exact same simple network installed. Unfortunately, the new versions of these routines have inherited some of that flakiness and require some tweaking, experimentation, and patience to get some of the scripts to work. The latest version of the network routines are nonetheless more reliable and much easier to use.

Conclusion

The network procedures offer another level of automated testing such that the tester can run scripts on multiple machines at the same time. This is helpful when running the same scripts on multiple machine configurations for compatibility testing, and is also helpful for simulating multiple users on a given application (for example, database access).

Two roles, that of the station and of the host, are played to allow for running of the different tasks, and for managing the tasks that are being passed to the multiple machines. Through this coordination, tasks can be dispatched and results collected from multiple machines running asynchronously. It is also possible to closely synchronize the tasks on multiple machines for the testing of mutual-exclusion situations, semaphores, and critical sections.

While capable and fairly straightforward to use, these procedures can be twitchy when moving from network to network. While they may run on one network protocol that supports NetBIOS, they may react differently on another protocol that also purports to support NetBIOS. While the situation can get frustrating, the feeling of accomplishment is very gratifying when the host and station scripts finally run and perform as expected.

Summary

This chapter discusses the two roles between the host and station scripts running on two or more machines across a network. The host is the controlling computer that issues tasks to any computer that has identified itself as an available station on the network. The station carries out the tasks assigned by the host and reports the results back to the host when completed.

Each of these roles have similar Test language routines making it easier on the Test programmer once he or she has learned how to use the routines for one of those two roles. A callback routine is the heart of both the station and host scripts, allowing the two players to process messages asynchronously while performing other tasks. The host can also work with the station to synchronize testing tasks for checking such things as critical sections in a program.

Finally, the network routines can be somewhat temperamental and require some patience from the Test programmer when initially setting up the network scripts. Patience continues to be required when maintaining those scripts, especially when moving them to another networked environment.

V

Appendixes

Products for Visual Test 4.0 Users

Videotapes

Though there are hands-on courses available on Visual Test, many people like to go the route of learning at their own pace, instead of the jump-start approach a hands-on class provides. If you are one of these people, you're in luck because there are a number of videotapes put out by Software Testing Laboratories, Inc. on Visual Test.

Learning and Using Microsoft Visual Test 4.0 Video Series

This is a series with three sections:

▶ Introduction

▶ Intermediate

▶ Advanced Topics

The student is introduced to Visual Test as a tool, when to use and not to use it, and how to take a realistic approach to automating testing.

The series comprises eight VHS videotapes, covering beginning to advanced topics in learning and using Microsoft Visual Test 4.0. Included with the product are:

▶ Five student handbooks

▶ A sample source code disk

▶ A site license for five students

Price: $995.00 for all three sections (all eight tapes). **$395.00** for each individual section. If you are an owner of STLabs' original Microsoft Test 3.0 video series, you may upgrade to this latest version for only **$395.00**.

Visual Test 4.0 for Microsoft Test 3.0 Users

This two-tape video course is for those who already know the basics of test automation through using Microsoft Test 3.0. This course focuses on features new to the Visual Test version of Microsoft Test and issues related to upgrading existing Microsoft Test 3.0 scripts to Visual Test 4.0.

This video course is also for managers who are trying to determine whether or not they want to upgrade to this latest version of Microsoft Test. Included with the product is one handbook and one 3½ inch sample source code disk.

Price: $395.00

Learning and Using Microsoft Test 3.0

Have you just purchased Microsoft Visual Test 4.0 and found that you're really only interested in the 16-bit version of Microsoft Test included on the installation CD-ROM? If so, this is the video course for you! The video series comprises six VHS videotapes covering beginning to advanced topics in learning and using Microsoft Test 3.0. Included with the product are:

▶ Five student handbooks

▶ Five sample source code disks

▶ A site license for five students

Price: $995.00

Add-On Tools

Test Now 2.0 — Microsoft Visual Test 4.0 Add-On Tool

This package includes:

▶ 101+ functions and subroutines

▶ An *XY* utility for pixel coordinates

▶ The Digger 1.0 utility for generating script templates based on a program's resources

▶ A sample test suite

All of the Visual Test "Testing Language" source code is included with the product so that you can modify the XY and Digger utilities to meet your specific needs. (A compiled form of Digger 1.0 is included on the disk that comes with this book).

Price: $189.00 (Upgrade for Test Now 1.0 owners — **$99**)

How to Order

The above products can be purchased directly from Software Testing Laboratories, Inc. If you send in a copy of this page and a copy of your receipt for this book, you will receive **15% off** the above prices! (That alone can cover the cost of this book!)

Software Testing Laboratories, Inc.
83 South King Street, Suite 414
Seattle, Washington 98104
Tel: 206-682-5832
Fax: 206-682-2373
e-mail: *Training@STLabs.com* and *TestNow@STLabs.com*
Web site: HTTP://WWW.STLabs.com/

James Bach's "Useful Features of a Test Automation System"[1]

James Bach

James Bach, Chief Scientist at Software Testing Laboratories, has been in the Software Quality Assurance industry for 13 years. An experienced tester for Apple Computer, James' most recent experience was as Borland International's QA Manager.

Over the past couple of years, James has been compiling a list of useful features of automated tests. That list is provided here in its entirety for your perusal.

Useful Features of a Test Automation System

"I've run test teams at Apple and Borland. We tried to automate our tests. We had some success with it, but mostly we failed. Test automation for modern GUI software is very challenging. Along the way, though, I've collected this list of useful features and caveats that you might want to consider in doing your automation." — James Bach

[1] Reprinted with permission from Software Testing Laboratories, Inc. Copyright 1995-1996, Software Testing Laboratories, Inc.

1. Suite is structured to support team development. Break large monolithic source files down into smaller, cohesive units. Put the system under source control to prevent team members from overwriting each other's work. Naturally, this applies only if the suite is being developed jointly, but beware of those small projects that become big projects: It might be worthwhile to plan ahead.

2. Suite can be distributed across a network of test execution systems. As your test suite grows in size, and as your organization gains more test suites and products to test, you will find it increasingly difficult to make efficient use of your test machines.

   One way of maximizing efficiency is to centralize a group of test machines (at Borland there is a lab with 50 or more identical, centrally controlled systems), and create test suites that can be distributed to a number of machines at once. This can substantially reduce the time needed for a test cycle, and eliminate the possibility that a problem with one machine will stop the whole suite from running.

   Another idea is to make the suite distributable to machines that are not otherwise dedicated to testing, such as computers normally used in development or administration. There are obvious risks to this strategy (such as the possibility of an automated test destroying a programmer's hard disk), but if your company has very few computers and a big need to test, it's useful to have the option of borrowing a few systems and getting each of them to run part of the test cycle.

3. Suite can execute tests individually, or by group. You might design the suite such that it can run an individual test, a set of specific tests, a group of related tests, all tests, all tests except specific tests or groups of tests, or only tests that failed the last time through. Also, allow the order of tests to be modified. You get the idea—the suite should provide flexibility in test execution.

4. Suite inter-operates with bug tracking system (bugs and tests are linkable). Depending on the kind of testing that you do, enabling the test suite to record a failure directly into your bug tracking system (whether that system is a flat file database or something more elaborate) may save time and effort. It may also waste time, if a high per-

centage of failures are due to automation problems and not defects in the product.

Another possible linkage might be the ability of the test automation to look in the bug tracking system for all fixed bugs and verify that they are still fixed. This requires that each bug report is accompanied by an automated test. Similar to that is the idea of marking a test as a "known failure until bug #3453 is fixed" and design the suite to execute that test, but ignore the failure until the associated bug is marked as fixed in the database.

The most feasible linkage I can think of is the ability to navigate directly from a bug in the tracking system to the part of the test suite that relates to it, and vice versa.

5.   Suite can perform hardware reset of test machines in case of system crashes. It's common for test machines to crash during testing, so you want some way to restart the hardware if that happens. In one project, we used a software-controllable power strip attached to each test machine, and used another computer to monitor the status of each test machine. If a crash was detected the monitoring computer would cycle the power on that system.

     With modern O/S's, it's sometimes possible to monitor the status of one process from within another process on the same computer. That may be easier and cheaper to arrange than the hardware reset.

6.   Suite can execute unattended. While a test suite that must be continually monitored can still be a lot better than manual testing, it's often more valuable to design it to run to completion without any help.

7.   Suite execution can be restarted from the point of interruption in case of catastrophic failure (for example, power loss). The more tests that you automate, the less you want your tests to start all over again from the beginning if the suite is halted in the middle of execution. This isn't as easy as it may sound, if your test drivers are dependent on variables and structures stored in memory.

By designing the system to write checkpoints out to disk, and to have an automatic start process that activates on reboot, and to have a means of resynchronizing to any other systems that it is connected to (such as file servers, which typically take longer to reset after the power goes out) your suite will survive a power outage and still be kicking.

8.   Suite can be paused, single-stepped, and resumed. In debugging the suite, or monitoring it for any reason, it's often important to be able to stop it or slow it down, perhaps so as to diagnose a problem or adjust a test, and then set it going again from where it left off.

9.   Suite can be executed remotely. Unless you live with your test machines, as some do, it's nice to be able to send a command from your workstation and get the test machines to wake up and start testing. Otherwise, you do a lot of walking to the lab. It's especially nice if you can query the status of a suite, start it, stop it, or adjust it over the phone. Even from home, you'd be able to get those machines cracking.

10. Suite is executable on a variety of system configurations to support compatibility testing. Automated suites should be designed with a minimum of assumptions about the configuration of the test machine. Since compatibility testing is so important, try to parameterize and centralize all configuration details, so that you can make the suite run on a variety of test machines.

11. Suite architecture is modular for maximum flexibility. This is as true for testware as it is for software. You will reuse your testware. You will maintain and enhance it. So build it such that you can replace or improve one part of it, say the test reporting mechanism, without having to rewrite every test.

Remember: TESTWARE IS SOFTWARE.

Just as software requires careful thought and design, you will discover that testware requires the same. Another aspect of good structure is to centralize all suite configuration parameters in one place. Here are some factors that might be controlled by a configurations file:

▶ Whether or not to log every navigational step taken during the test

▶ Whether or not to write out memory info before/after each test

▶ Where output is directed: common I/O, log file, debug monitor, nowhere

▶ Whether to perform screen comparisons or to rebuild capture files instead

▶ Which directory in which to place log files

▶ Which directories in which to read/write binary (capture) files

12. Suite can reset test machine(s) to known state prior to each test. There are good reasons to reset the test machine to a clean, known state, and there are also good reasons not to do that. Resetting helps in the process of investigating a problem, but not resetting is a more realistic test, since presumably your users will not be rebooting their computers between opening a file and printing it! A good idea is to make it a selectable option, so the tests can run either way.

13. Suite execution and analysis take less time and trouble than hand-testing. I know, it sounds pretty obvious. Alas, it needs to be said. Too many testers and managers approach test automation for its own sake. Instead, look critically at how much time and effort you are heaping on your automation. In the beginning automation costs more, yes, but too often even after a couple of years it still takes more effort to manage the automation than it would just to do the same thing by hand.

The most common problems, in my experience, are false fails. Every time the test suite reports a fail that turned out to be a problem with the suite itself, or a trivial misalignment between the test and the latest conception of the product, all the time needed to solve that problem is pure automation cost. Generally speaking, keep the suite architecture as simple as possible, to keep maintenance costs down.

14. Suite creates summary, coverage, result, debug, and performance logs.

    A summary log is an overview of the results of the test suite: how many tests were executed, how many passed, failed, are unknown, and so on.

    A coverage log shows what features were tested. You can achieve this by maintaining an electronic test outline that is associated with the test suite. If you have the appropriate tool, a coverage log should also report on code-level coverage.

    A result log records the outcome of each test.

    A debug log contains messages that track the progress of the test suite. Each entry should be time-stamped. This helps in locating problems with the suite when it mysteriously stops working.

    A performance log tracks how long each test took to execute. This helps in spotting absolute performance problems, as well as unexpected changes in relative performance.

15. Suite creates global (suite-wide) and local (test-specific) logs. Except for the summary log, all the logs should have global and local versions. The local versions of the logs should be cumulative from test cycle to test cycle. Each local log pertains to a single test and is stored next to that test. They form a history of the execution of that test. Global logs should be reinitialized at every test cycle, and include information about all of the tests.

16. Suite logs are accessible and readable. Logs ought to be both machine readable and human readable. I also recommend that they be tied into an icon or some other convenient front end, so that they are easy to get to.

17. Tests can be selectively activated or deactivated. There should be a mechanism (other than commenting out test code) to deactivate a test, such that it does not execute along with all the other tests. This is useful for when a test reveals a crash bug, and there is no reason to run it again until the bug is fixed.

18. Tests are easily reconfigured, replicated, or modified. An example of this is a functional test of a program with a graphical user interface that can be configured to simulate either mouse input or keyboard

input. Rather than create different sets of tests to operate in different modes and contexts, design a single test with selectable behavior.

Avoid hard-coding basic operations in a given test. Instead, engineer each test in layers and allow its behavior to be controlled from a central configuration file. Move sharable/reusable code into separate include files.

19. Tests are important and unique. You might think the best test suite is one with the best chance of finding a problem. Not so. Remember, you want to find a lot of important problems, and be productive in getting them reported and fixed. So, in a well-designed test suite, for every significant bug in the product, one and only one test will fail. This is an ideal, of course, but we can come close to it.

In other words, if an enterprising developer changes the background color of the screen, or the spelling of a menu item, you don't want 500 tests to fail (I call it the "500 fail scenario," and it gives me chills). You want one test to fail, at most.

Whenever a test fails, you know that at least one thing went wrong, but you can't know if more than one thing went wrong until you investigate. If 500 tests fail, it would help you to budget your time if you were confident that 500 different and important problems had been detected. That way, even before your investigation began, you would have some idea of the quality of the product. Likewise, you don't want tests to fail on bugs so trivial that they won't be fixed, while great big whopper bugs go unnoticed.

Therefore, I suggest automating interesting and important tests before doing the trivial ones. Avoid full-screen snapshots, and use partial screen shots or pattern recognition instead. Maybe have one single test that takes a series of global snapshots, just to catch some of those annoying little UI bugs. Also, consider code inspection, instead of test automation, to test data-intensive functionality, like online help. It's a lot easier to read files than it is to manipulate screenshots.

20. Dependencies between tests can be specified. Tests that depend on other tests can be useful. Perhaps you know that if one particular test fails, there's no reason to run any other tests in a particular

group. However, this should be explicitly specified to the test suite, so that it will skip dependent tests. Otherwise, many child tests will appear to fail due to one failure in a parent test.

21. Tests cover specific functionality without covering more than necessary. Narrowly defined tests help to focus on specific failures and avoid the 500 failure scenario. The downside is that overly narrow tests generally miss failures that occur on a system level. For that reason, specify a combination of narrow and broader tests. One way to do that is to create narrow tests that do individual functions, then create a few broad tests, dependent on the narrow ones, that perform the same functions in various combinations.

22. Tests can be executed on a similar product or a new version of the product without major modification. Consider that the test suite will need to evolve as the software that it tests evolves. It's common for software to be extended, ported, or unbundled into smaller applications. Consider how your suite will accommodate that.

    One example is localization. If you are called upon to test a French version of the software, will that require a complete rewrite of each and every test? This desirable attribute of test automation can be achieved, but may lead to very complex test suites. Be careful not to trade a simple suite that can be quickly thrown out and rewritten for a super-complex suite that is theoretically flexible but also full of bugs.

23. Test programs are reviewable. Tests must be maintained, and that means they must be revisited. Reviewability is how easy it is to come back to a test and understand it.

24. Test programs are easily added to suite. In some suites I've seen, it's major surgery just to add a new test. Make it easy and the suite will grow more quickly.

25. Tests are rapidly accessible. I once saw a test management system where it took more than 30 seconds to navigate to a single test from the top level of the system. That's awful. It discouraged test review and test development. Design the system such that you can access a given test in no more than a few seconds. Also, make sure the tests are accessible by anyone on the team.

26. Tests are traceable to a test outline. To some it's obvious, for me it was a lesson that came the hard way: Do not automate tests that can't already be executed by hand. That way, when the automation breaks, you will still be able to get your testing done. Furthermore, if your automated tests are connected to a test outline, you can theoretically assess functional test coverage in real time. The challenge is to keep the outline in sync with both the product and the tests.

27. Tests are reviewed, and their review status is documented in-line. This is especially important if several people are involved in writing the tests. Believe it or not, I have seen many examples of very poorly written tests that were overlooked for years. It's an unfortunate weakness (and most of us have it) that we will quickly assume that our test suite is full of useful tests, whether or not we personally wrote those tests. Many bad experiences have convinced me that it's dangerous to assume this!

    Test suites most often contain nonsense. REVIEW THEM!

    In order to help manage the review process, I suggest recording the date of review within each test. That will enable you to periodically re-review tests that haven't been touched in a while. Also, review tests that never fail, and ones that fail very often. Review, especially, those tests that fail falsely.

28. Test hacks and temporary patches are documented in-line. Adopt a system for recording the assumptions behind the test design, and any hacks or work-arounds that are built into the test code. This is important, as there are always hacks and temporary changes in the tests that are easy to forget about. I recommend creating a code to indicate hacks and notes, perhaps three asterisks, as in: "*** Disabled the 80387 switch until co-processor bug is fixed." Periodically, you should search for triple-asterisk codes, in order not to forget about intentionally crippled tests.

29. Suite is well documented. You should be able to explain to someone else how to run the test suite. At Borland I used the "Dave" test. When one of my testers claimed to have finished documenting how to run a suite I'd send Dave, another one of the testers, to try to run it. That invariably flushed out problems.

APPENDIX C

Other Materials Relating to Software Quality Assurance

The Internet

The Internet is a wealth of information for everyone, including those interested in quality assurance and test automation. Newsgroups, list-servers, and Web sites are among some of the most common ways to get information on areas of interest.

Newsgroups

The `comp.software.testing` newsgroup covers all areas of Software Quality Assurance, ranging from testing UNIX applications, to Macintosh applications, to Microsoft Windows applications. Use your favorite Internet provider—Microsoft Network (MSN), CompuServe, America Online (AOL), or a local provider—to get access to this newsgroup. If you're looking for a job in QA, have job openings in your group, want to know others' thoughts on a particular testing tool, or just want to share your opinion on testing methodologies, this is the place to come.

Also, since software testing is a subdiscipline of software engineering, you might find `comp.software-eng` helpful.

MT_Info

When a subject area isn't large enough to warrant a newsgroup, *list-servers* are created. A listserver is a large mailing list that people with Internet e-mail accounts can add themselves to. When someone sends a message to a given listserver, that message is then broadcast to the members of that list.

One such list was started in January, 1995, by Software Testing Laboratories, in the interest of providing a forum for the discussion of test automation using Microsoft Test. This list has continued to grow and currently has over 300 members.

To join in on the discussion, or to just "lurk" and read what others write, subscribe to the list by sending e-mail to *listproc@eskimo.com* with the following text in the body of your message:

subscribe mt_info *yourname*

(where *yourname* is replaced by your real name).

If you find that there is too much traffic and it's clogging your electronic mailbox, send a message to the same address with the following text that will remove you from the list:

unsubscribe mt_info

Web Sites

Marick's Corner

Brian Marick maintains the following Frequently Asked Questions (FAQs) lists and posts them periodically to the `comp.software.testing` newsgroup mentioned previously:

▶ Testing Contractors and Consultants

▶ Testing Courses

▶ Testing Tool Suppliers

If you are fortunate enough to have a Web browser, these FAQs are also available at both:

```
http://www.stlabs.com/marick/root.htm
ftp://cs.uiuc.edu/pub/testing/faqs/
```

Brian is working on getting his FAQs approved for news.answers and the standard repositories that go with it.

The Unofficial Visual Test Home Page

The following Web page provides tips on using Visual Test, and has links to other web pages relating to Visual Test:

```
http://www.stlabs.com/mst.htm
```

Previously, it was The Unofficial Microsoft Test Home Page, hence the updated graphic, shown in Figure C-1.

FIGURE C-1
STLabs hosts a page dedicated to Visual Test with links to other pages related to Visual Test.

Microsoft Web Pages

Microsoft has a number of helpful Web pages. Their main home page is at:

```
http://www.microsoft.com/default.htm
```

For general information about Visual Test, this is the Web site to visit:

```
http://www.microsoft.com/vtest/
```

FIGURE C-2
Visit the Microsoft Web site for information on Visual Test 4.0.

Software Productivity Center

SPC is an industry-driven, non-profit technical resource center for software developers. Founded in 1992, it has more than 100 members, and offers a wide range of courses, seminars, and products. Both products and services are offered nationally and internationally. The home page for the SPC is:

```
http://www.spc.ca/spc/Welcome.html
```

FIGURE C-3
Visit the SPC Web page for QA information.

Software Testing Laboratories (STLabs)

STLabs focuses on providing software quality assurance for developers of commercial packaged software. This company's philosophy is on helping companies build their own QA departments if they don't have one already, helping off-load work from QA departments during peak periods, and to provide training to help fill in a QA department's gaps to help them move to the next level. This includes training on some of the latest tools used in the SQA industry, including Visual Test. Its home page is:

```
http://www.stlabs.com/stl.htm
```

FIGURE C-4
STLabs is the place to go for your market-driven software testing needs.

NuMega Technologies

NuMega Technologies brings QA into the beginning of the development cycle by helping developers find bugs before releasing a build to the testing team. This is accomplished through their SoftICE and BoundsChecker products. Visit NuMega on the Web at:

```
http://www.numega.com
```

Software Testing Institute

STI provides access to industry research, surveys, seminars, publications, and online services. Its home page is:

```
http://www.ondaweb.com/sti/
```

FIGURE C-5
Another Web site for the development and testing professional to visit.

Data and Analysis Center for Software

The DACS is a Department of Defense (DOD) Information Analysis Center (IAC), administratively managed by the Defense Technical Information Center (DTIC) under the DOD IAC Program. It is technically managed by Rome Laboratory (RL). Kaman Sciences Corporation manages and operates the DACS, serving as a centralized source for current, readily available data and information concerning software engineering and software technology. The DACS home page is:

```
http://www.utica.kaman.com:8001/index.html
```

FIGURE C-6
Visit this group for information concerning software engineering and software technology.

Publications

If you're more of the type to avoid surfing the 'Net and prefer materials provided to you in hard copy form, then you'll be interested in the following newsletters and books on the subject of testing software.

Newsletters

Computing Trends. *The Software Practitioner.*
Address: 350 Dalkeith Avenue, Los Angeles, CA 90049
Tel: 310-440-9982

Ridgetop Publishing, Ltd. *Software QA Quarterly* .
Address: PO Box 379, Silverton, OR 97381-0379
Tel/Fax: 503-829-6806
e-mail: ridgetop@teleport.com

Software Maintenance News Inc. *Software Maintenance News.*
Address: B10, Suite 237, 4546 El Camino Real, Los Altos, CA 94022

Software Testing Laboratories, Inc. *STL Report.*
Address: 83 South King Street, Suite 414, Seattle, WA 98104
Tel: 206-682-5832
e-mail TrinaP@STLabs.com.

TTN. *Testing Techniques Newsletter.*
Tel: 415-957-1441 or 800-942-SOFT
Fax: 415-957-0730
e-mail: ttn@soft.com

Books

Beizer, Boris. *Software System Testing and Quality Assurance.* New York: Von Nostrand Reinhold, 1984. ISBN 0-442-21306-9.

Beizer, Boris. *Software Testing Techniques,* Second Edition. New York: Von Nostrand Reinhold, 1990. ISBN 0-442-20672-0.

DeMillo, R.A., McCracken, W.M., Martin, R.J., and Passafiume, J.F. *Software Testing and Evaluation*. Menlo Park, CA: Benjamin/Cummings, 1987. ISBN 0-8053-2535-2.

Deutsch, M.S. *Software Verification and Validation — Realistic Project Approaches*. Englewood Cliffs, NJ: Prentice Hall, 1982. ISBN 0-13-822072-7.

Dunn, Robert H. *Software Quality: Concepts And Plans*. Englewood Cliffs, NJ: Prentice Hall, 1990. ISBN 0-13-820283-4.

Friedman, Michael and Voas, Jeffrey M. *Software Assessment: Reliability, Safety, Testability*. New York: Wiley Press, 1995. ISBN 0-471-01009-X

Hetzel, B. *The Complete Guide to Software Testing*, Second Edition. Wellesley, MA: QED Information Sciences, 1988. ISBN 0-89435-242-3.

Ince, Darrel. *An Introduction to Software Quality Assurance and Its Implementation*. London, New York: McGraw Hill, 1994. ISBN 0-07-707924-8.

Kaner, Cem., Falk, and J., Nguyen, H.Q. *Testing Computer Software*, Second Edition. New York: Von Nostrand Reinhold, 1993. ISBN 0-442-01361-2.

Marick, Brian. *The Craft of Software Testing*. Englewood Cliffs, NJ: Prentice Hall, 1995. ISBN 0-13-177411-5.

Marks, D.M. *Testing Very Big Systems*. New York: McGraw Hill, 1992. ISBN 0-07-040433-X.

McConell, Steve. *Code Complete: A Practical Handbook of Software Construction*. Redmond, Washington: Microsoft Press, 1993. ISBN 1-55-615484-4.

Mosley, D.J. *The Handbook of MIS Application Software Testing*. Englewood Cliffs, NJ: Prentice Hall, 1993. ISBN 0-13-907007-9.

Myers, Glenford J. *The Art of Software Testing*. New York: John Wiley and Sons, 1979. ISBN 0-471-04328-1.

Ould, M.A. and Unwin, C., eds. *Testing in Software Development*. Cambridge: Cambridge University Press, 1986. ISBN 0-521-33786-0.

Parrington, Norman and Roper, Marc. *Understanding Software Testing.*
Ellis Horwood Limited, 1989. ISBN 0-7458-0533-7
Also: Ellis Horwood Limited. ISBN 0-470-21462-7 (Halsted Press).

Royer, T.C. *Software Testing Management — Life on the Critical Path.*
Englewood Cliffs, NJ: Prentice Hall, 1993. ISBN 0-13-532987-6.

Listing for notemain.inc

*T*he notemain.inc file is the main declaration or *include* file for the sample test suite discussed throughout this book. Declarations of constants, user-defined types, prototypes or links into external dynamic link libraries (DLLs) and macros that are common enough to be used by most test case files in the project, are placed into this top-level include file.

This file is a living file; it changes as more tests are added to the test suite. Sometimes declarations are moved to other include (.inc) files in the project if they only apply to a specific set of test cases. Other declarations find their way up to this top-level include file as it becomes apparent that the declarations are common enough to be applicable to many test case files in the test suite.

The source code file for this listing can be found on the disk included with this book under the name of "notemain.inc":

```
'****************************************************************
'* Copyright 1994-1996 Software Testing Laboratories, Inc.
'* All rights reserved. You may use this source code freely
'* as long as it is not included as part of a selling product
'* without prior written permission from STLabs.
'****************************************************************

'********************** notemain.inc **********************
'*
'* Purpose: Holds common declarations to be used by all test
'*          case files. Anything not common enough to be
'*          used by the majority of the test case files should
'*          be moved to an include file lower in the hierarchy,
'*          specific to the area it concerns.
'*
'* Author:  Tom Arnold
```

```
'*
'* Revision History:
'*
'* [ 0]  da-mon-year    email    action
'* [ 1]  29-FEB-1996    TomAr    Created notemain.inc to hold
'*                               common declarations.
'* [ 2]  29-FEB-1996    TVT      Moved in some common constants.
'* [ 3]  06-MAR-1996    TomAr    Added consts for rest of suite.
'****************************************************************

'$IFNDEF NOTEMAIN_INCLUDED
'$DEFINE NOTEMAIN_INCLUDED


'****************************************************************
'*********************** Constants ******************************
'****************************************************************


'********** General Application Info
const TEST_APP$        = "NOTEPAD.EXE" 'Exe file name of test subject

'********** Window captions/class names
const CAP_NOTEPAD$     = "- Notepad"   'Partial caption of main
                                        window
const CAP_SAVECHANGES$ = "Notepad"     'Caption of Save Chngs msg
                                        box
const TEST_APP_CLASS$  = "Notepad"     'Classname of app's main
                                        window


'********** Logging Detail Settings
const LVL_SUMMARY%     = 5             'Summary info after each
test                                    case
const LVL_MENUINFO%    = 10            'Give menu info if Detail >
                                        10
const LVL_STATUSINFO   = 20            'General status info
const LVL_VERBOSE%     = 100           'Have all calls to LOG
                                        enabled


'********** Edit control captions
const EDIT_NOTEPAD$    = "@1"          'Notepad's main edit window

'********** Button control captions
const BTN_NO$          = "No"          'Caption for No button
const BTN_YES$         = "Yes"         'Caption for Yes button
```

```
const BTN_CANCEL$        = "Cancel"        'Caption for Cancel button
const BTN_SAVE$          = "Save"          'Caption for Save button
const BTN_OK$            = "OK"            'Caption for OK button
const BTN_OPEN           = "Open"          'Caption for Open button

'********** Menu Bar and Menu Item captions
'***** Menu items for the File menu
const MNU_FILE_NEW$      = "File\New"
const MNU_FILE_OPEN$     = "File\Open..."
const MNU_FILE_SAVE$     = "File\Save"
const MNU_FILE_SAVEAS$   = "File\Save As..."
const MNU_FILE_PGSETUP$ = "File\Page Setup..."
const MNU_FILE_PRINT$    = "File\Print"
const MNU_FILE_EXIT$     = "File\Exit"

'***** Menu items for the Edit menu
const MNU_EDIT_UNDO$     = "Edit\Undo"
const MNU_EDIT_CUT$      = "Edit\Cut"
const MNU_EDIT_COPY$     = "Edit\Copy"
const MNU_EDIT_PASTE$    = "Edit\Paste"
const MNU_EDIT_DELETE$   = "Edit\Delete"
const MNU_EDIT_SELALL$   = "Edit\Select All"
const MNU_EDIT_TIMEDATE$= "Edit\Time\Date"
const MNU_EDIT_WRDWRAP$  = "Edit\Word Wrap"

'***** Menu items for the Search menu
const MNU_SEARCH_FIND$   = "Search\Find..."
const MNU_SEARCH_FNEXT$ = "Search\Find Next"

'***** Menu items for the Help menu
const MNU_HELP_TOPICS    = "Help\Help Topics"
const MNU_HELP_ABOUT     = "Help\About Notepad"


'********** Name of Temporary Files
const TEMPFILE1$             = "TEMP1.TXT"
const TEMPFILE2$             = "TEMP2.TXT"


'********** Other constants
const MAX_WAIT%          = 5      '# of secs to search for window
const MAX_GAP%           = 10     '# spaces gap used in logging out
                                  info
```

```
const DATA_TESTSTRING1$ = "Now is the time for all good people..."
const FW_NOTEPAD&       = FW_PART OR FW_ALL OR FW_FOCUS OR FW_RE-
                          STORE _
                        OR FW_EXIST    'Search criteria for finding
                                       'the Notepad main window


'****************************************************************
'********************** User Def'd Types ************************
'****************************************************************


'****************************************************************
'********************** Global Variables ***********************
'****************************************************************


global ghWndNotepad&     'Handle to Notepad's main window
global giTestCount%      'Incr. by strTestNum()
global giFailCount%      'Incr. by strFailNum()


'****************************************************************
'***************** Func/Proc Prototypes ********************
'****************************************************************



'$ENDIF NOTEMAIN_INCLUDED
```

APPENDIX

E

Listing for noteutil.inc

he noteutil.inc file is the main set of function and subroutine utilities for the sample test suite discussed throughout this book. Functions and subroutines that are common enough to be used by most test case files in the project are placed into this top-level include file.

Similar to the notemain.inc shown in Appendix D, this file is also a living file; it changes as more tests are added to the test suite. Sometimes functions and subroutines are moved to test case (.mst) files in the project if they only apply to those specific test cases. Other functions and subroutines find their way up to this top-level include file as it becomes apparent that they are common enough to be applicable to many test case files in the test suite.

The source code file for this listing can be found on the disk included with this book under the name of "noteutil.inc":

```
'****************************************************************
'* Copyright 1994-1996 Software Testing Laboratories, Inc.
'* All rights reserved. You may use this source code freely
'* as long as it is not included as part of a selling product
'* without prior written permission from STLabs.
'****************************************************************

'*********************** noteutil.inc ***********************
'*
'* Purpose: Common functions and subroutines that are useful
'*          to other test case files are placed into this
'*          file for our Notepad project. As this file grows
'*          other testing teams might be interested in using
'*          this file to get a head-start on their automation.
'*
'* Author:  Tom Arnold
'*
```

```
'* Revision History:
'*
'* [ 0]  da-mon-year     email    action
'* [ 1]  28-FEB-1996     TomAr    Created noteutil.inc to hold
'*                                common functions & subroutines.
'* [ 2]  29-FEB-1996     TVT      Moved in some common funcs.
'* [ 3]  06-MAR-1996     TomAr    Fixed TVT's bugs, added more
'*                                support routines.
'*******************************************************************

'$IFNDEF NOTEUTIL_INCLUDED
'$DEFINE NOTEUTIL_INCLUDED

'*********************** INCLUDES *****************************
'$include 'notemain.inc'



'*******************************************************************
'* Function:     fGrayMenu
'* Purpose:      Returns true if the menu item is grayed, false
'*               if not.
'*
'* Parameters:   strMenuItem$
'*                    String compatible with the wMenuSelect
'*                    command for a menu and its menu item.
'*
'* Returns:      INTEGER A boolean flag value is returned.
'*
'*******************************************************************

function fGrayMenu (strMenuItem$) as Integer
    dim strMenu$, strItem$

    'The backslash '\' separates the menu from the menu item.
    'This version of fGrayMenu doesn't currently work for
    'hierarchical menus.
    strMenu = left$(strMenuItem,instr(strMenuItem,"\")-1)
    strItem = right$(strMenuItem,len(strMenuItem)-
    instr(strMenuItem,"\"))

    wMenuEnd                        'Pop-up any open menus
    wMenuSelect(strMenu)            'Pop-down chosen menu
    if wMenuGrayed(strItem) then    'Check menu item
        fGrayMenu = TRUE
```

```
    else                              'Set appropriate return value
        fGrayMenu = FALSE
    end if
    wMenuEnd                          'Pop-up open menu
end function 'GrayMenu



'*****************************************************************
'* Function:    iFailCount
'* Purpose:     Returns current number of failures for current
'*              test case file. This only works if the test
'*              scenarios are using strFailNum() in conjunction
'*              with calls to the fail statement. Done this
'*              way to avoid Test programmers directly accessing
'*              the giFailCount global variable.
'*
'* Parameters:  NONE
'*
'* Returns:     INTEGER Current value of giFailCount, which is
'*                      a global value incremented every time
'*                      strFailNum is called.
'*
'*****************************************************************

function iFailCount() as integer
    iFailCount = giFailCount
end function 'iFailCount



'*****************************************************************
'* Function:    iTestCount
'* Purpose:     Returns current number of test scenarios executed
'*              for current test case file. This only works if
'*              the test scenarios are using strTestNum() in
'*              conjunction with calls to the scenario statement.
'*              Done this way to avoid Test programmers directly
'*              accessing the giTestCount global variable.
'*
'* Parameters:  NONE
'*
'* Returns:     INTEGER Current value of giTestCount, which is
'*                      a global value incremented every time
'*                      strTestNum is called.
'*
```

```
'******************************************************************

function iTestCount() as integer
    iTestCount = giTestCount
end function 'iTestCount



'******************************************************************
'* Subroutine:  PutString
'* Purpose:     Places a string into the Notepad editor at a
'*              specified line and character position. If the
'*              line or character doesn't exist, this routine adds
'*              the necessary carriage returns and spaces.
'*
'* Parameters:  strOut$ String to be written to the editor
'*              iLine%  Line at which string is to be written
'*              iChar%  Character/column position to place string
'*
'******************************************************************

sub PutString (strOut$, iLine%, iChar%)
    dim iCurrLine%      'Keeps track of what line the cursor is on
    dim iCurrChar%      'Tracks which column cursor is in
    dim iLoop%          'Used as index to for-loop
    dim iLoopLimit%     'Used to determine end value of for-loop
    dim strDirection$   'Set to which keystroke should be used

    'Get the current line and cursor position
    iCurrLine = wEditLine(EDIT_NOTEPAD)

    'Determine which direction to move based on
    'current position and desired position.
    if (iCurrLine < iLine) then
        iLoopLimit = (iLine - iCurrLine)
        strDirection = "{DOWN}"             'We need to move down
    else
        iLoopLimit = (iCurrLine - iLine)
        strDirection = "{UP}"               'We need to move up
    endif

    'Move to the desired position, adding lines
    'if necessary.
    for iLoop = 1 to iLoopLimit
        if (wEditLine(EDIT_NOTEPAD) < wEditLines(EDIT_NOTEPAD)) then
```

```
            Play strDirection
        elseif (strDirection = "{DOWN}") then
            Play "{END}"
            Play "{ENTER}"
        else
            Play strDirection
        endif
    next iLoop

    'Get the current character position
    iCurrChar = wEditPos(EDIT_NOTEPAD)

    'Based on the current position, determine which
    'direction to move.
    if (iCurrChar < iChar) then
        iLoopLimit = (iChar - iCurrChar)
        strDirection = "{RIGHT}"
    else
        iLoopLimit = (iCurrChar - iChar)
        strDirection = "{LEFT}"
    endif

    'Move to the desired position added spaces if needed.
    for iLoop = 1 to iLoopLimit
        if (wEditPos(EDIT_NOTEPAD) < _
            wEditLineLen(EDIT_NOTEPAD,wEditLine(EDIT_NOTEPAD))) then
            Play strDirection
        elseif (strDirection = "{RIGHT}") then
            Play " "
        else
            Play strDirection
        endif
    next iLoop

    Play strOut    'Type the string at the current location
end sub 'PutString()


'******************************************************************
'* Subroutine:  ResetApp
'* Purpose:     Attempts to reset the application to a known
'*              state. This routine will likely grow in
'*              complexity as strange circumstances are
'*              discovered where this routine isn't able to
```

```
'*              reset the application.
'*
'*****************************************************************

sub ResetApp()
   wMenuEnd
   SelMenu(MNU_FILE_NEW)

   if (GetText(NULL) = CAP_SAVECHANGES) then
      wButtonClick(BTN_NO)
   endif
end sub 'ResetApp()


'*****************************************************************
'* Subroutine:  SelMenu
'* Purpose:     This is a wrapper around the wMenuSelect
'*              statement, allowing us a level of detailed
'*              information if requested.
'*
'* Parameters:  STRING  A wMenuSelect-compatible string.
'*
'*****************************************************************

sub SelMenu(strMenu$)
      wMenuEnd                'Make sure a menu isn't already popped
                              down
   wMenuSelect(strMenu)    'Select the menu item

   'The detail level represented by the LVL_MENUINFO constant is
   'controlled from the Options dialog box in the Suite Manager.
   'If the level specified in the Suite Manager is greater than
   'the level specified by LVL_MENUINFO (below) then the information
   'will be logged out. Otherwise, the information isn't logged.
   'This is a way to control the level/detail of information
   'provided.
   Log #LVL_MENUINFO, "Selected menu: "+strMenu$
end sub 'SelMenu()


'*****************************************************************
'* Function:    strFailNum
'* Purpose:     Keeps a counter of the total number of failures
'*              that have occurred using the fail command for
```

```
'*              the current test case file. For this to work,
'*              it must be called for each failure and is
'*              therefore designed to work with the fail
'*              statement.
'*
'* Parameters:  NONE
'*
'* Returns:     STRING  The string that is returned is formatted
'*                      to fit in front of the text being
'*                      included in the fail statement.
'*
'* Format
'* returned:    "Fail #<num>: "
'*
'* Use:         FAIL strFailNum()+"<descrip-of-failure>"
'*
'******************************************************************

function strFailNum() as string
    giFailCount = giFailCount + 1
    strFailNum = "Fail #"+trim$(str$(giFailCount))+": "
end function 'strFailNum()


'******************************************************************
'* Function:    strTestNum
'* Purpose:     Keeps a counter of the total number of tests
'*              that have been executed for the current test
'*              case file. For this to work, it must be
'*              called for each test. It is designed to work
'*              with the scenario statement. This is why it
'*              returns a string.
'*
'* Parameters:  NONE
'*
'* Returns:     STRING  The string that is returned is formatted
'*                      to fit in front of the text being
'*                      included in the scenario statement.
'*
'* Format
'* returned:    "Test #<num>: "
'*
'* Use:         SCENARIO strTestNum()+"<descrip-of-test>"
'*
```

```
'*******************************************************************

function strTestNum() as string
    giTestCount = giTestCount + 1
    strTestNum = "Test #"+trim$(str$(giTestCount))+": "
end function 'strTestNum()



'*******************************************************************
'* Subroutine:  TestBegin
'* Purpose:     All initialization code that needs to be run
'*              before the scenarios of a test case are
'*              executed should be placed in this subroutine.
'*              This subroutine needs to be called first by
'*              each test case.
'*
'* Parameters:  NONE
'*
'*******************************************************************

sub TestBegin()
    log #LVL_VERBOSE, "Initializing Test Case and attempting to"
    log #LVL_VERBOSE, "find or run ";TEST_APP;" application."

    viewport clear       'Clean the contents of the Viewport tab
                         'in the Output window.

    'Get test application up and running. If it can be run
    'for whatever reason, print an error message and stop
    'the execution of the script.

    ghWndNotepad = wFndWndC(CAP_NOTEPAD, TEST_APP_CLASS, FW_NOTEPAD,
    MAX_WAIT)

    if (ghWndNotepad = 0) then
        log #LVL_VERBOSE, "Unable to find ";TEST_APP;"."
        if run(TEST_APP) then
            fail "Error: Unable to run notepad.exe"
        else
            ghWndNotepad = wFndWnd(CAP_NOTEPAD, FW_NOTEPAD,
            MAX_WAIT)
            log #LVL_VERBOSE, "Successfully ran ";TEST_APP
        endif
    else
```

```
        log #LVL_VERBOSE, "Found ";TEST_APP;" already running."
        ResetApp()
    endif

    'Note: Having a call to the fail statement will generate
    'a run-time error since it is not in a scenario block.
    'As a result, an error message box will be given, if you
    'are in Microsoft Developer Studio. If you are in the
    'Visual Test Suite Manager, the result will be the Suite
    'Manager moving on to the next test case file. This is
    'what you would want, as it doesn't make sense for the
    'rest of the tests to run, since the test application
    'can't be brought up.

end sub 'TestBegin()


'*****************************************************************
'* Subroutine:  TestEnd
'* Purpose:     Clean-up code that needs to be executed after
'*              all scenarios for a given test case file have
'*              been executed.
'*
'* Parameters:  NONE
'*
'*****************************************************************

sub TestEnd()
    dim iPPass%         'Percent passed
    dim strMetrix$      'Misc metrics

    '** Clean-up before the test case file ends **

    wMenuSelect(MNU_FILE_EXIT)      'Shut down Notepad application

    if GetText(NULL) = CAP_SAVECHANGES then
        wButtonClick(BTN_NO)        'Click 'No' to "Save changes?"
    endif

    'Set up info to be logged out
    iPPass = ((iTestCount - iFailCount) / iTestCount) * 100
    strMetrix = "Scenarios: "+trim$(str$(iTestCount)) + _
                SPACE$(MAX_GAP) + "Errors: "+trim$(str$(iFailCount))
                + _
```

```
                              SPACE$(MAX_GAP) + "Passed: " + _
                              trim$(str$(iPPass))+"%"

             'Log out final information for the test case file.
             'When doing the LEFT$() stuff a bunch of spaces are added
             'for padding and then are cropped off, so that the max size
             'of the line being written out is 70 characters. By cropping
             'like this the info can adjust its size and still have the
             'right-hand border of the box remain in line.
             log #LVL_SUMMARY,"************************* Test Case Results "
             + _
                          "*************************"
             log #LVL_SUMMARY,"*"+space$(68)+"*"
             log #LVL_SUMMARY,"* Test Case:
             "+(left$(NAME$(0)+space$(70),56))+"*"
             log #LVL_SUMMARY,"*"+space$(68)+"*"
             log #LVL_SUMMARY,"* "+left$(strMetrix+space$(70),67)+"*"
             log #LVL_SUMMARY,"*"+space$(68)+"*"
             log #LVL_SUMMARY,"* Test case completed testing at "+ _
                          left$(datetime$+space$(70),36)+"*"
             log #LVL_SUMMARY,"*"+space$(68)+"*"
             log #LVL_SUMMARY,STRING$(70,"*")
             end sub 'TestEnd()


        '$ENDIF NOTEUTIL_INCLUDED
```

APPENDIX

Listings of All Test Cases

The following listings are the test case files that make up the Notepad test suite which is discussed throughout this book. The test scenarios that make up the test case files are just a beginning to provide some structure and examples. By creating this structure and some beginning scenarios, other Test programmers have examples to follow when setting out to create their own tests for the different features of the Notepad application.

File Menu

The File menu is made up of seven menu items. These are: New, Open, Save, Save As, Page Setup, Print and Exit. Based on the approach that is being taken in this example (menu-based), the path followed by the automated tests traverse the menus that make up the Notepad product.

Based on these seven menu items, eight files should be created for testing those menu items: file.inc, new.mst, open.mst, save.mst, saveas.mst, page_su.mst, print.mst and exit.mst. In this example, print.mst has not been included.

The file.inc include file holds declarations common to the menu items that make up the File menu. Any declarations that might be used by the other test case files should be placed into the file.inc include file. Declarations that are even more generic, and useful to other menus and menu items, should be moved up higher into the notemain.inc file.

FILE.INC

Any declarations that aren't generic enough to go into the main header file for the Notepad test suite (notemain.inc) and are specific to the test case files that perform tests on the File menu are placed into this file.

```
'*****************************************************************
'* Copyright 1994-1996 Software Testing Laboratories, Inc.
'* All rights reserved. You may use this source code freely
'* as long as it is not included as part of a selling product.
'*****************************************************************


'*********************** FILE.INC ************************
'*
'* PURPOSE: Decls for the File menu tests.
'*
'*****************************************************************


'$ifndef FILE_INCLUDED
'$define FILE_INCLUDED


'*****************************************************************
'************************ CONSTANTS ************************
'*****************************************************************


'***** Dialog Control Names

const DCN_FILENAME$          = "File Name:"
const DCN_SPECIFICPRINTER$   = "Specific Printer:"
const DCN_OUTPUTFILENAME$    = "Output File Name:"


'***** Captions

const CAP_SAVEAS$            = "Save As"       'Save As Common DB
const CAP_OPEN$              = "Open"          'Open Common DB
const CAP_SAVE$              = "Save"          'Save Common DB
const CAP_PRINTTOFILE$       = "Print To File" 'print to file DB
const CAP_PAGESETUP$         = "Page Setup"    'page setup DB
const CAP_PRINTSETUP$        = "Print Setup"   'print setup DB

'***** Misc

const MAX_COUNT              = 15
```

```
'****************************************************************
'********************** User Def'd Types **********************
'****************************************************************



'****************************************************************
'********************** Global Variables **********************
'****************************************************************



'****************************************************************
'****************** Func/Proc Prototypes **********************
'****************************************************************


'$endif FILE_INCLUDED
```

NEW.MST

```
'****************************************************************
'* Copyright 1994-1996 Software Testing Laboratories, Inc.
'* All rights reserved. You may use this source code freely
'* as long as it is not included as part of a selling product.
'****************************************************************


'****************************************************************
'* Filename:    NEW.MST
'*
'* Purpose:     Tests the New menu item for the File menu in
'*              Notepad's main window.
'*
'* Revision History:
'*
'*  [ 0]   da-mon-year   email    : action
'*  [ 1]   28-FEB-1996   TomAr    First few scenarios for the New
'*                                  menu item to give some structure.
'*  [ 2]   29-FEB-1996   TVT      Created common constants, etc.
'*                                  and moved to notemain.inc. Made
'*                                  common subs & funcs and moved to
'*                                  noteutil.inc.
'*  [ 3]   01-MAR-1996   TomAr    Added some final test scenarios
'*                                  to fill in this first test case.
'*  [ 4]   06-MAR-1996   TomAr    Moved File menu-specific consts
'*                                  to file.inc and out of notemain.inc.
'*
```

```
'****************************************************************
'*********************** INCLUDES ****************************
'$include 'notemain.inc'    'Constants common enough to share with everyone
'$include 'noteutil.inc'    'Utilities generic/sharable with all tests
'$include 'file.inc'        'Constants/utils generic for testing the file menu


TestBegin()               'Initialize the test case

    '** Beginning of the test scenarios **
    scenario strTestNum()+"Test that 'Save changes' message box"+ _
                        " is displayed."
        PutString(DATA_TESTSTRING1, 1, 1)

        SelMenu(MNU_FILE_NEW)

        if (GetText(NULL) <> CAP_SAVECHANGES) then
            fail strFailNum()+"Error: Message box not found."
        endif
    scenario cleanup
        LOG #LVL_VERBOSE, "Cleaning up for test scenario #"+str$(iTestCount)
        if not(failed) then
            wButtonClick(BTN_CANCEL)
        endif
    end scenario


    scenario strTestNum()+"Verify that the original text remains"+ _
                        " unchanged after clicking Cancel."
        if EditText(EDIT_NOTEPAD) <> DATA_TESTSTRING1 then
            fail strFailNum()+"Original test string changed."
        endif
    end scenario

    ResetApp     'Clear contents of Notepad to get to known state


    scenario strTestNum()+"Click 'No' to 'Save Changes?' msg"
        PutString(DATA_TESTSTRING1, 10, 10)

        SelMenu(MNU_FILE_NEW)
        wButtonClick(BTN_NO)
        if EditText(EDIT_NOTEPAD) <> "" then
            fail strFailNum()+"Text was not cleared as expected."
```

```
            endif
    scenario cleanup
        LOG #LVL_VERBOSE, "Cleaning up for test scenario #"+str$(iTestCount)
        ResetApp
    end scenario


    scenario strTestNum()+"Click 'Yes' to 'Save changes?' msg"
        PutString(DATA_TESTSTRING1, 10, 10)

        SelMenu(MNU_FILE_NEW)
        wButtonClick(BTN_YES)    'Yes to save changes

        if (GetText(NULL) <> CAP_SAVEAS) then
            fail strFailNum()+"Save As dialog box not displayed."
        else
            'We don't want to test the Save As dialog box,
            'just make sure it displays.  We can determine
            'how we want to test it later.
            wButtonClick(BTN_CANCEL)
        endif
    scenario cleanup
        LOG #LVL_VERBOSE, "Cleaning up for test scenario #"+str$(iTestCount)
        ResetApp
    end scenario

TestEnd()
```

OPEN.MST

```
'*****************************************************************
'* Copyright 1994-1996 Software Testing Laboratories, Inc.
'* All rights reserved. You may use this source code freely
'* as long as it is not included as part of a selling product.
'*****************************************************************


'*****************************************************************
'* Filename:    OPEN.MST
'*
'* Purpose:     Tests the Open menu item for the File menu in
'*               Notepad's main window.
'*
'* Revision History:
'*
```

```
'*  [ 0]   da-mon-year  email   : action
'*  [ 1]   06-MAR-1996  TomAr   First few scenarios to give
'*                               some general structure.
'*
'****************************************************************


'*********************** INCLUDES *****************************
'$include 'notemain.inc'    'Constants common enough to share with everyone
'$include 'noteutil.inc'    'Utilities generic/sharable with all tests
'$include 'file.inc'        'Constants/utils generic for testing the File menu

TestBegin
    dim strText$

    '
    'Create a test file to use with the Open menu item.
    '
    LOG #LVL_STATUSINFO, "Creating temporary file to open."
    If not exists(TEMPFILE1) then
        PutString(DATA_TESTSTRING1,1,1)
        SelMenu(MNU_FILE_SAVEAS)
        wEditSetText(DCN_FILENAME,TEMPFILE1)
        wButtonClick(BTN_SAVE)
    EndIf


    '
    'Tests the "Open" menu item, dirty bit not set.
    '
    scenario strTestNum()+MNU_FILE_OPEN+" file when no text in editor exists."
        SelMenu(MNU_FILE_OPEN)   'Select menu item "Open".

        If(GetText(NULL) = CAP_OPEN) then              'Did "Open" db display?
            wEditSetText(DCN_FILENAME,TEMPFILE1)    'Enter the filename to open.
            wButtonClick(BTN_OPEN)

            'See If filename is in the caption.
            If INSTR(ucase$(GetText(NULL)),ucase$(TEMPFILE1)) = 0 then
                fail strFailNum()+ TEMPFILE1 + " was not opened."
            EndIf
        Else
            fail strFailNum()+MNU_FILE_OPEN+" without text didn't " + _
                "display dialog."
        EndIf
    end scenario
```

```
'
'Open menu item with text and click 'Cancel' to save changes message box.
'
scenario strTestNum()+MNU_FILE_OPEN+" file and select "+BTN_CANCEL+ _
        " to Save Changes prompt."
    PutString(DATA_TESTSTRING1, 2, 1)
    strText = EditText(EDIT_NOTEPAD)      'Grab contents of editor.
    SelMenu(MNU_FILE_OPEN)

    'Since text was added the Save Changes message box should appear.
    If (GetText(NULL) = CAP_SAVECHANGES) then
        wButtonClick(BTN_CANCEL)
    Else
        fail strFailNum()+MNU_FILE_OPEN+ _
            " w/ text didn't display Save Changes msgbox."
    EndIf
end scenario



scenario strTestNum()+"Verify text didn't change from previous scenario"
    If (strText <> EditText(EDIT_NOTEPAD)) then
        Fail strFailNum()+BTN_CANCEL+" to Save Changes."
    EndIf
end scenario



'
'Open menu item with text and clicking 'No' to save changes message box.
'

scenario strTestNum()+"'Open' file and 'No' to Save Changes msgbox."
    SelMenu(MNU_FILE_OPEN)

    If (GetText(NULL) = CAP_SAVECHANGES) then          'Did the "are you sure?"
                                                        'appear?
        wButtonClick(BTN_NO)                            'Click the "No" button
        If(GetText(NULL) = CAP_OPEN) then               'Did "Open" db display?
            wEditSetText(DCN_FILENAME,TEMPFILE1)        'Enter the filename to
                                                        'open.
            wButtonClick(BTN_OPEN)                      'Click "Open" button.

            'See If filename is in the caption.
            If INSTR(ucase$(GetText(NULL)),ucase$(TEMPFILE1)) = 0 then
                fail strFailNum()+ TEMPFILE1 + " was not opened."
```

```
            EndIf
        Else
            fail strFailNum()+MNU_FILE_OPEN+" with text didn't display."
        EndIf
    Else
        fail strFailNum()+MNU_FILE_OPEN+" w/ text didn't give Save" + _
            " Changes msgbox."
    EndIf
end scenario

'
'Open menu item with text and clicking 'yes' to save changes
'message box and click 'cancel' in save as db.
'
scenario strTestNum()+MNU_FILE_OPEN+" w/ text. "+BTN_YES+ _
        " to Save Changes, then "+BTN_CANCEL+" to Open dialog box."
    SelMenu(MNU_FILE_NEW)
    PutString(DATA_TESTSTRING1, 3, 1)
    strText = EditText(EDIT_NOTEPAD)                'Get contents of editor.
    SelMenu(MNU_FILE_OPEN)

    If (GetText(NULL) = CAP_SAVECHANGES) then    'Did the "are you sure?"
                                                 'appear?
        wButtonClick(BTN_YES)
        If(GetText(NULL) = CAP_SAVEAS) then      'Did "Saveas" db display?
            wButtonClick(BTN_CANCEL)

            'Make sure text did not change.
            If (strText <> EditText(EDIT_NOTEPAD)) then
                fail strFailNum()+BTN_CANCEL+" out of 'SaveAs' " + _
                    "caused text change."
            EndIf
        Else
            fail strFailNum()+MNU_FILE_OPEN+" with "+BTN_YES+ _
                " to Save Changes didn't display SaveAs DB."
        EndIf
    Else
        fail strFailNum()+MNU_FILE_OPEN+" w/ text didn't " + _
            "give Save Changes msgbox."
    EndIf
end scenario
```

```
'
'Open menu item with text and clicking 'Yes' to save changes
'message box and saving the file before opening another.
'
scenario strTestNum()+MNU_FILE_OPEN+" w/o text. Press "+BTN_YES+ _
        " then "+BTN_OK
    PutString(DATA_TESTSTRING1, 4, 1)
    SelMenu(MNU_FILE_OPEN)

    If (GetText(NULL) = CAP_SAVECHANGES) then          'Save Changes dialog?
        wButtonClick(BTN_YES)
        If(GetText(NULL) = CAP_SAVEAS) then               'Did "Saveas" db
                                                          'display?
            wEditSetText(DCN_FILENAME,TEMPFILE2)    'Enter the filename to
                                                          'save to.
            wButtonClick(BTN_SAVE)
            If(GetText(NULL) = CAP_OPEN) then       'Did "Open" db display?
                wEditSetText(DCN_FILENAME,TEMPFILE1)'Enter the filename to
                                                          'open.
                wButtonClick(BTN_OPEN)

                'See if filename is in the caption.
                If INSTR(ucase$(GetText(NULL)),ucase$(TEMPFILE1)) = 0 then
                    fail strFailNum()+TEMPFILE1 + " was not opened."
                EndIf
            Else
                fail strFailNum()+MNU_FILE_OPEN+" with text didn't display."
            EndIf
        Else
            fail strFailNum()+MNU_FILE_OPEN+", click "+BTN_YES+ _
                " to Save Changes didn't display SaveAs"
        EndIf
    Else
        fail strFailNum()+MNU_FILE_OPEN+" w/ new text didn't " + _
            "give Save Changes msgbox."
    EndIf
scenario cleanup
    log #LVL_VERBOSE, "Removing temporary text files for test scenario #"+ _
        str$(iTestCount)
    kill TEMPFILE1
    kill TEMPFILE2
end scenario
TestEnd()
```

SAVE.MST

```
'******************************************************************
'* Copyright 1994-1996 Software Testing Laboratories, Inc.
'* All rights reserved. You may use this source code freely
'* as long as it is not included as part of a selling product.
'******************************************************************


'******************************************************************
'* Filename:    SAVE.MST
'*
'* Purpose:      Tests the Save menu item for the File menu in
'*               Notepad's main window.
'*
'* Revision History:
'*
'* [ 0]    da-mon-year   email    : action
'* [ 1]    06-MAR-1996   TomAr    First few scenarios to give
'*                                 some general structure.
'*
'******************************************************************


'********************** INCLUDES ***************************
'$include 'notemain.inc'      'Constants common enough to share with everyone
'$include 'noteutil.inc'      'Utilities generic/sharable with all tests
'$include 'file.inc'          'Constants/utils generic for testing the file menu

TestBegin
    dim strText$


    '
    'Save with text untitled.
    '
    scenario strTestNum()+MNU_FILE_SAVE+" with text.  Untitled instance"
        PutString(DATA_TESTSTRING1,1,1)
        strText = EditText(EDIT_NOTEPAD)
        SelMenu(MNU_FILE_SAVE)

        If (GetText(NULL) = CAP_SAVEAS) then
            wEditSetText(DCN_FILENAME, TEMPFILE2)
            wButtonClick(BTN_SAVE)

            if (GetText(NULL) = CAP_SAVEAS) then  'File already exists?
```

```
                    wButtonClick(BTN_YES)
              endif

              If (INSTR(ucase$(GetText(NULL)),ucase$(TEMPFILE2)) <> 0) then
                  If (strText <> EditText(EDIT_NOTEPAD)) then
                        fail strFailNum+"Saving the file caused the text to change."
                  EndIf
              Else
                  fail strFailNum+TEMPFILE2+" was not Saved."
              EndIf
          Else
              fail strFailNum+MNU_FILE_SAVE+" with text didn't display "+ _
                  CAP_SAVEAS+" dialog."
          EndIf
end scenario


'
'Save with text in saved instance.
'
scenario strTestNum()+MNU_FILE_SAVE+" with text.  Saved instance"
    PutString(DATA_TESTSTRING1, 2, 1)
    strText = EditText(EDIT_NOTEPAD)
    SelMenu(MNU_FILE_SAVE)

    If (WGetActWnd(0) <> ghWndNotepad) then
        fail strFailNum+MNU_FILE_SAVE+" should not have displayed a dialog."
        Play("{Esc}")    'Dismiss the dialog.
    EndIf
scenario cleanup
    log #LVL_VERBOSE, "Cleaning up for test scenario #"+str$(iTestCount)
    ResetApp()
end scenario


'
'Verify text saved by opening file saved in previous
'scenario and comparing with text of previous scenario
'
scenario strTestNum()+"Verify text was saved to file."
    SelMenu(MNU_FILE_OPEN)  'Open up the saved file.
    wEditSetText(DCN_FILENAME,TEMPFILE2)
    wButtonClick(BTN_OPEN)
```

```
        If (strText <> EditText(EDIT_NOTEPAD)) then
            fail strFailNum+MNU_FILE_SAVE+" didn't save changes."
        EndIf
    scenario cleanup
        log #LVL_VERBOSE, "Cleaning up for test scenario #"+str$(iTestCount)
        ResetApp()
    end scenario



    '
    'Save to a file that already Exists.  Respond 'No'.
    '
    scenario strTestNum()+MNU_FILE_SAVE+" to existing file. Click "+BTN_NO
        PutString(DATA_TESTSTRING1, 1, 1)
        strText = EditText(EDIT_NOTEPAD)
        SelMenu(MNU_FILE_SAVE)

        If (GetText(NULL) = CAP_SAVEAS) then
            wEditSetText(DCN_FILENAME, TEMPFILE2)    'Enter filename
            wButtonClick(BTN_SAVE)                    'Click Save
            If (GetText(NULL) = CAP_SAVEAS) then     'Replace file?
                wButtonClick(BTN_NO)                   'No, don't replace
                If (GetText(NULL) = CAP_SAVEAS) then
                    wButtonClick(BTN_CANCEL)          'Cancel out of SaveAs
                    If (strText <> EditText(EDIT_NOTEPAD)) then
                        fail strFailNum+BTN_CANCEL+" "+MNU_FILE_SAVE+ _
                            " caused text to change."
                    EndIf
                Else
                    fail strFailNum+BTN_NO+" to 'Replace?' didn't " + _
                        "return to Save As db."
                EndIf
            Else
                fail strFailNum+"'File Exists' message box didn't appear."
            EndIf
        Else
            fail strFailNum+MNU_FILE_SAVE+" w/ text didn't give" + _
                " 'Save As' dialog."
        EndIf
    scenario cleanup
        log #LVL_VERBOSE, "Cleaning up for test scenario #"+str$(iTestCount)
        ResetApp()
    end scenario
```

```
'
'Save to existing file.  Respond 'Yes'.
'
scenario strTestNum()+("'Save' to an existing file.  Respond 'Yes'.")
    PutString(DATA_TESTSTRING1, 1, 1)
    strText = EditText(EDIT_NOTEPAD)
    SelMenu(MNU_FILE_SAVE)

    If (GetText(NULL) = CAP_SAVEAS) then
        wEditSetText(DCN_FILENAME, TEMPFILE2)
        wButtonClick(BTN_SAVE)
        If (GetText(NULL) = CAP_SAVEAS) then
            wButtonClick(BTN_YES)
            If (WGetActWnd(0) = ghWndNotepad) then
                If INSTR(ucase$(GetText(NULL)),ucase$(TEMPFILE2)) = 0 then
                    fail strFailNum+TEMPFILE2+" was not Saved."
                EndIf
            Else
                fail strFailNum+BTN_YES+" to replace file did go " + _
                    "back to main window."
            EndIf
        Else
            fail strFailNum+"File Exists msgbox didn't appear."
        EndIf
    Else
        fail strFailNum+MNU_FILE_SAVE+" with text didn't display "+ _
            CAP_SAVEAS+" dialog."
    EndIf
scenario cleanup
    log #LVL_VERBOSE, "Cleaning up for test scenario #"+str$(iTestCount)
    ResetApp()
end scenario


'
'Check to make sure the file that was overwritten was truely overwritten.
'

scenario strTestNum()+"Verify file was actually replaced."
    SelMenu(MNU_FILE_OPEN)
    wEditSetText(DCN_FILENAME,TEMPFILE2)
    wButtonClick(BTN_OPEN)
    If (strText <> EditText(EDIT_NOTEPAD)) then
        fail strFailNum+"The file was not overwritten."
```

```
        EndIf
    scenario cleanup
        kill TEMPFILE2
    end scenario
TestEnd()
```

SAVEAS.MST

```
'*****************************************************************
'* Copyright 1994-1996 Software Testing Laboratories, Inc.
'* All rights reserved. You may use this source code freely
'* as long as it is not included as part of a selling product.
'*****************************************************************


'*****************************************************************
'* Filename:    SAVEAS.MST
'*
'* Purpose:     Tests the SaveAs menu item for the File menu in
'*              Notepad's main window.
'*
'* Revision History:
'*
'*  [ 0]   da-mon-year   email   : action
'*  [ 1]   06-MAR-1996   TomAr   First few scenarios to give
'*                               some general structure.
'*
'*****************************************************************


'********************** INCLUDES *****************************
'$include 'notemain.inc'      'Constants common enough to share with everyone
'$include 'noteutil.inc'      'Utilities generic/sharable with all tests
'$include 'file.inc'          'Constants/utils generic for testing the file menu

TestBegin
    dim strText$

    '
    'SaveAs with text in an untitled instance
    '
    scenario strTestNum()+MNU_FILE_SAVEAS+" w/ text.  Untitled"
        ResetApp()
        PutString(DATA_TESTSTRING1, 1, 1)
        strText = EditText(EDIT_NOTEPAD)
        SelMenu(MNU_FILE_SAVEAS)
```

```
    If (GetText(NULL) = CAP_SAVEAS) then
        wEditSetText(DCN_FILENAME, TEMPFILE2)
        wButtonClick(BTN_SAVE)
        if (GetText(NULL) = CAP_SAVEAS) then       'File must already exist
            wButtonClick(BTN_YES)
        endif

        'See If filename is in the caption
        If INSTR(ucase$(GetText(NULL)),TEMPFILE2) = 0 then
            fail strFailNum+TEMPFILE2+" was not Saved."
        EndIf
    Else
        fail strFailNum+MNU_FILE_SAVEAS+" w/ text didn't display "+ _
            CAP_SAVEAS+" dialog."
    EndIf
end scenario


'
'SaveAs with text in an already saved instance.
'
scenario strTestNum()+MNU_FILE_SAVEAS+" w/ text.  Saved instance"
    PutString(DATA_TESTSTRING1, 2, 1)
    strText = EditText(EDIT_NOTEPAD)
    SelMenu(MNU_FILE_SAVEAS)

    If (GetText(NULL) = CAP_SAVEAS) then              'Did "SaveAs" db appear?
        wEditSetText(DCN_FILENAME, TEMPFILE1)
        wButtonClick(BTN_SAVE)
        if (GetText(NULL) = CAP_SAVEAS) then          'File must already exist
            wButtonClick(BTN_YES)
        endif
        If INSTR(ucase$(GetText(NULL)),TEMPFILE1) = 0 then
            fail strFailNum+TEMPFILE1 + " was not Saved."
        EndIf
    Else
        fail strFailNum+MNU_FILE_SAVEAS+" w/ text didn't give "+ _
            CAP_SAVEAS+" dialog box."
    EndIf
scenario cleanup
    log #LVL_VERBOSE, "Cleaning up for test scenario #"+str$(iTestCount)
    ResetApp()
end scenario
```

```
'
'Verify text saved in strText variable in previous scenario
'matches the text in the saved file.  This verifies the
'file was saved as reported.
'
scenario strTestNum()+"Verify text was saved."
    SelMenu(MNU_FILE_OPEN)                              'Open up the saved file.
    wEditSetText(DCN_FILENAME,TEMPFILE1)
    wButtonClick(BTN_OPEN)

    If strText <> EditText(EDIT_NOTEPAD) then    'See if saved file matches
                                                      'changed text.
        fail strFailNum+MNU_FILE_SAVEAS+" didn't save any changes."
    EndIf
scenario cleanup
    log #LVL_VERBOSE, "Cleaning up for test scenario #"+str$(iTestCount)
    ResetApp()

    if exists(TEMPFILE1) then
        kill TEMPFILE1
    endif

    if exists(TEMPFILE2) then
        kill TEMPFILE2
    endif
end scenario
TestEnd()
```

PAGE_SU.MST

```
'****************************************************************
'* Copyright 1994-1996 Software Testing Laboratories, Inc.
'* All rights reserved. You may use this source code freely
'* as long as it is not included as part of a selling product.
'****************************************************************
'****************************************************************
'* Filename:    PAGE_SU.MST
'*
'* Purpose:     Tests the Page Setup menu item for the File menu
'*                 in Notepad's main window.
'*
'* Revision History:
'*
```

```
'*  [ 0]   da-mon-year   email    : action
'*  [ 1]   06-MAR-1996   TomAr    First few scenarios to give
'*                                    some general structure.
'*
'****************************************************************

'$include 'notemain.inc'     'Constants common enough to share with everyone
'$include 'noteutil.inc'     'Utilities generic/sharable with all tests
'$include 'file.inc'         'Constants/utils generic for testing the file menu

TestBegin
    dim strText$

    '
    'Bring up "PageSetup" with no text. Click "Cancel".
    '
    scenario strTestNum()+MNU_FILE_PGSETUP+" w/o text in editor, "+_
            "click "+BTN_CANCEL
        SelMenu(MNU_FILE_PGSETUP)

        'See If "PageSetup" DB appears.
        If (GetText(NULL) = CAP_PAGESETUP) then
            wButtonClick(BTN_CANCEL)
        Else
            fail strFailNum()+CAP_PAGESETUP+" dialog didn't appear."
        EndIf
    end scenario


    '
    'Bring up the "PageSetup" with no text. click "OK".
    '
    scenario strTestNum()+MNU_FILE_PGSETUP+" w/o text in editor, click "+BTN_OK
        SelMenu(MNU_FILE_PGSETUP)

        'See If "PageSetup" DB appears.
        If (GetText(NULL) = CAP_PAGESETUP) then
            wButtonClick(BTN_OK)
        Else
            fail strFailNum+CAP_PAGESETUP+" dialog didn't appear."
        EndIf
    end scenario
```

```
                  '
                  'Bring up the "PageSetup" DB with text. Click "Cancel".
                  'Verify text in editor doesn't change.
                  '
                  scenario strTestNum()+MNU_FILE_PGSETUP+" w/ text, click "+BTN_CANCEL
                      PutString(DATA_TESTSTRING1, 1, 1)
                      strText = EditText(EDIT_NOTEPAD)
                      SelMenu(MNU_FILE_PGSETUP)

                      If (GetText(NULL) = CAP_PAGESETUP) then
                          wButtonClick(BTN_CANCEL)
                      Else
                          fail strFailNum()+CAP_PAGESETUP+" dialog didn't appear."
                      EndIf

                      If (strText <> EditText(EDIT_NOTEPAD)) then
                          fail strFailNum()+BTN_CANCEL+CAP_PAGESETUP+" caused the text "+_
                              "to change."
                      EndIf
                  end scenario

                  '
                  'Bring up the "PageSetup" DB with text. Click "OK"
                  'Verify text in editor doesn't change.
                  '
                  scenario strTestNum()+CAP_PAGESETUP+" w/ text. Click "+BTN_OK
                      PutString(DATA_TESTSTRING1, 2, 1)
                      strText = EditText(EDIT_NOTEPAD)
                      SelMenu(MNU_FILE_PGSETUP)

                      If (GetText(NULL) = CAP_PAGESETUP) then
                          wButtonClick(BTN_OK)
                      Else
                          fail strFailNum()+CAP_PAGESETUP+" dialog didn't appear."
                      EndIf
                      If (strText <> EditText(EDIT_NOTEPAD)) then
                          fail strFailNum()+CAP_PAGESETUP+" dialog caused the text to change."
                      EndIf
                  end scenario
              TestEnd()
```

EXIT.MST

```
'****************************************************************
'* Copyright 1994-1996 Software Testing Laboratories, Inc.
```

```
'* All rights reserved. You may use this source code freely
'* as long as it is not included as part of a selling product.
'******************************************************************


'******************************************************************
'* Filename:    EXIT.MST
'*
'* Purpose:     Tests the Exit menu item for the File menu in
'*              Notepad's main window.
'*
'* Revision History:
'*
'* [ 0]   da-mon-year  email   : action
'* [ 1]   06-MAR-1996  TomAr   First few scenarios to give
'*                             some general structure.
'*
'******************************************************************


'********************** INCLUDES *****************************
'$include 'notemain.inc'     'Constants common enough to share with everyone
'$include 'noteutil.inc'     'Utilities generic/sharable with all tests
'$include 'file.inc'         'Constants/utils generic for testing the file menu


TestBegin()
    dim strText$

    scenario strTestNum()+"'Exit' w/o text in editor"
        SelMenu(MNU_FILE_EXIT)

        sleep 1    'Give app time to shut down
        If (WGetActWnd(0) = ghWndNotepad) then   'See If app exited.
            fail strFailNum()+"'Exit' did not exit the app."
        endif
    scenario cleanup)
        log #LVL_VERBOSE, "Cleaning up for test scenario #"+str$(iTestCount)
        if not(failed) then
            If (Run(TEST_APP) = 0) then      'Rerun the app for next test.
                ghWndNotepad = wGetActWnd(0)
            Else
                Fail strFailNum()+"Unable to rerun the app."
            EndIf
        EndIf
    end scenario
```

```
scenario strTestNum()+"'Exit' with text.  Select 'Cancel'."
    PutString(DATA_TESTSTRING1, 1, 1)
    strText = EditText(EDIT_NOTEPAD)
    SelMenu(MNU_FILE_EXIT)

    If (GetText(NULL) = CAP_SAVECHANGES) then    '"Save Changes" msgbox?
        wButtonClick(BTN_CANCEL)
    Else
        fail "'Exit' didn't prompt to save changes."
        run TEST_APP
    EndIf
end scenario


scenario strTestNum()+"Verify text in editor didn't change."
    If (strText <> EditText(EDIT_NOTEPAD)) then
        fail "Cancel Exit caused the text to change."
    EndIf
end scenario


scenario strTestNum()+"'Exit' with text.  Select 'No'."
    PutString(DATA_TESTSTRING1, 2, 1)
    SelMenu(MNU_FILE_EXIT)

    If (GetText(NULL) = CAP_SAVECHANGES) then    '"Save Changes" msgbox?
        wButtonClick(BTN_NO)
    Else
        fail "'Exit' didn't prompt to save changes."
    EndIf

    if (wGetActWnd(0) = ghWndNotepad) then
        fail strFailNum()+"'Exit' did not exit the app"
    endif
scenario cleanup
    LOG #LVL_VERBOSE, "Cleaning up for test scenario #"+str$(iTestCount)
    if not(failed) then
        If (Run(TEST_APP) = 0) then       'Rerun the app for next test.
            ghWndNotepad = wGetActWnd(0)
        Else
            Fail strFailNum()+"Unable to rerun the app."
        EndIf
    EndIf
end scenario
```

```
scenario strTestNum()+"'Exit' w/ text. Select 'Yes' then 'Cancel'."
    PutString(DATA_TESTSTRING1, 3, 1)
    strText = EditText(EDIT_NOTEPAD)
    SelMenu(MNU_FILE_EXIT)

    If (GetText(NULL) = CAP_SAVECHANGES) then     'Save Chgs msgbox?
        wButtonClick(BTN_YES)
        If (GetText(NULL) = CAP_SAVEAS) then      'SaveAs DB appear?
            wButtonClick(BTN_CANCEL)
            If (WGetActWnd(0) = ghWndNotepad) then  'App still up?
                If (strText <> EditText(EDIT_NOTEPAD)) then 'Text change?
                    fail strFailNum()+"Cancel Exit caused the " + _
                        "text to change."
                EndIf
            Else
                fail strFailNum()+"'Cancel' SaveAs from Exit " + _
                    "still exited app."
            EndIf
        Else
            fail strFailNum()+"'Yes' did not bring up a Save As dialog."
        EndIf
    Else
        fail strFailNum()+"'Exit' didn't prompt to save changes."
    EndIf
end scenario


scenario strTestNum()+"'Exit' with text.  Select 'Yes' then 'OK'."
    PutString(DATA_TESTSTRING1, 4, 1)
    SelMenu(MNU_FILE_EXIT)
    If (GetText(NULL) = CAP_SAVECHANGES) then
        wButtonClick(BTN_YES)
        If (GetText(NULL) = CAP_SAVEAS) then
            wEditSetText(DCN_FILENAME,TEMPFILE1)
            wButtonClick(BTN_SAVE)
            If (GetText(NULL) = CAP_SAVEAS) then   'Replace existing file
                wButtonClick(BTN_YES)
            EndIf
            If (WGetActWnd(0) = ghWndNotepad) then  'App still running?
                fail strFailNum+"App didn't shut down."
            Else
                If not exists(TEMPFILE1) then       'Did file get created?
                    fail strFailNum()+"Exiting did not save the file."
                EndIf
```

```
                    EndIf
            Else
                fail strFailNum()+"'Yes' did not bring up a Save As DB."
            EndIf
        Else
            fail strFailNum()+"'Exit' didn't prompt to save changes."
        EndIf
    scenario cleanup
        LOG #LVL_VERBOSE, "Cleaning up for test scenario #"+str$(iTestCount)

        if exists(TEMPFILE1) then
            kill TEMPFILE1                'Delete test file
        endif

        if not(failed) then
            If (Run(TEST_APP) = 0) then       'Rerun the app for next test.
                ghWndNotepad = wGetActWnd(0)
            Else
                Fail strFailNum()+"Unable to rerun the app."
            EndIf
        EndIf
    end scenario
TestEnd()
```

Edit Menu

The Edit menu is made up of eight menu items. These are: Undo, Cut, Copy, Paste, Delete, Select All, Time/Date and Word Wrap. Based on the approach that is being taken in this example (menu-based), the path followed by the automated tests traverse the menus that make up the Notepad product.

Based on these eight menu items, nine files should be created for testing those menu items: edit.inc, undo.mst, cut.mst, copy.mst, paste.mst, delete.mst, slct_all.mst, timedate.mst and wordwrap.mst.

The edit.inc include file holds declarations common to the menu items that make up the Edit menu. Any declarations that might be used by the other test case files should be placed into the edit.inc include file. Declarations that are even more generic, and useful to other menus and menu items, should be moved up higher into the notemain.inc file.

EDIT.INC

Any declarations that aren't generic enough to go into the main header
file for the Notepad test suite (notemain.inc) and are specific to the test
case files that perform tests on the Edit menu are placed into this file.

```
'****************************************************************
'* Copyright 1994-1996 Software Testing Laboratories, Inc.
'* All rights reserved. You may use this source code freely
'* as long as it is not included as part of a selling product.
'****************************************************************


'************************* Edit.INC ***********************
'*
'* PURPOSE: Decls for the Edit menu tests.
'*
'****************************************************************


'$ifndef EDIT_INCLUDED
'$define EDIT_INCLUDED


'****************************************************************
'*********************** CONSTANTS **********************
'****************************************************************


'****************************************************************
'******************** Dialog Control Names *****************
'****************************************************************


'****************************************************************
'********************** Captions ***************************
'****************************************************************


'****************************************************************
'******************** User Def'd Types ******************
'****************************************************************



'****************************************************************
'********************* Global Variables *****************
'****************************************************************



'****************************************************************
'***************** Func/Proc Prototypes *****************
```

```
'*****************************************************************

'$endif EDIT_INCLUDED
```

UNDO.MST

```
'*****************************************************************
'* Copyright 1994-1996 Software Testing Laboratories, Inc.
'* All rights reserved. You may use this source code freely
'* as long as it is not included as part of a selling product.
'*****************************************************************


'*****************************************************************
'* Filename:    undo.mst
'*
'* Purpose:     Tests the Undo menu item for the Edit menu
'*              in Notepad's main window.
'*
'* Revision History:
'*
'*  [ 0]   da-mon-year   email    : action
'*  [ 1]   06-MAR-1996   TomAr    First few scenarios to give
'*                                some general structure.
'*
'*****************************************************************


'********************** INCLUDES *****************************
'$include 'notemain.inc'        'Common declarations for Notepad tests
'$include 'noteutil.inc'        'Common utilities for Notepad tests
'$include 'edit.inc'            'Decls specific to the Edit menu

TestBegin()
    dim strText$

    '
    '"Undo" should be disabled when starting.
    '
    scenario strTestNum+MNU_EDIT_UNDO+" is disabled after 'File/New'."
        if not fGrayMenu(MNU_EDIT_UNDO) then
            fail strFailNum()+MNU_EDIT_UNDO+" menu item is not disabled."
        end if
    end scenario
```

```
'
'"Undo" should be enabled when you enter text.
'
scenario strTestNum+MNU_EDIT_UNDO+" enabled after typing."
    PutString(DATA_TESTSTRING1, 1, 1)
    strText = EditText(EDIT_NOTEPAD)
    if fGrayMenu(MNU_EDIT_UNDO) then
        fail strFailNum()+MNU_EDIT_UNDO+" should be available after typing."
    end if
end scenario


'
'"Undo" after typing should leave editor blank.
'
scenario strTestNum+MNU_EDIT_UNDO+" typing in a string."
    SelMenu(MNU_EDIT_UNDO)
    if (EditText(EDIT_NOTEPAD) <> "") then
        fail strFailNum()+MNU_EDIT_UNDO+" did not clear."
    end if
end scenario
'
'"Undo" again should put the text back into the editor.
'
scenario strTestNum+MNU_EDIT_UNDO+" again should 'REDO' the typing."
    SelMenu(MNU_EDIT_UNDO)
    if (EditText(EDIT_NOTEPAD) <> strText) then
        fail strFailNum()+MNU_EDIT_UNDO+" a second time did not " + _
            "reenter the text."
    end if
end scenario


'
'"Cut" should be undoable.
'
scenario strTestNum+"Test "+MNU_EDIT_CUT+" is undoable."
    SelMenu(MNU_EDIT_CUT)

    if (EditText(EDIT_NOTEPAD) <> strText) then
        SelMenu(MNU_EDIT_UNDO)

        if (EditText(EDIT_NOTEPAD) <> strText) then
            fail strFailNum()+"Undoing a "+MNU_EDIT_CUT+ _
                " action changed the text."
        end if
```

```
        else
            fail strFailNum()+MNU_EDIT_CUT+" did not remove the text."
        end if
end scenario


'"Copy" then "Undo" should redo the "Cut" operation.
'
scenario strTestNum+"Undoing a "+MNU_EDIT_COPY+" action should redo the "+ _
        MNU_EDIT_CUT+" action."
    CLIPBOARD CLEAR
    SelMenu(MNU_EDIT_COPY)
    if (CLIPBOARD$ = strText) then
        SelMenu(MNU_EDIT_UNDO)
        if (EditText(EDIT_NOTEPAD) <> "") then
            fail strFailNum()+MNU_EDIT_COPY+" action changed the "+ _
                "Undo buffer."
        end if
    else
        fail strFailNum()+MNU_EDIT_COPY+" did not copy the text."
    end if
end scenario


'"Paste" should be undoable.
'
scenario strTestNum+"Test that "+MNU_EDIT_PASTE+" is undoable."
    ResetApp()
    SelMenu(MNU_EDIT_PASTE)
    SelMenu(MNU_EDIT_UNDO)
    if (EditText(EDIT_NOTEPAD) <> "") then
        fail strFailNum()+"Undoing a "+MNU_EDIT_PASTE+ _
            " action changed the text."
    end if
end scenario


'"Delete" should be undoable.
'
scenario strTestNum+"Test that "+MNU_EDIT_DELETE+" is undoable."
    SelMenu(MNU_EDIT_DELETE)
    if (EditText(EDIT_NOTEPAD) = "") then
        SelMenu(MNU_EDIT_UNDO)
        if (EditText(EDIT_NOTEPAD) <> strText) then
```

```
                              fail strFailNum()+"Undoing a "+MNU_EDIT_DELETE+ _
                                  " action changed the text."
                  end if
            else
                  fail strFailNum()+MNU_EDIT_DELETE+" did not delete the text."
            end if
      end scenario


      '
      '"Undo" again should "Redo" the delete action.
      '
      scenario strTestNum+MNU_EDIT_UNDO+" again should 'Redo' the delete"
            SelMenu(MNU_EDIT_UNDO)
            If (EditText(EDIT_NOTEPAD) <> "") then
                  fail strFailNum()+MNU_EDIT_UNDO+" a second time, "+ _
                        "did not 'Redo' the 'Delete action."
            end if
      end scenario


      '
      'Time/Date stamp should disable the "Undo" menu item.
      '
      scenario strTestNum+"Test Time/Date action disables 'Undo'."
            SelMenu(MNU_EDIT_TIMEDATE)
            if not fGrayMenu(MNU_EDIT_UNDO) then
                  fail strFailNum()+MNU_EDIT_UNDO+" menu item is not disabled."
            end if
      end scenario
TestEnd()
```

CUT.MST

```
'****************************************************************
'* Filename:    CUT.MST
'*
'* Purpose:     Tests the Cut menu item for the Edit menu in
'*              Notepad's main window.
'*
```

```
'* Revision History:
'*
'*  [ 0]   da-mon-year  email   : action
'*  [ 1]   06-MAR-1996  TomAr    First few scenarios to give
'*                               some general structure.
'*
'********************************************************************

'********************** INCLUDES ****************************
'$include 'notemain.inc'       'Common declarations for Notepad tests
'$include 'noteutil.inc'       'Common utilities for Notepad tests
'$include 'edit.inc'           'Decls specific to the Edit menu

TestBegin
    dim strText$

    '
    '"Cut" should be disabled when starting.
    '
    scenario strTestNum()+MNU_EDIT_CUT+" is disabled after "+MNU_FILE_NEW
        if not fGrayMenu(MNU_EDIT_CUT) then
            fail strFailNum()+MNU_EDIT_CUT+" menu item is not disabled."
        end if
    end scenario

    '
    '"Cut" should be disabled After you enter text.
    '
    scenario strTestNum()+"'Cut' still disabled after typing."
        PutString(DATA_TESTSTRING1, 1, 1)
        strText = EditText(EDIT_NOTEPAD)
        if not fGrayMenu(MNU_EDIT_CUT) then
            fail strFailNum()+MNU_EDIT_CUT+" should be grayed."
        end if
    end scenario

    '
    '"Cut" should be available after selecting text.
    '
    scenario strTestNum()+MNU_EDIT_CUT+" available after selecting text."
        SelMenu(MNU_EDIT_SELALL)
        if fGrayMenu(MNU_EDIT_CUT) then
            fail strFailNum()+MNU_EDIT_CUT+" should not be gray."
        end if
```

```
        end scenario

        '
        'Text should be blank after "Cut".
        '
        scenario strTestNum()+MNU_EDIT_CUT+" should remove the text."
            PutString(DATA_TESTSTRING1, 3, 10)
            strText = EditText(EDIT_NOTEPAD)
            SelMenu(MNU_EDIT_SELALL)
            SelMenu(MNU_EDIT_CUT)
            if (EditText(EDIT_NOTEPAD) <> "") then
                fail strFailNum()+MNU_EDIT_CUT+" did not remove the text."
            end if
        end scenario

        '
        'Test should be on clipboard
        '
        scenario strTestNum()+MNU_EDIT_CUT+" should put text onto clipboard."
            if (CLIPBOARD$ <> strText) then
                fail strFailNum()+MNU_EDIT_CUT+" did not put text onto clipboard."
            end if
        end scenario
TestEnd
```

COPY.MST

```
'****************************************************************
'* Copyright 1994-1996 Software Testing Laboratories, Inc.
'* All rights reserved. You may use this source code freely
'* as long as it is not included as part of a selling product.
'****************************************************************


'****************************************************************
'* Filename:    COPY.MST
'*
'* Purpose:     Tests the Copy menu item for the Edit menu in
'*              Notepad's main window.
'*
'* Revision History:
'*
'*  [ 0]   da-mon-year   email    : action
'*  [ 1]   06-MAR-1996   TomAr    First few scenarios to give
'*                                some general structure.
```

```
'*
'****************************************************************

'********************** INCLUDES *****************************
'$include 'notemain.inc'        'Common declarations for Notepad tests
'$include 'noteutil.inc'        'Common utilities for Notepad tests
'$include 'edit.inc'            'Decls specific to the Edit menu

TestBegin
    dim strText$

    '
    '"Copy" should be disabled when starting.
    '
    scenario strTestNum()+MNU_EDIT_COPY+" is disabled after "+MNU_FILE_NEW
        ResetApp()
        if not(fGrayMenu(MNU_EDIT_COPY)) then
            fail strFailNum()+MNU_EDIT_COPY+" menu item should be disabled."
        end if
    end scenario
    '
    '"Copy" should be disabled After you enter text.
    '
    scenario strTestNum()+MNU_EDIT_COPY+" still disabled after typing."
        PutString(DATA_TESTSTRING1, 1, 1)
        strText = EditText(EDIT_NOTEPAD)
        if not fGrayMenu(MNU_EDIT_COPY) then
            fail strFailNum()+MNU_EDIT_COPY+" should be grayed."
        end if
    end scenario


    '
    '"Cut" should be available after selecting text.
    '
    scenario strTestNum()+MNU_EDIT_COPY+" available after selecting text."
        SelMenu(MNU_EDIT_SELALL)
        if fGrayMenu(MNU_EDIT_COPY) then
            fail strFailNum()+MNU_EDIT_COPY+" should be available."
        end if
    end scenario
```

```
    '
    '"Copy" text to the clipboard
    '
    scenario strTestNum()+MNU_EDIT_COPY+" the selected text."
        SelMenu(MNU_EDIT_COPY)
        If (CLIPBOARD$ <> strText) then
            fail strFailNum()+MNU_EDIT_COPY+" did not copy the text" + _
                " to the clipboard."
        end if
    end scenario
TestEnd
```

PASTE.MST

```
'****************************************************************
'* Copyright 1994-1996 Software Testing Laboratories, Inc.
'* All rights reserved. You may use this source code freely
'* as long as it is not included as part of a selling product.
'****************************************************************


'****************************************************************
'* Filename:    PASTE.MST
'*
'* Purpose:     Tests the Paste menu item for the Edit menu in
'*              Notepad's main window.
'*
'* Revision History:
'*
'*  [ 0]   da-mon-year   email    : action
'*  [ 1]   06-MAR-1996   TomAr    First few scenarios to give
'*                                some general structure.
'*
'****************************************************************


'********************** INCLUDES ****************************
'$include 'notemain.inc'        'Common declarations for Notepad tests
'$include 'noteutil.inc'        'Common utilities for Notepad tests
'$include 'edit.inc'            'Decls specific to the Edit menu

TestBegin
    dim strText$

    '
    '"Paste" should be disabled when clipboard is empty.
    '
```

```
        scenario strTestNum()+MNU_EDIT_PASTE+" disabled when clipboard is empty."
            ClipBoard CLEAR          'clear contents of the clipboard.
            if not fGrayMenu(MNU_EDIT_PASTE) then
                fail strFailNum()+MNU_EDIT_PASTE+" should be disabled."
            end if
        end scenario

        '
        'Typing text should keep Paste disabled.
        '
        scenario strTestNum()+"Typing should not effect "+MNU_EDIT_PASTE
            PutString(DATA_TESTSTRING1, 1, 1)
            strText = EditText(EDIT_NOTEPAD)
            if not fGrayMenu(MNU_EDIT_PASTE) then
                fail strFailNum()+MNU_EDIT_PASTE+" should be disabled."
            end if
        end scenario

        '
        'Cutting text should enabled "Paste".
        '
        scenario strTestNum()+MNU_EDIT_CUT+" enables "+MNU_EDIT_PASTE
            SelMenu(MNU_EDIT_SELALL)
            SelMenu(MNU_EDIT_CUT)
            if (CLIPBOARD$ = strText) then
                if fGrayMenu(MNU_EDIT_PASTE) then
                    fail strFailNum()+MNU_EDIT_PASTE+" should be enabled."
                end if
            else
                fail strFailNum()+MNU_EDIT_CUT+" did not work."
            end if
        end scenario

        '
        '"Paste" the text.
        '
        scenario strTestNum()+MNU_EDIT_PASTE+" text into empty editor."
            SelMenu(MNU_EDIT_PASTE)
            if (EditText(EDIT_NOTEPAD) <> strText) then
                fail strFailNum()+MNU_EDIT_PASTE+ _
                    " text did not match original text."
            end if
        end scenario
```

```
'
'"Paste" text after text of editor.
'
scenario strTestNum()+MNU_EDIT_PASTE+" text after text."
    'Add strText to strText for second paste.
    strText = strText+strText
    SelMenu(MNU_EDIT_PASTE)
    if (EditText(EDIT_NOTEPAD) <> strText) then
        fail strFailNum()+MNU_EDIT_PASTE+" text did not match."
    end if
end scenario


'
'"Paste" text over selected text.
'
scenario strTestNum()+MNU_EDIT_PASTE+" before text."
    PutString("", 1, 1)
    strText = DATA_TESTSTRING1 + strText
    SelMenu(MNU_EDIT_PASTE)
    if (EditText(EDIT_NOTEPAD) <> strText) then
        fail strFailNum()+MNU_EDIT_PASTE+" before text did not match."
    end if
end scenario


'
'Paste should not be affected by File/New.
'
scenario strTestNum()+MNU_FILE_NEW+" then try "+MNU_EDIT_PASTE
    ResetApp()
    SelMenu(MNU_EDIT_PASTE)
    if (EditText(EDIT_NOTEPAD) <> DATA_TESTSTRING1) then
        fail strFailNum()+MNU_EDIT_PASTE+" text did not match."
    end if
end scenario
TestEnd
```

DELETE.MST

```
'*****************************************************************
'* Filename:    DELETE.MST
'*
'* Purpose:     Tests the Delete menu item for the Edit menu in
'*              Notepad's main window.
'*
'* Revision History:
'*
'* [ 0]   da-mon-year   email    : action
'* [ 1]   06-MAR-1996   TomAr    First few scenarios to give
'*                               some general structure.
'*
'*****************************************************************


'********************** INCLUDES ****************************
'$include 'notemain.inc'          'Common declarations for Notepad tests
'$include 'noteutil.inc'          'Common utilities for Notepad tests
'$include 'edit.inc'              'Decls specific to the Edit menu
TestBegin
    dim strText$

    '
    '"Delete" should be disabled in empty editor.
    '
    scenario strTestNum()+MNU_EDIT_DELETE+" is disabled in empty editor."
        if not fGrayMenu(MNU_EDIT_DELETE) then
            fail strFailNum()+MNU_EDIT_DELETE+" should be grayed."
        end if
    end scenario


    '
    '"Delete" should be disabled with no text selected
    '
    scenario strTestNum()+MNU_EDIT_DELETE+" is disabled with no text selected."
        PutString(DATA_TESTSTRING1, 1, 1)
        if not fGrayMenu(MNU_EDIT_DELETE) then
            fail strFailNum()+MNU_EDIT_DELETE+" should be grayed."
        end if
    end scenario


    '
    '"Delete" enabled with text selected."
    '
```

```
        scenario strTestNum()+MNU_EDIT_DELETE+" is enabled with text selected."
            SelMenu(MNU_EDIT_SELALL)
            if fGrayMenu(MNU_EDIT_DELETE) then
                fail strFailNum()+MNU_EDIT_DELETE+" should be enabled."
            end if
        end scenario


        '
        '"Delete" should remove the text."
        '
        scenario strTestNum()+MNU_EDIT_DELETE+" should clear the selected text."
            SelMenu(MNU_EDIT_DELETE)
            if (EditText(EDIT_NOTEPAD) <> "") then
                fail strFailNum()+MNU_EDIT_DELETE+" did not remove the text."
            end if
        end scenario
        '
        '"Delete first word of text."
        '
        scenario strTestNum()+MNU_EDIT_DELETE+" first word of text."
            PutString(DATA_TESTSTRING1, 1, 1)

            'Jump to beginning of first line (CTRL+Home)
            'Ctrl+Shift+Right-arrow to select first word
            Play "^{HOME}"
            Play "^+{RIGHT}"

            SelMenu(MNU_EDIT_DELETE)
            strText = right$(DATA_TESTSTRING1,(len(DATA_TESTSTRING1) _
                    - instr(DATA_TESTSTRING1," ")))
            if (EditText(EDIT_NOTEPAD) <> strText) then
                fail strFailNum()+MNU_EDIT_DELETE+" did not delete first word."
            end if
        end scenario
    end scenario
TestEnd
```

SLCT_ALL.MST

```
'*****************************************************************
'* Filename:    SLCT_ALL.MST
'*
'* Purpose:     Tests the Select All menu item for the Edit menu
'*                 in Notepad's main window.
'*
'* Revision History:
'*
'*  [ 0]   da-mon-year   email    : action
'*  [ 1]   06-MAR-1996   TomAr    First few scenarios to give
'*                                    some general structure.
'*
'*****************************************************************


'*********************** INCLUDES ***************************
'$include 'notemain.inc'          'Common declarations for Notepad tests
'$include 'noteutil.inc'          'Common utilities for Notepad tests
'$include 'edit.inc'              'Decls specific to the Edit menu

TestBegin

    '
    '"SelectAll" is enabled with no text.
    '
    scenario strTestNum()+ MNU_EDIT_SELALL+" enabled with no text."
        if fGrayMenu(MNU_EDIT_SELALL) then
            fail strFailNum()+MNU_EDIT_SELALL+" is not enabled."
        end if
    end scenario


    '
    '"SelectAll" is a no op with no text.
    '
    scenario strTestNum()+ MNU_EDIT_SELALL+" is a no-op with no text."
        SelMenu(MNU_EDIT_SELALL)

        'Make sure a dialog or another window did not appear.
        if (WGetActWnd(0) <> ghWndNotepad) then
            fail strFailNum()+MNU_EDIT_SELALL+" with no text is not a no-op."
        end if
    end scenario


    '
    '"SelectAll" enabled with text.
    '
```

```
    scenario strTestNum()+ MNU_EDIT_SELALL+" enabled with text."
        PutString(DATA_TESTSTRING1, 1, 1)
        if fGrayMenu(MNU_EDIT_SELALL) then
            fail strFailNum()+MNU_EDIT_SELALL+" is not enabled with text."
        end if
    end scenario


    '
    '"SelectAll" selects the text. 1 line.
    '
    scenario strTestNum()+ MNU_EDIT_SELALL+" selects 1 line of text."
        SelMenu(MNU_EDIT_SELALL)
        SelMenu(MNU_EDIT_DELETE)
        if (EditText(EDIT_NOTEPAD) <> "") then
            fail strFailNum()+MNU_EDIT_SELALL+" did not select all the text."
        end if
    end scenario


    '
    '"SelectAll" selects the text 3 lines.
    '
    scenario strTestNum()+ MNU_EDIT_SELALL+" selects 3 lines of text."
        PutString(DATA_TESTSTRING1, 1, 1)
        PutString(DATA_TESTSTRING1, 2, 1)
        PutString(DATA_TESTSTRING1, 3, 10)
        SelMenu(MNU_EDIT_SELALL)
        SelMenu(MNU_EDIT_DELETE)
        if (EditText(EDIT_NOTEPAD) <> "") then
            fail strFailNum()+MNU_EDIT_SELALL+" did not select all the text."
        end if
    end scenario
TestEnd
```

TIMEDATE.MST

```
'****************************************************************
'* Copyright 1994-1996 Software Testing Laboratories, Inc.
'* All rights reserved. You may use this source code freely
'* as long as it is not included as part of a selling product.
'****************************************************************


'****************************************************************
'* Filename:    Timedate.mst
'*
```

```
'* Purpose:      Tests the Time/Date menu item for the Edit menu
'*               in Notepad's main window.
'*
'* Revision History:
'*
'*  [ 0]   da-mon-year  email    : action
'*  [ 1]   06-MAR-1996  TomAr    First few scenarios to give
'*                                some general structure.
'*
'*******************************************************************


'********************** INCLUDES *****************************
'$include 'notemain.inc'        'Common declarations for Notepad tests
'$include 'noteutil.inc'        'Common utilities for Notepad tests
'$include 'edit.inc'            'Decls specific to the Edit menu

TestBegin
    dim strText$

    '
    '"Time/Date" menu is enabled.
    '
    scenario strTestNum()+MNU_EDIT_TIMEDATE+" menu is enabled."
        if fGrayMenu(MNU_EDIT_TIMEDATE) then
            fail strFailNum()+MNU_EDIT_TIMEDATE+" menu should not be gray."
        end if
    end scenario

    '
    'Put "Time/Date" into an empty editor.
    '
    scenario strTestNum()+"Put "+MNU_EDIT_TIMEDATE+" into an empty editor."
        SelMenu(MNU_EDIT_TIMEDATE)
        SelMenu(MNU_EDIT_SELALL)
        SelMenu(MNU_EDIT_CUT)
        SelMenu(MNU_EDIT_TIMEDATE)

        If (EditText(EDIT_NOTEPAD) <> CLIPBOARD$) then
            fail strFailNum()+MNU_EDIT_TIMEDATE+" string differs."
        end if
    end scenario
TestEnd
```

WORDWRAP.MST

```
'******************************************************************
'* Copyright 1994-1996 Software Testing Laboratories, Inc.
'* All rights reserved. You may use this source code freely
'* as long as it is not included as part of a selling product.
'******************************************************************


'******************************************************************
'* Filename:    wordwrap.mst
'*
'* Purpose:     Tests the Wordwrap menu item for the Edit menu
'*              in Notepad's main window.
'*
'* Revision History:
'*
'*   [ 0]   da-mon-year  email    : action
'*   [ 1]   06-MAR-1996  TomAr    First few scenarios to give
'*                                some general structure.
'*
'******************************************************************


'********************** INCLUDES ****************************
'$include 'notemain.inc'          'Common declarations for Notepad tests
'$include 'noteutil.inc'          'Common utilities for Notepad tests
'$include 'edit.inc'              'Decls specific to the Edit menu

TestBegin
    '
    'Type in long string with WordWrap off.
    '
    scenario strTestNum()+"Type text with WordWrap off."
        PutString(DATA_TESTSTRING1, 1, 1)    'Put in a lot
        PutString(DATA_TESTSTRING1, 1, 30)   'of test text.
        PutString(DATA_TESTSTRING1, 1, 60)

        if (wEditLines(EDIT_NOTEPAD) > 1) then
            fail strFailNum()+"Text wrapped when it shouldn't."
        end if
    end scenario


    '
    '"WordWrap" on with existing text.
    '
```

```
scenario strTestNum()+"Turn 'WordWrap' on with existing text."
    SelMenu(MNU_EDIT_WRDWRAP)
    if (wEditLines(EDIT_NOTEPAD) < 2) then
        fail strFailNum()+MNU_EDIT_WRDWRAP+" didn't wrap text."
    end if
end scenario


'
'Type text with WordWrap on.
'
scenario strTestNum()+"Type text with WordWrap on."
    ResetApp()
    PutString(DATA_TESTSTRING1, 1, 1)
    PutString(DATA_TESTSTRING1, 1, 30)
    PutString(DATA_TESTSTRING1, 1, 60)

    if (wEditLines(EDIT_NOTEPAD) < 2) then
        fail strFailNum()+"Typing text with wordwrap on did not wrap."
    end if
end scenario
TestEnd
```

Search Menu

The Search menu is made up of two menu items. These are: Find and
Find Next. Based on the approach that is being taken in this example
(menu-based), the path followed by the automated tests traverse the
menus that make up the Notepad product.

Based on these two menu items, three files should be created for testing
those menu items: search.inc, find.mst and findnext.mst.

The search.inc include file holds declarations common to the menu
items that make up the Search menu. Any declarations that might be
used by the other test case files should be placed into the search.inc
include file. Declarations that are even more generic, and useful to
other menus and menu items, should be moved up higher into the
notemain.inc file.

SEARCH.INC

Any declarations that aren't generic enough to go into the main header file for the Notepad test suite (notemain.inc) and are specific to the test case files that perform tests on the Search menu are placed into this file.

```
'****************************************************************
'* Copyright 1994-1996 Software Testing Laboratories, Inc.
'* All rights reserved. You may use this source code freely
'* as long as it is not included as part of a selling product.
'****************************************************************


'************************* Search.INC *********************
'*
'* PURPOSE: Decls for the Search tests.
'*
'****************************************************************


'$ifndef SEARCH_INCLUDED
'$define SEARCH_INCLUDED


'****************************************************************
'************************* CONSTANTS ***********************
'****************************************************************


'****************************************************************
'******************** Dialog Control Names *******************
'****************************************************************
const DCN_FINDWHAT$          = "Find What:"


'****************************************************************
'*********************** Captions ***************************
'****************************************************************
const CAP_FIND$            = "Find"
const CAP_NOTFOUND$        = "Notepad"

const BTN_DOWN             = "Down"              'Down option button in
                                                     FindNext
const BTN_FINDNEXT$        = "Find Next"         'Find Next button


'****************************************************************
'******************** User Def'd Types ********************
'****************************************************************
```

```
'*****************************************************************
'********************* Global Variables ************************
'*****************************************************************


'*****************************************************************
'****************** Func/Proc Prototypes **********************
'*****************************************************************


'$endif SEARCH_INCLUDED
```

FIND.MST

```
'*****************************************************************
'* Copyright 1994-1996 Software Testing Laboratories, Inc.
'* All rights reserved. You may use this source code freely
'* as long as it is not included as part of a selling product.
'*****************************************************************


'*****************************************************************
'* Filename:     find.mst
'*
'* Purpose:      Tests the Find menu item for the Search menu
'*                 in Notepad's main window.
'*
'* Revision History:
'*
'* [ 0]   da-mon-year   email    : action
'* [ 1]   06-MAR-1996   TomAr    First few scenarios to give
'*                                 some general structure.
'*
'*****************************************************************


'********************** INCLUDES ****************************
'$include 'notemain.inc'          'Common declarations for Notepad tests
'$include 'noteutil.inc'          'Common utilities for Notepad tests
'$include 'search.inc'            'Decls specific to the Search menu

TestBegin
    dim strSearchText$


    '
    '"Find" menu should be enabled with no text.
    '
    scenario strTestNum()+MNU_SEARCH_FIND+" menu enabled with no text."
```

```
        if fGrayMenu(MNU_SEARCH_FIND) then
            fail strFailNum()+MNU_SEARCH_FIND+" menu should not be grayed."
        end if
end scenario


'
'"Find" menu item brings up Find DB.
'
scenario strTestNum()+MNU_SEARCH_FIND+" brings up 'Find' DB with no text."
        SelMenu(MNU_SEARCH_FIND)
        if (GetText(NULL) <> CAP_FIND) then
            fail strFailNum()+MNU_SEARCH_FIND+" dialog did not appear."
        else
            wButtonClick(BTN_CANCEL)
        end if
end scenario


'
'"Find" the first char of a string.
'
scenario strTestNum()+MNU_SEARCH_FIND+" the first char of a string."
        strSearchText = MID$(DATA_TESTSTRING1,5,1)
        PutString(DATA_TESTSTRING1, 1, 1)
        PutString("", 0, 0)
        SelMenu(MNU_SEARCH_FIND)
        wEditSetText(DCN_FINDWHAT, strSearchText)
        wOptionClick(BTN_DOWN)
        wButtonClick(BTN_FINDNEXT)

        if (GetText(NULL) <> CAP_FIND) then
            fail strFailNum()+MNU_SEARCH_FIND+" DB did not stay up."
        end if
end scenario


'
'"Find" next occurance of strSearchText.
'
scenario strTestNum()+MNU_SEARCH_FIND+" next occurance of SearchText."
        wButtonClick(BTN_FINDNEXT)
        if (GetText(NULL) <> CAP_FIND) then
            fail strFailNum()+MNU_SEARCH_FIND+" did not find occurence 2."
            wButtonClick(BTN_OK)
        end if
end scenario
```

```
'
'"Find" next does not find anything.
'
scenario strTestNum()+MNU_SEARCH_FIND+" again will not find anything."
    wButtonClick(BTN_FINDNEXT)
    if (GetText(NULL) <> CAP_NOTFOUND) then
        fail strFailNum()+MNU_SEARCH_FIND+ _
            " did not display not Found msgbox."
    else
        wButtonClick(BTN_OK)        'Dismiss "Not Found" msgbox
        wButtonClick(BTN_CANCEL)    'Dismiss "Find" DB.
    end if
end scenario


'See if text found matches search text. .
'
scenario strTestNum()+"Check that text found matches search text."
    if (LCASE$(EditSelText(EDIT_NOTEPAD)) <> LCASE$(strSearchText)) then
        fail strFailNum()+"Found text did not match Search Text."
    end if
end scenario


'"Find" first word of string.
'
scenario strTestNum()+MNU_SEARCH_FIND+" first word of a string."
    strSearchText = LEFT$(DATA_TESTSTRING1,3)
    PutString("", 0, 0)
    SelMenu(MNU_SEARCH_FIND)
    wEditSetText(DCN_FINDWHAT, strSearchText)
    wButtonClick(BTN_FINDNEXT)

    if (GetText(NULL) <> CAP_FIND) then
        fail strFailNum()+MNU_SEARCH_FIND+" DB did not stay up."
    end if
end scenario


''Find Next' should display message.
'
scenario strTestNum()+MNU_SEARCH_FIND+" again should display message box."
    wButtonClick(BTN_FINDNEXT)
    if (GetText(NULL) <> CAP_NOTFOUND) then
```

```
                    fail strFailNum()+MNU_SEARCH_FNEXT+" did not display not Found msg."
        else
            wButtonClick(BTN_OK)            'Dismiss "Not Found" message box.
            wButtonClick(BTN_CANCEL)        'Dismiss "Find" DB.
        end if
end scenario

'
'See if text found matches search text.
'
scenario strTestNum()+"Check that text found matches search text."
        if (LCASE$(EditSelText(EDIT_NOTEPAD)) <> LCASE$(strSearchText)) then
            fail strFailNum()+"Found text did not match Search Text."
        end if
end scenario

'
'"Find" last word of a string.
'
scenario strTestNum()+MNU_SEARCH_FIND+" last word of a string."
        strSearchText = RIGHT$(DATA_TESTSTRING1,3)
        PutString("",0,0)
        SelMenu(MNU_SEARCH_FIND)
        wEditSetText(DCN_FINDWHAT, strSearchText)
        wButtonClick(BTN_FINDNEXT)

        if (GetText(NULL) <> CAP_FIND) then
            fail strFailNum()+MNU_SEARCH_FIND+" DB did not stay up."
        end if
end scenario

'
'"Find" again will not find anything.
'
scenario strTestNum()+MNU_SEARCH_FIND+ _
            " again will not find another occurance."
        wButtonClick(BTN_FINDNEXT)
        if (GetText(NULL) <> CAP_NOTFOUND) then
            fail strFailNum()+MNU_SEARCH_FNEXT+ _
                " did not display 'not found' msg."
        else
            wButtonClick(BTN_OK)            'Dismiss "Not Found" DB.
            wButtonClick(BTN_CANCEL)        'Dismiss "Find" DB.
        end if
```

```
            end scenario

            '
            'See if text found matches search text.
            '
            scenario strTestNum()+"Check that text found matches search text."
                if (LCASE$(EditSelText(EDIT_NOTEPAD)) <> LCASE$(strSearchText)) then
                    fail strFailNum()+"Found text did not match Search Text."
                end if
            end scenario
TestEnd
```

FINDNEXT.MST

```
'*****************************************************************
'* Copyright 1994-1996 Software Testing Laboratories, Inc.
'* All rights reserved. You may use this source code freely
'* as long as it is not included as part of a selling product.
'*****************************************************************


'*****************************************************************
'* Filename:    findnext.mst
'*
'* Purpose:     Tests the Find Next menu item for the Search
'*              menu in Notepad's main window.
'*
'* Revision History:
'*
'*  [ 0]   da-mon-year   email    : action
'*  [ 1]   06-MAR-1996   TomAr    First few scenarios to give
'*                                some general structure.
'*
'*****************************************************************


'********************** INCLUDES ***************************
'$include 'notemain.inc'        'Common declarations for Notepad tests
'$include 'noteutil.inc'        'Common utilities for Notepad tests
'$include 'search.inc'          'Decls specific to the Search menu

TestBegin
    dim strSearchText$

    '
    '"Find Next" should display the "Find" DB.
    '
```

```
scenario strTestNum()+MNU_SEARCH_FNEXT+" with 'Find' Buffer empty."
    SelMenu(MNU_SEARCH_FNEXT)
    if (GetText(NULL) <> CAP_FIND) then
        fail strFailNum()+MNU_SEARCH_FNEXT+" did not display."
    else
        wButtonClick(BTN_CANCEL)
    end if
end scenario

'
'"Find Next" with text.
'
scenario strTestNum()+MNU_SEARCH_FNEXT+" with next but Find buffer empty."
    strSearchText = MID$(DATA_TESTSTRING1,5,1)
    PutString(DATA_TESTSTRING1, 1, 1)
    PutString("", 0, 0)
    SelMenu(MNU_SEARCH_FNEXT)

    if (GetText(NULL) = CAP_FIND) then
        wEditSetText(DCN_FINDWHAT, strSearchText)
        wButtonClick(BTN_FINDNEXT)
        If (GetText(NULL) <> CAP_FIND) then
            fail strFailNum()+"'Find' DB did not stay up."
        end if
        wButtonClick(BTN_CANCEL)
    else
        fail strFailNum()+MNU_SEARCH_FNEXT+" did not display."
    end if
end scenario

'
'See if text found matches search text.
'
scenario strTestNum()+"Check that text found matches search text."
    if (LCASE$(EditSelText(EDIT_NOTEPAD)) <> LCASE$(strSearchText)) then
        fail strFailNum()+"Found text did not match Search Text."
    end if
end scenario

'
''Find Next' finds the next occurance without display the DB.
'
scenario strTestNum()+MNU_SEARCH_FNEXT+" with 'Find' buffer filled."
```

```
            SelMenu(MNU_SEARCH_FNEXT)
            if (WGetActWnd(0) <> ghWndNotepad) then
                fail strFailNum()+MNU_SEARCH_FNEXT+" did not find next occurence."
            end if
        end scenario
        '
        'See if text found matches search text.
        '
        scenario strTestNum()+"Check that text found matches search text."
            if (LCASE$(EditSelText(EDIT_NOTEPAD)) <> LCASE$(strSearchText)) then
                fail strFailNum()+"Found text did not match Search Text."
            end if
        end scenario

        '
        ''Find Next' should display "not found" message box.
        '
        scenario strTestNum()+MNU_SEARCH_FNEXT+ _
                " should display 'Not Found' message box."
            SelMenu(MNU_SEARCH_FNEXT)
            if (GetText(NULL) <> CAP_NOTFOUND) then
                fail strFailNum()+MNU_SEARCH_FNEXT+" did not display."
            else
                wButtonClick(BTN_OK)
            end if
        end scenario

        '
        'See if text found matches search text.
        '
        scenario strTestNum()+"Check that text found matches search text."
            if (LCASE$(EditSelText(EDIT_NOTEPAD)) <> LCASE$(strSearchText)) then
                fail strFailNum()+"Found text did not match Search Text."
            end if
        end scenario
    TestEnd
```

Help Menu

The Help menu is made up of two menu items. These are: Help Topics and About Notepad. Based on the approach that is being taken in this example (menu-based), the path followed by the automated tests traverse the menus that make up the Notepad product.

Based on these two menu items, three files should be created for testing those menu items: help.inc, topics.mst and about.mst.

The help.inc include file holds declarations common to the menu items that make up the Help menu. Any declarations that might be used by the other test case files should be placed into the help.inc include file. Declarations that are even more generic, and useful to other menus and menu items, should be moved up higher into the notemain.inc file.

HELP.INC

Any declarations that aren't generic enough to go into the main header file for the Notepad test suite (notemain.inc) and are specific to the test case files that perform tests on the Help menu are placed into this file.

```
'******************************************************************
'* Copyright 1994-1996 Software Testing Laboratories, Inc.
'* All rights reserved. You may use this source code freely
'* as long as it is not included as part of a selling product.
'******************************************************************


'************************* Help.INC ************************
'*
'* PURPOSE: Decls for the Help tests.
'*
'******************************************************************


'$ifndef HELP_INCLUDED
'$define HELP_INCLUDED


'******************************************************************
'************************* CONSTANTS ************************
'******************************************************************


'******************************************************************
'*********************** Captions ***************************
'******************************************************************
const CAP_TOPICS$          = "Help Topics: Notepad Help"
const CAP_ABOUT$           = "About Notepad"
```

```
'*****************************************************************
'********************** User Def'd Types ************************
'*****************************************************************



'*****************************************************************
'********************** Global Variables ************************
'*****************************************************************



'*****************************************************************
'****************** Func/Proc Prototypes ***********************
'*****************************************************************


'$endif HELP_INCLUDED
```

TOPICS.MST

```
'*****************************************************************
'* Copyright 1994-1996 Software Testing Laboratories, Inc.
'* All rights reserved. You may use this source code freely
'* as long as it is not included as part of a selling product.
'*****************************************************************


'*****************************************************************
'* Filename:    topics.mst
'*
'* Purpose:     Tests the Help Topics menu item for the Help
'*              menu in Notepad's main window.
'*
'* Revision History:
'*
'*  [ 0]   da-mon-year  email    : action
'*  [ 1]   06-MAR-1996  TomAr    First few scenarios to give
'*                                 some general structure.
'*
'*****************************************************************


'********************** INCLUDES ***************************
'$include 'notemain.inc'      'Common declarations for Notepad tests
'$include 'noteutil.inc'      'Common utilities for Notepad tests
'$include 'help.inc'          'Decls specific to the Help menu

TestBegin
```

```
'
'Select the "Contents" menu item
'
scenario strTestNum()+"Select the "+MNU_HELP_TOPICS+" menu item"
    SelMenu(MNU_HELP_TOPICS)
    wFndWnd(CAP_TOPICS, FW_ALL OR FW_FOCUS)
    If (GetText(NULL) = CAP_TOPICS) then
        wButtonClick(BTN_CANCEL)
    else
        fail MNU_HELP_TOPICS+" help did not open."
    end if
    wFndWnd(CAP_NOTEPAD, FW_ALL OR FW_FOCUS)
end scenario
TestEnd
```

ABOUT.MST

```
'****************************************************************
'* Copyright 1994-1996 Software Testing Laboratories, Inc.
'* All rights reserved. You may use this source code freely
'* as long as it is not included as part of a selling product.
'****************************************************************


'****************************************************************
'* Filename:     about.mst
'*
'* Purpose:      Tests the About menu item for the Help menu
'*               in Notepad's main window.
'*
'* Revision History:
'*
'* [ 0]   da-mon-year   email    : action
'* [ 1]   06-MAR-1996   TomAr    First few scenarios to give
'*                                some general structure.
'*
'****************************************************************


'********************** INCLUDES ****************************
'$include 'notemain.inc'         'Common declarations for Notepad tests
'$include 'noteutil.inc'         'Common utilities for Notepad tests
'$include 'help.inc'             'Decls specific to the Help menu

TestBegin
```

```
scenario strTestNum()+"Select the "+MNU_HELP_ABOUT+" menu item."
    SelMenu(MNU_HELP_ABOUT)

    if (GetText(NULL) = CAP_ABOUT) then
        wButtonClick(BTN_OK)
    else
        fail CAP_ABOUT+" dialog did not appear."
    end if
end scenario
TestEnd
```

APPENDIX

Log File Generated from Run of Notepad Test Suite

*T*he following log file was generated when the Notepad test script was run in its entirety. The detail level was set to zero (0) to show only the detail that Visual Test provides as a default. For more verbose information, refer to the different levels available as declared in the notemain.inc file (for example, Detail Level 5 would provide summary information after each test case file had completed its test run).

Use this log file to compare the output for the source code for the test case files shown in Appendix F, "Listings of All Test Cases."

```
[Start Suite Header]
[Suite Name]      Notepad Test Suite
[Machine]         TOMA
[Start Time]      03/06/1996 22:53:58
[End Suite Header]

  [Start Case Header]
  [Case Name]       C:\MSDEV\SAMPLES\Notepad\File\New.mst
  [Product Version] Windows 95
  [Language]        English
  [Machine]         TOMA
  [Start Time]      03/06/1996 22:53:59
  [End Case Header]

    [Start Scenario]
    [Name]            Test #1: Test that 'Save changes' message box is
                      displayed.
    [Test Location]   C:\MSDEV\SAMPLES\Notepad\File\New.mst (38)
    [Start Time]      03/06/1996 22:54:02
    [Result]          PASS
    [Elapsed Time]    1.180
    [End Scenario]
```

459

```
[Start Scenario]
[Name]            Test #2: Verify that the original text remains
                  unchanged after clicking Cancel.
[Test Location]   C:\MSDEV\SAMPLES\Notepad\File\New.mst (55)
[Start Time]      03/06/1996 22:54:03
[Result]          PASS
[Elapsed Time]    0.016
[End Scenario]

[Start Scenario]
[Name]            Test #3: Click 'No' to 'Save Changes?' msg
[Test Location]   C:\MSDEV\SAMPLES\Notepad\File\New.mst (65)
[Start Time]      03/06/1996 22:54:04
[Result]          PASS
[Elapsed Time]    2.883
[End Scenario]

[Start Scenario]
[Name]            Test #4: Click 'Yes' to 'Save changes?' msg
[Test Location]   C:\MSDEV\SAMPLES\Notepad\File\New.mst (79)
[Start Time]      03/06/1996 22:54:07
[Result]          PASS
[Elapsed Time]    4.029
[End Scenario]

[Case Result]     PASS
[Elapsed Time]    13.258
[End Case]

[Start Case Header]
[Case Name]       C:\MSDEV\SAMPLES\Notepad\File\Page_su.mst
[Product Version] Windows 95
[Language]        English
[Machine]         TOMA
[Start Time]      03/06/1996 22:54:13
[End Case Header]

[Start Scenario]
[Name]            Test #1: File\Page Setup... w/o text in editor,
                  click Cancel
[Test Location]   C:\MSDEV\SAMPLES\Notepad\File\Page_su.mst (31)
[Start Time]      03/06/1996 22:54:20
[Result]          PASS
[Elapsed Time]    2.216
[End Scenario]
```

```
[Start Scenario]
[Name]              Test #2: File\Page Setup... w/o text in editor,
                    click Ok
[Test Location]  C:\MSDEV\SAMPLES\Notepad\File\Page_su.mst (46)
[Start Time]     03/06/1996 22:54:22
[Result]         PASS
[Elapsed Time]   1.182
[End Scenario]


[Start Scenario]
[Name]              Test #3: File\Page Setup... w/ text, click Cancel
[Test Location]  C:\MSDEV\SAMPLES\Notepad\File\Page_su.mst (62)
[Start Time]     03/06/1996 22:54:23
[Result]         PASS
[Elapsed Time]   1.909
[End Scenario]


[Start Scenario]
[Name]              Test #4: Page Setup w/ text. Click Ok
[Test Location]  C:\MSDEV\SAMPLES\Notepad\File\Page_su.mst (82)
[Start Time]     03/06/1996 22:54:25
[Result]         PASS
[Elapsed Time]   2.065
[End Scenario]


[Case Result]    PASS
[Elapsed Time]   16.203
[End Case]


[Start Case Header]
[Case Name]        C:\MSDEV\SAMPLES\Notepad\File\Save.mst
[Product Version]  Windows 95
[Language]         English
[Machine]          TOMA
[Start Time]       03/06/1996 22:54:29
[End Case Header]


[Start Scenario]
[Name]              Test #1: File\Save with text.  Untitled instance
[Test Location]  C:\MSDEV\SAMPLES\Notepad\File\Save.mst (32)
[Start Time]     03/06/1996 22:54:36
[Result]         PASS
[Elapsed Time]   2.452
[End Scenario]
```

461

```
[Start Scenario]
[Name]          Test #2: File\Save with text.  Saved instance
[Test Location] C:\MSDEV\SAMPLES\Notepad\File\Save.mst (61)
[Start Time]    03/06/1996 22:54:39
[Result]        PASS
[Elapsed Time]  1.661
[End Scenario]

[Start Scenario]
[Name]          Test #3: Verify text was saved to file.
[Test Location] C:\MSDEV\SAMPLES\Notepad\File\Save.mst (80)
[Start Time]    03/06/1996 22:54:41
[Result]        PASS
[Elapsed Time]  1.986
[End Scenario]

[Start Scenario]
[Name]          Test #4: File\Save to existing file. Click No
[Test Location] C:\MSDEV\SAMPLES\Notepad\File\Save.mst (97)
[Start Time]    03/06/1996 22:54:43
[Result]        PASS
[Elapsed Time]  2.971
[End Scenario]

[Start Scenario]
[Name]          Test #5: 'Save' to an existing file.  Respond 'Yes'.
[Test Location] C:\MSDEV\SAMPLES\Notepad\File\Save.mst (130)
[Start Time]    03/06/1996 22:54:46
[Result]        PASS
[Elapsed Time]  2.873
[End Scenario]

[Start Scenario]
[Name]          Test #6: Verify file was actually replaced.
[Test Location] C:\MSDEV\SAMPLES\Notepad\File\Save.mst (163)
[Start Time]    03/06/1996 22:54:49
[Result]        PASS
[Elapsed Time]  1.646
[End Scenario]

[Case Result]   PASS
[Elapsed Time]  22.560
[End Case]
```

```
[Start Case Header]
[Case Name]        C:\MSDEV\SAMPLES\Notepad\File\Exit.mst
[Product Version]  Windows 95
[Language]         English
[Machine]          TOMA
[Start Time]       03/06/1996 22:54:52
[End Case Header]

  [Start Scenario]
  [Name]          Test #1: 'Exit' w/o text in editor
  [Test Location] C:\MSDEV\SAMPLES\Notepad\File\Exit.mst (30)
  [Start Time]    03/06/1996 22:54:59
  [Result]        PASS
  [Elapsed Time]  2.588
  [End Scenario]

  [Start Scenario]
  [Name]          Test #2: 'Exit' with text.  Select 'Cancel'.
  [Test Location] C:\MSDEV\SAMPLES\Notepad\File\Exit.mst (49)
  [Start Time]    03/06/1996 22:55:02
  [Result]        PASS
  [Elapsed Time]  1.301
  [End Scenario]

  [Start Scenario]
  [Name]          Test #3: Verify text in editor didn't change.
  [Test Location] C:\MSDEV\SAMPLES\Notepad\File\Exit.mst (63)
  [Start Time]    03/06/1996 22:55:03
  [Result]        PASS
  [Elapsed Time]  0.016
  [End Scenario]

  [Start Scenario]
  [Name]          Test #4: 'Exit' with text.  Select 'No'.
  [Test Location] C:\MSDEV\SAMPLES\Notepad\File\Exit.mst (70)
  [Start Time]    03/06/1996 22:55:03
  [Result]        PASS
  [Elapsed Time]  2.793
  [End Scenario]

  [Start Scenario]
  [Name]          Test #5: 'Exit' w/ text. Select 'Yes' then
                  'Cancel'.
  [Test Location] C:\MSDEV\SAMPLES\Notepad\File\Exit.mst (95)
```

```
            [Start Time]      03/06/1996 22:55:06
            [Result]          PASS
            [Elapsed Time]    2.437
            [End Scenario]

            [Start Scenario]
            [Name]            Test #6: 'Exit' with text.  Select 'Yes' then 'OK'.
            [Test Location]   C:\MSDEV\SAMPLES\Notepad\File\Exit.mst (120)
            [Start Time]      03/06/1996 22:55:08
            [Result]          PASS
            [Elapsed Time]    4.151
            [End Scenario]

        [Case Result]     PASS
        [Elapsed Time]    22.372
        [End Case]

        [Start Case Header]
        [Case Name]       C:\MSDEV\SAMPLES\Notepad\File\Open.mst
        [Product Version] Windows 95
        [Language]        English
        [Machine]         TOMA
        [Start Time]      03/06/1996 22:55:14
        [End Case Header]

            [Start Scenario]
            [Name]            Test #1: File\Open... file when no text in editor
                              exists.
            [Test Location]   C:\MSDEV\SAMPLES\Notepad\File\Open.mst (44)
            [Start Time]      03/06/1996 22:55:23
            [Result]          PASS
            [Elapsed Time]    1.476
            [End Scenario]

            [Start Scenario]
            [Name]            Test #2: File\Open... file and select Cancel to
                              Save Changes prompt.
            [Test Location]   C:\MSDEV\SAMPLES\Notepad\File\Open.mst (64)
            [Start Time]      03/06/1996 22:55:25
            [Result]          PASS
            [Elapsed Time]    1.388
            [End Scenario]
```

```
[Start Scenario]
[Name]              Test #3: Verify text didn't change from previous
                    scenario
[Test Location]  C:\MSDEV\SAMPLES\Notepad\File\Open.mst (78)
[Start Time]     03/06/1996 22:55:26
[Result]         PASS
[Elapsed Time]   0.016
[End Scenario]

[Start Scenario]
[Name]              Test #4: 'Open' file and 'No' to Save Changes msg
                    box.
[Test Location]  C:\MSDEV\SAMPLES\Notepad\File\Open.mst (89)
[Start Time]     03/06/1996 22:55:26
[Result]         PASS
[Elapsed Time]   1.711
[End Scenario]

[Start Scenario]
[Name]              Test #5: File\Open... w/ text. Yes to Save
                    Changes, then Cancel to Open dialog box.
[Test Location]  C:\MSDEV\SAMPLES\Notepad\File\Open.mst (114)
[Start Time]     03/06/1996 22:55:28
[Result]         PASS
[Elapsed Time]   2.639
[End Scenario]

[Start Scenario]
[Name]              Test #6: File\Open... w/o text. Press Yes then Ok
[Test Location]  C:\MSDEV\SAMPLES\Notepad\File\Open.mst (141)
[Start Time]     03/06/1996 22:55:31
[Result]         PASS
[Elapsed Time]   3.503
[End Scenario]

[Case Result]      PASS
[Elapsed Time]     21.860
[End Case]

[Start Case Header]
[Case Name]        C:\MSDEV\SAMPLES\Notepad\File\Saveas.mst
[Product Version]  Windows 95
[Language]         English
```

```
[Machine]            TOMA
[Start Time]         03/06/1996 22:55:36
[End Case Header]

  [Start Scenario]
  [Name]             Test #1: File\Save As... w/ text.  Untitled
  [Test Location]    C:\MSDEV\SAMPLES\Notepad\File\Saveas.mst (32)
  [Start Time]       03/06/1996 22:55:43
  [Result]           PASS
  [Elapsed Time]     2.799
  [End Scenario]

  [Start Scenario]
  [Name]             Test #2: File\Save As... w/ text.  Saved instance
  [Test Location]    C:\MSDEV\SAMPLES\Notepad\File\Saveas.mst (58)
  [Start Time]       03/06/1996 22:55:46
  [Result]           PASS
  [Elapsed Time]     2.862
  [End Scenario]

  [Start Scenario]
  [Name]             Test #3: Verify text was saved.
  [Test Location]    C:\MSDEV\SAMPLES\Notepad\File\Saveas.mst (86)
  [Start Time]       03/06/1996 22:55:49
  [Result]           PASS
  [Elapsed Time]     1.992
  [End Scenario]

[Case Result]        PASS
[Elapsed Time]       16.316
[End Case]

[Start Case Header]
[Case Name]          C:\MSDEV\SAMPLES\Notepad\Edit\Paste.mst
[Product Version]    Windows 95
[Language]           English
[Machine]            TOMA
[Start Time]         03/06/1996 22:55:53
[End Case Header]

  [Start Scenario]
  [Name]             Test #1: Edit\Paste disabled when clipboard is
                     empty.
  [Test Location]    C:\MSDEV\SAMPLES\Notepad\Edit\Paste.mst (32)
```

```
[Start Time]      03/06/1996 22:56:00
[Result]          PASS
[Elapsed Time]    0.369
[End Scenario]


[Start Scenario]
[Name]            Test #2: Typing should not effect Edit\Paste
[Test Location]   C:\MSDEV\SAMPLES\Notepad\Edit\Paste.mst (42)
[Start Time]      03/06/1996 22:56:00
[Result]          PASS
[Elapsed Time]    1.032
[End Scenario]


[Start Scenario]
[Name]            Test #3: Edit\Cut enables Edit\Paste
[Test Location]   C:\MSDEV\SAMPLES\Notepad\Edit\Paste.mst (53)
[Start Time]      03/06/1996 22:56:01
[Result]          PASS
[Elapsed Time]    1.346
[End Scenario]


[Start Scenario]
[Name]            Test #4: Edit\Paste text into empty editor.
[Test Location]   C:\MSDEV\SAMPLES\Notepad\Edit\Paste.mst (68)
[Start Time]      03/06/1996 22:56:03
[Result]          PASS
[Elapsed Time]    0.442
[End Scenario]


[Start Scenario]
[Name]            Test #5: Edit\Paste text after text.
[Test Location]   C:\MSDEV\SAMPLES\Notepad\Edit\Paste.mst (78)
[Start Time]      03/06/1996 22:56:03
[Result]          PASS
[Elapsed Time]    0.474
[End Scenario]


[Start Scenario]
[Name]            Test #6: Edit\Paste before text.
[Test Location]   C:\MSDEV\SAMPLES\Notepad\Edit\Paste.mst (90)
[Start Time]      03/06/1996 22:56:04
[Result]          PASS
[Elapsed Time]    4.550
[End Scenario]
```

```
            [Start Scenario]
            [Name]              Test #7: File\New then try Edit\Paste
            [Test Location]     C:\MSDEV\SAMPLES\Notepad\Edit\Paste.mst (102)
            [Start Time]        03/06/1996 22:56:08
            [Result]            PASS
            [Elapsed Time]      1.040
            [End Scenario]


        [Case Result]           PASS
        [Elapsed Time]          18.175
        [End Case]


        [Start Case Header]
        [Case Name]             C:\MSDEV\SAMPLES\Notepad\Edit\Slct_all.mst
        [Product Version]       Windows 95
        [Language]              English
        [Machine]               TOMA
        [Start Time]            03/06/1996 22:56:11
        [End Case Header]


            [Start Scenario]
            [Name]              Test #1: Edit\Select All enabled with no text.
            [Test Location]     C:\MSDEV\SAMPLES\Notepad\Edit\Slct_all.mst (31)
            [Start Time]        03/06/1996 22:56:18
            [Result]            PASS
            [Elapsed Time]      0.490
            [End Scenario]


            [Start Scenario]
            [Name]              Test #2: Edit\Select All is a no-op with no text.
            [Test Location]     C:\MSDEV\SAMPLES\Notepad\Edit\Slct_all.mst (40)
            [Start Time]        03/06/1996 22:56:19
            [Result]            PASS
            [Elapsed Time]      0.452
            [End Scenario]


            [Start Scenario]
            [Name]              Test #3: Edit\Select All enabled with text.
            [Test Location]     C:\MSDEV\SAMPLES\Notepad\Edit\Slct_all.mst (52)
            [Start Time]        03/06/1996 22:56:19
            [Result]            PASS
            [Elapsed Time]      1.032
            [End Scenario]
```

```
[Start Scenario]
[Name]            Test #4: Edit\Select All selects 1 line of text.
[Test Location]   C:\MSDEV\SAMPLES\Notepad\Edit\Slct_all.mst (62)
[Start Time]      03/06/1996 22:56:20
[Result]          PASS
[Elapsed Time]    0.957
[End Scenario]

[Start Scenario]
[Name]            Test #5: Edit\Select All selects 3 lines of text.
[Test Location]   C:\MSDEV\SAMPLES\Notepad\Edit\Slct_all.mst (73)
[Start Time]      03/06/1996 22:56:21
[Result]          PASS
[Elapsed Time]    3.585
[End Scenario]

[Case Result]     PASS
[Elapsed Time]    15.187
[End Case]

[Start Case Header]
[Case Name]       C:\MSDEV\SAMPLES\Notepad\Edit\Wordwrap.mst
[Product Version] Windows 95
[Language]        English
[Machine]         TOMA
[Start Time]      03/06/1996 22:56:26
[End Case Header]

[Start Scenario]
[Name]            Test #1: Type text with WordWrap off.
[Test Location]   C:\MSDEV\SAMPLES\Notepad\Edit\Wordwrap.mst (30)
[Start Time]      03/06/1996 22:56:33
[Result]          PASS
[Elapsed Time]    2.883
[End Scenario]

[Start Scenario]
[Name]            Test #2: Turn 'WordWrap' on with existing text.
[Test Location]   C:\MSDEV\SAMPLES\Notepad\Edit\Wordwrap.mst (43)
[Start Time]      03/06/1996 22:56:36
[Result]          PASS
[Elapsed Time]    0.594
[End Scenario]
```

```
[Start Scenario]
[Name]            Test #3: Type text with WordWrap on.
[Test Location]   C:\MSDEV\SAMPLES\Notepad\Edit\Wordwrap.mst (53)
[Start Time]      03/06/1996 22:56:37
[Result]          PASS
[Elapsed Time]    5.480
[End Scenario]


[Case Result]     PASS
[Elapsed Time]    17.838
[End Case]


[Start Case Header]
[Case Name]       C:\MSDEV\SAMPLES\Notepad\Edit\Copy.mst
[Product Version] Windows 95
[Language]        English
[Machine]         TOMA
[Start Time]      03/06/1996 22:56:44
[End Case Header]


  [Start Scenario]
  [Name]            Test #1: Edit\Copy is disabled after File\New
  [Test Location]   C:\MSDEV\SAMPLES\Notepad\Edit\Copy.mst (32)
  [Start Time]      03/06/1996 22:56:51
  [Result]          PASS
  [Elapsed Time]    0.803
  [End Scenario]


  [Start Scenario]
  [Name]            Test #2: Edit\Copy still disabled after typing.
  [Test Location]   C:\MSDEV\SAMPLES\Notepad\Edit\Copy.mst (43)
  [Start Time]      03/06/1996 22:56:52
  [Result]          PASS
  [Elapsed Time]    0.982
  [End Scenario]


  [Start Scenario]
  [Name]            Test #3: Edit\Copy available after selecting text.
  [Test Location]   C:\MSDEV\SAMPLES\Notepad\Edit\Copy.mst (55)
  [Start Time]      03/06/1996 22:56:53
  [Result]          PASS
  [Elapsed Time]    0.822
  [End Scenario]
```

```
[Start Scenario]
[Name]          Test #4: Edit\Copy the selected text.
[Test Location] C:\MSDEV\SAMPLES\Notepad\Edit\Copy.mst (66)
[Start Time]    03/06/1996 22:56:54
[Result]        PASS
[Elapsed Time]  0.393
[End Scenario]

[Case Result]   PASS
[Elapsed Time]  . 12.127
[End Case]

[Start Case Header]
[Case Name]       C:\MSDEV\SAMPLES\Notepad\Edit\Cut.mst
[Product Version] Windows 95
[Language]        English
[Machine]         TOMA
[Start Time]      03/06/1996 22:56:56
[End Case Header]

  [Start Scenario]
  [Name]          Test #1: Edit\Cut is disabled after File\New
  [Test Location] C:\MSDEV\SAMPLES\Notepad\Edit\Cut.mst (32)
  [Start Time]    03/06/1996 22:57:03
  [Result]        PASS
  [Elapsed Time]  0.413
  [End Scenario]

  [Start Scenario]
  [Name]          Test #2: 'Cut' still disabled after typing.
  [Test Location] C:\MSDEV\SAMPLES\Notepad\Edit\Cut.mst (41)
  [Start Time]    03/06/1996 22:57:04
  [Result]        PASS
  [Elapsed Time]  0.919
  [End Scenario]

  [Start Scenario]
  [Name]          Test #3: Edit\Cut available after selecting text.
  [Test Location] C:\MSDEV\SAMPLES\Notepad\Edit\Cut.mst (52)
  [Start Time]    03/06/1996 22:57:05
  [Result]        PASS
  [Elapsed Time]  0.879
  [End Scenario]
```

471

```
[Start Scenario]
[Name]            Test #4: Edit\Cut should remove the text.
[Test Location]   C:\MSDEV\SAMPLES\Notepad\Edit\Cut.mst (62)
[Start Time]      03/06/1996 22:57:06
[Result]          PASS
[Elapsed Time]    2.195
[End Scenario]

[Start Scenario]
[Name]            Test #5: Edit\Cut should put text onto clipboard.
[Test Location]   C:\MSDEV\SAMPLES\Notepad\Edit\Cut.mst (75)
[Start Time]      03/06/1996 22:57:08
[Result]          PASS
[Elapsed Time]    0.009
[End Scenario]

[Case Result]     PASS
[Elapsed Time]    13.168
[End Case]

[Start Case Header]
[Case Name]       C:\MSDEV\SAMPLES\Notepad\Edit\Delete.mst
[Product Version] Windows 95
[Language]        English
[Machine]         TOMA
[Start Time]      03/06/1996 22:57:09
[End Case Header]

[Start Scenario]
[Name]            Test #1: Edit\Delete is disabled in empty editor.
[Test Location]   C:\MSDEV\SAMPLES\Notepad\Edit\Delete.mst (32)
[Start Time]      03/06/1996 22:57:17
[Result]          PASS
[Elapsed Time]    0.428
[End Scenario]

[Start Scenario]
[Name]            Test #2: Edit\Delete is disabled with no text
                  selected.
[Test Location]   C:\MSDEV\SAMPLES\Notepad\Edit\Delete.mst (42)
[Start Time]      03/06/1996 22:57:17
[Result]          PASS
[Elapsed Time]    0.979
[End Scenario]
```

```
[Start Scenario]
[Name]              Test #3: Edit\Delete is enabled with text
                    selected.
[Test Location]  C:\MSDEV\SAMPLES\Notepad\Edit\Delete.mst (53)
[Start Time]     03/06/1996 22:57:18
[Result]         PASS
[Elapsed Time]   0.808
[End Scenario]


[Start Scenario]
[Name]              Test #4: Edit\Delete should clear the selected
                    text.
[Test Location]  C:\MSDEV\SAMPLES\Notepad\Edit\Delete.mst (63)
[Start Time]     03/06/1996 22:57:19
[Result]         PASS
[Elapsed Time]   0.583
[End Scenario]


[Start Scenario]
[Name]              Test #5: Edit\Delete first word of text.
[Test Location]  C:\MSDEV\SAMPLES\Notepad\Edit\Delete.mst (73)
[Start Time]     03/06/1996 22:57:20
[Result]         PASS
[Elapsed Time]   1.255
[End Scenario]


[Case Result]    PASS
[Elapsed Time]   13.234
[End Case]


[Start Case Header]
[Case Name]         C:\MSDEV\SAMPLES\Notepad\Edit\Timedate.mst
[Product Version]   Windows 95
[Language]          English
[Machine]           TOMA
[Start Time]        03/06/1996 22:57:23
[End Case Header]


[Start Scenario]
[Name]              Test #1: Edit\Time/Date menu is enabled.
[Test Location]  C:\MSDEV\SAMPLES\Notepad\Edit\Timedate.mst (32)
[Start Time]     03/06/1996 22:57:30
[Result]         PASS
[Elapsed Time]   0.435
[End Scenario]
```

```
[Start Scenario]
[Name]           Test #2: Put Edit\Time/Date into an empty editor.
[Test Location]  C:\MSDEV\SAMPLES\Notepad\Edit\Timedate.mst (41)
[Start Time]     03/06/1996 22:57:31
[Result]         PASS
[Elapsed Time]   1.911
[End Scenario]

[Case Result]    PASS
[Elapsed Time]   11.525
[End Case]

[Start Case Header]
[Case Name]        C:\MSDEV\SAMPLES\Notepad\Edit\Undo.mst
[Product Version]  Windows 95
[Language]         English
[Machine]          TOMA
[Start Time]       03/06/1996 22:57:34
[End Case Header]

  [Start Scenario]
  [Name]           Test #1: Edit\Undo is disabled after 'File/New'.
  [Test Location]  C:\MSDEV\SAMPLES\Notepad\Edit\Undo.mst (32)
  [Start Time]     03/06/1996 22:57:42
  [Result]         PASS
  [Elapsed Time]   0.388
  [End Scenario]

  [Start Scenario]
  [Name]           Test #2: Edit\Undo enabled after typing.
  [Test Location]  C:\MSDEV\SAMPLES\Notepad\Edit\Undo.mst (42)
  [Start Time]     03/06/1996 22:57:42
  [Result]         PASS
  [Elapsed Time]   0.976
  [End Scenario]

  [Start Scenario]
  [Name]           Test #3: Edit\Undo typing in a string.
  [Test Location]  C:\MSDEV\SAMPLES\Notepad\Edit\Undo.mst (53)
  [Start Time]     03/06/1996 22:57:43
  [Result]         PASS
  [Elapsed Time]   0.416
  [End Scenario]
```

```
[Start Scenario]
[Name]           Test #4: Edit\Undo again should 'REDO' the typing.
[Test Location]  C:\MSDEV\SAMPLES\Notepad\Edit\Undo.mst (64)
[Start Time]     03/06/1996 22:57:44
[Result]         PASS
[Elapsed Time]   0.430
[End Scenario]

[Start Scenario]
[Name]           Test #5: Test Edit\Cut is undoable.
[Test Location]  C:\MSDEV\SAMPLES\Notepad\Edit\Undo.mst (74)
[Start Time]     03/06/1996 22:57:44
[Result]         PASS
[Elapsed Time]   0.838
[End Scenario]

[Start Scenario]
[Name]           Test #6: Undoing a Edit\Copy action should redo
                 the Edit\Cut action.
[Test Location]  C:\MSDEV\SAMPLES\Notepad\Edit\Undo.mst (91)
[Start Time]     03/06/1996 22:57:45
[Result]         PASS
[Elapsed Time]   0.941
[End Scenario]

[Start Scenario]
[Name]           Test #7: Test that Edit\Paste is undoable.
[Test Location]  C:\MSDEV\SAMPLES\Notepad\Edit\Undo.mst (107)
[Start Time]     03/06/1996 22:57:46
[Result]         PASS
[Elapsed Time]   1.436
[End Scenario]

[Start Scenario]
[Name]           Test #8: Test that Edit\Delete is undoable.
[Test Location]  C:\MSDEV\SAMPLES\Notepad\Edit\Undo.mst (119)
[Start Time]     03/06/1996 22:57:48
[Result]         PASS
[Elapsed Time]   0.853
[End Scenario]

[Start Scenario]
[Name]           Test #9: Edit\Undo again should 'Redo' the delete
[Test Location]  C:\MSDEV\SAMPLES\Notepad\Edit\Undo.mst (134)
```

```
[Start Time]      03/06/1996 22:57:49
[Result]          PASS
[Elapsed Time]    0.436
[End Scenario]


[Start Scenario]
[Name]            Test #10: Test Time/Date action disables 'Undo'.
[Test Location]   C:\MSDEV\SAMPLES\Notepad\Edit\Undo.mst (144)
[Start Time]      03/06/1996 22:57:49
[Result]          PASS
[Elapsed Time]    0.935
[End Scenario]


[Case Result]     PASS
[Elapsed Time]    17.051
[End Case]


[Start Case Header]
[Case Name]       C:\MSDEV\SAMPLES\Notepad\Search\Find.mst
[Product Version] Windows 95
[Language]        English
[Machine]         TOMA
[Start Time]      03/06/1996 22:57:52
[End Case Header]


  [Start Scenario]
  [Name]            Test #1: Search\Find... menu enabled with no text.
  [Test Location]   C:\MSDEV\SAMPLES\Notepad\Search\Find.mst (32)
  [Start Time]      03/06/1996 22:57:59
  [Result]          PASS
  [Elapsed Time]    0.411
  [End Scenario]


  [Start Scenario]
  [Name]            Test #2: Search\Find... brings up 'Find' DB with
                    no text.
  [Test Location]   C:\MSDEV\SAMPLES\Notepad\Search\Find.mst (41)
  [Start Time]      03/06/1996 22:57:59
  [Result]          PASS
  [Elapsed Time]    0.633
  [End Scenario]


  [Start Scenario]
  [Name]            Test #3: Search\Find... the first char of a string.
```

```
[Test Location]   C:\MSDEV\SAMPLES\Notepad\Search\Find.mst (53)
[Start Time]      03/06/1996 22:58:00
[Result]          PASS
[Elapsed Time]    3.545
[End Scenario]


[Start Scenario]
[Name]            Test #4: Search\Find... next occurance of
                  SearchText.
[Test Location]   C:\MSDEV\SAMPLES\Notepad\Search\Find.mst (70)
[Start Time]      03/06/1996 22:58:04
[Result]          PASS
[Elapsed Time]    0.110
[End Scenario]


[Start Scenario]
[Name]            Test #5: Search\Find... again will not find any
                  thing.
[Test Location]   C:\MSDEV\SAMPLES\Notepad\Search\Find.mst (81)
[Start Time]      03/06/1996 22:58:04
[Result]          PASS
[Elapsed Time]    0.445
[End Scenario]


[Start Scenario]
[Name]            Test #6: Check that text found matches search
                  text.
[Test Location]   C:\MSDEV\SAMPLES\Notepad\Search\Find.mst (94)
[Start Time]      03/06/1996 22:58:04
[Result]          PASS
[Elapsed Time]    0.018
[End Scenario]


[Start Scenario]
[Name]            Test #7: Search\Find... first word of a string.
[Test Location]   C:\MSDEV\SAMPLES\Notepad\Search\Find.mst (103)
[Start Time]      03/06/1996 22:58:04
[Result]          PASS
[Elapsed Time]    1.606
[End Scenario]


[Start Scenario]
[Name]            Test #8: Search\Find... again should display mes
                  sage box.
```

```
[Test Location]  C:\MSDEV\SAMPLES\Notepad\Search\Find.mst (118)
[Start Time]     03/06/1996 22:58:06
[Result]         PASS
[Elapsed Time]   0.433
[End Scenario]


[Start Scenario]
[Name]           Test #9: Check that text found matches search
                 text.
[Test Location]  C:\MSDEV\SAMPLES\Notepad\Search\Find.mst (131)
[Start Time]     03/06/1996 22:58:07
[Result]         PASS
[Elapsed Time]   0.019
[End Scenario]


[Start Scenario]
[Name]           Test #10: Search\Find... last word of a string.
[Test Location]  C:\MSDEV\SAMPLES\Notepad\Search\Find.mst (140)
[Start Time]     03/06/1996 22:58:07
[Result]         PASS
[Elapsed Time]   1.013
[End Scenario]


[Start Scenario]
[Name]           Test #11: Search\Find... again will not find
                 another occurance.
[Test Location]  C:\MSDEV\SAMPLES\Notepad\Search\Find.mst (155)
[Start Time]     03/06/1996 22:58:08
[Result]         PASS
[Elapsed Time]   0.496
[End Scenario]


[Start Scenario]
[Name]           Test #12: Check that text found matches search
                 text.
[Test Location]  C:\MSDEV\SAMPLES\Notepad\Search\Find.mst (168)
[Start Time]     03/06/1996 22:58:08
[Result]         PASS
[Elapsed Time]   0.022
[End Scenario]


[Case Result]    PASS
[Elapsed Time]   18.025
[End Case]
```

```
[Start Case Header]
[Case Name]        C:\MSDEV\SAMPLES\Notepad\Search\Findnext.mst
[Product Version]  Windows 95
[Language]         English
[Machine]          TOMA
[Start Time]       03/06/1996 22:58:10
[End Case Header]

  [Start Scenario]
  [Name]           Test #1: Search\Find Next with 'Find' Buffer
                   empty.
  [Test Location]  C:\MSDEV\SAMPLES\Notepad\Search\Findnext.mst (32)
  [Start Time]     03/06/1996 22:58:17
  [Result]         PASS
  [Elapsed Time]   0.645
  [End Scenario]


  [Start Scenario]
  [Name]           Test #2: Search\Find Next with next but Find
                   buffer empty.
  [Test Location]  C:\MSDEV\SAMPLES\Notepad\Search\Findnext.mst (44)
  [Start Time]     03/06/1996 22:58:18
  [Result]         PASS
  [Elapsed Time]   3.631
  [End Scenario]


  [Start Scenario]
  [Name]           Test #3: Check that text found matches search
                   text.
  [Test Location]  C:\MSDEV\SAMPLES\Notepad\Search\Findnext.mst (65)
  [Start Time]     03/06/1996 22:58:22
  [Result]         PASS
  [Elapsed Time]   0.018
  [End Scenario]


  [Start Scenario]
  [Name]           Test #4: Search\Find Next with 'Find' buffer
                   filled.
  [Test Location]  C:\MSDEV\SAMPLES\Notepad\Search\Findnext.mst (75)
  [Start Time]     03/06/1996 22:58:22
  [Result]         PASS
  [Elapsed Time]   0.442
  [End Scenario]
```

479

[Start Scenario]
[Name]   Test #5: Check that text found matches search
                  text.
[Test Location]   C:\MSDEV\SAMPLES\Notepad\Search\Findnext.mst (85)
[Start Time]   03/06/1996 22:58:22
[Result]   PASS
[Elapsed Time]   0.019
[End Scenario]

[Start Scenario]
[Name]   Test #6: Search\Find Next should display 'Not
                  Found' message box.
[Test Location]   C:\MSDEV\SAMPLES\Notepad\Search\Findnext.mst (94)
[Start Time]   03/06/1996 22:58:22
[Result]   PASS
[Elapsed Time]   0.662
[End Scenario]

[Start Scenario]
[Name]   Test #7: Check that text found matches search
                  text.
[Test Location]   C:\MSDEV\SAMPLES\Notepad\Search\Findnext.mst (106)
[Start Time]   03/06/1996 22:58:23
[Result]   PASS
[Elapsed Time]   0.018
[End Scenario]

[Case Result]   PASS
[Elapsed Time]   14.830
[End Case]

[Start Case Header]
[Case Name]   C:\MSDEV\SAMPLES\Notepad\Help\About.mst
[Product Version] Windows 95
[Language]   English
[Machine]   TOMA
[Start Time]   03/06/1996 22:58:25
[End Case Header]

[Start Scenario]
[Name]   Test #1: Select the Help\About Notepad menu item.
[Test Location]   C:\MSDEV\SAMPLES\Notepad\Help\About.mst (27)
[Start Time]   03/06/1996 22:58:32
[Result]   PASS

```
    [Elapsed Time]    0.938
    [End Scenario]

[Case Result]     PASS
[Elapsed Time]    9.789
[End Case]

[Start Case Header]
[Case Name]       C:\MSDEV\SAMPLES\Notepad\Help\Topics.mst
[Product Version] Windows 95
[Language]        English
[Machine]         TOMA
[Start Time]      03/06/1996 22:58:35
[End Case Header]

    [Start Scenario]
    [Name]           Test #1: Select the Help\Help Topics menu item
    [Test Location]  C:\MSDEV\SAMPLES\Notepad\Help\Topics.mst (30)
    [Start Time]     03/06/1996 22:58:42
    [Result]         PASS
    [Elapsed Time]   4.084
    [End Scenario]

[Case Result]     PASS
[Elapsed Time]    12.670
[End Case]

[Suite Result]    PASS
[Elapsed Time]    289.548
[End Suite]
```

Using the Disk

*T*he following three directories are provided on this disk:

▶ Listings

▶ Suite

▶ TestNow

Listings

The Listings directory contains text files created from the chapters in this book. These are provided to you so that when you find a script that you'd like to try, or some code that you'd like to use in your own automated tests, you can more easily do this.

The naming convention followed identifies the text file as a listing, the chapter number, and position of the listing in that chapter. For example, "LST01-02.TXT" is a source code listing taken from Chapter 1 and is the second listing in that chapter.

Suite

The Suite directory contains the final version of the Test Suite that is developed throughout this book. If you have Visual Test installed correctly, you will be able to double-click on the Notepad.vtp file to open the project. This project file is also used by the Microsoft Suite Manager that comes with Visual Test.

The sample driver (driver.mst) uses an initialization file to keep track of the test case files it has been configured to run. This initialization file (test.ini) assumes a particular directory structure. The test.ini file can either be edited to match the directory structure where you place these sample files, or the files and directories found in the Suite directory can be copied to c:\msdev\samples\notepad. This only must be done if you plan to use the driver.mst example program.

TestNow

Test Now 2.0 is a product created by Software Testing Laboraties in Seattle, WA. This product is an add-on tool that works with the Visual Test product. One of the tools (digger.pcd) has been included in this directory. It is fully functional and will not expire. It is one of the more popular tools of the Test Now product. You are free to use it as the owner of this book on Visual Test. You may not copy it or redistribute it to others without written permission from Software Testing Labs.

Also in this directory is the online help file for the Test Now product. This has been provided to give you online documentation for the Digger 1.0 tool. It also provides you with a list of the other features included in the full version of Test Now 2.0. The full version of Test Now 2.0 can be purchased from STL for $189, plus shipping and handling. Refer to the back of your book for ordering information, or see the readme file in the TestNow directory.

From the Author

I hope you find this book and the files included on the disk helpful to you and your work. STL was kind enough to allow me to include the Digger utility in full with this book because it is such a useful tool. I hope you find it helpful when creating your automation templates.

The files that make up the test suite are based on the latest feedback we've received from Microsoft and students from our classes. These approaches have saved us a considerable amount of time as we've created automated scripts for our clients. It's especially noticeable when our clients later want things changed. The key is keeping this as flexible as possible. I invite you to share you ideas on making things even more flexible. You can send your comments to me at TomA@STLabs.com or TomA@WebSoln.com.

While I cannot provide any technical support help, I can direct you to a mailing list I set up that currently has nearly 300 subscribers. This e-mail list (or *listserver*) allows you to send a question or comment to the discussion group. That message is then broadcast to the members of the group, allowing others to answer your questions. Or, hopefully, it allows you to help others with their Visual Test problems. Subscribe to this group by sending e-mail to LISTPROC@ESKIMO.COM. In your message, type in **subscribe mt_info *yourname*** (where *yourname* is your first name). To unsubscribe, send e-mail to the same address with the message: **unsubscribe mt_info**.

When you subscribe, you will receive confirmation e-mail describing how to use this service. I hope you find this to be an ongoing help. This book can only take you so far. Perhaps this e-mail group can pick up where the book leaves off.

Tom Arnold June 1996

Index

Numbers and Symbols

& **(ampersand)**, 78, 300
* **(asterisk)**, 102, 123
@ **(at symbol)**, 100
\ **(backslash)**, 106
^ **(caret)**, 110
{} **(curly braces)**, 110, 162
$ **(dollar sign)**, 78
... **(ellipses)**, 99, 106
= **(equal sign)**, 101
! **(exclamation point)**, 78
- **(hyphen)**, 170
% **(percent sign)**, 78, 109
+ **(plus sign)**, 110
# **(pound sign)**, 78, 100, 291
' **(single quotes)**, 80, 99, 165
[ ] **(square brackets)**, 77
_ **(underline character)**, 83, 304

16-bit programming, 28, 30, 240, 311
32-bit programming, 28, 30, 311
  variable declarations and, 78
  Windows Software Development Kit
    (Win32 SDK) for, 52, 308, 316, 343

A

about.mst, 60, 455, 457–458
About Notepad menu item, 454–455,
    457–458
accelerator keys, 106, 111, 218
  basic description of, 347

  creating, with the Accelerator Editor,
    328
  DAM keys and, comparison of, 344
Access (Microsoft), 21
Add Multi-User dialog box, 123
add-ons, 373
Add Verification... button, 123
AHostMsgHandler() function, 355
allocate statement, 301
America Online (AOL), 385
ampersand (&), 78, 300
APIs (application programming
    interfaces), 34, 304–318
append mode, 290
Apple Computer, 375
approach(es)
  basic description of, 195–214
  defining what's to be testing, 199–207
  dialog-centric, 198
  functionality, 198, 209–210, 215
  menu-based, 198
  toolbar-based, 198
  types of, 197–199
arguments, 257–259
asterisk (*), 102, 123
Asymetrix Corporation, 103,
    107–108, 165
asynchronous events, 354
aTest() function, 317–318
at symbol (@), 100

B

Bach, James, 375
backslash (\), 106
base state, 232

C

file extensions
.mst, 58, 184
.pcd, 61
.scn, 114–115
.vts, 281
file.inc, 182–183, 187, 189, 298, 407–409
File menu, 60, 106, 108, 111, 122,
209–210, 217–218, 407–428
Exit menu item, 407, 424–428
New menu item, 55–57, 144–157,
183–187, 216–224, 245, 248–266,
269, 326, 332, 407, 409–411
Open menu item, 407, 411–415
Page Setup menu item, 407, 422–424
Save As menu item, 407, 420–421
Save menu item, 407, 416–420
filename.inc, 167
FILTDELIM constant, 313
filters, 313, 315
Find dialog box, 198
Finder tool, 127, 129
Find in Files tab, 47
Find menu item, 181, 446, 448–452
find.mst, 446, 448–452
Find Next menu item, 446, 452–454
findnext.mst, 446, 452–454
flags, basic description of, 148–149
folder(s)
adding new files to, 58
entry scripts, 59–60
MSDEV folder, 33–35
FOO function, 173
for/next loops, 91–92
**foreign countries, localizing your
product in,** 189, 244
FORTRAN, 75, 222
France, 244
freefile() function, 289, 291
Friedman, Michael, 391
Fuchs, Steve, 22
fullpass.vts, 281
functionality approach, 198,
209–210, 215
functional specifications, 5

functions. *See also* functions (listed by
name)
basic description of, 82–83
callback functions, 316–318
includes files and, 60
wrapper functions, 188, 192–193
functions (listed by name). *See also*
functions
AHostMsgHandler() function, 355
aTest() function, 317–318
CPTR() function, 315
DoKeys() function, 108
DriverProc() function, 343
EditText function, 153
EOF() function, 291
ERF() function, 321
FOO function, 173
freefile() function, 289, 291
GetOpenFileName() function, 306,
308–315
GetText() function, 154, 219
GetTickCount() function, 299
iFailCount() function, 270–272, 273
iTestCount() function, 270–272, 273
LEN() function, 296, 314
main() function, 79–80
MessageBox() function, 305
MessageBoxA() function, 305
QueMouse*() function, 108
RES$ function, 331, 349
ScnSetExcludeRects() function, 139
SetDefaultWaitTimeout function, 98, 99
SetMenu() function, 345–346
SetTimer() function, 364
STR$() function, 263
strFailNum() function, 227, 272–273
strGetFile() function, 311–312
strTestNum() function, 226–227,
272–273
TalkCallHost() function, 361–362
TalkCreateHost() function, 353–356,
359
TalkGetStationCount() function, 357
TalkGetStationName() function, 357

(continued)

(continued)

temporary files, 64
test1.txt, 120–124
TEST_ALL_CLASS constant, 242
TestBegin() function, 226, 227, 228
TestBegin() routine, 186–187, 191, 247, 263–266, 275, 298
test drivers, 23–24, 26–27, 39
TestEnd() routine, 227, 266, 274–275, 298
test.ini, 484
Testing Techniques Newsletter **(TTN),** 390
Test Locals window, 66–67, 293–294
Test menu, 51, 61–68, 80, 119–121, 127
  stepping through code with, 64–66
  tracking down problems with, 63–64
  watching variables with, 66–67
Test Now, 35, 70, 288, 373, 484
TestRes1 folder, 326
Test tab, 66
Test toolbar, 49, 52
TestView tab, 55
TestView window, 211
Test Watch window, 66–67
ThunderCommandButtons, 102
Time/Date menu item, 428, 443–444
timedate.mst, 428, 443–444
time-out parameters, 97
Timer() function, 299
TimerProc() function, 316–317
tiTestOne variable, 85
toolbar(s), 69, 126–128. *See also* toolbars (listed by name)
  basic description of, 48–55
  context-sensitive help and, 76
  declaring variables and, 76–79
toolbars (listed by name). *See also* toolbars
  Debug toolbar, 49, 51–52, 66
  Edit toolbar, 49, 50–51, 67–68
  InfoViewer Contents toolbar, 49, 55
  InfoViewer toolbar, 49, 52–54, 308
  Resource toolbar, 48, 50
  Standard toolbar, 48, 49–50

Test toolbar, 49, 52
Toolbars dialog box, 49
Toolbars tab, 69
ToolBook, 103, 107–108
tool palettes, 126–128, 199
Tools menu, 30, 48, 71
Tools tab, 70
topics.mst, 455, 456–457
TPL files, 56–57
TRIM$() function, 263

U

UI (user interface), 24, 100
  overview of, 43–74
  the Screen Utility and, 133–139
UINTs (unsigned integers), 316
unconditional branching, 91, 176–177
underline character (_), 83, 304
Undo menu item, 428, 430–433
undo.mst, 428, 430–433
UNIX, 162, 366, 385
The Unofficial Visual Test Web site, 387
unrecoverable application errors, 131
until option, 93
Unwin, C., 391
user-defined types, 60, 84–85, 171–172
User Interface Editor, 26, 132
utilities. *See also* specific utilities
  basic description of, 119–142
  the final test suite and, 270–276
  noteutil.inc and, 248–266

V

variable(s). *See also* variables (listed by name)
  declarations, 76–79, 147–148
  double, 78
  global, 60, 76–78, 171–172, 228, 263, 321
  in-scope, 66
  integer, 77–78, 171–172, 175–176, 354–355
  local, 77, 172
  long, 77–78, 147, 299, 311
  naming conventions for, 174–176
  out-of-scope, 67
  scopes, 66–67, 76–79
  short, 78, 311, 354–355
  single, 78
  static, 77–78, 262
  string, 77–78, 147
  watching, 66–67
variables (listed by name). *See also* variables
  execScripts variable, 344
  ghWndNotepad variable, 228, 247, 265
  iBook% variable, 79
  iCount variable, 175, 176
  iDescription variable, 175
  iIndex variable, 93
  iLoop variable, 91
  in-scope variables, 67
  ITimer variable, 175, 176
  pstrTestType variable, 175
  rectWindow variable, 175, 176
  strDescription variable, 175
  strfParse variable, 175, 176
  strText variable, 153
  strText$ variable, 147
  tiTestOne variable, 85
VarPtr() function, 300, 315
VCR (Versatile Computer Recorder), 21–22
vData parameter, 360, 362

videos series, 371–374
Viewport, 153, 154, 278
VIEWPORT CLEAR statement, 149
Viewport tab, 47, 290
vInfo parameter, 322
Visual BASIC, 29, 76, 94, 206
  encapsulation and, 191–192
  pointers and, 303
Visual C++, 30, 43, 327
Visual Test (Microsoft)
  basic description of, 9
  history of, 21–31
  version 1.0, 23–25
  version 2.0, 24–27, 132
  version 3.0, 27–29, 372
  version 4.0, 29–30, 371–372, 373
VM (Virtual Machine), 26
Voas, Jeffrey M., 391
void data type, 81
Vt4setup folder, 35
VTP (Visual Test Project) files, 56, 57, 132, 276–277, 483–484
VTR files, 325. *See also* resources

W

watch window, 66–67
WATT (Windows Application Testing Tool), 22
wButtonClassLen function, 96
wButtonClick statement, 96, 97, 121, 128, 153, 218, 219
wButtonDefault function, 96
wButtonDefaults function, 96
wButtonEnabled function, 96
wButtonExits function, 96
wButtonFind function, 96
wButtonFocus function, 96
wButtonGetClass statement, 96
wButtonMoveTo statement, 96
wButtonSetClass statement, 96, 129
wButtonSetFocus statement, 96

About the Author

Tom Arnold graduated from Purdue University in 1990 with a Bachelor of Science degree in computer science. He began his career in the computer industry at Asymetrix Corporation where, after two and a half years, he was the Senior Test Lead for their Multimedia & Tools Group, responsible for such products as ToolBook 3.0, Multimedia ToolBook 3.0 and MediaBlitz! 2.0. In addition, he contributed to the development of ToolBook 3.0 by writing DLLs to support Microsoft Windows common dialogs and parts of the ToolBook 3.0 menu editor feature.

One of his main tasks at Asymetrix was developing a strategy for automating test cases for each individual project. Involved in using Microsoft Test since the 1.0 version was released in Beta form, he had the opportunity to build elaborate and extensive automation libraries.

In August 1993, Arnold accepted a position in the Microsoft Consulting Services department at Microsoft Corporation. He was responsible for writing the underlying utilities used by the test automation team and working on a project for the multimedia passenger services for the passenger terminals placed in the new Boeing 777. The automated tests were used to not only exercise the passenger-side of the product, but to emulate multiple users on the airplane's internal network as well.

Arnold began working with Software Testing Laboratories (STLabs) and Microsoft Corporation in December 1993 to develop a course on Microsoft Test 2.0 and 3.0. This gave him access to the key people on the Microsoft Test 3.0 team to ask questions and seek guidance in addressing as many issues as possible for the Microsoft Test user. After three months of course development, Microsoft employees began receiving instruction from Arnold and other STLabs instructors that he managed. Because Microsoft Test 3.0 wasn't a released product, however, course instruction was limited to Microsoft employees.

After the release of Version 3.0 in September 1994, Arnold continued to instruct employees from Microsoft and other companies (such as MCI, IBM, Traveling Software, Spry/CompuServe, Attachmate, Hewlett-Packard, Delrina, Asymetrix, Aldus/Adobe, PeachTree, Compaq, Entergy, and Corel).

After accepting the position of Vice President at Software Testing Laboratories, Inc., he led the development teams for STLabs' add-on products, Test Now 1.0 and 2.0, for Microsoft Test 3.0 and Microsoft Visual Test 4.0. These add-on products provide routines that commonly must be written when starting an automation project, in addition to utilities to help the productivity of the Visual Test programmer.

Arnold continues in his role as Vice President heading up STLabs' Training and Tools group providing new courses and videotape products in the areas of Visual Test 4.0 and quality assurance in general. In his spare time, he enjoys flying, motorcycle touring, and downhill skiing.

Credits

Senior Vice President & Group Publisher
Brenda McLaughlin

Managing Editor
Terry Somerson

Publishing Director
Walter Bruce

Director of Marketing
Deb Burns

Marketing Manager
Jill Reinemann

Acquisitions Editor
John Osborn

Development Editors
Tim Lewis
Jim Sumser

Copy Editor
Kevin Shafer

Technical Reviewer
Dan Hodge

Production Director
Andrew Walker

Production Associate
Christopher Pimentel

Supervisor of Page Layout
Craig A. Harrison

Media/Archive Coordination
Leslie Popplewell
Melissa Stauffer

Project Coordinator
Ben Schroeter

Production Staff
Diann Abbott
Mary Ellen Moran
Andreas F. Schueller

Proofreader
Mary C. Oby

Quality Control Specialist
Mick Arellano

Indexer
Elizabeth Cunningham

Cover Design
Liew Design

IDG BOOKS WORLDWIDE, INC.
END-USER LICENSE AGREEMENT

Read This. **You should carefully read these terms and conditions before opening the software packet(s) included with this book ("Book"). This is a license agreement ("Agreement") between you and IDG Books Worldwide, Inc. ("IDGB"). By opening the accompanying software packet(s), you acknowledge that you have read and accept the following terms and conditions. If you do not agree and do not want to be bound by such terms and conditions, promptly return the Book and the unopened software packet(s) to the place you obtained them for a full refund.**

1. **License Grant.** IDGB grants to you (either an individual or entity) a nonexclusive license to use one copy of the enclosed software program(s) (collectively, the "Software") solely for your own personal or business purposes on a single computer (whether a standard computer or a workstation component of a multiuser network). The Software is in use on a computer when it is loaded into temporary memory (i.e., RAM) or installed into permanent memory (e.g., hard disk, CD-ROM, or other storage device). IDGB reserves all rights not expressly granted herein.

2. **Ownership.** IDGB is the owner of all right, title, and interest, including copyright, in and to the compilation of the Software recorded on the disk(s)/CD-ROM. Copyright to the individual programs on the disk(s)/CD-ROM is owned by the author or other authorized copyright owner of each program. Ownership of the Software and all proprietary rights relating thereto remain with IDGB and its licensors.

3. **Restrictions on Use and Transfer.**

    (a) You may only (i) make one copy of the Software for backup or archival purposes, or (ii) transfer the Software to a single hard disk, provided that you keep the original for backup or archival purposes. You may not (i) rent or lease the Software, (ii) copy or reproduce the Software through a LAN or other network system or through any computer subscriber system or bulletin-board system, or (iii) modify, adapt, or create derivative works based on the Software.

(b) You may not reverse engineer, decompile, or disassemble the Software. You may transfer the Software and user documentation on a permanent basis, provided that the transferee agrees to accept the terms and conditions of this Agreement and you retain no copies. If the Software is an update or has been updated, any transfer must include the most recent update and all prior versions.

4. **Restrictions on Use of Individual Programs.** You must follow the individual requirements and restrictions detailed for each individual program in Appendix H of this Book. These limitations are contained in the individual license agreements recorded on the disk(s)/CD-ROM. These restrictions may include a requirement that after using the program for the period of time specified in its text, the user must pay a registration fee or discontinue use. By opening the Software packet(s), you will be agreeing to abide by the licenses and restrictions for these individual programs. None of the material on this disk(s) or listed in this Book may ever be distributed, in original or modified form, for commercial purposes.

5. **Limited Warranty.**

(a) IDGB warrants that the Software and disk(s)/CD-ROM are free from defects in materials and workmanship under normal use for a period of sixty (60) days from the date of purchase of this Book. If IDGB receives notification within the warranty period of defects in materials or workmanship, IDGB will replace the defective disk(s)/CD-ROM.

(b) **IDGB AND THE AUTHOR OF THE BOOK DISCLAIM ALL OTHER WARRANTIES, EXPRESS OR IMPLIED, INCLUDING WITHOUT LIMITATION IMPLIED WARRANTIES OF MERCHANTABILITY AND FITNESS FOR A PARTICULAR PURPOSE, WITH RESPECT TO THE SOFTWARE, THE PROGRAMS, THE SOURCE CODE CONTAINED THEREIN, AND/OR THE TECHNIQUES DESCRIBED IN THIS BOOK. IDGB DOES NOT WARRANT THAT THE FUNC-**

TIONS CONTAINED IN THE SOFTWARE WILL MEET YOUR REQUIREMENTS OR THAT THE OPERATION OF THE SOFT-WARE WILL BE ERROR FREE.

(c)   This limited warranty gives you specific legal rights, and you may have other rights which vary from jurisdiction to jurisdiction.

6.   **Remedies.**

(a)   IDGB's entire liability and your exclusive remedy for defects in materials and workmanship shall be limited to replacement of the Software, which may be returned to IDGB with a copy of your receipt at the following address: Disk Fulfillment Department, Attn: Software Testing with Visual Test 4.0, IDG Books Worldwide, Inc., 7260 Shadeland Station, Ste. 100, Indianapolis, IN 46256, or call 1-800-762-2974. Please allow 3-4 weeks for delivery. This Limited Warranty is void if failure of the Software has resulted from accident, abuse, or misapplication. Any replacement Software will be warranted for the remainder of the original warranty period or thirty (30) days, whichever is longer.

(b)   In no event shall IDGB or the author be liable for any damages whatsoever (including without limitation damages for loss of business profits, business interruption, loss of business information, or any other pecuniary loss) arising from the use of or inability to use the Book or the Software, even if IDGB has been advised of the possibility of such damages.

(c)   Because some jurisdictions do not allow the exclusion or limitation of liability for consequential or incidental damages, the above limitation or exclusion may not apply to you.

7.   **U.S. Government Restricted Rights.** Use, duplication, or disclosure of the Software by the U.S. Government is subject to restrictions stated in paragraph (c) (1) (ii) of the Rights in Technical Data and Computer Software clause of DFARS 252.227-7013, and in subparagraphs (a) through (d) of the Commercial Computer—Restricted Rights clause at FAR 52.227-19, and in similar clauses in the NASA FAR supplement, when applicable.

8. **General.** This Agreement constitutes the entire understanding of the parties and revokes and supersedes all prior agreements, oral or written, between them and may not be modified or amended except in a writing signed by both parties hereto which specifically refers to this Agreement. This Agreement shall take precedence over any other documents that may be in conflict herewith. If any one or more provisions contained in this Agreement are held by any court or tribunal to be invalid, illegal, or otherwise unenforceable, each and every other provision shall remain in full force and effect.

The Internet For Macs® For Dummies® 2nd Edition	by Charles Seiter	ISBN: 1-56884-371-2	$19.99 USA/$26.99 Canada
The Internet For Macs® For Dummies® Starter Kit	by Charles Seiter	ISBN: 1-56884-244-9	$29.99 USA/$39.99 Canada
The Internet For Macs® For Dummies® Starter Kit Bestseller Edition	by Charles Seiter	ISBN: 1-56884-245-7	$39.99 USA/$54.99 Canada
The Internet For Windows® For Dummies® Starter Kit	by John R. Levine & Margaret Levine Young	ISBN: 1-56884-237-6	$34.99 USA/$44.99 Canada
The Internet For Windows® For Dummies® Starter Kit, Bestseller Edition	by John R. Levine & Margaret Levine Young	ISBN: 1-56884-246-5	$39.99 USA/$54.99 Canada

MACINTOSH

Mac® Programming For Dummies®	by Dan Parks Sydow	ISBN: 1-56884-173-6	$19.95 USA/$26.95 Canada
Macintosh® System 7.5 For Dummies®	by Bob LeVitus	ISBN: 1-56884-197-3	$19.95 USA/$26.95 Canada
MORE Macs® For Dummies®	by David Pogue	ISBN: 1-56884-087-X	$19.95 USA/$26.95 Canada
PageMaker 5 For Macs® For Dummies®	by Galen Gruman & Deke McClelland	ISBN: 1-56884-178-7	$19.95 USA/$26.95 Canada
QuarkXPress 3.3 For Dummies®	by Galen Gruman & Barbara Assadi	ISBN: 1-56884-217-1	$19.99 USA/$26.99 Canada
Upgrading and Fixing Macs® For Dummies®	by Kearney Rietmann & Frank Higgins	ISBN: 1-56884-189-2	$19.95 USA/$26.95 Canada

MULTIMEDIA

Multimedia & CD-ROMs For Dummies® 2nd Edition	by Andy Rathbone	ISBN: 1-56884-907-9	$19.99 USA/$26.99 Canada
Multimedia & CD-ROMs For Dummies® Interactive Multimedia Value Pack, 2nd Edition	by Andy Rathbone	ISBN: 1-56884-909-5	$29.99 USA/$39.99 Canada

OPERATING SYSTEMS:

DOS

MORE DOS For Dummies®	by Dan Gookin	ISBN: 1-56884-046-2	$19.95 USA/$26.95 Canada
OS/2® Warp For Dummies® 2nd Edition	by Andy Rathbone	ISBN: 1-56884-205-8	$19.99 USA/$26.99 Canada

UNIX

MORE UNIX® For Dummies®	by John R. Levine & Margaret Levine Young	ISBN: 1-56884-361-5	$19.99 USA/$26.99 Canada
UNIX® For Dummies®	by John R. Levine & Margaret Levine Young	ISBN: 1-878058-58-4	$19.95 USA/$26.95 Canada

WINDOWS

MORE Windows® For Dummies® 2nd Edition	by Andy Rathbone	ISBN: 1-56884-048-9	$19.95 USA/$26.95 Canada
Windows® 95 For Dummies®	by Andy Rathbone	ISBN: 1-56884-240-6	$19.99 USA/$26.99 Canada

PCS/HARDWARE

Illustrated Computer Dictionary For Dummies® 2nd Edition	by Dan Gookin & Wallace Wang	ISBN: 1-56884-218-X	$12.95 USA/$16.95 Canada
Upgrading and Fixing PCs For Dummies® 2nd Edition	by Andy Rathbone	ISBN: 1-56884-903-6	$19.99 USA/$26.99 Canada

PRESENTATION/AUTOCAD

AutoCAD For Dummies®	by Bud Smith	ISBN: 1-56884-191-4	$19.95 USA/$26.95 Canada
PowerPoint 4 For Windows® For Dummies®	by Doug Lowe	ISBN: 1-56884-161-2	$16.99 USA/$22.99 Canada

PROGRAMMING

Borland C++ For Dummies®	by Michael Hyman	ISBN: 1-56884-162-0	$19.95 USA/$26.95 Canada
C For Dummies® Volume 1	by Dan Gookin	ISBN: 1-878058-78-9	$19.95 USA/$26.95 Canada
C++ For Dummies®	by Stephen R. Davis	ISBN: 1-56884-163-9	$19.95 USA/$26.95 Canada
Delphi Programming For Dummies®	by Neil Rubenking	ISBN: 1-56884-200-7	$19.99 USA/$26.99 Canada
Mac® Programming For Dummies®	by Dan Parks Sydow	ISBN: 1-56884-173-6	$19.95 USA/$26.95 Canada
PowerBuilder 4 Programming For Dummies®	by Ted Coombs & Jason Coombs	ISBN: 1-56884-325-9	$19.99 USA/$26.99 Canada
QBasic Programming For Dummies®	by Douglas Hergert	ISBN: 1-56884-093-4	$19.95 USA/$26.95 Canada
Visual Basic 3 For Dummies®	by Wallace Wang	ISBN: 1-56884-076-4	$19.95 USA/$26.95 Canada
Visual Basic "X" For Dummies®	by Wallace Wang	ISBN: 1-56884-230-9	$19.99 USA/$26.99 Canada
Visual C++ 2 For Dummies®	by Michael Hyman & Bob Arnson	ISBN: 1-56884-328-3	$19.99 USA/$26.99 Canada
Windows® 95 Programming For Dummies®	by S. Randy Davis	ISBN: 1-56884-327-5	$19.99 USA/$26.99 Canada

SPREADSHEET

1-2-3 For Dummies®	by Greg Harvey	ISBN: 1-878058-60-6	$16.95 USA/$22.95 Canada
1-2-3 For Windows® 5 For Dummies® 2nd Edition	by John Walkenbach	ISBN: 1-56884-216-3	$16.95 USA/$22.95 Canada
Excel 5 For Macs® For Dummies®	by Greg Harvey	ISBN: 1-56884-186-8	$19.95 USA/$26.95 Canada
Excel For Dummies® 2nd Edition	by Greg Harvey	ISBN: 1-56884-050-0	$16.95 USA/$22.95 Canada
MORE 1-2-3 For DOS For Dummies®	by John Weingarten	ISBN: 1-56884-224-4	$19.99 USA/$26.99 Canada
MORE Excel 5 For Windows® For Dummies®	by Greg Harvey	ISBN: 1-56884-207-4	$19.95 USA/$26.95 Canada
Quattro Pro 6 For Windows® For Dummies®	by John Walkenbach	ISBN: 1-56884-174-4	$19.95 USA/$26.95 Canada
Quattro Pro For DOS For Dummies®	by John Walkenbach	ISBN: 1-56884-023-3	$16.95 USA/$22.95 Canada

UTILITIES

Norton Utilities 8 For Dummies®	by Beth Slick	ISBN: 1-56884-166-3	$19.95 USA/$26.95 Canada

VCRS/CAMCORDERS

VCRs & Camcorders For Dummies™	by Gordon McComb & Andy Rathbone	ISBN: 1-56884-229-5	$14.99 USA/$20.99 Canada

WORD PROCESSING

Ami Pro For Dummies®	by Jim Meade	ISBN: 1-56884-049-7	$19.95 USA/$26.95 Canada
MORE Word For Windows® 6 For Dummies®	by Doug Lowe	ISBN: 1-56884-165-5	$19.95 USA/$26.95 Canada
MORE WordPerfect® 6 For Windows® For Dummies®	by Margaret Levine Young & David C. Kay	ISBN: 1-56884-206-6	$19.95 USA/$26.95 Canada
MORE WordPerfect® 6 For DOS For Dummies®	by Wallace Wang, edited by Dan Gookin	ISBN: 1-56884-047-0	$19.95 USA/$26.95 Canada
Word 6 For Macs® For Dummies®	by Dan Gookin	ISBN: 1-56884-190-6	$19.95 USA/$26.95 Canada
Word For Windows® 6 For Dummies®	by Dan Gookin	ISBN: 1-56884-075-6	$16.95 USA/$22.95 Canada
Word For Windows® For Dummies®	by Dan Gookin & Ray Werner	ISBN: 1-878058-86-X	$16.95 USA/$22.95 Canada
WordPerfect® 6 For DOS For Dummies®	by Dan Gookin	ISBN: 1-878058-77-0	$16.95 USA/$22.95 Canada
WordPerfect® 6.1 For Windows® For Dummies® 2nd Edition	by Margaret Levine Young & David Kay	ISBN: 1-56884-243-0	$16.95 USA/$22.95 Canada
WordPerfect® For Dummies®	by Dan Gookin	ISBN: 1-878058-52-5	$16.95 USA/$22.95 Canada

Macworld® Mac® & Power Mac SECRETS,™ 2nd Edition
by David Pogue & Joseph Schorr

HOT!

This is the definitive Mac reference for those who want to become power users! Includes three disks with 9MB of software!

WINNERS 1994-95 TECHNICAL PUBLICATIONS AND ART COMPETITIONS OF THE SOCIETY FOR TECHNICAL COMMUNICATION

ISBN: 1-56884-175-2
$39.95 USA/$54.95 Canada

Includes 3 disks chock full of software.

NEWBRIDGE BOOK CLUB SELECTION

Macworld® Mac® FAQs™
by David Pogue

HOT!

Written by the hottest Macintosh author around, David Pogue, *Macworld Mac FAQs* gives users the ultimate Mac reference. Hundreds of Mac questions and answers side-by-side, right at your fingertips, and organized into six easy-to-reference sections with lots of sidebars and diagrams.

ISBN: 1-56884-480-8
$19.99 USA/$26.99 Canada

Macworld® System 7.5 Bible, 3rd Edition
by Lon Poole

ISBN: 1-56884-098-5
$29.95 USA/$39.95 Canada

NATIONAL BESTSELLER!

Macworld® ClarisWorks 3.0 Companion, 3rd Edition
by Steven A. Schwartz

ISBN: 1-56884-481-6
$24.99 USA/$34.99 Canada

NATIONAL BESTSELLER!

Macworld® Complete Mac® Handbook Plus Interactive CD, 3rd Edition
by Jim Heid

BMUG SPRING 1995 CHOICE PRODUCT

ISBN: 1-56884-192-2
$39.95 USA/$54.95 Canada

Includes an interactive CD-ROM.

NEWBRIDGE BOOK CLUB SELECTION

Macworld® Ultimate Mac® CD-ROM
by Jim Heid

ISBN: 1-56884-477-8
$19.99 USA/$26.99 Canada

CD-ROM includes version 2.0 of QuickTime, and over 65 MB of the best shareware, freeware, fonts, sounds, and more!

Macworld® Networking Bible, 2nd Edition
by Dave Kosiur & Joel M. Snyder

ISBN: 1-56884-194-9
$29.95 USA/$39.95 Canada

Macworld® Photoshop 3 Bible, 2nd Edition
by Deke McClelland

ISBN: 1-56884-158-2
$39.95 USA/$54.95 Canada

Includes stunning CD-ROM with add-ons, digitized photos and more.

WINNERS 1994-95 TECHNICAL PUBLICATIONS AND ART COMPETITIONS OF THE SOCIETY FOR TECHNICAL COMMUNICATION

NEW!

Macworld® Photoshop 2.5 Bible
by Deke McClelland

ISBN: 1-56884-022-5
$29.95 USA/$39.95 Canada

NATIONAL BESTSELLER!

Macworld® FreeHand 4 Bible
by Deke McClelland

ISBN: 1-56884-170-1
$29.95 USA/$39.95 Canada

Macworld® Illustrator 5.0/5.5 Bible
by Ted Alspach

ISBN: 1-56884-097-7
$39.95 USA/$54.95 Canada

Includes CD-ROM with QuickTime tutorials.

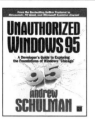